Life in the Posthuman Condition

Life in the Posthuman Condition

Critical Responses to the Anthropocene

Edited by S. E. Wilmer and
Audronė Žukauskaitė

EDINBURGH
University Press

Edinburgh University Press is one of the leading university presses in the UK. We publish academic books and journals in our selected subject areas across the humanities and social sciences, combining cutting-edge scholarship with high editorial and production values to produce academic works of lasting importance. For more information visit our website: edinburghuniversitypress.com

Edinburgh University Press Ltd
The Tun – Holyrood Road
12(2f) Jackson's Entry
Edinburgh EH8 8PJ

Typeset in 11/13 Bembo by
IDSUK (DataConnection) Ltd, and
printed and bound in Great Britain

A CIP record for this book is available from the British Library

ISBN 978 1 3995 0527 7 (hardback)
ISBN 978 1 3995 0529 1 (webready PDF)
ISBN 978 1 3995 0530 7 (epub)

Contents

Acknowledgements

This book emanates from a conference on 'Art in the Anthropocene' held at Trinity College Dublin in 2019. We wish to thank the School of Creative Arts headed by Matthew Causey, the Long Room Hub, Players Theatre and the Science Gallery at Trinity College Dublin for hosting and supporting the conference and for the assistance of our scientific committee of Anna Barcz, Ruth Brennan, Poul Holm, Radek Przedpełski, Cordula Scherer and Yvonne Scott. We are also grateful for the support from the Trinity College Association and Trust, the Visiting Professors Fund, the Arts and Social Sciences Benefaction Fund, the Visual and Performing Arts Fund and the Faculty Event Grant. We also wish to thank the Trinity Institute for Neuroscience and the Wellcome Trust ISSF Award for supporting the 'Neurohumanities Symposium: A tribute to the work of Catherine Malabou' in 2021. We are grateful to *e-flux journal* for granting permission to reproduce 'Climate Control: From Emergency to Emergence' by T. J. Demos that originally appeared in *e-flux journal*, 104 (November 2019), and to *Configurations* for permission to reproduce parts of 'A Recursive Web of Models: Studio Tomás Saraceno's Working Objects' by Jussi Parikka that originally appeared in *Configurations*, 28(3) (summer 2020), and Studio Tomás Saraceno for the images accompanying Parikka's article. We also want to thank Aran Kleebaur for his help in copy-editing the text before its delivery to the publisher.

Illustrations

Notes on Contributors

Anna Barcz works as an Assistant Professor at the Institute of History of the Polish Academy of Sciences in Warsaw; she was the Marie Sklodowska-Curie Fellow at the Trinity Long Room Hub (Trinity College Dublin) in 2018–2019, and Rachel Carson Centre Fellow (LMU, Munich) in 2019–2020. She is the author of books: *Environmental Cultures in Soviet East Europe: Literature, History and Memory* (Bloomsbury 2020); *Animal Narratives and Culture: Vulnerable Realism* (CSP 2017) and *Ecorealism: From Ecocriticism to Zoocriticism in Polish Literature* (in Polish, 2016). Her recent research promotes theoretical approaches that reconceptualise human-rivers relations and terracentrism. She published her last flood-related studies with *Space and Culture and Environmental Hazards* journals.

Bruce Clarke is Paul Whitfield Horn Distinguished Professor of Literature and Science in the Department of English at Texas Tech University. He was Baruch S. Blumberg/NASA Chair in Astrobiology at the Library of Congress in 2019; Senior Fellow at the Center for Literature and the Natural Sciences, Friedrich Alexander University Erlangen-Nürnberg for 2015; and Senior Fellow at the International Research Institute for Cultural Technologies and Media Philosophy, Bauhaus-University Weimar in 2010–11. His latest book is *Gaian Systems: Lynn Margulis, Neocybernetics, and the End of the Anthropocene* (2020); other books include *Neocybernetics and Narrative* (2014), *Posthuman Metamorphosis: Narrative and Systems* (2008) and *Energy Forms: Allegory and Science in the Era of Classical Thermodynamics* (2001). He co-edits the book series *Meaning Systems*, published by Fordham University Press, and is the editor or co-editor of seven essay collections, most recently

Writing Gaia: The Scientific Correspondence of James Lovelock and Lynn Margulis, co-edited with Sébastien Dutreuil, *Posthuman Biopolitics: The Science Fiction of Joan Slonczewski* (2020), and with Manuela Rossini, *The Cambridge Companion to Literature and the Posthuman* (2017).

Michael Cronin is the Chair of French 1776 at Trinity College Dublin. He taught in the Université of Tours, the École Normale Supérieure (Cachan) and was Director of the Centre for Translation and Textual Studies at Dublin City University. He has published extensively on language, culture, translation and travel writing. Among his works are *Across the Lines: Travel, Language, Translation* (2000), *Translation and Identity* (2006), *The Expanding World: Towards a Politics of Microspection* (2012) and *Eco-Translation: Translation and Ecology in the Age of the Anthropocene* (2017). His current interests are in developing eco-criticism in relation to modern languages and translation, exploring the notion of 'translation trauma' in relation to population displacement and investigating language identities as mediated through travel. He is an elected Member of the Royal Irish Academy, the Academia Europaea and is an Officer in the *Ordre des Palmes Académiques*.

T. J. Demos is Professor of History of Art and Visual Culture and Director of the Center for Creative Ecologies at University of California at Santa Cruz. He has served on the *Art Journal* editorial board (2004–8), and currently is on the editorial board of *Third Text* and on the advisory board of *Grey Room*. His current research focuses on contemporary art and visual culture, investigating in particular the diverse ways that artists and activists have negotiated crises associated with globalisation, including the emerging conjunction of post-9/11 political sovereignty and statelessness, the hauntings of the colonial past, and the growing biopolitical conflicts around ecology and climate change. His books include: *Against the Anthropocene: Visual Culture and Environment Today* (2017); *Decolonizing Nature: Contemporary Art and the Politics of Ecology* (2016); *Return to the Postcolony: Spectres of Colonialism in Contemporary Art* (2013); *The Migrant Image: The Art and Politics of Documentary During Global Crisis* (2013); *Dara Birnbaum: Technology/Transformation: Wonder Woman* (2010); and *The Exiles of Marcel Duchamp* (2007).

Mintautas Gutauskas is an Associate Professor at the Philosophy Faculty of Vilnius University, Lithuania. He is the author of the monographs *Space of Dialogue: A Phenomenological Approach* (in Lithuanian, 2010) and *Human and Animal: The Anthropological Difference in the Phenomenological Hermeneutical Philosophy* (in Lithuanian, 2021), and the co-author of collective monographs *Secularization and Contemporary Culture* (edited by Rita Šerpytytė, in Lithuanian, 2013) and *Transformations of Nature: Modernity and the Anthropocene* (with Gianluca Cuozzo, Danutė Bacevičiūtė and Vaiva Daraškevičiūtė (in Lithuanian, 2020). His current research interests include phenomenology, hermeneutics, eco-phenomenology, human-animal relations, liminal subjects, animality, critique of anthropocentrism, anthropological difference, and the Anthropocene.

Graham Harman is Distinguished Professor of Philosophy at SCI-Arc in Los Angeles, California, following sixteen years at the American University in Cairo. He is the author of more than twenty books, most recently *Art and Objects* (2020), *Architecture and Objects* (2022), and *The Graham Harman Reader*, edited by Jon Cogburn and Niki Young (2022), as well as more than 300 articles. He is editor-in-chief of the journal *Open Philosophy*, editor of the Speculative Realism book series at Edinburgh University Press and co-editor (with Bruno Latour) of the New Metaphysics book series at Open Humanities Press. In 2016 he was named by The Best Schools as one of the world's fifty most influential living philosophers.

Catherine Malabou is Professor of Philosophy at the Centre for Research in Modern European Philosophy, at Kingston University, UK, and in the departments of Comparative Literature and European Languages and Studies at UC Irvine. Her most recent books include *Before Tomorrow: Epigenesis and Rationality* (2016, trans. Carolyn Shread), *Morphing Intelligence, From IQ to IA*, (2018, trans. Carolyn Shread), *Pleasure Erased: The Clitoris Unthought,* (2022, trans. Carolyn Shread), and *Au Voleur! Anarchisme et Philosophy* (2022).

Thomas Nail is Professor of Philosophy at the University of Denver and author of numerous books, including *The Figure of the Migrant* (2015), *Theory of the Border* (2016), *Marx in Motion* (2020), *Theory of the Image* (2019), *Theory of the Object* (2021), *Theory of the Earth* (2021), *Lucretius I: An Ontology of Motion* (2018), *Lucretius II: An Ethics of Motion* (2020), *Lucretius III: A History of Motion* (2022), *Returning to Revolution* (2012) and *Being and Motion* (2018). His research focuses on the philosophy of movement.

Agnė Narušytė is Professor in the Vilnius Academy of Arts in Lithuania, photography and art critic, exhibition curator, and a columnist for the weekly *7 Days of Art (7 meno dienos)*. Her doctoral dissertation at the Vilnius Academy of Arts formed the basis of her monograph *Aesthetics* *of Boredom in Lithuanian Photography* (in Lithuanian and English, 2010). From 2006–9 she taught at the Napier University of Edinburgh, and from 2009–14 was the Head of the Department of Art History and Theory at the Vilnius Academy of Arts. She is currently researching the anthropological and philosophical aspects of contemporary photography, and together with Dr Margarita Matulytė has published *Camera Obscura: The History of Lithuanian Photography 1839–1945* (in Lithuanian, 2016).

John Ó Maoilearca is a Professor in the Department of Critical and Historical Studies at Kingston University, London. He has previously lectured in philosophy departments at the University of Sunderland, England, and the University of Dundee, Scotland. He has published twelve books, including (as author), *Post-Continental Philosophy: An Outline* (2006), *Philosophy and the Moving Image: Refractions of Reality* (2010), *All Thoughts Are Equal: Laruelle and Nonhuman Philosophy* (2015) and *Vestiges of a Philosophy* (forthcoming 2022). He works in the areas of continental philosophy (Bergson, Deleuze, Henry, Laruelle, Badiou), metaphysics (especially of time and identity), film philosophy, and metaphilosophy. He is currently working on ordinary forms of time travel (so far with only modest success).

Jussi Parikka is Professor in Digital Aesthetics and Culture at Aarhus University in Denmark. He is also Visiting Professor at Winchester School of Art (University of Southampton) and at FAMU at the Academy of Performing Arts in Prague where he leads the project Operational Images and Visual Culture (2019–23, funded by the Czech Science Foundation). In 2021 he was elected as member of Academia Europaea. His published books include *Insect Media* (2010), *Digital Contagions* (2007/2016), *A Geology of Media* (2015) and *A Slow, Contemporary Violence* (2016). Recently, he co-edited *Photography Off the Scale* (2021) and is the co-author of *The Lab Book: Situated Practices in Media Studies* (2022). His book *Operational Images* is forthcoming in 2023. Parikka is also the co-editor of the book series Technicities at Edinburgh University Press.

Małgorzata Sugiera is a Full Professor at Jagiellonian University in Cracow, Poland, and Head of the Department for Performativity Studies. She was a Research Fellow of the Alexander von Humboldt Foundation, DAAD, Institut für die Wissenschaften vom Menschen in Vienna, the Andrew Mellon Foundation, and the International Research Centre 'Interweaving Performance Cultures' at the Freie Universität in Berlin. Her research concentrates on performativity theories and speculative and decolonial studies, particularly in the context of the history of science. She has published twelve single-authored books, the most recent of which are *Non-Humans: Reports from Nonnatural Natures* (in Polish, 2015) and, together with Mateusz Borowski, *Artificial Natures: Performances of Technoscience and Arts* (in Polish, 2017). She has co-edited several books in English and German, most recently *Crisis and Communitas: Performative Concepts of Commonality in Art and Politics* (2022), and translates scholarly books and theatre plays from English, German and French. She is carrying out a three-year international research project, 'Epidemics and Communities in Critical Theories, Artistic Practices and Speculative Fabulations of the Last Decades', funded by the National Science Centre (NCN).

S. E. Wilmer is Professor Emeritus in Drama at Trinity College Dublin, former editor-in-chief of *Nordic Theatre Studies* and former Head of the School of Drama, Film and Music at Trinity College Dublin. Recent books and edited volumes include *Deleuze and Beckett* (2015) and *Resisting Biopolitics: Philosophical, Political and Performative Strategies* (2016) (both co-edited with Audronė Žukauskaitė), *Performing Statelessness in Europe* (2018) and *Deleuze, Guattari and the Art of Multiplicity* (co-edited with Radek Przedpełski). He is currently co-editing with Yana Meerzon *The Palgrave Handbook on Theatre and Migration* (forthcoming from Palgrave Macmillan).

Cary Wolfe currently holds the Bruce and Elizabeth Dunlevie Chair in English at Rice University, where he is Founding Director of 3CT: The Center for Critical and Cultural Theory. His books include *Animal Rites: American Culture, The Discourse of Species, and Posthumanist Theory* (2003), and the edited collections *Zootologies: The Question of the Animal* (2003), *The Other Emerson* (with Branka Arsic, 2010), *What Is Posthumanism?* (2010) and *Before the Law: Humans and Other Animals in a Biopolitical Frame* (2012). He has also participated in two recent multi-authored collections: *Philosophy and Animal Life* (2008) with Cora Diamond, Ian Hacking, Stanley Cavell and John McDowell, and *The Death of the Animal: A Dialogue* (2009), with philosophers Paola Cavalieri, Peter Singer, Harlan Miller, Matthew Calarco and novelist J. M. Coetzee. He is founding editor of the series *Posthumanities* at the University of Minnesota Press, which has published more than forty volumes by noted authors such as Donna Haraway, Roberto Esposito, Isabelle Stengers, Michel Serres, Vilem Flusser, and many others.

Patricia Ybarra is Professor of Theatre Arts and Performance Studies at Brown University, USA. Her books include *Performing Conquest* about the persistence of colonialism in present day Mexico, and *Latinx Theatre in the Times of Neoliberalism*. One of her concerns is about how and when a conception of the Anthropocene is useful (or not) to thinking about the larger history of political economy in the Americas.

Audronė Žukauskaitė is Chief Researcher at the Lithuanian Culture Research Institute. Her recent publications include the monographs: *From Biopolitics to Biophilosophy* (in Lithuanian, 2016) and *Gilles Deleuze and Félix Guattari's Philosophy: The Logic of Multiplicity* (in Lithuanian, 2011). She has also co-edited (with S. E. Wilmer) *Interrogating Antigone in Postmodern Philosophy and Criticism* (2010); *Deleuze and Beckett* (2015); and *Resisting Biopolitics: Philosophical, Political and Performative Strategies* (2016). Her latest monograph *Organism-Oriented Ontology* is forthcoming from Edinburgh University Press.

Forms of Life in the Posthuman Condition: An Introduction

Audronė Žukauskaitė and S. E. Wilmer

Posthumanist critical theory has made many attempts to question the humanistic and anthropocentric foundations of our thinking. The 'posthuman turn' not only questions human exceptionalism but invites us to rethink our relationships with non-human others and environments, and to reconsider our exteriorisations in technological tools. However, posthumanist critical theory does not represent a coherent position, built on consensus. It can be easily undermined by new forms of essentialism, such as transhumanism, or the theory of the Anthropocene. Transhumanism represents the same old human exceptionalism which is enhanced with the help of technological advancement. The Anthropocene thesis requires a much closer examination. On the one hand, the Anthropocene thesis is close to posthumanist critical theory in its concern with the environment and endangered species; on the other hand, it is at odds with it because it brings the 'Anthropos' back in an oblique way.

The Anthropocene is a term suggested by Paul Crutzen and Eugene Stoermer to name a new geological epoch, which marks the irreversible effects on the planet produced by human activity (Crutzen and Stoermer 2000: 17–18). As the theory of the Anthropocene has developed, it has become clear that it is not only descriptive but also performative, actually performing the action it intends to describe. Anthropocene theory creates a normalising discourse and a specific visuality which makes the climate catastrophe aesthetically acceptable. As Mirzoeff points out, 'Anthropocene visuality keeps us believing that somehow the war against nature that Western society has been waging for centuries is not only right; it is beautiful and it can be won' (Mirzoeff 2014: 217). In presenting catastrophic but at the same time beautiful images, its aesthetic and anaesthetic functions distance us from the real consequences of what's happening.

> Anthropocene visuality allows us to move on, to see nothing and keep circulating commodities, despite the destruction of the

biosphere. We do so less out of venal convenience, as some might suggest, than out of a modernist conviction that 'the authorities' will restore everything to order in the end. (Mirzoeff 2014: 217)

This means that to represent or visualise the catastrophic effects of human activity is satisfying but not sufficient practice to address it.

While it might seem that Anthropocene theory is a new apparatus of thinking which would allow us to change the conditions of living, the problem is that this theory, in bringing the 'Anthropos' back into the scene, masks the fact that the real agent behind the climate disaster is not 'universal humanity'. As T. J. Demos points out in *Against the Anthropocene*, it is important to ask what ideological function the word 'Anthropocene' serves (Demos 2017: 16). On the one hand, the Anthropocene effects are related to the military-state-corporate apparatus; on the other hand, we can ask to what degree the Anthropocene itself – as a discursive and optical tool or apparatus – is a function of that system. As Demos points out, 'Anthropocene rhetoric – joining images and texts – frequently acts as a mechanism of universalization [. . .] which enables the military-state-corporate apparatus to disavow responsibility for the differentiated impacts of climate change [. . .] inadvertently making us all complicit in its destructive project' (Demos 2017: 17). Thus, the theory of the Anthropocene allows us to outsource the responsibility to universal human activity.

However, as Jason W. Moore proposes in *Anthropocene or Capitalocene: Nature, History, and the Crisis of Capitalism*, the real agent behind the Anthropocene is not universal humanity, but corporate capitalism; therefore, he suggests replacing the word 'Anthropocene' with the term 'Capitalocene'. As Moore argues,

> capitalism is a way of organizing *nature as a whole* . . . a nature in which human organizations (classes, empires, markets, etc.) not only make environments, but are simultaneously made by the historical flux and flow of the web of life. In perspective, capitalism is a world-ecology that joins the accumulation of capital, the pursuit of power, and the co-production of nature in successive historical configurations. (Moore 2016: 7)

Thus, the term Capitalocene refers to corporate capitalism as a specific agent which not only appropriates, consumes and exhausts natural and human resources but also manages to pass down the catastrophic consequences on to the poorest and the most underprivileged populations. As Demos points out, 'in such narratives as these, Anthropos serves to distract attention from the economic class that has long benefitted from the financial system responsible for the catastrophic environmental change' (Demos 2017: 49).

Moreover, Anthropocene theory masks not only the agency of corporate capitalism but also the effects of colonialism. As Mirzoeff argues, 'the Anthropos in *Anthropocene* turns out to be our old friend the (imperialist) white male' (Mirzoeff 2018: 123). In this sense Anthropocene theory is not an objective representation of nature but a scene of colonial biopolitical regulation. If we accept that the 'golden spike', marking the beginning of the Anthropocene, can be related to the arrival of Europeans in the Americas in 1610, the decimation of the indigenous population, and the burgeoning slave trade from Africa, then it follows that 'the Anthropocene began with a massive colonial genocide' (Mirzoeff 2018: 138). In other words, the alleged neutrality of Anthropocene theory masks the fact that climate injustice is a consequence of long-lasting racist and colonial politics that enslaved, oppressed, displaced or eradicated millions of indigenous people in Africa and the Americas. Kathryn Yusoff complains of attending 'too many Anthropocene events, where the absence of discussions of race allowed the smooth flow of patriarchal reason to make its earth anew' (Yusoff 2018: 109). Therefore, as Mirzoeff points out, 'it seems that white supremacy, not content with being the übermensch, has settled on the ultimate destiny of being a geological agent' (Mirzoeff 2018: 142). In this sense it is important to acknowledge that the Anthropocene is a scene of (mis)representation and redistribution of power, where the coloniser takes 'responsibility' to represent those who are not worthy to represent themselves.

Furthermore, Anthropocene theory effectively erases not only the reality of race but also of gender. As Joanna Zylinska pointed out in *The End of Man: A Feminist Counterapocalypse*, the Anthropocene narrative, with its messianic-apocalyptic undertones, is saturated with masculinist ambitions (Zylinska 2018). What becomes a problem here is that the discourse on the Anthropocene, in bringing back the universal subject, immediately erases all theoretical efforts to differentiate every subject as being racialised and gendered. As Claire Colebrook observes, 'after years of theory that contested every naturalization of what was ultimately historical and political, "man" has returned' (Colebrook 2016: 90). It is as if the danger and urgency to react to the climate emergency pushed back all theoretical efforts in postcolonialist, decolonial and feminist discourses and created the conditions to rehabilitate a new type of hyper-humanism. In other words, the Anthropocene can be seen as a certain 'Anthropopolitics' (Colebrook 2016) which continues the work of biopolitics: if biopolitics seeks to subject and manage both human and animal lives, turning them into disposable biological resources, then the Anthropocene (or Anthropo-politics) seeks to colonise and subject the whole of nature and all natural resources. If biopolitics works by sorting out individuals deciding which lives are worth living, then the Anthropocene works by outsourcing responsibilities and deciding which forms of life are worth being taken into account. To confront this, we need to reconceptualise our research methodologies and the whole apparatus of thinking.

In this context posthumanist theory can counter-theorise the 'Anthropos' of the Anthropocene as a damaging force, threatening to destroy other living systems and environments. Although posthumanism is more like a patchwork of insights rather than a unified and coherent theory, what all its insights have in common is a disbelief in a universal humanity and a universal human knowledge, based on appropriation, colonisation and objectification of human and non-human others and natural environments. Here the perspective is reversed, and the human subject is seen as being haunted by non-human and inhuman forces, and entangled in larger biological and technological systems. In this sense posthumanism, as Rosi Braidotti has extensively demonstrated, is a critical methodology aiming to question both humanism and anthropocentrism (Braidotti 2013, 2018; Braidotti and Bignall 2019). First, posthumanism can be seen as a critique of the humanist model of 'Man', which is based on the project of Enlightenment and expresses 'the Eurocentric, masculinist universalism that is still operative in the most knowledge production scientific systems' (Braidotti and Bignall 2019: 2). By contrast, posthumanism offers partial and perspectival 'situated knowledges', which take into account feminism, gender theory, postcolonialism and emerging indigenous philosophies. Second, posthumanism can be seen as a critique of anthropocentrism and human exceptionalism, based on species hierarchy and the subjection and exclusion of non-human others. Posthumanism raises 'the question of the animal' and asks what place animals take in our all-too-human ontology (Derrida 2008; Despret 2016). It questions the rigid boundaries between human and non-human animals and demonstrates that they share such capacities as sentience, inventiveness, memory, cognition and (in some cases) consciousness. Moreover, instead of projecting human characteristics onto animals, humans have to admit that they themselves belong to the continuum of living beings. Therefore, as Brian Massumi suggests, anthropocentrism should be replaced by 'animo-centrism' (Massumi 2014: 52). That would mean that the logic of exclusion which was underlying both biopolitics and anthropo-politics could be replaced by a logic of mutual inclusion. In this respect posthumanism can be seen as an inclusive way of thinking, which attempts to conceptualise what is 'more-than-human'.

Such a conceptualisation is not an easy task. As Cary Wolfe suggests, 'when we talk about posthumanism, we are not just talking about a thematics of the decentering of the human [. . .]; rather [. . .] we are talking about *how* thinking confronts that thematics, what thought has to become in the face of those challenges' (Wolfe 2010: xvi). This implies the need to rethink our research methodologies and the necessity to redefine human subjectivity in such a way that it would include multiple modes of existence. As Wolfe points out, 'What we call "we" is in fact a multiplicity of relations between "us" and "not us", "inside" and "outside", organic and non-organic, things "present" and things "absent"' (Wolfe 2018: 357–8). In other words, posthumanism is a new way of thinking, oriented towards the multiplicity of connections between inorganic and organic, human and non-human, human and technological beings. To be more precise, posthumanism is oriented not only towards the multiplicity of connections, but also towards the zones of indistinction between human and non-human actors, which might be both biological or technological. However, this does not mean leaving out the notion of the human. The posthuman doesn't mean the disappearance of the human. This is why Richard Grusin argues that the phrase 'nonhuman turn' would be more precise than the 'posthuman turn'. As Grusin explains,

> the very idea of the posthuman entails a historical development from human to something after the human, even as it invokes the imbrication of human and nonhuman in making up the posthuman turn. The nonhuman turn, on the other hand, insists (to paraphrase Latour) that 'we have never been human' but that the human has always coevolved, coexisted, or collaborated with the nonhuman. (Grusin 2015: ix)

We have never been human because our bodies have always been interconnected with other species and extended with the help of technological prostheses.

Such a reconceptualisation of the (non)human forces us to think not in terms of identities and individuals, but in terms of processes, entanglements and networks. Are these processes material, or are they driven by some vital immaterial force? This issue is driving so-called 'new' materialism which questions the conventional notion of matter as a passive and inert substance and asserts materiality as a self-organising force. 'For materiality is always something more than "mere" matter: an excess, force, vitality, relationality, or difference that renders matter active, self-creative, productive, unpredictable' (Coole and Frost 2010: 9). Matter is not opposed to form; rather, matter is understood as a self-forming and self-organising activity. However, new materialists differ in their attempts to define what underlies this materiality. For example, Jane Bennett in *Vibrant Matter: A Political Ecology of Things* pursues the project of vital materialism and theorises a vitality intrinsic to materiality as such. By vitality she means 'the capacity of things – edibles, commodities, storms, metals – not only to impede or block the will or designs of humans but also to act as quasi agents or forces with trajectories, propensities, or tendencies of their own' (Bennett 2010: viii). Bennett interprets vitality as immanent to matter: matter is vibrant and lively and is in no need of any transcendence. However, the problem is that to explain the notion of vitality we have to know what life is. Can life be explained merely in materialistic terms or does it need a recourse to ideality? As Elizabeth Grosz argues in *The Incorporeal: Ontology, Ethics, and the Limits of Materialism*, 'there is always already something in the organization of matter – matter at its most elementary – that contains the smallest but perhaps most significant elements of ideality' (Grosz 2017: 250). Even the most elementary life forms could not develop if they would not carry within themselves some ideality, incorporeality, directionality or purposiveness. Life is composed of these material-ideal relations, and it always oscillates between its virtual, incorporeal dimension and its actual, material incarnations.

This edited volume explores these new conceptualisations of life in the posthuman condition. The first part of the book critically questions Anthropocene theory and outlines alternative scenarios, such as Gaia theory, or post-Anthropocene forms of life on Earth and other planets. Bruce Clarke discusses Gaia theory, developed by James Lovelock and Lynn Margulis. Gaia theory suggests that the Earth regulates its own temperature and keeps it in homeostasis, which humans have been disrupting with disastrous consequences. Clarke closely reviews Lovelock's dire predictions from a 1988 article, pointing out its prescient conclusions, and suggests that, while the planet will survive, we will become desperate spectators of our own demise unless we make 'massive and difficult adjustments' that will 'realign our ways of life in concert with the nonlinear dynamics by which Gaia's symbiotic contingencies unfold'. The only possible solution to this self-inflicted Anthropocene is the 'Gaian being', which means solidarity with non-human life and non-organic Earth.

By contrast, Małgorzata Sugiera and Patricia Ybarra outline alternative scenarios of life after the Anthropocene. Sugiera discusses the Mars trilogy by Kim Stanley Robinson as 'Climate Fiction', inventing a world on Mars that defamiliarises the earthbound human perspective and imagines alternative forms of life and behaviour to interrogate the catastrophic systems that have produced today's world. Robinson's trilogy portrays life on a planet that is beyond human mastery and control, revealing by comparison the inability of humans to control their own destiny on an overpopulated earth. Sugiera concludes by comparing Robinson's approach with that of Donna Haraway, seeing the need for being in the world as sympoietic rather than as master of the earth, 'the humus of a speculated future'.

Patricia Ybarra invokes an indigenous perspective and reveals that indigenous people in North America have for centuries experienced the destruction of their habitat and lifestyle. Ybarra analyses the work of two playwrights who depict an apocalyptic future in Japan and the USA. Aya Ogawa, a Japanese-born writer, evokes two ecological disasters (Chernobyl and Fukushima) in her play *Ludic Proxy* to demonstrate the fragility of mankind from its destructive technologies and the need for an ethics of care. Yvette Nolan, a Metis/Algonquin playwright, focuses in *The Unplugging* on the need to recover fading indigenous knowledge of how to cope with limited resources. Ybarra observes that both playwrights project a feminist ethics of interdependency between humans and the natural world as a way forward in the current environmental emergency.

Mintautas Gutauskas and T. J. Demos discuss those aspects of Anthropocene destruction that change our understanding of human subjectivity. Gutauskas uses a phenomenological approach to reconsider waste as a simple phenomenon, a fundamental phenomenon and, finally, as a phenomenon which changes our self-awareness. In our everyday life waste is a simple phenomenon which can be defined by its readiness-to-hand. However, in the Anthropocene, waste is accumulated in such quantity that it becomes a life-changing condition and should be analysed as a fundamental phenomenon. Finally, waste becomes a trace through which humans can recognise themselves, thus it becomes a phenomenon of self-awareness. Similarly, T. J. Demos examines the effects of Anthropocene through another substance – a gas – which is seen as the exemplary medium both of climate emergency and of authoritarian oppression. Demos highlights an asymmetry between typical greenhouse gases, such as carbon dioxide, that mostly remain invisible, and the tear gas, directed against insurgencies and rebellions (such as Extinction Rebellion), that is strategically visible and experientially affective. In this respect we can see two different uses of gas: carbon emission is the effect of consumer capitalism, whereas tear gas is the expression of climate control to manage crowds and oppress insurrections. Thus the ecological demand to diminish greenhouse gas emission should have an additional political dimension – to stop the weaponisation of air.

The second part of the book investigates the obscure boundary between life and non-life, and between human and non-human animal life forms. By pointing out the inadequate attempts by philosophers in the past to differentiate various forms of life, Graham Harman asks, 'how many crucial divisions are there, really, between life and non-life?' Harman investigates Helmuth Plessner's *Levels of Organic Life and the Human* and discusses his theory of 'punctuations'. Plessner argues that life – as opposed to non-life – consists in positionality, meaning that the living body has a special relation to its own boundary and also a special relation to time. However, in trying to differentiate between different forms of life, Plessner distinguishes between unicellular and multicellular life and between decentralised animals and animals with a central nervous system. In this respect Plessner contributes to human exceptionalism, because, once a central nervous system has evolved, we must await the advent of a human being.

Anna Barcz and Michael Cronin consider post-human modes of translation as engaging forms of communication with and between non-human animals. This leads them to merge ideas on interspecies communication with eco-translation to anticipate how species may respond to climate catastrophe in a telling way. By merging an ecosemiotic approach and the need for more extensive and effective translation in reaction to the Anthropocene's changing ecological conditions, they argue for exploring the resilient elements of animal and human-animal (interspecies) communication in such gigantic, innovative and ambitious work-in-progress projects as the Interspecies Internet.

The next two chapters by Jussi Parikka and Agnė Narušytė explore the artistic collaborations between humans and non-human animals. Jussi Parikka focuses on Tomás Saraceno's works, which stage spider webs as living sculptural diagrams. These webs are seen as 'working objects' situated between cognitive architecture and extended cognition. Parrika interprets Saraceno's diagrammatic webs 'not as a *reflection* of theoretical work on extended cognition and the cognitive nonconscious, but as a more complex *working with* of the shared objects of research – and the staging and producing of working objects'. The strategy of working with non-human partners is at the centre of Agnė Narušytė's chapter. Narušytė reviews an ongoing project 'The Landscape Partisan: Castor Fiber' by the Lithuanian artist Aurelija Maknytė, who photographs the dam-building of beavers and interprets them as the partisans of landscaping in trying to fight back against the destructive effects of the Anthropocene. Narušytė argues that the artist herself also uses specific partisan practices to assure that beavers have a proper status. One of these partisan practices is to photograph the landscape from the perspective of beavers and thus present them as perceiving subjects. Another practice is to claim for beavers a creator's status by presenting their 'working objects' in prestigious art institutions under the name 'Castor Fiber'. By presenting 'working objects' created by Castor Fiber, Maknytė seeks to convince the *Homo sapiens* that beavers are not pests to be gotten rid of, but equal living beings.

The third part of the book discusses the question of life in terms of ideality and materiality. Cary Wolfe argues that the discourses of Gaia and the Anthropocene have abandoned 'the question of the animal' prematurely, because it is 'the animal' which exposes the qualitatively different orders of causality in biological versus physical systems. Wolfe points out that biological systems have an unpredictable, 'creative' character, which differentiates them from physical systems. Wolfe criticises Latour for being unable to conceptualise the contingency of Gaia (and of self-referential biological systems) and describes it as an 'outlaw' and 'anti-system'. Therefore, Wolfe insists on creating a new 'jagged' ontology which consists of contingency, constraint closure, complexity and creativity. This 'jagged' ontology would explain the unpredictable and unruly character of biological life forms and their environmental relations. Wolfe argues that 'paying serious attention to the question of "the animal" forces us to think more clearly and more rigorously about the biosphere in all its singularity and uniqueness in ways that reach far beyond the question of climate change and the Anthropocene'. On a similar trajectory, John Ó Maoilearca questions contemporary definitions of ontology by asking what is new about new materialism. He points out that new materialists describe matter as 'vital', 'lively' and 'vibrant', in contrast to passive and inert matter described by old materialists. New materialist ontologies emphasise such questions as movement, vitality, duration and contingency; however, as Ó Maoilearca points out, these are exactly the same questions which were discussed by earlier spiritualists, from 'French Spiritualism' to Henri Bergson. This means that neither a spiritualism devoid of matter nor a materialism devoid of spirit could explain the continuing activity that life is. Life is to be understood not as opposed substances but as 'covarying levels (parts and wholes) of change, creativity, and freedom'.

Thomas Nail continues the dispute about how to define the nature of life in the posthuman condition. He critically reconsiders the premises of Deleuzian 'neo-vitalism' and Jane Bennett's 'vital materialism' and argues that this approach is politically insufficient, historically suspicious, unnecessarily metaphysical and conceptually vague. In contrast to a 'neo-vitalist' approach, Nail suggests thinking about movement as a more ontologically primary concept than life or vital forces. Instead of making claims about matter's vitality, he suggests that 'everything is in motion'. Such a movement-oriented perspective could examine emergent motion patterns at any scale without ontologically privileging one scale or another. In a similar vein, Audronė Žukauskaitė examines the notion of form in the philosophies of Simondon, Ruyer and Malabou, seeking to reconstruct a certain morphing ontology. Discussing such notions as individuation, transduction, morphogenesis or plasticity, she defines life as a form-taking activity. In this respect a morphing ontology encompasses both organic and inorganic life forms, although maintaining their differences, and traces a certain continuity between cellular plasticity of the body and neuronal plasticity of the brain. In this sense life is seen as a formation, a form-taking activity, which possesses its own mode of self-transformation and self-organisation. In the final chapter, Catherine Malabou introduces her 'plastic ontology' related to the 'epigenetic turn' in the history of neurology and in contemporary philosophy. The epigenetic plasticity of the brain was considered an exceptional feature of human creativity in contrast to the functioning of machines. However, some recent developments in AI make this distinction more problematic because machines are becoming more and more plastic and can create artificial neurons that mimic neurobiological models. This poses difficult philosophical questions: is technology just imitating the nature of the neurobiological self, or is this technological self just relating to itself through the mediation of nature? Perhaps these questions cannot be answered right now but they definitely give contours of our posthuman condition and point towards a posthuman future.

References

Bennett, Jane (2010), *Vibrant Matter: A Political Ecology of Things*, Durham, NC and London: Duke University Press.

Braidotti, Rosi (2013), *The Posthuman*, Cambridge: Polity Press.

Braidotti, Rosi (2018), 'A Theoretical Framework for the Critical Posthumanities', *Theory, Culture & Society*, Special Issue: Transversal Posthumanities: 1–31.

Braidotti, Rosi and Simone Bignall (eds) (2019), *Posthuman Ecologies: Complexity and Process After Deleuze*, New York and London: Rowman and Littlefield.

Colebrook, Claire (2016), 'What Is the Anthropo-Political?', in Tom Cohen, Claire Colebrook and J. Hillis Miller (eds), *Twilight of the Anthropocene Idols*, London: Open Humanities Press, pp. 81–125.

Coole, Diana and Samantha Frost (eds) (2010), *New Materialisms. Ontology, Agency, and Politics*, Durham, NC and London: Duke University Press.

Crutzen, Paul J. and Eugene F. Stoermer (2000), 'The Anthropocene', *Global Change News Letter*, 41: 17–18.

Demos, T. J. (2017), *Against the Anthropocene: Visual Culture and Environment Today*, New York and Berlin: Sternberg Press.

Derrida, Jacques (2008), *The Animal That Therefore I Am*, trans. David Wills, New York: Fordham University Press.

Despret, Vinciane (2016), *What Would Animals Say If We Asked the Right Questions?*, trans. Brett Buchanan, Minneapolis: University of Minnesota Press.

Grosz, Elizabeth (2017), *The Incorporeal: Ontology, Ethics, and the Limits of Materialism*, New York: Columbia University Press.

Grusin, Richard (2015), 'Introduction', in Richard Grusin (ed.), *The Nonhuman Turn*, Minneapolis and London: University of Minnesota Press, pp. vii–xxix.

Massumi, Brian (2014), *What Animals Teach Us about Politics*, Durham, NC and London: Duke University Press.

Mirzoeff, Nicholas (2014), 'Visualizing the Anthropocene', *Public Culture*, 26(2): 213–32.

Mirzoeff, Nicholas (2018), 'It's Not the Anthropocene, It's the White Supremacy Scene; or, The Geological Color Line', in Richard Grusin (ed.), *After Extinction*, Minneapolis and London: University of Minnesota Press, pp. 123–49.

Moore, Jason (ed.) (2016), *Anthropocene or Capitalocene: Nature, History, and the Crisis of Capitalism*, Oakland, CA: PM Press.

Wolfe, Carey (2010), *What Is Posthumanism?*, Minneapolis: University of Minnesota Press.

Wolfe, Carey (2018), 'Posthumanism', in Rosi Braidotti and Maria Hlavajova (eds), *Posthuman Glossary*, New York and London: Bloomsbury, pp. 356–9.

Yusoff, Kathryn (2018), *A Billion Black Anthropocenes or None*, Minneapolis: University of Minnesota Press.

Zylinska, Joanna (2018), *The End of Man: A Feminist Counterapocalypse*, Minneapolis: University of Minnesota Press.

Part I

Life Beyond the Anthropocene

1

Anthropocene Desperation in Gaian Context

Bruce Clarke

Years before COVID-19 hit, American evolutionary theorist and major Gaia proponent Lynn Margulis sized up the 'pandemic we call progress' in noting that 'what has been called "the Earth's environment" is no externality' (Margulis 2006: 12). That is, in a Gaian view, the environment is not 'out there'; we are inside it. Our despoilments are thus self-mutilations.[1] Especially when it comes to Gaia, we cannot help but include ourselves within the sytem to be observed, not at all as primary agents, but fundamentally as distributed geobiological elements intricately bound up with the whole system. Moreover, in the rhetorical theatre of this statement, Gaia also looks back at us, but with a diminishing gaze:

> The environment is part of the body. Therefore, for us, the talkative, lying, quarrelsome but endlessly manipulative, social ape, the disrespectful act of despoilment, the self-mutilation, the pandemic we call progress (e.g., deforestation, desertification) are, for Gaia, only petty activities, a masochism writ large of the mammalian kind that Gaia has seen before. Gaia continues to smile: *Homo sapiens*, she shrugs, soon will either change its wayward ways or, like other plague species, will terminate with a whimper in the current scourge, in this same accelerated Holocene extinction it initiated and has sustained over the past 10,000 years. (Margulis 2006: 12)

Personifying Gaia as somewhat irritated by human annoyances, Margulis issued a blanket condemnation of anthropic folly. Composing this passage in 2006, she was likely aware of the onset of 'the Anthropocene' as a new geological description of contemporary planetary dynamics. If so, she was having none of it. Through a leap of identification with Gaia's planetary perspective, a view in the making since joining forces with British scientist James Lovelock at the start of the 1970s, Margulis saw through our 'human age' to perceive the leading edge of an extinction event for which humans have indeed been the primary agents – not just since the steam engine or Hiroshima, as indicated by some Anthropocene chronologies, but at least since the recession of the last ice age – and to which humans have now put themselves in peril of succumbing (Rull 2022).

> The current rate of extinctions compared to the geological norm is now several thousandfold faster, making this the sixth great mass extinction event in Earth's history, and thus the start of the Anthropocene in its clearest demarcation, which is to say, we are in a biosphere catastrophe that will be obvious in the fossil record for as long as the Earth lasts. Also the mass extinction is one of the most obvious examples of things done by humans that cannot be undone, despite [. . .] the general robustness of life on Earth. (Robinson 2020: 43)

This passage from *The Ministry for the Future* has the generic curiosity of presenting scientific statements about the Anthropocene situation along with plausible conclusions based on those constructions, while stationed within the invented story of a climate-fiction novel. My chapter is largely addressed to the former, the nonfiction discourse rather than the fictive imagination of our time of climate crisis, although I will eventually bring these two threads together. The apocalyptic content to be explored here is largely drawn from the same stock of documentation as the plausible conclusions that inform Robinson's narrative. I approach the topical theme of cultural desperation as a reasonable affect and not at all ironically as an overheated response. But sheer desperation left to itself is likely to drive bad decisions and so to compound both itself and its causes. One way to defuse the negative amplifications of such positive feedbacks, as I hope to explain, is by placing them in Gaian context.

1. Toys of desperation

As I began to write up this chapter on a December day, *The Washington Post* pushed an article into my inbox titled 'Climate change has destabilized the Earth's poles, putting the rest of the planet in peril'. The takeaway was this:

> The rapid transformation of the Arctic and Antarctic creates ripple effects all over the planet. Sea levels will rise, weather patterns will shift and ecosystems will be altered. Unless humanity acts swiftly to curb emissions, scientists say, the same forces that have

destabilized the poles will wreak havoc on the rest of the globe. (Kaplan 2021)

This was hardly the first downbeat news article to reach me by the same route. Two months earlier another *Post* article, bemoaning 'a sad reality about our halfhearted war on climate change', offered a version of the term this essay puts into play: 'We are losing, the effects of global warming are becoming ever-more glaring, and we are desperately groping for solutions, including far-fetched schemes that we might have avoided or dismissed in the past' (Appell 2021). Coming back to December, numb from the disruption of the poles, I returned to the academic article already up on my screen:

> What is this truth of our time? Perhaps one can start with its causes, which are multiple: the global climate and ecological crisis, resource depletion, military development, digital industrialization and a runaway consumerism accelerating daily through the intense exploitation of people's attention and desires – there is a whole range of phenomena that seem to inevitably lead towards an apocalyptic end. If we are not able to reverse these destructive trends, humanity may soon confront its own extinction. (Lemmens and Hui 2017)

These are desperate times: over and above the great derangements in our planetary systems, an ambient frenzy grips the globe.[2] Everyone seems to be angry at something or someone and the worst are criminally acting out. Starring its current stealth bomber, COVID-19, and the chaotic uptake of the virus and its vaccines into human populations and social systems, climate change in the time of the Anthropocene has induced a vicious collective malaise. Bruno Latour sees something similar in the sociopolitical affect of climate-change denial: 'The absence of a *common world* we can share is driving us crazy' (2018: 2).

The *Oxford English Dictionary* defines *desperation* as a partial or complete loss of hope in matters as they stand, spurring incautious responses that risk being futile or destructive in their own right: 'Despair leading to recklessness, or recklessness arising from despair; a desperate state of mind in which, on account of hopelessness or extremely small chance of success, one is ready to do any violent or extravagant action, regardless of risks or consequences' (*OED*). A passage from Shakespeare's *Hamlet* provides a classical example. Describing the dizzying view of the sea from the battlements of the royal castle, Horatio implores Hamlet to be mindful how the very height alone (let alone a dubious spectre) makes the mind reel. The place itself breeds 'toys of desperation', a good place for a ghost to lure someone to their doom:

> What if it tempt you toward the flood, my lord,
> Or to the dreadful summit of the cliff
> That beetles o'er his base into the sea,
> And there assume some other horrible form,
> Which might deprive your sovereignty of reason
> And draw you into madness? Think of it.
> The very place puts toys of desperation,
> Without more motive, into every brain
> That looks so many fathoms to the sea
> And hears it roar beneath. (*Hamlet* I. iv. 75–84)

However, let us go beyond Hamlet's tragic story of terminal indecision and adopt this scene as a collective allegory of fear and inaction as Anthropocene humans gaze from above, so to speak, upon the climate crisis, down there where nature lies, somewhere below them. The debacle of the Anthropocene is filled with all-too-real materialisations of horrible forms.[3] Within the specifically geological remit of the Anthropocene concept, however, the anthropogenic technosphere is said to overtake natural 'forces' – physical, thermodynamic, tectonic, sedimentary.[4] Less distinctly observed if equally palpable are geobiological agencies that the technosphere cannot possibly overtake – for instance, the imperiled biospheric efficacies of forests – whose loss or removal diminishes the affordances of complex natural systems. While human activities can augment or damage but not control or replace these Gaian agencies, ecosystem destruction diminishes the cohesion of Gaian systems.[5]

Climate aberrations leading to and arising from extinctions and die-offs, in the aftermath of fatal inundations from sea-level rise and extreme weather events: these are the ever more mundane disasters that most threaten to pull humanity down off its battlements and cancel its prior immunities to immediate harm merely from occupying one's place of dwelling. As I will discuss further on, Gaian science brought the climate crisis into focus decades before the dissemination of its current Anthropocene profile. More importantly, its preview of current anthropogenic environmental disruptions derived in good part from its profound purchase on prior climatic vagaries over geological time. Whether the Anthropocene era is measured in decades, centuries or even millennia, it is but a blip within the Gaiacene, which has been around well over two aeons.

2. Countercultural apocalypse and scientific consensus

A prior state of modern environmental desperation came about under the shadow of *Silent Spring* and nuclear annihilation. Its remediation at that moment was assisted by the fall 1968 debut of the *Whole Earth Catalog*, offering 'access to tools' for off-grid and communal lifestyles that were themselves radical responses to apocalyptic fears of social and ecological collapse. The name 'Whole Earth' – itself a gesture of systemic restoration to counter a fragmented Cold-Warring global polity – came from pictures of Earth taken from space, in particular, the Earthrise photograph taken from lunar orbit on Christmas Eve of 1968, which spectacularly confirmed the evocative power of this technologically realised vista of our planet as a whole system.[6] The *Catalog*'s deeply informed cultivation of ecological and whole-systems thinking carried on with its reboot in 1974 as the periodical *CoEvolution Quarterly*. Its prescient Gaian intimations were famously confirmed in 1975 with an elaborate cover article on the veritable Gaia hypothesis, lead-authored by Margulis in collaboration with Lovelock (Margulis and Lovelock 1975; Clarke 2020: 112–18).

A decade later, *CoEvolution Quarterly* was rebranded the *Whole Earth Review*, somewhat displacing its ecological motif with a pioneering interest in global cyberculture (Turner 2006). Its Winter 1988 number celebrated the twentieth anniversary of the *Catalog*'s creation by gathering a cohort of contributors largely from the American countercultural intelligentsia of that moment.[7] However, nestled among these luminaries was also the name of James Lovelock. After their first appearance in *CoEvolution Quarterly*, both Margulis and Lovelock became occasional contributors to its pages. The Winter 1988 number of the *Whole Earth Review* afforded them facing pages linked by a picture of them sitting at a table side by side, with Margulis smilingly pointing a finger at Lovelock. His headnote explains: 'In this photograph Lynn accuses Jim of being the true author of the Gaia notion' (Lovelock 1988b). This was an inside joke concerning the precise provenance of the Gaia hypothesis, given that their names had been consistently linked in the earliest run of Gaia publications in the mid-1970s, in both scientific and popular venues, occasionally with Margulis as lead author. But by the end of the 1980s, Lovelock had fully documented his right to first authorship (Lovelock 1979, 1988a).

To be sure, Lovelock invoked his notion of Gaia on this twentieth-anniversary occasion (1988b).[8] But he did so only after situating that concept in geopolitical and starkly environmental contexts invoking human activities as both 'ecocidal' and 'geocidal'. It still would have been possible at that moment to read his observations as alarmist. But with over thirty years of hindsight and the unremitting onslaught of climate disruptions upon us, Lovelock's acrid birthday gift to the readership of the *Whole Earth Review* anticipated by several decades the current strain of desperation in Anthropocene climate discourse.

The unsettling confidence of Lovelock's remarks on this occasion may well express Gaian projections he was drawing from a sharply converging scientific consensus on anthropogenic global heating, punctuated in 1988 by the United Nation's creation of the Intergovernmental Panel on Climate Change (IPCC). Earlier that year, several days after the atmospheric physicist James Hansen's famous presentation to a US Senate committee nailing the anthropogenic source of the strengthening climate greenhouse, a major conference met in Toronto on 'The Changing Atmosphere: Implications for Global Security'. Here Michael B. McElroy, an eminent atmospheric chemist well-known to both Lovelock and Margulis, gave an austere presentation on 'global change', a slogan that arose in 1982 in work that his Harvard colleague, professor of planetary physics Richard Goody, led on behalf of NASA (McElroy 1989; Goody 1982). The Gaia hypothesis itself was also incubated in NASA's nurseries, a milieu shared by Lovelock and Margulis, Goody and McElroy (Clarke 2020: 245–9). McElroy picked up that theme with a straightforwardly Gaian statement while proceeding to emphasise the human portion of the biosphere as the source of the current anomalies:

> The atmosphere may be considered in many respects an extension of the biosphere. Its composition is changing rapidly at the present time, for a variety of reasons linked ultimately to pressures exerted by an expanding population, and the aspirations of this population for an enhanced quality of life. The human species is now a force of consequence for change on a global scale. Its presence is evident from pole to pole, from the depths of the ocean to the heights of the stratosphere. We face an immediate and important challenge: to understand and predict the consequences of our actions, and to bring this knowledge to bear on policy so as to preserve the viability of the planet for ourselves and for generations yet unborn. (McElroy 1989: 106)

3. Natural non-linearity

Lovelock (1988b) picks up and prognosticates upon this already advanced consensus regarding matters that will fall under the Anthropocene label over a decade later. I will quote Lovelock's article in its entirety to let its resonances echo in full across the third of a century since its publication.

The lucidity of his view into the near future of 1988 – that is, our world now – derives in part from the mature state to which Lovelock and Margulis by then had brought the heuristic integrity of Gaian science. Lovelock (1988a) argues that the Gaian system's age-old efficacy as a climate regulator keeping the planet cool for the current biota has already been coping with natural stresses throughout the Pleistocene epoch; in his view, the ice ages' repeated glaciations and thaws are the sign and outcome of a wobbly regulatory regime whose oscillations suggest a weakening of the overall system. In that case, the human colonisation of the Holocene epoch – civilisation and its accelerating demands for domesticated land and energy extraction and combustion – has only thrown an already-challenged system into further imbalance. These views added force to Lovelock's long-standing conviction that contemporary climate changes will be hard to reverse.

Seemingly Anthropocenic *avant la lettre*, Lovelock's affirmations of modern humanity's share of responsibility for deteriorating planetary conditions also place the human technosphere in truer proportion to the rest of the biosphere and its deep backstory. Whereas Earth System Science (ESS) and the International Geosphere/Biosphere Programme (IGBP) would inject a Gaian conception of the Earth into the Anthropocene concept, the Anthropocene stages humanity in the foreground of its eponymous geological epoch (Steffen et al. 2020). Gaia's difference rests in its radical demotion of the human contribution. Both Lovelock and Margulis diminish humanity's importance by contrast with the longue durée of Earth history. Nevertheless, this Gaian correction does not remediate the dire content of Lovelock's contemporary climate predictions, which, he assured his readers, 'are near certain and not the fashionable fiction of doom scenarios'.

Lovelock begins by situating his remarks in the geopolitical lull of the late 1980s, the moment of Mikhail Gorbachev's political reforms in the Soviet Union and the partial winding down of the Cold War. As an erstwhile British summer resident of County Cork, Ireland, with significant connections to the UK military, Lovelock felt under personal threat from the IRA. Lovelock places the Irish conflict under a figure drawn from his own activities as a naturalist and expert in sensitive measurement apparatus such as his fabled electron capture device. These local troubles, then, are like a gauge by which to measure the lessening of geopolitical hostilities elsewhere in the world. His article begins:

For the moment it seems that peace has broken out all over the world; conciliatory noises are coming from almost all of the erstwhile combatants from the super-powers to purely tribal

confrontations. Perhaps as an example to monitor the intensity
of peace, Northern Ireland continues the monstrous irrelevance
of its permanent war. (Lovelock 1988b)

With the suggestion that the superpower détente of that moment allows
one to turn one's attention towards more important and truly existential
matters, now Lovelock takes up his own construction of environmental
concerns. He drops in his contrarian credentials by minimising other
strains of alarmism over the ecological threats posed by nuclear energy
generation and mundane industrial pollution – perhaps seeing these as
relatively tractable problems – in favour of an implicitly Gaian view of
truly 'vast' – global rather than local – perils to the viability of the planet.

> In this new political climate there has been time to stand back
> and wonder what looms ahead. There is a growing realization
> that the future political agenda will be filled with environmen-
> tal concern. Not those minor problems, like nuclear radiation,
> nuclear waste, or the fearful non-event of Three Mile Island or
> the noxious effluents of chemical industries, or indeed anything
> that might titillate the public fear of cancer. The problems that lie
> ahead are vast, perilous, and certain. (Ibid.)

Lovelock now cuts to the heart of his message: climate change is coming,
it's going to be bad, and its deliberate mitigation is unlikely. As just
discussed, his prediction is implicitly drawn from his Gaian reading of
the succession of ice ages as a vacillation in Gaia's homeostatic function
as a global temperature regulator. He ironically suggests that human
'privilege' obtains not in any possession of control over these processes,
but strictly insofar as we may partake – as spectators, but really, as
participants – in a conscious spiritual awareness of their occurrence:

> In the next few decades the Earth will pass through one of its
> major transitions and we, its first social intelligent species, are
> privileged to be among the spectators. The event is an imminent
> major climate change, one that will be twice and could be six
> times as great as the change from the last ice age until now. (Ibid.)

The Gaian perspective enhances the long view of geobiological turbu-
lence under the ultimate criterion of habitability, biological viability.
When, relatively recently, the upper latitudes were under massive sheets
of ice, nevertheless the tropics were larger than now and often lush.
Making its living where it could, *Homo* had already learned the trick of

fire and was leaving extensive marks, wreaking anthropogenic upheaval on the forested lands to the south. Lovelock continues:

> So let's look at the depth of the last glaciation, some tens of thousands of years ago. When the glaciers reached St. Louis in America, and London in Europe, the sea level was some 400 feet lower than now and as a consequence an area of land as large as Africa was above water and covered with vegetation. The tropics were like the warm temperate regions now. In all, it was a rather pleasant planet to live on and was the home of simple natural humans just beginning to try such neat ecocidal tricks as fire-drive hunting: set the forest on fire and a free effortless barbecue is provided. (Ibid.)

The onset of the Holocene thaw opened up vast new landscapes for general repatriation. And while all geological eras undergo climate changes at some pace, earlier humanity already had a hand in the acceleration of the recession of the glaciers. But in another ironic reversal of the overall triumph of that process, we have driven the pendulum in the opposite direction. Where once were blizzards and frigid dry spells, heat waves, hurricanes and tornadoes shall be:

> Just imagine a change in climate at least twice as great as that from then until now, the start of a heat age. The temperature and the sea level will climb decade by decade, until eventually the world will become torrid, ice free, and all but unrecognizable. Eventually is a long time ahead, it might never happen, and need not worry us now; what we do have to prepare for are the events of the transition itself, events that are just about to begin. These are likely to be surprises in the way of extremes, like storms of great ferocity, and unexpected atmospheric events like the ozone hole over Antarctica. Nature is non-linear and unpredictable and never more so than in a period of transition. So sit back and enjoy the show – it is all but unstoppable now. (Ibid.)

Much that was once only imaginable has now come to pass, more or less as Lovelock sketched it here. The Gaian frame of Lovelock's vision tells in the statement that 'Nature is non-linear'. This is the proper Gaian understanding of planetary feedback mechanisms. Yes, the Gaian system (the theory goes) acts to maximise habitability over geological time by achieving a homeostasis in key planetary flows of energies and materials. But the 'stasis' of homeostasis is simply an ideal mean, not a fixed condition. It is the average over eons around which lesser or greater oscillations play out. Lovelock satirises the simplistic idea of Gaia that misperceives it as a balance-of-nature warrantee:

> But what of Gaia? Will she not respond and keep the status quo? Before we expect Gaia to act, we should realise that the present interglacial warm period could be regarded as a fever for Gaia and that left to herself she would be relaxing into her normal, comfortable for her, ice age. She may be unable to relax because we have been busy removing her skin and using it as farm land, especially the trees and the forests of the humid tropics, which otherwise are among the means for her recovery. But also we are adding a vast blanket of greenhouse gases to the already feverish patient. In these circumstances Gaia is much more likely to shudder and move over to a new stable state fit for a different and more amenable biota. It could be much hotter or much colder, but whatever it is, no longer the comfortable world we know. (Ibid.)

Lovelock extrapolates from the Pleistocene epoch by reading anthropogenic climate change as forcing hotter oscillations, impeding Gaia's efficacy as a planetary air cooler. His foresight connecting diverse phenomena induced by global heating – such as 'drought and floods' – rings true today. As McElroy laid out the situation that same year:

> There is an important synergism between CO_2 and H_2O (Hansen et al. 1981). Carbon dioxide itself absorbs but a small fraction of the energy radiated by the surface. Water vapour is much more significant. The abundance of water vapour, however, is controlled ultimately by temperature; an increase in CO_2 would be expected to cause an increase in temperature, allowing more water vapour to enter the atmosphere, leading to a further increase in temperature. (1989: 106–7)

This is the positive feedback scenario to be averted, or more realistically now, to be planned for. The global increase in CO_2 and methane heats up the planet; greater heat produces a rise in humidity strongly augmenting an atmospheric suffocation that, like a pressure cooker, keeps the heat in rather than allowing its radiation to exit the system. Lovelock continues:

> The onset of the human and political consequences of these two geocidal acts, forest clearance and suffocation by the greenhouse

gases, will be the news. News that will usurp the political agenda. Soon, and suddenly, in the regions that are now the humid tropical forests, there could be a billion or more humans enduring drought and floods, perhaps with mean temperatures of 120° F. They would be without support, in a vast arid region around the earth. All this could happen at a time when we in the North, who might otherwise come to their rescue, are facing rising sea levels and major changes in our own climate, and the most amazing surprises. (Lovelock 1988b)

On schedule, climate refugees from the South and the East are being refused or held in internment by the North. An anthropogenic surfeit of greenhouse gases is amplifying the positive feedback between humidity and heat. Brutal heat waves have arrived and only need to go up another notch before the opening scene of *The Ministry for the Future*, in which a single heat event leaves millions dead across a wide swath of India, becomes reportage rather than fiction. One of the novel's didactic narrators mentions 'wet-bulb temperatures'. In an actual Indian heat wave in 2015 in which thousands died, the wet-bulb temperature – a measure of heat stress due to saturation of water vapour – hit 30° C:

> And a wet-bulb temperature of 35 will kill humans, even if unclothed and sitting in the shade; the combination of heat and humidity prevents sweating from dissipating heat, and death by hypothermia soon results. And wet-bulb temperatures of 34 have been recorded since the year 1990. (Robinson 2020: 29)

Lovelock concludes his 1988 piece with an assurance of predictive reliability drawn, I speculate, from his confidence in the veracity of his cybernetic descriptions of Gaia's climate mechanisms. He wrapped his remarks in a Biblical image to match Horatio's picture of the edge of doom. In our desperation to stay inside a flawed technosphere built on unsupportable levels of combustion, our demons are driving us over the cliff:

> These predictions of events are near certain and not the fashionable fiction of doom scenarios. We are like a modern version of the Gadarene swine, driving our polluting cars heedlessly down the slope into a sea that is rising to drown us. (Lovelock 1988b)

And here we are. Lovelock's predictions of 1988 eerily echo in his remarks just last November on the occasion of COP26, in a parting shot that evokes something like Gaia's desperation to be done with the Anthropocene:

> Warnings that once seemed like the doom scenarios of science fiction are now coming to pass. We are entering into a heat age in which the temperature and sea levels will be rising decade by decade until the world becomes unrecognisable. We could also be in for more surprises. Nature is non-linear and unpredictable, never more than at a time of transition [. . .] But my fellow humans must learn to live in partnership with the Earth, otherwise the rest of creation will, as part of Gaia, unconsciously move the Earth to a new state in which humans may no longer be welcome. The virus, Covid-19, may well have been one negative feedback. Gaia will try harder next time with something even nastier. (Lovelock 2021)

It seems that living in partnership is something most humans have seldom done all that well. For Lovelock to speculate in our present moment that COVID-19 could be 'one negative feedback' among others likely to follow is to conceive the spread of that virus through the human population as a Gaian stab at bolstering its dedicated efficacy as a self-regulating system holding the planet altogether in a state fit for the continuation of life by diminishing its Anthropocene agents. It would certainly be preferable at this stage of affairs to partner up as Gaian beings producing our own self-regulation as a planetary participant.

4. Gaian being and Gaian time

In 'The Future in the Anthropocene: Extinction and the Imagination', Claire Colebrook develops a cultural chronology of the idea of extinction, largely as that has been reflected in imaginative literature – novels, poems and movies. The conclusion of Darwin's *Origin of Species* merits a key role in her construction: she sees it as culminating a pre-modern tradition in which apocalyptic ends revealed the beginning of a new set of encompassing conditions. In the classical evolutionary view, for instance, the destruction wrought by the extinction of species cleared the field for new forms that could now have their own day in the sun:

> What ties traditional, mythic, and pre-modern apocalyptic thought to the Darwinian conception of extinction is a notion of ends as redemptive and inhuman: life's grandeur makes its way through forms that are an expression of a power for formation or creativity that is bound up with destruction. (Colebrook 2019: 280)

In contrast, Anthropocene imaginations are 'post-apocalyptic' in that the matter of extinction tends to refer exclusively to human beings, and even more so to the contemporary 'world' of affluent accommodations, to those enjoying the ways of life that have the farthest to fall if the climate crisis brings the contemporary technosphere crashing down. In the literary and cinematic disaster narratives Colebrook reviews,

> the end of Western urbanity reveals nothing other than the desire to save or mourn the very world of hyper-consumption that brought about its own end, and that of many others, precisely because no other form of existence counts as a world. (Ibid.: 265–6)

If we position the place of extinction in the Gaian imaginary as brought forward by Margulis and Lovelock in relation to Colebrook's account, it would seem to go against the typical Anthropocene constriction of concern to the precarious state of the developed world. The remarkable thing about their decades of Gaian discourse on the climate crisis is its equanimity, or, again, its literal evocation of a posthuman condition. While it does not return to anything like the scriptural tones of Darwin's evocation of evolutionary grandeur, nor does the notion of redemption have a place here, nevertheless, it does restore the primary themes of continuation under new circumstances. As Margulis stated unequivocally, 'Gaia continues to smile' (2006: 12) even when confronting the prospect of 'a new state in which humans may no longer be welcome' (Lovelock 2021). In other words, in the Gaian imaginary, apocalypse is radical transformation but not disaster. It is a disaster and a dead end only for those forms of life whose depredations upon other life forms have also rendered them no longer viable within the changed conditions they have brought upon themselves. The villains of the piece will suffer their just deserts.

States of desperation can form only around points of hope, however minute. If the responses incited by desperate affairs can pull back from sheer recklessness and exercise due compassion for communal dilemmas, they might still succeed in setting matters on a viable course. After all, although the choice does appear to be in our hands, human beings need not go extinct any time soon (Grinspoon 2016). All the same, in the terms laid out by Colebrook, human life in a planetary ecology of radically diminished biodiversity would certainly be post-apocalyptic: we might save a remnant of ourselves but would still come to the end of the world as we know it. In a recent post-lecture conversation with environmental narrative scholar Ursula Heise, novelist Kim Stanley

Robinson framed his view on the calamity of the current extinction event as a crime against humanity and nature at once:

> Human extinction is not quite possible given our cleverness and our ability to get by. We could have mass deaths. We could lose a big percentage of humanity and it would be a disaster and a crime forever. But it wouldn't be extinction for us. It's the other species. That is the crime we can't come back from. (Robinson 2021)

Against these sombre vistas of guilt and remorse, Gaia extends a steadying hand and a long view whose non-human durations could calm the ambient madness. In this extended moment of Anthropocene desperation, it could help to some small degree to have a Gaian perspective on the past extinction events that have punctuated the prehuman aeons. As Dorion Sagan reminds us, Gaia 'is essentially a microbe-based system that has come roaring back after several mass extinctions and appears to be able to take care of itself through complex feedbacks' (2020: 144). Of course, the temporality of such recoveries is itself Gaian, and so measured in millions of years. However, time measured on the human scale could encompass a complementary view towards the posthuman condition to follow upon the Anthropocene event (Gibbard et al. 2021). For those who arrive there, it need not be a state of utter desolation. Elsewhere I have called this prospective posthuman condition *Gaian being* (Clarke 2017, 2020).

Where human being in all the suppositious glory of its distinction from the rest of life has been, there Gaian being shall be, one way or another, in settled acknowledgement of its dependence upon the flourishing of the biosphere altogether and of its obligatory participation with non-human life and non-organic Earth. Gaian being denotes planetary solidarity. In whatever way we resolve or accommodate self-inflicted Anthropocene threats to our collective existence, or botch that job, the Gaian system will hold on as long as cosmologically possible, seeking out and buffering a planetary state of general viability that plays no favourites. In this view, the supreme value is the continuation of the life that has arisen on the Earth and taken the planet to itself, its continuation right here on the same Earth, in whatever forms can keep that alliance going. Off-planet adventures can wait until a post-Anthropocene humanity gets right with Gaia and so stabilises its own long-term survival prospects.

As the Anthropocene event plays out, massive and difficult adjustments will be necessary to realign our ways of life in concert with the non-linear dynamics by which Gaia's symbiotic contingencies unfold. The Gaian beings I envision will ally the positivity of their own mortality with the cosmological longevity of the Gaian system. In this sense, Gaian being complements Donna Haraway's evocation of planetary compost, in which the posthuman condition itself merges into a matrix of inorganic and post-organic constituents, decomposing and recomposing forms. This would be akin to Colebrook's Darwinian evocation of Gaian time as 'an expression of a power for formation or creativity that is bound up with destruction':

> We are not posthuman; we are compost. We are not homo; we are humus. We are terran; we are earthlings; we are many; we are indeterminate. We bleed into each other in chaotic fluid extravagance. We eat our own snakey tails in sympoietic whorls to generate polymorphic ongoingness; we are enmeshed with the ouroboroi of diverse interlaced netherworlds. We are chthonic, of and for the earth, of and for its unfinished times. We live and die in its ruins. (Haraway 2018: 79)

We will call this being-to-come into being by reorganising human being around its inextricable immersion in Gaian cycles of life and death.

Acknowledgement

Thanks to Sébastien Dutreuil, Robert Salter, Henry Sussman and Tyler Volk for helpful comments on preliminary versions of this article.

Notes

1. One may read in such a statement an ecological application of the principle of the self-reference of cognition. See Clarke (2014: 177–81).
2. To the usual list of planetary stresses associated with the Anthropocene era, Pieter Lemmens and Yuk Hui add apocalyptic notes arising from a register of governmental, economic and technocultural crises. Introducing the complex critique of the Anthropocene and the arcane blueprints for its reversal in Stiegler (2018), Daniel Ross cites the Trump era as 'evidence of a deterioration of political faith, belief, trust, hope and will, and a corresponding rise of a desperate, reactionary and xenophobic anti-politics all too willing to designate scapegoats and appeal at every opportunity to fear and stupidity' (2018: 11).
3. The International Union of Geological Sciences has provided a helpful list: 'An order-of-magnitude increase in erosion and sediment transport associated with urbanization and agriculture; marked and abrupt anthropogenic perturbations of the cycles of elements such as carbon, nitrogen, phosphorus and various metals together with new chemical compounds; environmental changes generated by these perturbations, including global warming, sea-level rise, ocean acidification and spreading oceanic "dead

zones"; rapid changes in the biosphere both on land and in the sea, as a result of habitat loss, predation, explosion of domestic animal populations and species invasions' (Working Group on the Anthropocene, no date).

4. Anthropocene discourse foregrounds the accumulation of human leavings within the geological strata. The dynamism associated with the material momentum of this effluence is abstracted, as in Newtonian physics, as a *force*. The authorised literature ranges from rhetorical questionings (Steffen, Crutzen and McNeill 2007) to claims of ownership (Cooper et al. 2018). The Anthropocene: hey, we got this.

5. I draw my evocations of Gaia and its subsystems from the scientific and speculative discourses now labelled Gaia theory, as developed since the 1970s by James Lovelock with his collaborators and a multidisciplinary cadre of Earth and life scientists and critical theorists (Lovelock 1979, 1988a; Volk 2003; Harding 2006; Stengers 2015; Stolz 2017; Dutreuil 2018; Latour and Lenton 2019; Clarke 2017, 2020; Žukauskaitė 2020).

6. Shortly thereafter, that image appeared on the cover of the *Catalog*'s spring 1969 iteration (Clarke 2020: 102–6).

7. That roster confirmed the primarily old-school environmentalist nexus of the Whole Earth network's current mix of existential desperadoes, poets and politicos, psychonauts and pranksters. Those listed on the front cover included Mary Catherine Bateson, Wendell Berry, Jerry Brown, R. Crumb, Ram Dass, Lawrence Ferlinghetti, Wavy Gravy, Ivan Illich, Ken Kesey, Timothy Leary, Ralph Nader, Ted Nelson, Gary Snyder, Paolo Soleri, William Irwin Thompson and Anne Waldman.

8. Margulis herself left Gaia aside to write up her recent move from Boston University to the University of Massachusetts, Amherst, where she hoped to press ahead with her signature work on the serial evolution of the eukaryotic cell (1988).

References

Appell, David (2021), 'The climate crisis is spawning weird ideas to fix it. They might be all we have', *The Washington Post*, 8 October: https://www.washingtonpost.com/outlook/2021/10/08/mammoths-climate-ideas-desperation (last accessed 5 January 2022).

Clarke, Bruce (2014), *Neocybernetics and Narrative*, Minneapolis: University of Minnesota Press.

Clarke, Bruce (2017), 'Rethinking Gaia: Stengers, Latour, Margulis', *Theory, Culture and Society*, 34(4): 3–26.

Clarke, Bruce (2020), *Gaian Systems: Lynn Margulis, Neocybernetics, and the End of the Anthropocene*, Minneapolis: University of Minnesota Press.

Colebrook, Claire (2019), 'The Future in the Anthropocene: Extinction and the Imagination', in Adeline Johns-Putra (ed.), *Climate and Literature*, Cambridge: Cambridge University Press, pp. 263–80.

Cooper, Anthony H., Teresa J. Brown, Simon J. Price, Jonathan R. Ford and Colin N. Waters (2018), 'Humans are the Most Significant Global

Geomorphological Driving Force of the 21st Century', *The Anthropocene Review*, 5(3): 222–9.

Dutreuil, Sébastien (2018), 'James Lovelock's Gaia Hypothesis: "A New Look at Life on Earth" . . . for the Life and the Earth Sciences', in Oren Harman and Michael R. Dietrich (eds), *Dreamers, Visionaries, and Revolutionaries in the Life Sciences*, Chicago: University of Chicago Press, pp. 272–87.

Gibbard, Philip L., Andrew M. Bauer, Matthew Edgeworth, William F. Ruddiman, Jacquelyn L. Gill, Dorothy J. Merritts, Stanley C. Finney, Lucy E. Edwards, Michael J. C. Walker, Mark Maslin and Erle C. Ellis (2021), 'A Practical Solution: The Anthropocene is a Geological Event, Not a Formal Epoch', *Episodes: Journal of International Geoscience*, 15 November: https://www.episodes.org/journal/view.html?doi=10.18814/epiiugs/2021/021029 (last accessed 29 December 2021).

Goody, Richard (1982), *Global Change: Impacts on Habitability*, Jet Propulsion Laboratory, California Institute of Technology, Pasadena, CA: NASA.

Grinspoon, David (2016), *Earth in Human Hands: Shaping Our Planet's Future*, New York: Grand Central Publishing.

Hansen, James, D. Johnson, A. Lacis, S. Lebedeff, P. Lee, D. Rind and G. Russell (1981), 'Climate Impact of Increasing Atmospheric Carbon Dioxide', *Science* 213: 957–66.

Haraway, Donna (2018), 'Capitalocene and Chthulucene', in Rosi Braidotti and Maria Hlavajova (eds), *Posthuman Glossary*, London: Bloomsbury Academic, pp. 79–83.

Harding, Stephan (2006), *Animate Earth: Science, Intuition and Gaia*, White River Junction, VT: Chelsea Green.

Kaplan, Sarah (2021), 'Climate change has destabilized the Earth's poles, putting the rest of the planet in peril', *The Washington Post*, 14 December: https://www.washingtonpost.com/climate-environment/2021/12/14/climate-change-arctic-antarctic-poles (last accessed 6 January 2022).

Latour, Bruno (2018), *Down to Earth: Politics of the New Climatic Regime*, Cambridge: Polity.

Latour, Bruno and Timothy M. Lenton (2019), 'Extending the Domain of Freedom, or why Gaia is So Hard to Understand', *Critical Inquiry*, 45(3): 659–80.

Lemmens, Pieter and Yuk Hui (2017), 'Apocalypse, Now! Peter Sloterdijk and Bernard Stiegler on the Anthropocene', *boundary 2*, 16 January: https://www.boundary2.org/2017/01/ pieter-lemmens-and-yuk-hui-apocalypse-now-peter-sloterdijk-and-bernard-stiegler-on-the-anthropocene/ (last accessed 14 December 2021).

Lovelock, James (1979), *Gaia: A New Look at Life on Earth*, London: Oxford University Press.

Lovelock, James (1988a), *The Ages of Gaia: A Biography of Our Living Earth*, New York: Norton.

Lovelock, James (1988b), 'James Lovelock', *Whole Earth Review*, 61: 87.

Lovelock, James (2021), 'Beware: Gaia may destroy humans before we destroy the Earth', *The Guardian*, 2 November: https://www.theguardian.com/

commentisfree/2021/nov/02/ beware-gaia-theory-climate-crisis-earth (last accessed 30 December 2021).

McElroy, Michael (1989), 'The Challenge of Global Change', in *The Changing Atmosphere: Implications for Global Security*, Geneva: World Meteorological Organization, pp. 106–15.

Margulis, Lynn (1988), 'Lynn Margulis', *Whole Earth Review*, 61: 86.

Margulis, Lynn (2006), 'Foreword', in Harding 2006, pp. 7–12.

Margulis, Lynn and James Lovelock (1975), 'The Atmosphere as Circulatory System of the Biosphere: The Gaia Hypothesis', *CoEvolution Quarterly*, 6: 31–40.

Robinson, Kim Stanley (2020), *The Ministry for the Future*, New York: Orbit.

Robinson, Kim Stanley (2021), 'Optopia: From Fiction to Action on Climate Change', Possible Worlds Lecture presented by the Berggruen Institute, UCLA, 7 December, available at: https://www.youtube.com/watch?v=-4WqG4sLaBU (last accessed 9 January 2022).

Ross, Daniel (2018), 'Introduction', in Stiegler 2018, pp. 7–32.

Rull, Valentí (2022), 'Biodiversity Crisis or Sixth Mass Extinction? Does the Current Anthropogenic Biodiversity Crisis Really Qualify as a Mass Extinction?', *EMBO Reports*, 23: e54193.

Sagan, Dorion (2020), 'Gaia Versus the Anthropocene: Untimely Thoughts on the Current Eco-catastrophe', *Ecocene: Cappadocia Journal of Environmental Humanities*, 1(1): 137–46.

Steffen, Will, Paul J. Crutzen and John R. McNeill (2007), 'The Anthropocene: Are Humans Now Overwhelming the Great Forces of Nature?', *AMBIO: A Journal of the Human Environment*, 36(8): 614–21.

Steffen, Will, Katherine Richardson, Johan Rockström, Hans-Joachim Schellnhuber, Opha Pauline Dube, Sébastien Dutreuil, Timothy M. Lenton, and Jane Lubchenco (2020), 'The Emergence and Evolution of Earth System Science', *Nature Reviews – Earth and Environment*, 1: 54–63.

Stengers, Isabelle (2015), *In Catastrophic Times: Resisting the Coming Barbarism*, trans. Andrew Goffey, Ann Arbor, MI: Open Humanities Press.

Stiegler, Bernard (2018), *The Neganthropocene*, trans. Daniel Ross, London: Open Humanities Press.

Stolz, John (2017), 'Climate Change and the Gaia Hypothesis', in Gerard Magill and Kiarash Aramesh (eds), *The Urgency of Climate Change: Pivotal Perspectives*, Newcastle upon Tyne: Cambridge Scholars, pp. 50–72.

Turner, Fred (2006), *From Counterculture to Cyberculture: Stewart Brand, the Whole Earth Network, and the Rise of Digital Utopianism*, Chicago: University of Chicago Press.

Volk, Tyler (2003), *Gaia's Body: Toward a Physiology of Earth*, Cambridge: The MIT Press.

Working Group on the Anthropocene (no date), Subcommission on Quaternary Stratigraphy, available at: http://quaternary.stratigraphy.org/working-groups/anthropocene (last accessed 21 December 2021).

Žukauskaitė, Audronė (2020), 'Gaia Theory: Between Autopoiesis and Sympoiesis', *Problemos*, 98: 141–53.

2

Making Worlds Beyond Human Scale and Perspective

Małgorzata Sugiera

Increasing anxiety about anthropogenic changes and their catastrophic effects has visibly undermined the credibility of C. P. Snow's concept of the two cultures, introduced at the very beginning of the Great Acceleration, more than sixty years ago (Snow 2019). In his famous essay, Snow lamented the growing cultural divide that separated two great areas of human intellectual activity – 'science' and 'the arts' – hoping for bridges to be built by practitioners on both sides of this divide. In the late 1990s the issue of two cultures, this time figured predominantly as a divide between 'sciences' and 'humanities', returned on the wave of heated debates about what Bill Readings rightly addressed in the title of his book *The University in Ruins* (1997). What, however, changed the situation was the approaching eco-catastrophe, multipronged and complex, and therefore calling for global yet locally specific transdisciplinary approaches.

Writing in the hard times of another growing wave of the COVID-19 pandemic, I will refer briefly to the notion of 'syndemic' to give an example of new transversal and transdisciplinary tendencies in today's cultures. The American medical anthropologist Merrill Singer offered the notion a decade ago in order to demonstrate that the emergence and spread of a contagious disease reflects not only human activities, modes of production and residence as well as environmental transformations, but also what he aptly called cultural factors: beliefs, meanings, norms, values, various lifeways and cultural narratives (Singer 2016). This crucial entanglement of biological, social and cultural factors, specific also for many kinds of anthropogenic changes, has made visible how cultural narratives not only represent the world around us, imagining worlds by analogy which in a Shakespearian manner should 'hold [. . .] the mirror up to nature'. Cultural narratives could also actively act towards transforming reality. Indeed, nothing can better illustrate it than a new wave of novels, already called Anthropocene Fiction (Trexler 2015) or Climate Fiction (Streeby 2018). Not only do they make climate change the central problem in imagining a future, but they also try to design such in-depth economic, political and ecological transitions as are needed to face the interrelated crises of climate, food, energy, poverty and meaning. This is one of the reasons, I posit, why arts, literatures included, have started to change gradually into more or less metaphoric laboratories. What is important to stress is that these laboratories function not so much as places of experience that produce scientific knowledge, but rather as places of experience understood in the way in which Chris Salter elaborated upon in *Alien Agency*, referring to the French term 'expérience'. Unlike the English notion, the French term has a double meaning, that is 'that of experiment or speculation and that of experience, of something that happens to us' (Salter 2015: 241). Although Salter writes primarily about contemporary performance practice, I would like to take his perspective a step further to include other cultural narratives, across genres and media. In my view, they also make a kind of practice that is 'the affective and improvisatory assemblage of conditions that operates on and transforms us [. . .]. It destabilizes both the phenomena and its perception/affection – keeping things moving, unsettled' (ibid.). To reach this aim, therefore, artists still make worlds beyond human scale and perspective but do it differently.

In what follows, I will start with Edwin Abbott's *Flatland* as a classic example of early science fiction in which a non-human, mathematically instantiated world has been made by analogy to the contemporary Victorian society. It is in this context that I will then look closer at Kim Stanley Robinson's best-selling *Mars* trilogy. Although the author located the action primarily on the eponymous red planet, his trilogy is the epitome of Climate Fiction, as it designs a non-human (or rather more-than-human) world in order to face a contemporary eco-crisis in a speculative laboratory of the alien planet. What is of importance is that Robinson's trilogy not only demonstrates a complex and long-lasting process of the terraforming of Mars. It also interrelates this process with multilevel changes of what we used to define as the human (or even Man). However, instead of depicting these slowly alter(ed) humans, especially the ones born on Mars, as a new posthuman species, in my reading of the trilogy the author had rather prefigured what in 'The Camille Stories' Donna Haraway described as deeply anti-anthropogenic compostist practices over two decades later (Haraway 2016: 134–68). These practices could fundamentally transform humanity which, step by step, learns 'to appreciate the sheer semiotic materiality of those who came before' (ibid.: 157). They do it actually in both Robinson's trilogy and Haraway's fabulation.

Making non-human worlds (by analogy)

In his influential mathematical phantasy *Flatland* Edwin Abbott, a headmaster and teacher-scholar from London, skilfully merged social satire on the Victorian class system, an introduction to non-Euclidean geometry and a meditation on science in the face of new developments. This classic of early science fiction, which challenged the existing division into literary and scientific genres, was published in 1884 as 'a romance of many dimensions' and dedicated among others: 'To the Enlargement of THE IMAGINATION' (Abbott 2010: 61). This enlargement of the imagination was – and still is – by far the most significant gain for its readers, because the action of *Flatland* takes place mainly in the eponymous world of two dimensions. Each character is a different geometrical shape with President Circle as head of the state, and the book clearly denies even a possibility of existence of other worlds of three or more dimensions. To emphasise how this central tenet establishes the limits of both their perception and knowledge, Abbott published his novel under the name of A Square, who is at the same time the main character, the narrator and our guide in the alien flat universe. Nevertheless, this flat universe, inhabited by geometrical shapes, represented the Victorian society, close to the first readers of the novel. In so doing, Abbott allowed them to see their contemporaries in an alien perspective. Although he addressed a much-needed enlargement of the imagination already in the dedication, he wanted his readers to do more – to genuinely incorporate this new perspective. That is why A Square, a mathematician of no mean standing, repeatedly asks the readers to look with their 'eye exactly on the edge of the table' (ibid.: 69), because only then will they be able to perceive Flatland as a real Flatlander does – only straight lines, no figures. Through this apparently simple exercise, which requires a certain amount of physical effort, he intended to demonstrate the difference between being in a two-dimensional world and looking at it from above, as if one was bending over a flat surface.[1] The view from above, offering a large field of vision, allows one to see all that has been hidden before. At the same time, it gives the observer command and mastery over all that is seen and recognised. There is a good reason why in the second part of the novel Abbott decided to temporarily move the action of the novel to two other realms: in a dream to Lineland and then, in reality, to Spaceland, a universe in three dimensions much closer to the readers' reality. As a result, A Square, having learned to think according to the rules of analogy, can boldly demand of Sphere, his host in the second world, to 'see the insides of all solid things' (ibid.: 148). Closely examining how the inhabitants of other worlds reach conclusions on the basis of sensory experiences, A Square is able to identify the cognitive limitations of their and his readers' perception and prove the existence of different orders of reality.

Featuring mathematics as a model for critical reasoning, Abbott's *Flatland* participated in a heated debate of its time about the limits of human knowledge. Darko Suvin rightly calls these types of early science fiction novels 'cognitive parables' and explains: 'They create an alternative world, treat it with verisimilitude, and use it analogically to challenge the standards of author's own societies' (Suvin 1983: 26). Although Abbott indeed used this recipe to create an alternative world, he did it in a specific manner – he employed mathematics in order to demonstrate the limitations of the naturalised human scale and perspective. In doing so he intentionally undermined the supposed human mastery over the world and himself (the male gender is in full accord with the marginalisation of Victorian women criticised in *Flatland*). However, I am less interested in providing an updated interpretation of the novel, adequate to the recently defined era of the Anthropocene (or even the Androcene as some critics call it). I would rather treat *Flatland* as a prism to take a closer look at debates continuing for at least two decades about re-establishing new and non-hierarchical connections between humans and biotic and abiotic entities and/or forces. Otherwise, we will not be able to do away with all cognitive habits and biases, resulting from the fact that the basic dichotomy between the hegemonic knowing subject and the subaltern known object seems to be still intrinsic to human perception (Clarke and Wittenberg 2017). It is not only that the anthropogenic climate changes have a variety of scale effects and demands and therefore demand multiscale approaches, as I have already indicated. Moreover, the medium of perception profoundly shapes what we are able to know at each scale. Thus, the Anthropocene challenges us to conceive of the human as a being whose naturalised limited perspective needs to be defamiliarised, among others also in speculative works that make worlds beyond human scale and perspective in order to imagine the human outside of Man.

'Master of himself' (and everything else)

Within the last few years, when a speculated-upon 'climate change' turned into an increasingly alarming 'climate emergency', a diversified search for possibilities of alternate ways of inhabiting the gradually degraded world has gained momentum. It resulted, among others, in the recent embrace of what is more-than-human in the area of cultural studies, especially in such fields as posthumanism, eco-criticism, animal and plant studies, new materialism and object-oriented realism. At the same time, new ideas of what it means (or should/would mean) to be human as a relational being beyond the regulatory discourse of the modern/colonial world, and long-held dichotomies between nature and culture or the humanities and the sciences, have started to crop up. Such an approach is best exemplified by Dipesh Chakrabarty's argument that anthropogenic climate change 'spells the collapse of the age-old humanist distinction between natural history and human history' (Chakrabarty 2009: 201). That is why, to be able to adequately address the climate changes, regardless of a specific name given to the current era in the Earth's history, we should operate on various scales, although not all the scales could be recognised as both 'human' and equally significant to all disciplines. For, as historian Julia Adeney Thomas (2014) rightly points out, different ways of knowing have produced (and still produce) a considerable diversity of human figures and ideas of what it amounts to being human, even within the same scientific discipline. In her article 'History and Biology in the Anthropocene: Problems of Scale, Problems of Value', Thomas focuses on diverse and well-established branches of biology – paleobiology, microbiology and biochemistry – in order to distinctly articulate their specific modes of understanding 'the human'. Whereas the first one operates on an enormous temporal and spatial scale, tracing our 'universal biological substrate', the other two focus on phenomena on microscales but raise equally perplexing issues. Thomas explains:

> Microbiologists jettison the idea of 'the human' as a single species, while biochemists examine the industrial toxins suddenly infiltrating our bodies, including our brains, raising questions about the continuity of 'the human' in the ways we think and respond to the world. (Thomas 2014: 1592)

Mindful that not only history but also each of the biological sciences defamiliarises 'the human' in its own mode, Thomas argues further that 'in addressing contemporary anthropogenic climate change, political histories are as pertinent as the biological sciences' (ibid.: 1605). For this reason, the sciences cannot define 'the human' better than the humanities, even today when we face 'climate emergency'.

The appropriate consideration of the Anthropocene requires all kinds of different scales, not only these 'naturalised' in Western cultures and sciences. This point is convincingly proven by Timothy Morton in his recent book *Hyposubjects: On Becoming Human*, intended as 'an exercise in flimsy and chaotic thinking' (Morton and Boyer 2021: 13). The well-known American eco-philosopher undertook this exercise together with media maker and anthropologist Dominic Boyer over lunch and a bottle of kombucha, subsequently registering it in writing in the form of a Woolfesque stream of consciousness. Already in his book *Hyperobjects* (2013), Morton declared that – despite all the warnings against a rapidly approaching global ecocatastrophe – we have been living after the end of the familiar, 'natural' world, already for several decades, at least since the 1990s when an increasingly intensive feeling of a dislocatedness became ubiquitous in Western porous migrant societies. Or most probably already since the turn of twentieth century when it became obvious that Euclidean space-time is admittedly a convenient way of conceiving the 'homely' world but certainly it is not the only one possible. Surrounded and simultaneously permeated for several decades by a large number of the eponymous hyperobjects (things which seem extremely huge to us), we still hardly know how to digest non-human scales and relate to these large-scale entities such as, for example, a black hole, global warming or the more recent phenomenon of coronavirus. In the meantime, they have effectively eroded our sense of specialness and mastery. They are simply 'too massive and multiphasic in their distribution in time and space for humans to fully comprehend or experience them in a unitary way', as the authors of *Hyposubjects* remind the reader (Morton and Boyer 2021: 13). Therefore, they recommend their contemporaries, who used to think that they are the masters of the world, to shrink down. To become squatters and bricoleurs who make do with what is available around in order to fabricate a possible future out of ruins, because only in this way do we have a chance to become human again. Morton and Boyer call this new human species they speculate about hyposubjects, the native species of the Anthropocene, and they intend each hyposubject to be an entity that is less than a sum of its parts. Also in this sense, while voicing that which should remain unspoken so that the contemporary world can carry on as it uneasily does, the authors continue the line of argument, which Morton started in his book *Hyperobjects*, about our living after the end of the 'homely' world. However, in the recent book he changes the scale, demonstratively shrinking it down. Now, together with Boyer, they urge their contemporaries 'not to take a savior position but to try to commit ourselves to a program of rebecoming as something less dangerous. To reprogram' (ibid.: 82).

While urging the reader to become a hyposubject, Morton and Boyer do not lose sight of their fellow researchers and take into account the possibility of squatting within authoritarian discourses, the discourses of science among others. Therefore, if I understand them correctly, their book is itself an exemplary demonstration of an 'exercise in flimsy and chaotic thinking' and in making use of 'a certain playful kind of epistemic excess' (ibid.: 13 and 26). Nevertheless, this epistemic exercise is firmly located within Western thinking. Thus, their eponymous hyposubjets are limited to former subjects of the Western episteme. Although the authors refer to sugar plantations and Susan Buck-Morss's writing on the Haitian Revolution, they do it in the context of Hegel's philosophy and the desire for sugar as a basic reason for colonial imperialism (ibid.: 80–2). This means that Morton and Boyer, while talking *en passant* about Eduardo Kohn's or Elizabeth Povinelli's projects of an anthropology beyond the human, leave out the possibilities for being and knowing that have otherwise been opened up by anti-hegemonic critical approaches towards the historical modern/colonial matrix by, for instance, black feminist theories as well as indigenous and decolonial studies. As recently demonstrated, for example, by Mark Rifkin, these, and many more well-established or emerging fields in the area, differ from each other no less than the above-mentioned branches of biological sciences (Rifkin 2019). Nevertheless, for several decades all these fields (in their specific theoretical and methodological idioms) have discussed a radical move beyond the doctrine of Man on which the idea of the human (and, indirectly, of the hyposubject) has been premised (Drexler-Dreis and Justaert 2020). Although the Anthropocene has become a subject only recently in these domains, the necessity of what Morton and Boyer call 'shrinking down' and 'reprogramming' as an important part of giving up on human mastery and specialness has been present in these fields from the outset. Obviously, what has been so widely discussed is not so much the universal idea of the human as is the case in *Hyposubjects*. The Man designates here the Western, secular, imperial version of the human, and is defined as the being which is, or can be, 'Master of himself' (and everything else) (Singh 2018: 13). Therefore, not every human being is permitted to be recognised as the human within Western modernity. This insight distinguishes minoritarian studies, which contrary to the mainstream disciplines try to open up new possibilities of defining a human of a (better) future.

Undoubtedly, the best example of the way that the crucial difference between the Man and the human can be conceptualised in anti-hegemonic studies is Alexander Weheliye's *Habeas Viscus* (2014). In his book, he identifies a complex and historically changing conglomerate of sociopolitical relations that 'discipline humanity into full humans, not-quite-humans, and not-humans' (Weheliye 2014: 3). Demonstrating tight bonds between humanity and racialising assemblages in the modern era, he critically assesses the discourse of bare life and biopolitics, predominant in current mainstream studies that imagine an indivisible biological substance anterior to racialisation. In so doing, he searches for alternative ways of conceptualising the place of race and posits 'the atrocity of flesh as a pivotal arena for the politics emanating from different traditions of the oppressed' (ibid.: 2). Introducing enfleshment as a necessary starting point for thinking about new genres of the human, Weheliye radically opposes the category of the human as it has been performed in the modern West. He continues this enquiry in his recent article 'Black Life/Schwarz Sein: Inhabitations of the Flesh' (Weheliye 2020). Here, he reclaims the eponymous Black Life as 'the negative ontological ground for the Western order of things' (Weheliye 2020: 237), and underlines that only when conceived as such could it open possibilities for being otherwise. However, I consider his approach too binary due to being firmly locked in the logic of domination it would like to relinquish, and therefore it cannot be a useful framework in the context of problems that I address. More so I intend to read closely a trilogy which manifestly inscribes itself in the Western tradition of critically knowing, writing and speculating about other worlds and ways of being, namely Kim Stanley Robinson's *Red Mars* (1992), *Green Mars* (1993) and *Blue Mars* (1996).

Therefore, I would here rather follow the lead of Julietta Singh, an expert in decolonial literature, ecological humanities and queer studies who, just like Weheliye, is critical of Western subjectivities founded on and through mastery. Nevertheless, she remains similarly critical of postcolonial studies and their fundamental dichotomies, mirroring the Western mode of defining the human, to which they have been strictly opposed at least since Frantz Fanon's *The Wretched of the Earth*. In her *Unthinking Mastery* (2018), in which she skilfully addresses the contemporary entanglements of dehumanism and decoloniality, Singh remains clear on one fundamental point: all projects of remaking the human have to be aware of how pervasive and intimately ingrained mastery is in the fabric of modern thought, living and politics. They are too pervasive and too ingrained to be rejected in one radical move as Weheliye would like to do. Looking for other performances of the human, Singh abides by Jacques Derrida's insistence that 'one cannot simply reverse binaries but must displace them' if one wants to gradually disentangle mastery (Singh 2018: 22). As Singh argues, we must keep on trying to displace them not only while thinking and writing, but also while reading. That is why she demonstrates how reading could become a practice 'driven by an aim to unearth the (other) ethico-political possibilities that remain active within their thought' – and within her own (ibid.: 24).

Following Singh's dehumanist guidance, while reading Robinson's trilogy I focus exactly on ways of displacing mastery in order to rethink and remake the human. Obviously, I can take into consideration only a tiny part of the complex problem of how 'natural' scales and perspectives, which strongly influence first-person sensory experience, inform our conceptions of human identity. To demonstrate this Abbott and Robinson created worlds beyond human scale and perspective in their novels. They did it in order to both displace and defamiliarise the concept of the human dominant in their respective times and open up possibilities of thinking about it otherwise. *Flatland* offers a kind of epistemological riddle, showing an entirely alien reality to which we gain access only through its representative and narrator. At the same time, this reality remains closely familiar in a gesture typical of the nascent science fiction at the turn of the nineteenth century (Rieder 2008). The action of the *Mars* trilogy begins in a not-too-distant future in a world very similar to our own when in 2027 one hundred (and one additional, Tobagonian stowaway) well-chosen people, mainly American and Russian scientists and engineers, are sent to the red planet. Thus, the trilogy belongs to the kind of contemporary speculative fabulations that engages less with a future that could be predicted on a probabilistic logic of science, progress and modernity than with the intense issues of our present that might otherwise go unnoticed. Robert Markley rightly points this out, writing that Robinson's trilogy is 'not a blueprint for the future but a way to think about the interanimating logics of economics, labor, ecology, politics, and culture as they currently exist on Earth' (Markley 2019: 95). In other words, the future serves here only as a narrative convention that makes it possible to present a displaced present in a landscape that resists earth-bound categories. In this way, it attempts to interrogate the systems that have produced the contemporary world and, among others, defined the human as 'master of himself' (and everything else).

Unthinking the human (speculatively)

No wonder that terraforming (or rather areoforming) is the topic of 'speculative problem-solving' (Jameson 2005: 394) that almost all critics who wrote about Robinson's trilogy have pondered about (Heise 2011; Markley 2019; Pak 2016). However, as Elizabeth Leane rightly pointed out, the author actually tightly intertwines two notions – 'Mars as a colony and Mars as a "planet for science"' (Leane 2002: 84). Robinson persuasively demonstrates parallels between scientific and colonialist metaphors of conquest premised on a recognition that not only colonisers but also scientists operate through a process of mastering and othering. In other words, the physical world is posited in the *Mars* trilogy as 'other' to the observers who treat it as an object of their cognitive practices. However, the author shows this entanglement of Western imperialism and knowledge systems in order to make his 'Martians' seek new possibilities of thinking, knowing and doing – all constituting a kind of long-term experiment realisable only in the alien, 'unhomely' environment of the red planet. That is exactly why the already-mentioned Jameson underlines, in his reading of the trilogy, that Mars 'is a unique laboratory in which the variables can never be isolated in the ordinary ways, but always coexist in a multiplicity which can scarcely be mastered by equations let alone by the computer itself' (Jameson 2005: 395). He is particularly interested in how Robinson presents the dynamics of the laboratory without losing sight of the multiplicity of its tightly entangled, multipronged variables. The Jamesonian comparison of Robinson's Mars to an extraordinary laboratory could be, however, dangerously misleading since it still presupposes both the purification of experimental practices and the human mastery. Yet, as it seems, Robinson decided to displace the First Hundred and other Terrans with a different aim in view.

Robinson's Mars is not so much a laboratory, but rather a virtual world made beyond human scale and perspective wherein the author could speculate more freely about a (better) future and other modes of being human. One of the main characters of the First Hundred, a Russian engineer from Siberia, retrospectively compares Earth to Mars as 'a gravity-driven fractal' to 'impact randomness' in order to formulate the key difference between the two: 'In the inchoate meteoric landscape, almost anything was possible, because nothing was obvious' (Robinson 1996: 323). In this setting nothing is also obvious to the reader, first because Mars has no 'nature' in the terrestrial sense; this 'nature' which has always been the main subject of human mastery. For this reason the *Mars* trilogy is able to persuasively demonstrate the slow and complex processes of unsettling the 'natural' human/Man mastery in many tightly connected practices and domains of life. Nothing makes it clearer than another citation, which compares life on Earth to life on Mars, in the last instalment of the trilogy, *Blue Mars*:

> No different than life on Earth had ever been, in other words; but here all happening at a much faster rate, pushed by the human-driven changes, modifications, introductions, transcriptions, translations – the interventions that worked, the interventions that backfired – the effects unintended, unforeseen, unnoticed – to the point where many thoughtful scientists were giving up any pretense of control [. . .] They didn't know what they were doing. It took some getting used to. (Robinson 1996: 412)

Obviously, I have no space here to dwell on how exactly Robinson reached his aim, or to provide an extensive review of the plethora of structural and rhetorical means he employed in each of his three comprehensive novels. However, a glance at the *Mars* trilogy suffices to see that although the author did not give voice to his main characters, he used their subjective perspectives and sensoriums, their motives, prior agendas, biographies, personalities and professional expertise in order to create many different temporalities and simultaneities, and then to carefully juxtapose them. Nevertheless, humans hardly ever get a good hold over this multiplicity of variables. Rather, they themselves are one of the variables which Jameson wrote about, and not master-engineers who dictate the ways of areoforming as if the red planet were a scientific laboratory. The more so that, as Elaine Gan and Anna Tsing argue in 'How Things Hold' (2018), in most cases juxtapositions of humans and more-than-humans become dynamic, polyphonic assemblages that hold together through coordinations – without a unified purpose or design.[2]

Writing on the specificity of Satoyama village forest in Japan, Gan and Tsing focus on what they call coordinations; that is, 'temporal rhythms across varied practices that together produce a new capacity or emergence', the new capacity or emergence sometimes made even through frictions and contingencies (Gan and Tsing 2018: 103). What is important in the context of this article is that they point out the critical difference between gardening as an incorporation of human dreams of mastery over nature and Satoyama, which practises hope for the restoration of particular interspecies arrangements if – and only if – other species coordinations follow. To properly present this difference, they turn to the diagram as a graphic form to help them 'foreground coordination and multispecies assemblages rather than autonomous humans' (ibid.: 104). Their diagram is a series of pen-and-ink sketches and field photographs that allow them to visualise coordinations as a series of tightly connected events, their continuity or change through layering, shifts in scale and changes in transparency. Alongside the sketches they provide, however, extensive verbal descriptions showing the encounters across incommensurable differences and without the homogenisation through which the traced coordinations arise. Mindful of all differences, I see Gan and Tsing's intention to 'show how a landscape assembles in ways that exceed human management and intention' (ibid.: 112) as analogous to the way Robinson depicted continuity and change in the deep time of his Mars's assemblages. In a sense, he also used a similar diagrammatic analysis of coordination while not only providing many maps of a given Mars region where he had located a series of events. He also situated chosen moments of the red planet's history from a discrete vantage point of a fictional character, in this way framing decisive events and encounters that matter for his unthinking the human in alien, unruly and predominantly mineral environments which cannot be changed by humans – they change together with them.

One of the reasons I have chosen to employ Gan and Tsing's diagrammatic analysis of coordination to read Robinson's *Mars* trilogy, is to foreground how he makes his readers think across temporal scales while telling the story of a possible development of humankind and the transformations of an alien world that span more than two centuries, from the landing on Mars in 2027 till the beginning of the twenty-third century which sees new settlements on Mercury, the asteroids and moonlets, and even starts to reach to the outer systems. One thing is evident all along: the *Mars* trilogy is by no means a story of progress and increasing human mastery over the universe. It should rather be read as a warning against those who would like to recreate Earth on other planets. Although in *Red Mars* the First Hundred landed on an uninhabited, empty planet, it had been hardly alien to them as it hardly is to the reader, despite its unique gravity, geology and chemistry. Leane stresses: 'Mars was in the constant process of being both read and written over, before the terraforming began: planet as palimpsest' (Leane 2002: 93). Robinson recognises the ancestry of both astronomers who drew maps, named mountain ranges, mesas and volcanoes (Morton 2002), and science fiction writers who depicted fantastic indigenous people and various First Contacts. But not only that. Moreover, he writes his trilogy in such a way as to demonstrate that terraforming involves physical and intellectual processes of giving it symbolic meaning, historical and aesthetic significance – both needed to make newcomers feel at home.

Yet, Robinson leaves no doubt that these processes are irresolvably ambiguous. In *Green Mars*, for instance, he writes that his Martians 'walk about in a horrendous mishmash of the dreams of the past, causing who knew what disastrous misapprehensions of the real terrain' (Robinson 1994: 121). Commenting on the burden of the earthly past in the trilogy, Chris Pak in *Terraforming* rightly refers to Stephen J. Gould's term 'exaptation'. It originally meant the way in which the biological structures of Darwinian pre-adaptations evolve into entirely new structures with capacities that predominantly could not have been pre-stated or predicted. However, Pak employs the Gouldian term to point out a specific way in which socioeconomic and political practices from Earth are exapted in new environments on Mars. He rightly regards such a 'fusion between physical adaptation of the environment and the transformation of social practices and institutions' as composting in both a real and metaphorical sense (in terms of both closed life-support systems, air and topsoil which have to be engineered, as well as socioeconomic and political practices and attitudes from Earth) (Pak 2016: 170). In the *Mars* trilogy composting provides grounds for a much-needed realisation that making a planet inhabitable does not necessarily entail a well-known landscaping, understood as an intentional modification of physical space and its interpretation for human-oriented ends. Rather, it means to get rid of earthbound images of the planet and learn how to see Mars in other ways than as an anthropocentric projection. That is why Arkady repeats not only that their obligation as scientists is to think everything anew, but also that 'we must terraform not only Mars, but ourselves' (Robinson 1993: 89). That is, change together in a reciprocal arrangement. To this end Robinson dedicated the first instalment of his trilogy – *Red Mars*.

On the one hand everything is alien on Mars, far from human scale and proportion: a longer day and year; a practical lack of magnetic field and atmospheric pressure; a much lower gravity of .38 g; much higher radiation; a closer horizon, sizes of mountain peaks and craters off the scale; wild colours that 'made it hard to figure out what was what, and how big it was, and how far away' (ibid.: 261), and many others. On the other hand, however, many migrants who came after the First Hundred from the overpopulated Earth, where sea levels rose about six metres, start to imitate an earlier form of community. For instance, Robinson depicts Bedouin Arabs who travel in caravans, in a deliberate recreation of a life that had disappeared on Earth. Shortly, new generations are about to be born to whom Martian alien environment is of human scale, and for them there will be nothing unnatural about it. Nevertheless, before presenting Marsborn humans, the author focuses on how to unlearn any earthbound perspective. And he does it for at least one reason – to properly introduce the so-called ecopoiesis, that is terraforming redefined, subtilised and localised. No longer powered by heavy industrial global methods but by the slow, steady and intensely local process of working on individual patches of land. A handful of examples should be enough to demonstrate this.

No wonder that when the psychologist Michel Duval compares 'the stony waste of this reality' to the 'living landscape, a landscape infinitely more beautiful and humane' of his native Provence, he misses it so much that he cannot adjust nor adapt to his current reality (ibid.: 223). Nevertheless, many a time something reminds him of home because, for instance, Avignon's tree-shaded plaza in the summer had the colour of Mars just after sunset. But it is not only memory which plays its trick on the characters. Their bodies remember as well. This is shown, for example, in a scene in which an American politician Frank Chalders comes back to Mars from the moon of Phobos in the elevator. When his decelerating car is passing momentarily through earthly one g, he sees an image 'of running out a long pier, wet uneven boards splashed with silver fish scales; he could even smell the salt fish stink' (ibid.: 448). Moreover, a perceptual issue is also an aesthetic appreciation of the alien environment which gives you a sense of being home. In the *Mars* trilogy it is primarily a geologist with the telling name of Ann Clayborne who, while strictly opposing any terraforming, sublimes the strange beauty of the Martian mineral world as an unconscious strategy of adjusting to its unhuman scale. In other words, Ann sees the wilderness on the red planet as a kind of natural work of art as many humans before her did, still appreciating it in an earthly way. It is only after the first Martian revolution for independence from Earth and its transnational corporations and giant floods of 2061, which alter 'every single feature of the primal Mars' (ibid.: 550), that Ann Clayborne has to change her way of perceiving the red planet:

> The landscape itself was now speaking kind of glossolalia [. . .] And it was visual chaos as well, a meaningless jumble that she couldn't seem to focus on, to distinguish near from far, or vertical from horizontal, or moving from still, or light from dark. She was losing the ability to read meaning from her senses. (Ibid.: 545–6)

Sharing with the reader her impression that in fact the landscape of Valles Marineris looked like a world in which regular shapes were impossible, Ann points out that physical space is not only constituted by anthropomorphic perspectives. However, to learn this, she had to see not the Mars from the human imaginary, but a new Mars as a chaotic waterscape, never seen or imagined in such a way before. Robinson represents this particular experience as a turning point in Mars's history and a springboard to some new biological and social order which he depicts concisely at the beginning of the second instalment, *Green Mars*: 'All the genetic templates for our new biota are Terran; the minds designing them are Terran; but the terrain is Martian' (Robinson 1994: 2).

Unthinking the human (as humus)

In an exemplary way Saxifrage Russel, a British model scientist in Robinson's trilogy, sums up the complex and long-term process of an emergence of new, synthetic and sympoietic ecologies on Mars in the last instalment by saying: 'Not nature, not culture: just Mars' (Robinson 1996: 679). The very name 'Mars' stands here for dynamic assemblages of human and more-than-human, animate and inanimate, planetary and extraplanetary, biological and technological elements that are impossible to tell apart anymore. Sax Russel's evolution from an apostle of a pure science, which has an indisputable right to know and master everything in its own way, to somebody who has learned a new way of seeing that a common liveable world must be composed, bit by bit, progresses in an analogous way to the history of Mars, with a decisive caesura of the 2061 floods and revolution. In the case of Sax it was an aphasia caused by his capture, tortures and mental seizure. Combating the aphasia's effects, Sax has to learn anew how to formulate and speak out his thoughts which went alongside gradually getting rid of old stereotypes and prejudices, conventional ways of putting things together: 'Then cutting through these comfortable formulations, as if from a separate language entirely, were the new perceptions, and the new phrases groping to express them' (Robinson 1994: 408). This has enabled him to see and appreciate the complex, dynamic assemblages and manifold incarnations of local 'Satoyama', of which people are merely a part of layers upon layers of life and death, not even the most important one. Thanks to this Sax not only got more lucky than other scientists while trying to understand how the human mind works in order to find a treatment for memory failures, tormenting the handful left of the First Hundred in their advanced age. Thanks to this Robinson could also both present his characters looking back and seeing their past in every detail in the ending of *Blue Mars*, as well as show the reader how to summarise the long way they had gone since 2027, the year of their landing on Mars.

However, Robinson in his *Mars* trilogy does not focus only on this move towards a colonisation/science that refuses the imperial/patriarchal impulse to naturalise and objectify the biotic and abiotic other. Equally important is a long-term confrontation of humans with an environment that no evolutionary process has prepared their bodies to inhabit. He shows this confrontation time and again, especially when a new wave of immigrants from Earth comes to Mars. Clearly, it is not a problem which bothers new generations of people born on the red planet. If you were born on Mars your look and outlook were different, and that is why some of Robinson's characters talk even about two different species: *Homo sapiens* and *Homo ares*. It is not only that for the Marsborn Terran cultural and biological vastness and diversity became simply unimaginable. When Nirgal, a representative of the first generation of the Marsborn, visits Earth, it turns out that the Martians' bodies are hardly able to adapt to earthly conditions. When in Trinidad, the birthplace of his father, the former stowaway, Nirgal feels pain when breathing in wet air, and he weighs more than twice of what he used to on Mars. It seems, however, that Robinson depicts these kinds of experiences predominantly as a useful background on which he shows how the First Hundred (and other migrants) adapt to new conditions. Initially they have to use advanced supporting technologies and then introduce certain genetic modifications that culminate in gerontological treatments which allow them to live decades longer. As I posit, a key reason for introducing these treatments was for the author to convincingly entangle larger processes of decisive but rather slowly progressing ecological and sociopolitical changes with changes of human modes of thinking, knowing and living. The aforementioned genetic modifications notwithstanding, they therefore have not become an incorporation of typical science fiction cyborgs or even posthumans who incarnate a possibility of starting over and beginning anew. Rather they demonstrate how humanity could be imagined and lived by displaced subjects who, even while not identifying with the figure of the human as the Master subject, have learned how to rethink and reconnect their heritage. In other words, they are not so much posthumans as rather dehumans because they have materialised in the (new for heuristic reasons) world of the red planet in different ways to those modelled by a central topos of the Western modernity since the Renaissance. Therefore, if I have written about processes of sedimentation in a literal and metaphorical sense, referring to Pak's term of areoforming as composting in the previous section, following Donna Haraway I would like to speak here about analogous long-term material-semiotic changes of Robinson's First Hundred – not only on the level of 'Werteswandel' but also of their bodies and minds – of becoming Children of Compost. That is, they became not so much human, but rather humus, 'that worker of and in the soil' (Haraway 2016: 11) who lives in symbiosis with all other biotic and abiotic beings.

Haraway speaks about Children of Compost in the already-mentioned speculative fabulation 'The Camille Stories', which conclude her *Staying with the Trouble* (ibid.: 134–68) and were created during a writing workshop at Cerisy in summer 2013. She defines her eponymous Camille as consecutive generations of people who have started a practice of repairing damaged places by actively living kin relations with threatened species, in this case monarch butterflies. Bodily modifications are normal here but what counts more are the subtle sensory similarities to their animal partners with which they live in symbiosis. Nevertheless, focusing on symbiogenetic transformations of five generations of Camille, Haraway offers a rather traditional, linear master-narrative of one hero's life in each of the stories, which follows one after another and is narrated by an 'objective' historical writer against the background of much broader progressive developments of catastrophic ecological changes. No wonder that several photographs serve here only as pure illustrations of the author's argument – not an intrinsic means of fabulation. In this respect a future world of 'The Camille Stories' is made differently to the one from Robinson's trilogy.

Interestingly enough, however, while locating all the narrated events in damaged worlds of Earth, Haraway begins her stories with the birth of Camille 1 in West Virginia, devastated by coal mining in 2025. Having narrated the lives of Camille's four consecutive generations, she ends her stories with the death of Camille 5 in 2425, who has to become a Speaker for the Dead as a consequence of the extinction of the monarch butterfly. That is, not only do 'The Camille Stories' unfold in the same time as Robinson's trilogy and make the overpopulation of the Earth one of their leitmotivs, they also depict a not-too-distant multispecies future of our world which may become habitable again. What is more, Haraway underlines that 'Camille is one of the children of compost who ripen in the earth to say no to the posthuman of every time' (ibid.: 134). Hence, both Haraway and Robinson are strictly opposed to the idea of starting anew. Rather, they focus on symbiotic and sympoietic commitments that urge the reader to rethink relationality, perspective and being human as living-with and dying-with, as humus of sympoiesis.

Making more-than-human worlds (to conclude)

In a sense, in her *Staying with the Trouble* Haraway has summed up her postulates of the last decades, put forward at least since 'Situated Knowledges' (1988). It is clearly visible in her stressing that not only from the narrative, but also the visual and mathematical point of view, it matters very much 'which figures figure figures, which systems systematize systems' (ibid.: 101). For this reason she has chosen to be a compostist rather than a posthumanist. If I rightly understand her move, she distinguishes between posthumanism and what she calls the era of Chthulucene, which may as well, I posit, be named dehumanism, to use the already-mentioned notion introduced by Singh in her *Unthinking Mastery* (2018) as they both aim at the eponymous goal. What is more, both oppose the confrontational way, so dear, as it seems, to Weheliye and – more broadly – black studies in general. Strongly believing that it is only as humus that humans have a potential, Haraway formulates a fundamental question in her *Staying with the Trouble*: 'What are the effects of bioculturally, biotechnically, biopolitically, historically situated people (not Man) relative to, and combined with, the effects of other species assemblages and their biotic/abiotic forces?' (ibid.: 99). Although the question was asked a few years ago, numerous answers to it had been tested much earlier, and one of them, as I argue, is to be seen in Robinson's *Mars* trilogy. Whereas Abbott created an alternative world to critically mirror his contemporaries in his *Flatland*, Robinson did something else, in a sense exapting the method of his predecessor. Similarly, he made a world beyond human scale and perspective, but did it in order to create not so much an un-human but rather a more-than-human world. Thus, Robinson aimed at unthinking his contemporaries as a new mode of humans in these 'unhomely' settings: the human as humus of a speculated future.

Notes

1. *Flatland* (2007), a computer-animated film based on Abbott's novel, directed by Ladd Ehlinger Jr, demonstrates how challenging this exercise is. In this screen adaptation the two-dimensional world, populated by geometrical figures, is shown only from above. Therefore it lacks the perspective of a Flatlander which the author attempted to introduce in his fantasy.
2. Critically following the Moderns, Tsing focused her attention on one kind of coordination – disciplined control – in her earlier writings. She offered a competitive name for the Anthropocene – the Plantatiocene – and argued against scalability which blocks our ability to notice the heterogeneity of the world (Tsing 2012). In Satoyama, she sees thus an alternative to plantation planning.

References

Abbott, Edwin (2010), *Flatland*, ed. Lila Marz Harper, London–Ontario: Broadview Editions.

Chakrabarty, Dipesh (2009), 'The Climate of History: Four Theses', *Critical Inquiry*, 35: 197–222.

Clarke, Michael Tavel and David Wittenberg (2017), 'Introduction', in Michael Tavel Clarke and David Wittenberg (eds), *Scale in Literature and Culture*, London: Palgrave Macmillan.

Drexler-Dreis, Joseph and Kristien Justaert (eds) (2020), *Beyond the Doctrine of Man: Decolonial Visions of the Human*, New York: Fordham University Press.

Gan, Elaine and Anna Tsing (2018), 'How Things Hold: A Diagram of Coordination in Satoyama Forest', *Social Analysis*, 62(4): 102–45.

Haraway, Donna (1988), 'Situated Knowledges: The Science Question in Feminism and the Privilege of Partial Perspective', *Feminist Studies*, 14(3): 575–99.

Haraway, Donna J. (2016), *Staying with the Trouble: Making Kin in the Chthulucene*, Durham, NC: Duke University Press.

Heise, Ursula K. (2011), 'Martian Ecologies and the Future of Nature', *Twentieth Century Literature*, 57(3–4): 447–71.

Jameson, Fredric (2005), '"If I Can Find One Good City, I Will Spare the Man": Realism and Utopia in Kim Stanley Robinson's *Mars* Trilogy', in Fredric Jameson, *Archaeologies of the Future: The Desire Called Utopia and Other Science Fictions*, London and New York: Verso, pp. 393–416.

Leane, Elizabeth (2002), 'Chromodynamics: Science and Colonialism in Kim Stanley Robinson's Mars Trilogy', *Ariel*, 33(1): 83–104.

Markley, Robert (2019), *Kim Stanley Robinson*, Urbana, Chicago and Springfield: University of Illinois Press.

Morton, Oliver (2002), *Mapping Mars: Science, Imagination, and the Birth of a World*, New York: Picador.

Morton, Timothy (2013), *Hyperobjects: Philosophy and Ecology after the End of the World*, Minneapolis and London: University of Minnesota Press.

Morton, Timothy and Dominic Boyer (2021), *Hyposubjects: On Becoming Human*, London: Open Humanities Press.

Pak, Chris (2016), *Terraforming. Ecopolitical Transformations and Environmentalism in Science Fiction*, Liverpool: Liverpool University Press.

Readings, Bill (1997), *The University in Ruins*, Cambridge, MA: Harvard University Press.

Rieder, John (2008), *Colonialism and the Emergence of Science Fiction*, Middletown, CT: Wesleyan University Press.

Rifkin, Mark (2019), *Fictions of Land and Flesh: Blackness, Indigeneity, Speculation*, Durham, NC: Duke University Press.

Robinson, Kim Stanley (1993), *Red Mars*, New York: Bantam Books.

Robinson, Kim Stanley (1994), *Green Mars*, New York: Bantam Books.

Robinson, Kim Stanley (1996), *Blue Mars*, New York: Bantam Books.

Salter, Chris (2015), *Alien Agency: Experimental Encounters with Arts in the Making*, Cambridge: The MIT Press.

Singer, Merrill (2016), *Anthropology of Infectious Disease*, London and New York: Routledge.

Singh, Julietta (2018), *Unthinking Mastery: Dehumanism and Decolonial Entanglements*, Durham, NC: Duke University Press.

Snow, C. P. (2019), *The Two Cultures*, Cambridge: Cambridge University Press.

Streeby, Shelley (2018), *Imagining the Future of Climate Change: World-Making through Science Fiction and Activism*, Berkeley: University of California Press.

Suvin, Darko (1983), *Victorian Science Fiction in the UK: The Discourses of Knowledge and Power*, Boston, MA: G. K. Hall.

Thomas, Julia Adeney (2014), 'History and Biology in the Anthropocene: Problems of Scale, Problems of Value', *The American Historical Review*, 119(5): 1587–1607.

Trexler, Adam (2015), *Anthropocene Fictions: The Novel in a Time of Climate Change*, Charlottesville: University of Virginia Press.

Tsing, Lowenhaupt Anna (2012), 'On Nonscalability: The Living World Is Not Amenable to Precision-Nested Scales', *Common Knowledge*, 18(3): 505–24.

Weheliye, Alexander (2014), *Habeas Viscus: Racializing Assemblages, Biopolitics, and Black Feminist Theories of the Human*, Durham, NC: Duke University Press.

Weheliye, Alexander (2020), 'Black Live/Schwarz-Sein: Inhabitations of the Flesh', in Joseph Drexler-Dreis and Kristien Justaert (eds), *Beyond the Doctrine of Man: Decolonial Visions of the Human*, New York: Fordham University Press, pp. 237–62.

3

For Whom is Apocalypse a New Idea?: Thoughts on Staging the End

Patricia Ybarra

We are currently surrounded with discourses about the inevitable end of the planet. There seemingly will be an end; and our everyday actions are only forestalling its emergence. In the Euroamerican reality we are in a climate crisis or we are nearing a moment of apocalypse. Imagining that end is a regular part of cultural production. This chapter considers two recent plays that imagine the end in ways that question the temporalities and ideologies based in Euroamerican coloniality. These two plays, Aya Ogawa's *Ludic Proxy* and Yvette Nolan's *The Unplugging*, were both written at the same time – 2010–12 – and one feels a synergy between them (Ogawa 2015; Nolan 2014). Although the plays and their dramaturgies are strikingly different, Ogawa and Nolan open up the possibility of thinking about how a post-Anthropocenic world might be lived, gesturing towards the ethics we will need to embody as we reimagine or remember. These plays consider the importance of organic matter, knowledge sharing and care as the pillars of life on earth. On the chopping block are our stubborn attachment to the idea of the human; risk management through individualistic rational choice; clinging to an outdated notion of futurity as imbedded within teleological progressive time; and the idea of knowledge production as a form of mastery or transactional exchange. It is not an accident that the ideologies these plays ask us to abandon are suffused throughout with Euroamerican ('Western') philosophies of coloniality, enlightenment humanism and neoliberal ideologies. As a scholar of colonialism, I come late to the idea of the Anthropocene and eco-criticism. As such, my consideration of *Ludic Proxy* and *The Unplugging* is deeply indebted to scholars who have been working within this field for much longer than I have, whose contributions I discuss below before moving into my analysis of the plays.

Anthropocene, or ending with a different relationship to endings

The concept of the Anthropocene is an attempt to demarcate the era in which human behaviour has been the dominant influence on the climate and the environment so as to understand the crisis of the present. There are many possible beginnings to this era: the post-1945 emergence of nuclear energy, the emergence of the steam engine in 1784, the mid-eighteenth-century emergence of the idea of human freedom, or the acceleration of the colonial project to intensified modes of extraction at the beginning of the seventeenth century. Each argument can be defended in its own way, but it should be noted, as categorised by Arun Saldanha, that each of these theorisations gesture to, if not replicate, pre-existing modes of histori-cising capitalism from within traditional Euroamerican categories: Post-War Liberalism, the Industrial Revolution, the Enlightenment, the Early Modern (Saldanha 2020: 15–19). Saldanha, with some restraint, succinctly states: 'different thematic foci can correspond to different starting dates for our planetary emergency' (ibid.: 15). I, with less restraint, might suggest that for non-European scholars, Anthropocenic conditions emerge with the timelines of colonisation of their countries of origin or heritage. Own-ing my own Latinx heritage, I gravitate to the date posited by Heather Davis and Zoe Todd in their efforts to 'decolonize the Anthropocene': 1610 (Davis and Todd 2017).[1] This is the year we see a peak after a tem-porary downward trend in CO_2 levels, which gradually begins to rise after that time. The temporary lull we see likely stems from reforestation that occurred after the death of 50 million indigenous Americans, who were no longer cultivating, burning or trading. The subsequent rise of course, is pegged to the emergence of global capitalism. Meaning that, as Saldanha claims: 'the newly systemized racism of early modernity, will be legible in tree rings and ice cores thousands or millions of years into the future' (Saldanha 2020: 26). I would argue that Todd and Davis's emphasis on 1610 as the beginning of the Anthropocene aligns with Anibal Quijano and Michael Ennis's conceptions of the coloniality of power, which tether racial othering, subordination and capitalism to the colonisation of the Americas (Quijano and Ennis 2000). Perhaps the most compelling argu-ment within the decolonial, indigenous critique of some utilisations of the Anthropocene is an obvious one, but it bears exploring: the idea that extinction is not 'new' or not 'not yet', but in the present and the past rather than in the future. As Kali Simmons states:

> Scholars such as Kim Tallbear, Grace Dillon, and Kyle Powys
> Whyte have argued that indigenous people are already post-

apocalyptic. That is indigenous peoples have already faced cata-strophic violence, the loss of relationships, and the fundamental alteration of their ways of life to survive in spaces that are psychi-cally, emotionally and spiritually toxic. (Simmons 2019: 175)

Or, as Potawatomi scholar Kyle P. Whyte himself says, 'the same colonial practices that opened up indigenous territories for deforestation and extrac-tive industries are the ones that make adaptation difficult for indigenous people today' (Whyte 2017a: 156–7). This mode of thinking is decolonial and engaged with the conception of the Anthropocene in a deeply ethi-cal way that does not ignore racial capitalism as a primary driver of misery making and destruction, without which the Anthropocene is reduced to simply being a displaced and universalising mode of talking about racial capitalism without race. Although I hew close to the 1610 date for all of the reasons above, Dipesh Chakrabarty's idea that the idea of freedom coalesces with the emergence of fossil fuels as a primary mode of energy is important, because it links freedom of movement made possible through fossil fuels to the idea of human liberty (Chakrabarty 2009: 207–13). The correlation between the ideological and the material is important to keep in mind so as to avoid a narrative that prioritises natural resources as an *a priori* category rather than a product of liberal humanism, with its gesture to freedom, or at least free choice of movement, with its attendant deeply toxic by-products. Ultimately, however, all scholars, despite their differ-ences, advocate for a new set of relationalities between humans and their global inhabitants, including scholars who offer different terms for this era, such as the Chthulucene (Haraway 2016), or the Capitalocene (Moore 2016). T. J. Demos, following Moore and Haraway, argues against the Anthropocene entirely because of its universalising tendencies in fram-ing the era as a result of 'human action' rather than particular subsets of humans' actions, who use resources at the expense of most other living things on the planet. His examination of the ways in which visual repre-sentations of the Earth buttress rather than contest this reality is adjacent to this study on theatrical production and dramatic literature that questions this universality (Demos 2017: 212).

Ecocriticism and its critical role

Recent scholarship on the theatre and the Anthropocene includes essays framing melodrama and its dependence on oil as petrodrama and early modern drama as drama of the Anthropocene, in addition to scholar-ship on contemporary performance (Griffiths 2018; Gillen 2018). These works, however, follow a longer legacy of thinking about ecology and theatre by scholars such as Una Chaudhuri and Theresa J. May. For most theatre scholars, Chaudhuri represents the emergence of eco-criticism in the theatre. Her 1994 essay, 'There Must Be a Lot of Fish in that Lake: Toward an Ecological Theatre', traces the rupture between nature and culture that has been so destructive to the earth as being at the bedrock of modern drama (Chaudhuri 1994). The title of her essay comes from her doubled reading of a line from Chekhov's *The Seagull*. Chaudhuri writes:

> *The Seagull* pictures the rupture between nature and culture pre-cisely through the image of a stage, thus identifying the theater as the site of both ecological alienation and potential ecological consciousness. After young Treplev's ghastly pseudo-symbolist playlet, staged on the grounds of the Sorin estate, Trigorin says to Nina, 'I didn't understand it at all. But I enjoyed watching. You acted *so* genuinely. And the scenery was beautiful. *Pause*. There must be a lot of fish in that lake.' The various gaps and non sequiturs of Trigorin's speech actually contain the prospect of an ambitious theater ecology, locating the constitutive disjunctions of drama – those between text and meaning, acting and being, performance and place – that fundamental rift, which intrudes here so unexpectedly and so comically, between humankind and nature, and which, in terms of the drama (but not only in those terms), makes of nature a mere setting – 'scenery'. (Ibid.: 25–6)

Chaudhuri is less sure of *Uncle Vanya*'s Ostrov. Written as a character with a great interest in forests and ecology, he is also a character who lapses into a belief in social human progress which asks for domina-tion and dispossession of nature by human actors, ultimately lapsing into what Chaudhuri calls 'resourcism' (ibid.: 25). Ultimately, she asks for us to adjust our attitude, stating,

> First: we are well past the stage in ecological history when things could correct themselves by being left alone; ecological action is an urgent necessity, and the nature and course of that action – or continued inaction – will inevitably be deeply political and will strongly impact every aspect of our lives. Second: if one thing has become clear from a century of ecological thought and effort, it is that the earth cannot now be saved by half-measures, by tinkering and puttering and fiddling around with rules and regulations and practices and customs; whether we like it or not, the ecological crisis is a crisis of values. Ecological victory will require a trans-valuation *so* profound as to be nearly unimaginable at present.

> And in this the arts and humanities – including the theater – must
> play a role. (Ibid.)

Chaudhuri's 1997 book *Staging Place*, and her conception of geopathol-
ogy, solidified her transition to being an eco-critical scholar of theatre
even as she contributed to the theoretical consideration of space so
crucial to 1990s theatre historiography (Chaudhuri 1997: 251). In this
final chapter of the book, Chaudhuri thinks about the apocalypse in
José Rivera's *Marisol*, and Tony Kushner's *Angels in America*, both of
which imagine 'the end' at the end of the millennium in New York
City. Chaudhuri's attention to these plays, however prescient, reveals
that her eco-critical critique is beholden to an apocalyptic vision of
the world with an overarching teleology. Both plays' eco-critical crises
are speculative and default to solutions that primarily protect human
beings. In *Angels in America*, the gestures to ecological apocalypse are
displaced to altered states due to pharmaceutical use or to the metaphysical space of Heaven (Kushner 1995). Thus, while as Katie Hogan
suggests, *Angels in America* expanded the idea of toxicity by linking
the biomedical apocalypse of gay men, racism and ecological destruction (Hogan 2012), the play still lapses into a rights framework at *Pere-
stroika*'s end. Rivera's *Marisol* reveals as apocalyptic the consequences of
the intersectional oppressions that emerged from the US Reagan era,
including the discontinuation of care for the mentally ill, debt acceleration and the mortality rates of black and brown children, making *Marisol* a brilliant mediation of racialised capitalism (Rossini 2008: 155–6).
Yet, excepting Theresa May (and my students), critics have ignored
the play's representation of endangered ecology, which lurks beneath
the surface (May 2020: 203). As insightful as pairing violent roving
skinheads and the extinction of coffee is, Rivera stops short of indict-
ing anthropocentric thinking, even when he imagines revolution. Like
most Millennial plays, they end with hope or futurity. Lindsay Goss, in
her essay 'Ending and Excess: Theatre as Being in Crisis', replaces the
idea of working towards a future hope with the recognition that excessive action combined with a hopeless expectation of anything but the
end is more realistic (Goss 2021: 52–3). Goss argues that theatre production teaches us how to do this because of the very excessive labour
it entails even when there is a known finite end in sight. Both authors
share a commitment to a state of emergency and teleology as they carefully render the harms of racial capitalism (although Chaudhuri, writing
some 25 years earlier, does not call it that). Perhaps this is mostly due to
their allegiance to Western climate scientists who do not engage with
indigeneity or temporality in a sustained way.

Theresa May's *Earth Matters on Stage* in contrast, heavily relies on indigenous scholars in her analysis of twentieth-century US theatre through an environmental lens (May 2020: 1–2). I will engage with her book continually throughout the chapter, but it bears noting that her final chapter on Metis playwright Marie Clements's *Burning Vision* and Quebecois settler Chantal Bilodeau's *Sila* is equally sceptical of apocalyptic teleology. May's engagement with differential conceptions of time and possibility in plays written by or in collaboration with indigenous artists allows her to stand with scholar Kyle Powys Whyte who asks: For whom is apocalypse a new Idea?

Ludic Proxy

Ogawa's *Ludic Proxy*, 2015, is a triptych play that links two past nuclear disasters, Chernobyl and Fukushima, with an imagined world in which people live inside the earth unable to travel to its surface. In the first 'act' of the play, called the 'past', we meet Nina, a survivor of the Chernobyl disaster who now lives in Brooklyn. Her memories of her teen years are brought back when she sees her younger relatives playing a video game about escape from the Chernobyl catastrophe whose virtual village is based on her own hometown, Pripyat. The second act, called 'present', takes place in Japan near the Fukushima reactor. This act concentrates on the actions of two sisters: Maho, visiting from Tokyo, and pregnant Maki, living near Fukushima. Audience members vote to decide whether Maki should have the child or not, stay in Fukushima or go to Tokyo with Maho. The third act, titled 'future', takes place under the 'surface' in which a nearly extinct organic human named Trepple decides whether or not to lose her organic material in order to better survive. Ultimately, she decides to go to the surface with her companion Astro, arriving in a futuristic New York. The play concludes when Trepple removes her radiation suit and bangs on a door on the other side of which Maki, now very pregnant, is waiting. Maki covers Trepple with a blanket when she enters the room. The play ends with all of the characters singing a lullaby.

Ogawa, the play's playwright and director, was born in Japan, but has lived primarily in the US for much of her adult life. *Ludic Proxy* was inspired by the combination of her agony watching the Fukushima disaster and her research into placemaking in video games. *Ludic Proxy*'s relevance, however, is not in how it questions the line between real and virtual or between past and present, but how it revises Chekhovian humanism through a re-suturing of the concerns of and for human and non-human organic matter. Ogawa stages the neoliberal period as an extension of a nuclear age, whose reality upends the idea of 'rational choice' so crucial to the era's ideology of risk management. Despite staging the apocalypse, Ogawa's depiction of advanced capitalism rejects Euroamerican notions of despair. In its place, she offers gestures of care and the making of kin – reproductive and not, engaging with and revising Donna Haraway's dictum: make kin not babies. For Haraway, making kin means rejecting pronatalism in favour of creating relations of care in larger networks, which might result in non-violent immigration policies, creating families with extended caregiving circles and including non-humans in such enclosures of care (Haraway 2016: 103n18). Ogawa does not entirely reject the hope of heterosexual procreation; she does however find ways to make connections outside of heteropatriarchal family structures as a final gesture.

Ogawa's critique of futurity is interlaced with the recognition of toxicity from *Ludic Proxy*'s first act. Nina's father, who works at the reactor, has a utopic view of nuclear energy; yet he also poisons himself through his drinking and smoking. Before the accident, he indulges while opining about the future. After the reactor explodes, he drinks vodka to counter the effects of radiation. This character is a nod to *Seagull*'s doctor Dorn, who links toxicity and Chekhovian Euroamerican despair at not understanding the future. Ogawa's Nina not only references Nina in *Seagull* but is playing her namesake in the school play in 1986 Chernobyl. When young Nina is learning her lines she recites this monologue from Treplev's symbolist play:

> People and lions, eagles and partridges. The horned deer, the geese, and the spiders. Silent fishes dwelling silently in the seas. Starfish and every unseen star in the sky – all life, all life, all life turning round and round in its sad, ceaseless circle, has been extinguished [. . .] Already for a thousand centuries, the world has not known a single living creature, and the sorrowful moon vainly lights her pale lamp. The meadows no longer stir to the cry of the cranes, and the hum of the june bugs is silent in the linden grove. Cold, cold, cold. Hollow, hollow, hollow. Horror, horror. . . . (Ogawa 2015: 8)

On the surface, this dramaturgical gesture may seem a little too obvious. The text references the end of life for many creatures on the planet in ways that echo the cessation of life after Chernobyl. The grandiosity of this cosmological vision of the second half of the monologue which Present Nina delivers is tempered by an exchange that references the 'thousands of years' in said monologue. Present Nina in *Ludic Proxy* can't conceive of the fact that Chernobyl will not be habitable by humans for another 20,000 years. She says: 'fifty, one hundred, two hundred . . . but beyond that? . . . Beyond that my consciousness cannot go' (ibid.: 22). Echoing her namesake, Nina's last words express that the most important thing in life is not success or love but 'the ability to survive' (ibid.: 84). Ogawa undermines Present Nina's fatalism in two ways: by interrupting this speech with a lullaby, and by juxtaposing this speech with the Maki and Trepple's moment of physical connection. It is notable that Present Nina is played by a white actress and Maki and Trepple are played by Asian American and African American actresses respectively. The play, in this sense, reveals the racialisation of care and cynicism in the Anthropocene.

The play's intertextual relationship to Chekhov extends to the third act. Connie Trepple references Constantine Treplev from *Seagull*; her work partner, Michael Astro, references *Uncle Vanya*'s Mikhail Astrov. Trepple, like her predecessor, is looking for a new kind of world through art, imagining the surface more than experiencing it; Astro explores as a form of adventure, if not of domination or modernisation. Eventually, Trepple decides to join Astro on a trip to the surface, despite the fact that she has cancer, and the trip is a risk. The protagonist's desire to stay organic is neither technophobia nor nostalgia for a sovereign human subject, but the fight for organic matter's right to exist. This desire performs the interconnectedness of organic matter without privileging the human, so important to scholars such as Haraway and Simpson. Even if the play is ambiguous about the possibility of its characters' survival (strikingly, in *Ludic Proxy*, one can be made sick by imagining the surface rather than actually having to encounter it). Thus, when Trepple cites Nina's monologue, we hear not fatalism but an attempt to connect – just as she does with Maki. Ogawa's selective citation of Chekhov also displaces the emphasis on work and progress displayed by many of Chekhov's philosophical characters (for example, Irina's 'we must work' at the end of *Three Sisters* and Astrov's own investment in progress) and interrogates the very idea of linear time and speculative futurity by continually moving between past, present and future and ultimately conjoining them at the end of *Ludic Proxy*.

This is not to say that the play is completely optimistic. It does, after all, contemplate the end of organic matter on earth. And, as my students astutely suggested, in Ogawa's play – unlike Rivera's *Marisol* – the threats to life are invisible. As Present Nina muses, 'I remember thinking to myself, what is it like, radiation? Has anyone seen it? People say it has no color, and no smell. But if you can't see it and it's everywhere, it must be like God' (ibid.: 21). In the second act we perceive radiation through the sound of a dosimeter. Much of the anxiety in the play arises around the danger that comes from toxicity of organic matter in food, a subject of great concern for both Maho and Maki. Maki is especially excited about eating the next-door neighbour's homegrown organic food; Maho is worried it might be poisoned because of the reactor. The sisters discuss the fact that schoolchildren eat the local rice in their school lunches, weighing the risk of radiation with the support of local agriculture; they also discuss an especially delicious and expensive peach from the grocery store. These details are notable – Fukushima Province is known for its fruit, especially peaches, in addition to rice and fish; it is odd that the fruit is so pricey. Maki eventually gags from the food, not because it is bad, but because she is pregnant. This revelation fuels the major obstacle or conflict of the scene – whether Maki should stay in or leave Fukushima. Maki is bound to the land because of family and history; Maho thinks this should be disregarded. The rest of the act becomes a meditation on radiation anxiety and risk calculation in the face of connection to place. Although thyroid cancer was later traced in survivors and children born near to both sites, the more widespread adverse health outcome common to Fukushima and the Chernobyl accident was/is *anxiety* about radiation (Bromet 2012).

This anxiety, and the very structure of the play – in which characters try to make a rational choice and audience members are given a choice about the actions and reactions of the characters – is where Ogawa reveals the great limitations in human rational choice in the face of the situation. The only choice the characters can make is staying in the apartment or leaving it. The earthquake arrives despite the character's decisions. Meaning the audience, while allowed to direct the actions of the characters, cannot change the catastrophic event which is to come. This mechanism, not unlike that offered by such mechanisms in video games, bring us to the same end, even as different decisions might give players an illusion of control. In the frame of neoliberal realities, the idea that rational choice based on individual risk analysis is an appropriate way to make choices about survival and ethical living on the planet falls away. That said, it is heartening to know that in what little choice the audience has, it has always chosen care: one of the final choices an audience member can make is deciding whether Maho saves herself or helps her sister. In a recent interview, Ogawa reports that every audience has chosen the latter (Ogawa 2021).

It should be noted that *Ludic Proxy* does tarry with the idea of reproductive futurity as part of its mediation on life during the Anthropocene. Maki's pregnancy is what necessitates a choice in relation to radiation; the medical intervention recommended in relation to Connie Trepple's cancer is a hysterectomy; Nina's childlessness is even referenced in relation to her sister's decision to reproduce once she left the Soviet Union. I mention this as a contrast to *The Unplugging*, which centres on two post-menopausal indigenous women, for whom reproduction is not a metaphorical or material condition to be considered. In this sense, Nolan pushes harder into Donna Haraway's suggestion that we should be making kin rather than making children in our current time (Haraway 2016: 99–103).

The Unplugging

The Unplugging, written by Metis/Algonquin playwright Yvette Nolan, imagines a different threshold moment: the cessation of electricity in a northern clime in the middle of winter. The play's two protagonists, Bern and Elena, are two Native American women who are left to try to manage the situation by using cultural memory to provide sustenance for survival. They are joined by Seamus, a young man of Irish heritage, who attempts to steal their knowledge. *The Unplugging* is based on a legend retold and published by Velma Wallis called *Two Old Women*. Nolan revised this story by moving it from a time before European contact to a time after; changing the reason for the women's exile from being about them being too weak to survive a winter in a community where food was scarce, to being about their non-reproductivity, and shifting their ages from their eighties to their fifties/sixties (Wallis 2004; Syron 2021: 64). The original narrative is Athabaskan, while Bern and Elena are likely Anishinaabe (Syron 2021: 64–5 and 74–6).[2] Yet both these nations share interdependency with animal and plant nations of Northern Turtle Island/the Far North, making the adaptation respectful and successful (Syron 2021: 75–6; Whyte 2017b).[3]

Ultimately, the play is not about the drama of whether or not the women will survive, (notably, the play's second scene, not its last, is called survival) or whether the earth will. Instead, *The Unplugging* asks us to reassess our conceptions of knowledge, intimacy and reciprocity in order to reimagine a world we can all live in together. Losing electricity is what allows the characters to go through that process; the play allows us to do so. As Kyle Whyte, Ryan Gunderson and Brett Clark claim, technology use not only has an impact on the environment in terms of toxic harm, but also on familial and community intimacy and knowledge (Whyte, Gunderson and Clark 2017: 46). They consider the hearth, which requires the collaborative work of many people and creates intimacy through its centrality in a home as a source of warmth and of community. Fire or the hearth is crucial to the unplugging as evidenced by the attention to acting with fire in the 2015 production of the play

(Syron 2021: 98). Note Nolan's description of the stove owned earlier by a survivalist known as the monk: 'Bern tends a simple, old airtight wood stove. It might be a top loader. It has no glass, no way to watch the fire within, its primary function to heat the house quickly' (Nolan 2014: 9). The characters praise the stove's functionality and its lack of need for retrofitting given that it pre-dated the area being electrified. Yet functional fire for a solo dweller, or isolationist living, is not valorised throughout the play any more than mere survival is. In *The Unplugging*, fire and light, as sources of heating, cooking and replenishment, are always imbedded within social relations of intimacy and trust. Bern teaches Seamus the responsible use of this stove; a lantern allows Bern and Elena to tell stories together; the open glass of the monk's house that allowed him to commune with non-human nations is reimagined as a greenhouse to create different relations between plants and sunlight, releasing the trees from existing as scenery in Chaudhuri's sense. Nature and culture are rejoined through the fusion of non-harmful technologies.

Rather than gesture to catastrophic events, or frame contemporary knowledge as dystopian, Nolan thinks about memory and knowledge as a quotidian practice. For example:

> Bern: I don't think tea goes bad . . . I don't recall ever hearing of anyone dying of tea that has gone off. Bern pours herself a cup of tea and smells it.
> Smells okay. Woodsy. I wonder if that is normal?
> Elena: google it
> Bern: ha
> Elena: think of all the information that disappeared in a blink. All the things we quit writing down and putting in books, all the things we stopped teaching our children, all the things we need to know now, like what is the shelf life of tea, and if it passes its best before date can it kill you. (Nolan 2014: 9–10)

This scene and others lapse not into nostalgia about vanishing indigenous knowledge but the importance of committing to the slow and steady act of (re-)learning how to create the relations to obtain food, warmth and shelter, such as trapping rabbits; (re-)membering Anishinaabe words for things; and understanding certain cycles of physical and metaphysical transformation though the marking of moons (Syron 2021: 75–8). As Nolan states in her presciently titled essay, 'A Hopeful Present':

> The things they [Bern and Elena] remember will move them forward in a way that memory dressed as nostalgia will not. This is

the way that we are going forward as a community, too. Even as we reclaim what was – traditions, knowledges, practices – we are aware that those things have transformed, that they cannot help but transform on their journey through the years. They are transformed by time and regret. They are transformed by our own growth. (Nolan 2011: 34)

In the play, Elena and Bern access different, complementary knowledges. Elena has the knowledge of trapping, cooking and cleaning. Bern gathers cast-off tools and food that can sustain them. This means that while Elena has more access to Anishinaabe cultural knowledge, Bern is more fluent in European epistemological knowledge systems, which sometimes help even as they can also harm. The women's conversation on libraries exemplifies this complexity:

> Bern: I love libraries. Loved. Full of other people's lives, full of other people's thoughts.
> Elena: ohh no. too quiet, everyone tiptoeing around, all those dead people lined up beside each other on the shelves, librarians frowning at you for touching anything like all of those stories are theirs . . . (Nolan 2014: 20)

The women's disagreement about books engages a critique of knowledge wrested from the body while also acknowledging the harm of library looting during the unplugging. In the end, Bern and Elena exemplify the right relation to knowledge and sacrifice – a deep respect for all living things and their knowledges. In an odd nod to Chekhov, the gun on the wall never goes off at the wrong time. Neither of the women kill any being with which they do not have a right relation. As Bern notes of the skinny hare they trap, 'it was generous of him to step into your noose', recognising the hare's agency in the matter (ibid.: 18). Thus the conclusion of the play, titled 'Harvest', is about planting what one sows, not imagining new technologies of resource extraction, restoring 'pure' indigenous knowledges or ridding oneself of conflictual beings.

Being in right relation means that Nolan's characters engage with, without defining themselves by, ideologies of coloniality or traumatic responses to them. This is true even in relation to the threat posed by Irish settler Seamus who takes off with the women's supplies and knowledge after Bern becomes intimate with him. When Seamus returns to make a peace offering in the form of a fish, it is Elena who welcomes him, and the family members accompanying him in for tea. Elena demands Bern put the gun down, reversing their earlier actions.

Revising the dynamics of settler colonial extraction, in which Euro-peans took indigenous knowledge and returned unspeakable violence, Nolan, through Elena and Bern, opts for the possibility of new modes of relation. They imagine not survival but survivance.[4]

Seamus's commitment to remembering at the play's close is a first step. By the play's end, *The Unplugging* mirrors the possibility of mutuality between indigenous and settler collaborators, which Whyte suggests as the best possibility for working together to save the planet (Whyte 2017a: 158–9). The focus of the play is not Seamus, although he has the last words in the play, 'Wait, just a moment. I want to remember everything' (Nolan 2014: 68). This line is one that Elena and Bern have manifested. These two old women are decolonising themselves and healing their own wounds so they can be intimate with each other and others so as to change the world. (The source book, one must remember, had more emphasis on the old women's transformation than that of those who exiled them.) The transformation of this trauma knowledge – from coloniality and other related violence – occurs within the personal relationships, but the larger implications are social and global. Elena and Bern demonstrate the values of relationality, trust and interdependency which the entire world must embody to change. *The Unplugging* is not simply an allegory about colonial violence in the past or its effects in the present. Instead, the play shows the temporal persistence of coloniality and Deep Time (Lane 2010; Quijano and Ennis 2000) as relations that are less causal than continuing over past, present and future. More relevant here, the space times explored in *The Unplugging* resonate with Anishinaabe modes of temporality in which an ancestor can also be a descendent and in which historical time exists as a spiral (Coperance and Miner, quoted in Whyte 2018: 228–9). This conception is sited in Anishinaabe knowledge but speaks to how the idea of a singular apocalypse can be decentred, and the ways these narratives enact epistemological harm on native and non-native peoples. Nolan's conceptions of time also participate in what Paula Allen Gunn calls 'ceremonial time', as Theresa May underscores in her analysis of Marie Clement's *Burning Vision* (May 2020: 246). Thus, although for many indigenous groups, particularly those in the North, the apocalypse has already happened, and knowing how to endure is a daily reality, one need not lapse into Euroamerican cynicism about the apocalypse.[5] A dialogue between Bern and Seamus makes this epistemological shift clear:

> Seamus: the unplugging? That is what you call it? An apocalypse
> destroys half the world, and you call it the unplugging?

Bern shrugs

Bern: I used to think of it as the earth waking and shaking like
some great dog, and all the machines and wires being shaken
off like so many fleas. The earthquakes in Haiti and Japan, the
disappearance of the Maldives. But that was really negative.
The Unplugging is more – benign.

Seamus: benign?

Bern: yeah. Like – mild. Harmless, kind of. (Nolan 2014: 29)

Only Seamus uses the word apocalypse. Bern jokes more about the
apocalypse, 'apocalyptists' and 'back to landers' as she makes relationships with those around her (ibid.: 8). Nolan's critique of temporality
and her commitment to decolonising knowledge production are inter-
woven, inspiring the structure of the play. *The Unplugging*'s lack of driving urgency and suspense in relation to Seamus's actions is not a fault of
the play, as at least one reviewer suggested, but one of its assets (Cole
2015). In summary, *The Unplugging* does not revolve around the threat
of Seamus's violence, or a reaction to it in unidirectional time. The plot
is not structured around sudden recognition, but Bern and Elena's slow
and evolving transformations: a mode of being offered to us as audience
members. This is a decolonial dramaturgy born of women's knowledge,
which, even within indigenous cultures, has often been pushed away
and is only now being reconsidered.[6] As non-Anishinaabe readers and
audience members, we are being asked to submerge ourselves in the
learning process, *in relation to the Anishinaabe knowledge we are allowed to
know*, so as to understand the protocol and ethic of care we must use as
we go on.[7] The modes of care modelled by the characters in these plays
are indigenous and feminist modalities of moral commitment which we
are asked to undertake (Whyte and Cuomo 2017).

While different, the ethics of care gestured to at the end of *Ludic
Proxy* and *The Unplugging* open up possibilities of what Haraway called
'moving on together' and Leanne Betasamosake Simpson, in relation to
her own nation's work, calls 'Nishnaabeg Internationalism' (Haraway
2016: 28; Simpson 2017: 55–70). Neither lapses into settler logics of apocalyptic inevitability by erasing the colonialities, imperialisms and complex
violences of nuclear age, nor compartmentalises histories that erase our
shared interconnectivity and responsibility. After all, as Nolan's fellow
Metis playwright Marie Clement suggests, in *Burning Vision*, Northern
indigenous and Japanese people are linked through the testing of and
use of nuclear weapons (May 2020: 242–5).[8] Ultimately, *Ludic Proxy*
and *The Unplugging* ask us, as they ask their characters, to make kin,
in Theresa May's and Donna Haraway's senses, in new and interesting

ways (Haraway 2016: 99–103; May 2020: 251–2). Maki's pregnancy aside, the relationship of care between Maki and Trepple suggests a new form of interdependency based on non-biological sisterhood. Bern, Elena, her family and Seamus also model a new form of relationality, which includes not only non-human animals, but air, fire and fruit. My offering for this collection on the post-Anthropocene is to open up the possibility of sitting near the hearth together so as to reimagine the present as well as the future, while respecting the indigenous knowledge that allows us to do so. In my conclusion, I resist the desire to prescribe a procedure or to offer a fungible theoretical modality of care; instead, I suggest that the thinking is in the listening, the gathering and the doing.

Notes

1. Kyle Whyte rightfully points out that indigenous peoples' sense of temporality and time contrast with 'highly disruptive colonial, capitalist and industrial periods' (Whyte 2017a: 159). Nonetheless Whyte centres his understanding of the Anthropocene around coloniality in ways that underscore my commitment to this date/period. Scholar Mark Maslin and Simon Lewis also underscore the colonial period as the beginning of the Anthropocene (Maslin and Lewis 2015).
2. I will be using the term Anishinaabe to refer to the cultural knowledge in *The Unplugging*. This term can be used to refer to people of a number of nations including Ojibwe and Algonquin, both of which are used at times to identify Nolan or the language she uses in her work. I refer to the terminology used by indigenous scholars in each instance throughout this work.
3. I use the term nations here in a manner consistent with Leanne Betasamosake Simpson.
4. Survivance is a concept created by Anishinaabe cultural theorist and writer Gerald Vizenor that adds agency such as the notion of resistance to the concept of survival (Vizenor 1999).
5. In addition to Kyle Whyte's critique of science fiction in Whyte (2017b), Theresa May makes a similar point about Clement's work; see May (2020).
6. In Whyte and Cuomo (2017: 239–42), it is suggested that the most important environmental ethics work is being done by female Anishinaabe and Ojibwe elders, knowledge keepers and activists. See also Simpson (2017: 83–94). Both writers also remind readers of gender fluidity and the importance of inclusion of women, queer and non-binary people within the movement.
7. The only indigenous reviewer of the play, S. Amy Dejarlais (Ojibwe), was somewhat disappointed by the smattering of cultural knowledge and the lack of a deeper connection between the two women, 'though, perhaps, this type of creative interpretation is an appropriate and safe space for these conversations to take place between Indigenous and non-Indigenous people'

(Dejarlais 2015). Syron, who was present for the process, seems to have a similar sense of disconnection between settlers and non-settlers. However, I don't think this problem lessens the strength of Nolan's dramaturgy.

8. See May (2020) for more on this relationship; see also Betasamosake Simpson, in her chapter on Nishnaabeg internationalism in Simpson (2017: 69).

Bibliography

Bromet, E. J. (2012), 'Mental Health Consequences of the Chernobyl Disaster', *Journal of Radiological Protection*, 32(1): N71.

Chakrabarty, Dipesh (2009), 'The Climate of History: Four Theses', *Critical Inquiry*, 35: 197–222.

Chaudhuri, Una (1994), 'There Must be a Lot of Fish in that Lake: Toward an Ecological Theatre', *Theater*, 25(1): 23–31.

Chaudhuri, Una (1997), *Staging Place: The Geography of Modern Drama*, Ann Arbor: Michigan University Press.

Chekhov, Anton (2017), *Seagull*, trans. Curt Columbus, New York: Dramatist Play Service.

Cole, Susan (2015), 'Review: *The Unplugging*', *Now Magazine*, 25 March: https://nowtoronto.com/review-the-unplugging (last accessed 6 December 2021).

Davis, Heather and Zoe Todd (2017), 'On the Importance of a Date, or Decolonizing the Anthropocene', *ACME: An International Journal for Critical Geographies*, 16(4): 761–80.

Dejarlais, S. Amy (2015), '*The Unplugging*: Post-Apocalyptic Stereotypes or Creative Interpretation', *Muskrat Magazine*, 26 March: http://muskratmagazine.com/the-unplugging-post-apocalyptic-stereotypes-or-creative-interpretation (last accessed 6 December 2021).

Demos, T. J (2017), *Against the Anthropocene*, Berlin: Sternberg Press.

Gillen, Katherine (2018), 'Shakespeare in the Capitalocene: Titus Andronicus, Timon of Athens, and Early Modern Eco-Theater', *Exemplaria*, 30(4): 275–92.

Goss, Lindsay (2021), 'Ending and Excess Theatre as Being in Crisis', *TDR* 65(4): 51–66.

Griffiths, Devin (2018), 'Petrodrama: Melodrama and Energetic Modernity', *Victorian Studies*, 60(4): 611–38.

Haraway, Donna (2016), *Staying with the Trouble: Making Kin in the Chthulucene*, Durham, NC: Duke University Press.

Hogan, Katie (2012), 'Green Angels in America: Aesthetics of Equity', *The Journal of American Culture*, 35(1): 4–14.

JapanSocietyNYC (2021), 'Ludic Proxy: Fukushima – Q&A with director/playwright Aya Ogawa' [video], *YouTube*: https://www.youtube.com/watch?v=UraCwPBqhMQ (last accessed 6 December 2021).

Kushner, Tony (1995), *Angels in America*, New York: Theatre Communications Group.

Lane, Jill (2010), 'Hemispheric America in Deep Time', *Theatre Research International*, 35(2): 11–25.

Maslin, Mark and Simon Lewis (2015), 'Defining the Anthropocene', *Nature*, 519: 171–80.

May, Theresa (2020), *Earth Matters on Stage: Ecology and Environment in American Theatre*, London and New York: Routledge.

Moore, Jason (2016), *Capitalism and the Web of Life: Ecology and Accumulation of Capital*, New York: Verso.

Nolan, Yvette (2011), 'A Hopeful Present', *Canadian Theatre Review*, 145: 31–4.

Nolan, Yvette (2014), *The Unplugging*, Toronto: Playwrights Canada Press.

Ogawa, Aya (2015), *Ludic Proxy*, unpublished text, courtesy of the author.

Ogawa, Aya, *Ludic Proxy*, directed by Aya Ogawa, Walker Art Space NYC, 1 April–2 May 2015, video of full performance available at: https://vimeo.com/209430385 (last accessed 6 December 2021).

Quijano, Anibal and Michael Ennis (2000), 'The Coloniality of Power', *Nepantla: Views from the South*, 1(3): 533–80.

Rivera, José (2005), *Marisol and Other Plays*, New York: Theatre Communications Group.

Rossini, Jon (2008), *Wrighting Ethnicity*, Carbondale, IL: Southern University Press.

Saldanha, Arun (2020), 'A Date with Destiny: Racial Capitalism and the Beginnings of the Anthropocene', *Society and Space*, 38(1): 12–34.

Simmons, Kali (2019), 'Reorientations; or An Indigenous Feminist Reflection on the Anthropocene', *JCMS: Journal of Critical and Media Studies*, 58(2): 174–9.

Simpson, Leanne Betasamosake (2017), *As We Have Always Done*, Minneapolis: University of Minnesota Press.

Syron, Liza-Mare (2021), *Rehearsal Practices of Indigenous Woman Theatre Makers: Australia, Aotearoa, and Turtle Island*, Cham, Switzerland: Palgrave Macmillan.

Vizenor, Gerald (1999), *Manifest Manners. Narratives on Postindian Survivance*, Lincoln: University of Nebraska Press.

Wallis, Velma (2004), *Two Old Women: An Alaska Legend of Betrayal, Courage and Survival*, 2nd edn, Kenmore, WA: Epicenter Books.

Whyte, Kyle Powys (2017a), 'Indigenous Climate Change Studies: Indigenizing Futures, Decolonizing the Anthropocene', *English Language Notes*, 55(1–2): 153–62.

Whyte, Kyle (2017b), 'Our Ancestors' Dystopia Now: Indigenous Conservation and the Anthropocene', in Ursula K. Heise, Jon Christensen and Michelle Niemann (eds), *Routledge Companion to the Environmental Humanities*, London and New York: Routledge, pp. 206–18.

Whyte, Kyle Powys (2018), 'Indigenous Science (Fiction) for the Anthropocene: Ancestral Dystopias and Fantasies of Climate Change Crises', *Environment and Planning E: Nature and Space*, 1(1–2): 224–42.

Whyte, Kyle Powys and Chris Cuomo (2017), 'Ethics of Caring in Environmental Ethics: Indigenous and Feminist Philosophies', in Stephen M. Gardiner and Allen Thompson (eds), *The Oxford Book of Environmental Ethics*, Oxford: Oxford University Press, pp. 234–47.

Whyte, Kyle Powys, Ryan Gunderson and Brett Clark (2017), 'Is Technology Use Insidious?', in David M. Kaplan (ed.), *Philosophy, Technology and the Environment*, Boston: The MIT Press, pp. 41–62.

4

Phenomenology of Waste in the Anthropocene

Mintautas Gutauskas

Introduction

The discussions surrounding the phenomenon of waste do not have an established theoretical tradition in philosophy, therefore the question of a methodological approach is of great importance. My research is phenomenological, which means that its main focus lies on waste as a phenomenon. What appears as waste, what do we conceive as waste? On the one hand, waste seems to be a simple phenomenon: everyone wastes more or less every day, we encounter waste in cities, parks and so on. It would seem that a phenomenological description could describe waste as phenomena appearing right in front of one's eyes. In the Anthropocene, however, waste does not only appear but also changes the environment by means of high-scale pollution, and thus indirectly begins to reshape our view of the world, of others and of the self. Waste is not only a simple object of experience; it is a phenomenon that gains the power to form the *horizon* of our experience. Therefore, waste requires a multifaceted approach. If we are concerned with 'the things themselves', this phenomenon has to be examined within several different dimensions. I will focus on the aspects of the individual's and of society's consciousness and attitude towards waste. Three dimensions of waste's participation in our experience will be distinguished. First, waste will be looked at as a simple phenomenon, then as a fundamental phenomenon and, finally, as a category of self-awareness. By examining the sense of waste as a simple phenomenon, I will determine the most basic structure. Following the footsteps of Martin Heidegger, attention will be drawn to the everyday meaning of waste and examined in terms of its readiness-to-hand. Since waste is no longer only a simple phenomenon and is gaining more and more weight in the perception of the world in the Anthropocene, I will draw on Eugen Fink's notion of a fundamental phenomenon to show the shift in the sense of waste. This shift is from that of a simple phenomenon to a fundamental one. Finally, to go beyond the boundaries of phenomenology, I will discuss how waste is involved in human self-awareness, as well as in the relationship between humans and other living beings.

Waste as a simple phenomenon

In order to understand why we waste so easily and do not notice the simple things which are at hand and under our feet, waste needs to be looked at in terms of everyday consciousness. Phenomenology begins with what is closest to us: with the familiar common practices and meanings. What kind of things are waste in the everyday, 'known to everyone' attitude? The latter is inseparable from the question of how things become waste and how we handle them. Lithuanian philosopher Arūnas Sverdiolas described the consciousness of littering as follows:

> It seems that a most regular everyman, on having drank the last sip of his yoghurt, beer, champagne, or vodka, and having smoked the last of his cigarettes, at that very moment, completely spontaneously and unaware of his own actions, launches a bottle or a packet out of his hands because it has just become useless. The *Zuhandenheit* of the packet, or its readiness-to-hand, is very narrow and episodic, the trajectory of its movement takes a very limited room of space, while beyond it there is the horizon of complete uncertainty: the empty containers slipping out of one's fingers simply disappear from the field of attention and that is that. (Sverdiolas 2006: 143)[1]

Sverdiolas marks the relationship between waste and certain modes of consciousness. The disappearance of waste from *the field of attention* and its *readiness-to-hand* are essential concepts when describing waste as a simple phenomenon. The first explains not only the ease and simplicity of littering, but also how we treat waste in general – waste is pushed out of the field of attention in various forms. The second shows waste's structuring of sense. Heidegger's term – *Zuhandenheit* – is of great significance as it points in the right direction: waste appears through the practical relationship with the world. Here, a few important things need to be marked.

Heidegger states that equipmentality is our primary relationship with things, and our relation to the world is firstly practical. According to him, things open up to us through their readiness-to-hand. Each piece of equipment is not defined by its material properties, but by its 'in-order-to'. Its sense is constituted in the network of relations. As Heidegger puts it, 'Equipment – in accordance with its equipmentality – always is *in terms of [aus]* its belonging to other equipment' (Heidegger 1962: 97, emphasis in original). A hammer points to a nail, the nail to a plank, and so to the whole world of building. A pen to a sheet of paper, the sheet to a desk, the desk is in the room, and so the room of a writer forms the practical structure of space. As Heidegger notes, the life-world is made up of such fields of sense in which we participate, understand and do something. For Heidegger, even nature is discovered through usability. Animals appear as suppliers of 'materials' (e.g. leather), and the 'power of nature' also emerges primarily through its usability: 'The wood is a forest of timber, the mountain a quarry of rock; the river is water-power, the wind is wind "in the sails"' (Heidegger 1962: 100).

And what about the equipmentality of waste? A thing becomes waste when it is not usable anymore and is disposed of. The sense of waste is constituted in a practical relationship with the world, but the structuring of sense is already different. Waste is simply thrown into certain places, piled up or placed in bags. It becomes *undifferentiated mass*, and its essential properties are its *materiality*, *resistibility* and *accumulability*. Even these properties are not easily noticeable if the disposal process of waste runs smoothly. It is important to mark how waste shapes the field of attention in the horizon of activity. The field of attention, just as the whole practical living space, has its own order in which something is constituted as normal, good, orderly and logical, or bad, abnormal and disorderly. When a tool loses its equipmentality, that craftwork has no place, and an attempt is made to remove it. This action can be spontaneous. Probably the most fitting example of spontaneous littering is waste thrown out of cars. Something that has been used up – a disposable cup of coffee or a cigarette butt – is thrown out of the 'orderly space' (for example the inside of a car). The car drives away, no waste is visible, there seems to be no problem and the field of attention remains in order. If the field of attention is narrow, then even the rubbish under the feet does not break the order because what is under the feet for the one who litters is beyond the horizon of their perception. This structure of the field of attention also applies to the more orderly consciousness. At home, waste is placed in certain places – put in black bags, taken away to garbage bins and then to landfills. The field of attention of these consciousnesses is wider and the actions are less spontaneous. As will be discussed later, such consciousnesses have a larger field of order, but not a new approach to waste.

It should be noted that waste as a simple phenomenon appears to the consciousness in two ways – through the modes of *disappearing* and *encounter*. During the actual encounter waste is clearly constituted as waste through the aspect of disorder. For example, while taking a walk in the park, waste often appears unexpectedly; it angers, shocks and bewilders how on earth such a beautiful place can be littered that much. Here waste does not disappear from but returns into the field of attention again, demonstrating that it is resistant and sticks out despite the fact that consciousness has pushed it out of the field of attention. When defining tools, Heidegger introduced the term 'ready-to-hand', so for waste the term 'under-the-feetness' can be suggested. Waste is not useful equipment; it does not have its 'in order to'. We step on it, kick it – waste just lying there under our feet – like a quantitative mass of material things that our consciousness seems to have pushed out of the field of attention. However, the 'under-the-feetness' of waste is its claim that waste has not disappeared anywhere and is not going to, especially if waste material is non-degradable or non-recyclable. The under-the-feetness of waste appears as the structuring of a sense of disorder which demands a course of action – waste needs to be tidied up, taken some-where further outside the field of attention. As long as the order of the field of attention is easily restored waste remains a simple phenom-enon. However, in the encounter with large quantities of waste – when waste is no longer an element in the field of attention but fills the entire horizon – the resistibility and accumulability of waste creates precondi-tions for it to become a fundamental phenomenon. But what is waste as a fundamental phenomenon?

Waste as a fundamental phenomenon

Let us begin firstly with defining what fundamental phenomena are. The term itself was coined by Eugen Fink. In *Grundphänomene des menschli-chen Daseins* [Basic phenomena of human existence], Fink distinguishes five phenomena of this kind: death, work, rule, love, and play. Each of these manifests as things that happen in life, as simple phenomena: people die, produce something, rule, love, and play. However, Fink points out that fundamental phenomena cannot be understood from what is manifested alone. Take death for instance. For one thing, we see our loved ones dying and different movies provide a wide variety of stories about death. But is this a way to grasp the phenomenality of death? As Fink writes, '[Death], in a strict sense, is not a phenomenon which you can display and put to show or can somehow bring to your-self as a vivid givenness at any time' (Fink 1979: 199).[2] Thus, rather than a simple phenomenon, death is a fundamental one: the expression of death cannot be reduced to simple manifestations, for it is not only what manifests but also what creates *the horizon* of human life. As Fink notes, fundamental phenomena are 'the ways of a human being'; 'the manners of understanding in which the man understands himself as the mortal, the worker, the fighter, the lover, and the player'; they are 'the horizons of sense, where the man interprets the being of all things' (Fink 1979: 358). Fundamental phenomena create the 'sense-structured space' (*Sinn-Raum*) which provides a structure for action and understanding (Fink 1979: 90). Unexperienced death creates mortal beings, life events gain meaning in the horizon of death and finitude. Other fundamental phenomena are more experiential. Work and the results of work, the manifestations of love and relationships, play and its processes are clearly visible. For Fink, play is the best example. It has its own rules and must be entered and played as intended by the rules. Therefore, the fundamental phenomena are not just simple phenomena. They are structures of sense of a certain medium in which people's lives unfold. It should be emphasised that the fundamental phenomena include epistemological as well as ontological dimensions which are the modes of a human's existence. A human being *exists* by working, playing, and so on. It is just as important that fundamental phenomena create the sense-structured space for perceiving not only phenomena but also oneself. Death creates the mortal, work creates the worker and love creates the lover. In such a horizon, a human being perceives not only things, but also one's own actions, as well as relationships with other people and oneself.

According to Fink, the ability to move from one space of the phenomenon's meaning to another constitutes the heterogeneity, even contradiction and conflict, of human existence. This is perhaps the most significant insight of Fink's philosophical anthropology today: the human being exists as a field of tensions. The fundamental phenomena compete or are in conflict with each other. Play, from the perspective of work, may look like a waste of time, in comparison to learning or preparation for serious work. Football may seem sheer folly: crowds squander money on fan tickets, merchandise and drinks; players waste energy running to and fro on the pitch; and the prize, a cup, is such a non-functional vessel that one cannot even conveniently drink from it. But this only seems to be the case if one does not take into account the specific meaning created in the play-space. Love, in turn, gives sense to various 'banalities' and 'trifles'. Flowers for your loved one may seem like an unnecessary thing and a waste of money: there are neither calories nor vitamins in them. Yet again, this is an attitude which disregards the *Sinn-Raum* of love.

Fundamental phenomena establish a field of activity, project values, aspirations and totalities of sense, and also give meaning to every object and action. Furthermore, for Fink, fundamental human phenomena are phenomena without which specifically human life would not be possible. Would the human community be possible if human relationships were not built in the sense-structured space of love, work, rule and play? Probably not. These fundamental phenomena are the conditions of being a human. And is waste a necessary condition for being a human? Would human life not be human without waste? How come waste may be treated as a new fundamental phenomenon? It is evident that waste is not necessary for defining humanity. But let us not rush to conclusions. Today, such a strong claim as that of Fink's on the humanity of a human cannot be made, but it can be said that waste is a fundamental phenomenon of the *Anthropocene*. Waste is not a universal and 'supertemporal' human phenomenon of life, but its *power to form the horizon* in the Anthropocene is of no less value. Waste might generally appear not only as a non-fundamental phenomenon, but as an inessential, marginal phenomenon. After all, for Fink, fundamental phenomena are those that distinguish the human being from other living beings. Humans live in the *Sinn-Raum*. Waste, in turn, is material and lies meaningless and unintentionally under-the-feet. But waste is a very special fundamental phenomenon. As a phenomenon it is primarily negative: it either disappears from the field of attention or returns as an element of disorder. Yet in the Anthropocene, from the negativity of waste grows a positive power to form a horizon. This by no means suggests that the treating of waste becomes positive. It continues to be negative, but waste becomes a part of human concern, it begins to form the horizon, a distinctive sense-structured space where each thing takes on meaning. Waste becomes not the liminal but the central and fundamental phenomenon. It forms a new foundation which prompts us to reconsider all our actions and choices. It is not only the relation with things that is important here, but also the relationship with oneself, the moment of self-understanding. Just as the phenomenon of death creates the mortal, so does the phenomenon of waste create the *waster*. I will return to self-awareness later, but here I want to point out once again that this is namely a phenomenon of the Anthropocene. Only in this epoch does it become possible and even necessary to interpret most of the things in the horizon of waste. This is due to the changed natural, physical and social living conditions and the awareness of them. The abundance and surplus of things and their rapid aging and consumption produce much more waste in comparison to other epochs. In the Anthropocene, waste emerges as a phenomenon which cannot be ignored. So, what are the most significant changes in our relationship with waste?

It has already been mentioned that perhaps the most significant change in the relationship with waste is the awareness of its *resistibility* and *accumulability*. The accumulation of the floating islands of plastic in oceans, such as The Great Pacific garbage patch, shows how far waste can 'travel' without human activity. It has to do with the expansion of the field of attention and the emergence of a global consciousness. This implies that waste does not disappear anywhere, and its movement trajectory is such that it almost always comes back. For example, the new 'food chain' can be regarded as follows: discarded plastic bottle → plastic in the ocean → microplastic → krill → small fish → large fish on a table which shows that the discarded plastic bottle, after completing the cycle, can easily end up on our dinner plate in the form of nano-plastic particles which remain in the fish. The most important point is the apprehension of this cycle, the awareness that this resistant and accumulative waste returns and requires us to reconsider ordinary actions in terms of sense, goals, values and consequences.

A new consciousness is emerging, one that sees everything not only as a piece of equipment, but as future waste. The pioneer of the Zero Waste movement, Bea Johnson, is a good example of that new consciousness for which waste is already a fundamental phenomenon. Here is how she describes her own relationship with waste:

> We drag the trash can to the curb at night, and by the time we get up the next morning, the cereal liners and dirty paper towels have disappeared, as if by magic. But when we say 'we threw something away', what do we really mean? 'Away' might take trash out of our sight, but that doesn't mean it should be out of our minds. After all, our discards don't just evaporate because the garbageman whisked them off. Our waste ends up in our landfills, spoiling our precious environment, leaching toxic compounds into our air and soil, wasting the resources used to create the discarded goods, and costing us billions of dollars each year in processing. (Johnson 2013: 14)

The 'old' consciousness of littering is characterised by the idea that a piece of trash 'evaporates' after disappearing from the field of attention. For the new consciousness, the act of 'throwing the trash away' is no longer obvious, as everything is interpreted not through the disposal of waste, but in terms of its resistibility, accumulability, recyclability and possible trajectories of movement. It is a consciousness that never lets waste 'be out of our minds'. This consciousness anticipates the possible, albeit often unpredictable, trajectories of the movement of waste and even differentiates craftworks according to their qualities of decomposability and pollution. Phenomenologically, the latter is particularly significant as it opens a new dimension of the sense of craftworks: not only of their equipmentality, but also of their trashiness, i.e. the future transformation of craftworks into hardly or easily decomposable waste. From the perspective of a consciousness, what matters is not so much the material composition of a craftwork but, rather, the inclusion of its decomposability into the sense structure of the craftwork. And when waste becomes a fundamental phenomenon, it turns into a medium through which all things, actions and even human relationships can be seen, as in Johnson's book. *Zero Waste Home* is almost a perfect example of such an attitude. It shows how all things and activities – school, work, leisure, holidays, entertainment and games – can be reinterpreted from the point of view of waste. Of course, waste is not the sole factor here. As mentioned before, waste has a meaning in terms of consumption and wastefulness, so these aspects are important too. I will stress only two points. Firstly, consumption multiplies waste, so that stopping the act itself becomes greatly significant; and secondly, an ethical relationship with nature and other living beings emerges. Production is understood as the *deprivation* of something from nature, or the *killing* of something. Therefore, the production process must not only be weighed in terms of a multiplication of waste, but also in terms of evaluating the need for that particular action or product, and whether it would be worth killing something over. Here is what Johnson says:

> Every bit we accept, or take, creates a demand to make more. In other words, compulsive accepting (versus refusing) condones and reinforces wasteful practices. When we let waiters fill our glass with water that we won't be drinking and a straw that we won't use, we are saying: 'Water is not important' and 'Please make more disposable straws'. When we take a 'free' shampoo bottle from a hotel room, more oil will be rigged to make a replacement. When we passively accept an advertising flyer, a tree is cut down somewhere to make more flyers, and our time is unwisely spent dealing with and recycling something that is trivial. (Johnson 2013: 16)

Of course, Johnson somewhat exaggerates. Are we not connecting routine everyday actions to global problems too fast? What assumptions lead to such conclusions so quickly? And yet, this is distinctive of the Anthropocene epoch: to understand everyday actions in the context of global processes. However, this is not that simple. Johnson herself admits that she went slightly overboard trying to lead a completely zero waste life (despite the fact of her family's annual trash managing to fit in a small glass jar being highly impressive). She realised that it was detrimental not only to her household, but also to social relationships. Johnson's example is important to us as an extreme example which shows that everything can be interpreted in the horizon of waste. The meaningfulness of her actions is not being questioned in any way, and it can be assumed that her proposed principles of action, within the limits of common sense, are necessary for today's daily life. But there are other phenomena of human existence without which human life would hardly be possible. This is where the tensions of human life and the conflicts between fundamental phenomena manifest themselves. Is it possible not to give presents and buy toys for your children at all? Hardly any child would be satisfied with receiving a gift every ten years. Is it possible to give your lover consumable produce such as carrots, cabbages or beets as a present, instead of flowers? Possibly, if agreed upon. Is it possible to give up candles at a funeral, and bury or burn the dead in their 'birthday suit' alone? Hardly. As we see, these questions are not easy and there are hardly any unequivocal answers. Of course, some daily habits can be changed, and this change can happen with the help of such initiators like Johnson, but everything cannot be changed by one fundamental phenomenon alone. Johnson's suggested principles of action – refuse, reduce, reuse, recycle, rot – are necessary in today's outlook (Johnson 2013: 15). However, this does not make our daily life any simpler, for it is permeated by conflicts between the fundamental phenomena or at least by the 'negotiations' in between them.

The important question for us is whether with the birth of a new consciousness the 'old' one still remains? When waste becomes a fundamental phenomenon, does it still continue to be the thing that disappears from the field of attention? Everyday consciousness tends to confine itself to a limited, cosy and familiar field, especially when a global viewpoint is threatening, apocalyptic and requires a lot of effort and far-reaching calculations. The main idea of everyday consciousness has been well described by the theorist of modernity Anthony Giddens in his description of the 'sequestration of experience'. As he writes, '[t]he term "sequestration of experience" refers here to the connected processes of concealment which set apart the routines of ordinary life from the following phenomena: madness; criminality; sickness and death; sexuality; and nature' (Giddens 1991: 157). Therefore, the everyday experience is 'ontologically secure' if it is isolated from the unknown, threatening processes that question the order of everyday life. According to Giddens, individuals are not the only ones who sequester their experiences. The sequestration of experiences and daily security is ensured by institutions which isolate elements of potential threat in madhouses, prisons and funeral homes. Waste is also taken to places which are hard to access physically; it requires a special effort to get to a landfill or to think about the release of toxic chemicals in the landfills when at the breakfast table. Everyday life tends to enclose itself in a cosy routine where waste continues to exist as discarded unwanted things. People relax from the tiring talks and threatening statistics of global climate change and the extinction of species by indulging in shopping, buying another piece of attractive clothing, or creating a homely environment in their households by renovating furniture and/or other elements of interior design. Who would not want a cosy home and relaxing leisure? When cosiness and ontological security are created through consumption, material waste only accumulates. On the other hand, daily life in the Anthropocene has become greatly heterogeneous. It requires people *to choose a scale or measure* by which daily activities will be perceived and assessed. Johnson and other pioneers of ecological movements offer a whole new scale: to understand that everyday actions partake in a global process, even if the direct consequences of these actions do not seem to be bad. What is wrong with collecting garbage and taking it to the waste containers? And yet, this depends on the chosen scale. If one confines oneself to one's own environment, the sequestration of experience allows waste to remain a simple phenomenon. Of course, various strategies of waste prevention and management are becoming daily habits, so waste as the horizon of the fundamental phenomenon is not that uncommon. We should, rather, acknowledge that in modern everyday life there are many different attitudes, habits and activities regarding waste, so there are two distinct poles here. On one side rests a simple consciousness which is limited to a narrow field of attention that pushes waste out of the horizon; on the other, a hyperactive ecological consciousness which realises that waste does not disappear beyond the horizon but wanders uncontrollably on the planet in various different forms. Our daily lives unfold exactly in between these poles. This can be understood not only as two poles, but also as two pure modes of consciousness according to which waste is either a simple or a fundamental phenomenon. With the growth of ecological self-awareness, we would like to see our daily lives as a movement from one mode to the other. But the current daily life is hybrid rather than pure.

Waste as a category of self-awareness

In the Anthropocene, waste can no longer be considered solely as a simple phenomenon. Newest trends of thinking and action – recycling waste, reduction of consumption, circular economy and the attempts to turn waste into resources – are becoming the latest necessities and directions of education. However, the atmosphere of the Anthropocene is a crisis in which the change of the horizon, when interpreting waste, is under constant tension both with other approaches and uncontrolled natural processes. For instance, despite the growth of ecological self-awareness, the scale of pollution and wastefulness is not declining; and the COVID-19 pandemic has shown that reducing medical waste loses out in the need to protect human lives. Medical masks are already turning into a new wave of waste. So all that is needed is a crisis which threatens people's lives and a far-sighted approach to waste becomes secondary. And yet, this does not mean that waste disappears from our sight. The accumulation of waste exposes our helplessness and begins to form a new self-awareness of the Anthropocene's *anthropos*. A few important things need to be addressed from the immense flow of Anthropocene narratives.

Although the Anthropocene is becoming a category of self-awareness, it is a *geological term* first. As a geological term, the Anthropocene refers to how human activities have developed to such an extent that they act as a *geological force* which produces changes that can no longer be reversed. The most visible signs of the Anthropocene are on the Earth's surface. In no other geological epoch has it changed so rapidly. Urban development, house building, constructions of roads and dams, artificial islands and mineral mines have changed the Earth's surface severely and irreversibly. However, it is the change in air composition and not the change on the Earth's surface that is more significant when dating the Anthropocene. As Jeremy Davies points out, Paul Crutzen's and Eugene Stoermer's idea was to link the beginning of the Anthropocene with the invention of the James Watt steam engine in 1784 (Davies 2016: 43). The steam engine allows for changes in air composition, and the increase in the number of engines leads to a gradual rise in the amount of carbon dioxide in the air. All this continues to determine not only the levels of air pollution but also the acidification of oceans, which in turn reduces the diversity of animal species, and so on. Of course, the steam engine is not the only acting agent here. Of equal significance is increased consumption, which has been taking place since the middle of the twentieth century and is now almost uncontrollable, as well as the constant growth of the population. For the geological dating of the Anthropocene, the importance of the changes in the *air*, rather than the *land*, signal an important factor. The transformation of the Earth's surface demonstrates the power of *voluntary* and *purposive* human activity: how mankind is able to transform the natural environment and connect it to its own needs. But the changes in air composition point to the *uncontrollable consequences* of human activity. The increase of carbon dioxide in the air is not a planned and purposively implemented thing, and it appears that humans cannot exactly cope with this by-product. Therefore, paradoxically, in the Anthropocene – in the human epoch – what matters is not what humans can do, but what they cannot do. The Anthropocene signifies the global unplanned changes which are brought about not so much by mankind as it takes over nature, but by the species which depletes resources, pollutes the environment, and fails to control its activities on a planetary scale.

The aspect of accumulation is of great importance here. Geological changes, when counted in years and not in centuries, occur with very slight and insignificant shifts. Only the accumulation of those processes becomes significant. However, Timothy Clark describes the Anthropocene as a threshold event:

> The Anthropocene is itself an emergent 'scale effect'. That is, at a certain, indeterminate threshold, numerous human actions, insignificant in themselves (heating a house, clearing trees, flying between the continents, forest management) come together to form a new, imponderable physical event, altering the basic ecological cycles of the planet. (Clark 2015: 72)

Therefore, the Anthropocene is an accumulative consequence of 'insignificant' actions. Domestic heating is a daily matter which maintains the standard of living conditions and everyday order. It is globally insignificant as long as it does not accumulate. The disposal of waste is also a daily matter which ensures living conditions and order, and is also globally insignificant as long as it does not accumulate. When heating a home or driving a car, there is no intention to cause harm. And when waste is removed from a home, the order is maintained. As a separate action, the removal of waste is treated as a positive thing. However, the consequences of these local, globally insignificant, actions – the resistance and accumulation of waste – are damaging. And it is this kind of damage that one cannot control on a planetary scale. Such helplessness encourages the emergence of a new self-awareness. Certain definitions are radical. Here is what Clark says:

> The newly recognized agent of humanity as a geological force is something indiscernible in any of the individuals or even large groups of which it is composed. It is a power that barely recognizes itself as such and which is not really capable of voluntary action or planning, as it arises from the often unforeseen consequences of the plans and acts of its constituents. (Clark 2015: 15)

But what do the unforeseen consequences of human actions mean for mankind? It is clear that a radical change is taking place here – a reversal of basic definitions. When analysing the changes in self-awareness, the researchers of the Anthropocene usually refer to the concept of humanity formed during the Enlightenment, which is defined by the idea of a man as a living being of a special quality. The human recognises himself through the life of mind and spirit, ideas, aspirations, ideals and intentions. The Anthropocene and waste force the human to meet with the material and seemingly least human side. The human begins to recognise oneself from one's own material traces. The concept of trace becomes particularly significant here. The human begins to know himself in new ways from his traces. Human traces on Earth – reshaped terrains, destroyed natural environments, polluted and littered areas – constitute what the human is. The human is a polluting being, a culprit, a species that cannot control the consequences of its actions. It is important to emphasise that through pollution, waste and the destruction of the environment, the human being accepts itself as an object that seems to be completely detached from the intentions of the subject. On one hand, the human who controls itself and the world with reason; on the other, the unconscious geological force. The subjectivity of the first one seems to have collapsed or at least been compromised, while the subjectivity of the second seems not to appear at all. Maybe that is why the self-awareness of humanity is formed as the 'power that barely recognizes itself as such and which is not really capable of voluntary action or planning'.

But here one has to ask: from what place is humanity defined as a geological force? It is rather obvious that this is not a self-awareness of geological forces, but a self-aware consciousness that has felt responsibility, and has also experienced frustration with its own incapacity. A new consciousness of guilt and responsibility emerges, which comprehends itself through the relationship with vulnerable nature. When questioning what is causing such change, it should be noted that the concepts of *encounter* and *event* are the most significant here. *Encounter* is particularly important from a phenomenological point of view and refers to personal experience and the bodily encounter with the other, whereas *event* refers to the new condition and constitution of humanity.

Through the dimension of a personal, bodily encounter, we can consider a new approach to the experience of waste. What do we experience when we encounter a seabird tangled in a plastic bag, a fish choking on plastic? Here, waste appears not only as an element of disorder that was supposed to disappear from the field of attention, but as something that remained and did not decay. An animal entangled in plastic shows that waste pollutes, as well as *kills* and *destroys* its environment. The animal's suffering and its inability to escape demand me to take action. The animal's appeal becomes a reference to the self. Emmanuel Levinas's insight on the identity of the self as constituted by the other is significant here. The self is not given, and only by encountering the other, in the 'not-being-able-to-slip-away', is the self constituted as a responsive and responsible one (Levinas 1998: 92). It is waste in nature that shows how and to what extent the other is damaged, pointing to the self as the one who did the damage. The animal that cannot get out of plastic constraints constitutes the self as the human who cannot escape responsibility. It is important to highlight that this is not only an interpersonal relationship. When we see an animal tangled in plastic and unable to move, we recognise that this damage was caused by humans. Someone else might have thrown out the plastic, but it is still human activity, and I as a human being become the polluter's collaborator. Waste as something that may or may not have been but still appeared points to the human. Animals can live only in their own environment, so the polluted coasts are understood not as the disorder of the human world, but as destruction of other living beings' environment. In this way, the self does not only stand in relation to the damaged animal, but also to the whole affected environment in which the natural habitat of many living beings is either damaged or completely destroyed.

Many researchers of the Anthropocene describe the Anthropocene as a critical event that established a new understanding of the human. Despite the fact that physically the Anthropocene unfolded as a consequence of accumulations, for us the Anthropocene occurs as a new self-awareness event. What is shocking is that the human's power to change the environment becomes dire due to its uncontrollable consequences. Anxiety becomes the atmosphere in which every individual not only seeks solutions but also has to answer to questions of guilt and responsibility. The emerging new ecological consciousness shows that not only can things, actions and social relations be interpreted through the horizon of waste, but also that the individual takes responsibility for global processes. We might ask, why do humans take the blame for global waste and even climate change? Why is the human to blame for what no individual is able to control? The relationship between guilt and responsibility is well explained by Paul Ricoeur. The limits of responsibility are closely linked to the increasing human power to cause harm. As Ricoeur put it, 'our responsibility for harm done extends as far as does our capacity to do harm' (Ricoeur 2000: 30). Hence, to the extent that power arises to do damage that would affect the entire planet, so too does the responsibility extend with it. This responsibility would remain a purely abstract or declarative commitment if it were not a shocking event: a crisis on a planetary scale along with the awareness of it. Enormous power is conceived – the human acts as a geological force. However, as we have seen, this power is twofold: it testifies not only to the power to change, but also to the inability to cope with unwanted consequences. Inability to deal with consequences does not relieve one from responsibilities, as the power to cause harm remains the same. This establishes the state of the human in which the human is defined not by the power but by the inability to deal with harm. Human self-awareness is awakened by a conscious perception of the obligation and the event where the damage is seen in the face of the other, in the eyes of an animal or on the surface of polluted nature. Therefore, although the Anthropocene itself cannot be accurately dated as an event, we can conceive that we have already established an event that points to the perpetrator and constitutes it.

Conclusion

As we have seen, waste has become a multidimensional phenomenon in the Anthropocene. On the one hand, it still remains a simple phenomenon, encountered corporeally in the modes of disappearing and under-the-feetness. As long as we sequester our experience and close ourselves within the bubble of comfort waste remains in the field of attention for only a short period of time; only for as long as it takes to dispose of what has become unneeded and unnecessary, before it is then taken care of by the relevant services. On the other hand, the resistibility and accumulability of waste turn it into a big thing changing the natural environment and the notion of the human. Furthermore, waste as a fundamental phenomenon of the Anthropocene changes the horizon of our daily lives, and we begin to understand things in terms of their wastability. We begin to see things anew, not only from the viewpoint of what we can do with them, but also in terms of what kind of waste they will become when we have thrown them away. What is more: things which are consumed gain another dimension – they not only turn into potential waste, but also into potential destroyers. Waste kills: dying animals entangled in waste become witnesses of uncontrolled human activity. Of course, it may seem quite paranoid to see both potential waste and destruction in every craftwork, but the awareness of the accumulability of waste requires that these dimensions be included in the horizon of perception of each of them. Due to high accumulability and pollution, waste becomes our relationship with other living beings.

Finally, waste transcends the boundaries of any phenomenon. Waste is not just a simple phenomenon appearing in experience, it is not just a fundamental phenomenon forming the horizon of interpretation for things, the self and others. Waste becomes a material trace from which the human recognises oneself. It forces the human to know oneself not so much through what was customary in Western thought – subjectivity, spirit, ideas, ideals, aspiration and creation of meaning – but through what seemed beyond the field of human culture and did not belong to human self-awareness – through material traces. The scale of these traces leads humans to be treated as a geological force that is as irrational and uncontrollable as the human's inability to cope with the consequences. The Anthropocene as an event constitutes the human, and the human identifies itself through waste which through harm shows who one is. Waste shows the paradoxical, in-between state of being: the human is in-between the extended responsibility for the whole planet and total irresponsibility for it; between the power to build and the inability to control the consequences; as well as between the destructive species and the responsible subject that takes the blame.

Notes

1. Translated from Lithuanian by Greta Kaikarytė.
2. All translations of quotes from Fink's book *Grundphänomene des menschlichen Daseins* (1979) are made by Greta Kaikarytė and myself.

References

Clark, Timothy (2015), *Ecocriticism on the Edge: The Anthropocene as a Threshold Concept*, London: Bloomsbury.

Davies, Jeremy (2016), *The Birth of the Anthropocene*, Oakland: University of California Press.

Fink, Eugen (1979), *Grundphänomene des menschlichen Daseins*, Freiburg: Alber.

Giddens, Anthony (1991), *Modernity and Self-Identity: Self and Society in the Late Modern Age*, Cambridge: Polity Press.

Heidegger, Martin (1962), *Being and Time*, trans. John Macquarrie and Edward Robinson, Oxford and Cambridge: Blackwell.

Johnson, Bea (2013), *Zero Waste Home: The Ultimate Guide to Simplifying Your Life by Reducing Your Waste*, New York: Scribner.

Levinas, Emmanuel (1998), *Of God Who Comes to Mind*, trans. Bettina Bergo, Stanford, CA: Stanford University Press.

Ricoeur, Paul (2000), *The Just*, trans. David Pellauer, Chicago and London: University of Chicago Press.

Sverdiolas, Arūnas (2006), 'Lėkštutėlė lėkštelė', in *Apie pamėklinę būtį: Ir kiti etiudai*, Vilnius: Baltos lankos.

5

Climate Control: From Emergency to Emergence

T. J. Demos

What if we consider tear gas as the exemplary medium of climate emergency, which environmentalist organisations are calling on governments worldwide to urgently recognise? We would face an entirely different politico-ecological calculus than carbon's, referencing not only a regime of socioeconomic inequality, but explicit repression and violence, too. Compared to greenhouse gases' usual suspects – carbon dioxide, methane (dubbed 'freedom gas' recently in the US [see Rueb 2019]), nitrous oxide and hydrofluorocarbons – on which climate emergency groups like Extinction Rebellion (XR) focus, the chemical weapon more directly exposes the nefarious side of global capital and thus leads immediately to an entirely different political analysis. Its toxic environment defines a conflicted war zone where unauthorised challenges to the ruling order – an order that is itself bringing about climate chaos, profound inequality and systemic violence – are met with the weaponisation of air, a formulation that proposes a very different way to consider the reality behind the otherwise banal phraseology of 'climate change'. As we are now seeing all over the world, counterinsurgency increasingly answers popular sovereignty demands in the age of post-democratic and ecological breakdown, indexed by an authoritarian atmospherics, a militarised ecology, of strategically enforced climate control. At the same time, these attempts are directed at forces that are ultimately uncontrollable.

The recent mass uprisings in Hong Kong; the anti-colonial rage expressed on the streets of San Juan; uprisings in war-torn Iraq; anti-neoliberal revolts in Chile; Central American migrants fleeing agricultural failure and gang violence crossing the US–Mexico border zone – all have been answered with tear gas, an integral component in the liberal-become-authoritarian state's response to opposition that bypasses conventional routes of negotiation. Its (supposedly) non-lethal crowd control is clearly post-political, maintaining the state's monopoly on violence. Nonetheless, these worldwide revolutions rise up against everything tear gas represents, and it is these struggles that can offer important lessons for the politics of climate emergency, beginning with a necessary expansion of our terminology.

With atmospheric carbon, conversely, the source is vastly distributed, rendering environmentalist demands and science's politics complex and inarticulate, with causality and culpability hard to ascertain. Sure, there are powerful fossil fuel corporations, and devious backroom lobbyists, but are we not also all carbon subjects, thoroughly enmeshed in an interconnected web of consumer complicity and guilt? So we often hear, even though we know that the wealthiest emit the largest share by far. With tear gas, the enemy is clear: Safariland CEO Warren B. Kanders, for instance, ousted recently from the Whitney Museum's Board of Trustees after sustained mass protests around the so-called 'Teargas Biennial', his weapons' profiteering seen as complicit in police actions against Black Lives Matter in Ferguson, migrants at the US–Mexico border, Turkish pro-democracy activists in Gezi Park, and Gazans opposing Israeli occupation of Palestinian lands. Safariland's Triple Chaser tear gas grenades – and the institutions that support and enable their use – bear a clearer signature of repressive order than fossil fuels more generally, even while the two remain intimately intertwined, with energy, infrastructure and security all essential components of the petro-capitalist complex.

Of course, there is also glyphosate, micropolymers, carbon monoxide, sulfur dioxide, neonicotinoids, chlorpyrifos, and more – all enacting untold damage, and for massive profits (Safariland has had annual *revenues* of $500 million in recent years). There are bullets too, the kind that have killed 167 environmentalists this year alone, according to Global Witness (see Global Witness 2019). Guns join white supremacist violence and anti-immigrant racism, as in Christchurch and El Paso, resulting in what Naomi Klein terms 'climate barbarism', the repressive state and the lone shooter two distinct positions on its spectrum (Stephenson 2019; Klein 2019). One can and should perform a critical analysis of all of them – and their systemic interconnectivity – but tear gas has gained particular visibility as of late as one key element of climate barbarism. Yet for many environmentalists, it remains invisible, and this is a strategic error.

For XR, climate emergency threatens civilisational collapse, attributed most immediately – and tellingly – to atmospheric carbon. Indeed there are fewer than twelve years to act, we are told (in a recent IPCC science report), before cascading tipping points of multispecies disaster overtake all (see Watts 2018). The human die-off – a massive population 'correction' for a contracting biosphere of habitat destruction, desertification and drought – could number *billions* in the next eighty years (the crash owing to shrinking resources, failing agribusiness and consequent resource wars).[1] This alone legitimates XR's macabre funereal obsessions, a prefigurative aesthetics of emergency overflowing into the streets, a recognition too that institutional containment of the becoming-activist of creative expression, of the structural transformation of collective practice in the era of emergency, is increasingly impossible in these circumstances. The sense of urgency driving multitudes to action all over the world is surely inspiring, but also potentially misdirected. But rather than dismissing the movement, let us contribute to this growing energy so that it foregrounds a just transition – meaning a radical restructuring of our politics and economics by prioritising equality, social justice and multispecies flourishing – rather than another depoliticised, single-issue environmental initiative, or worse, part of the growing project of green neoliberalism. To do so, a change of focus is necessary.

XR demands that governments 'tell the truth' about climate emergency, 'act now' to decarbonise by 2025, and become 'beyond political' by empowering 'citizens assemblies' to enact climate justice. 'We live in a toxic system, but no one individual is to blame', they claim, completely bypassing the justice-oriented arguments and historical gains of such groups as Black Lives Matter UK, Indigenous Environmental Network, Global Grassroots Justice Alliance and the Climate Justice Alliance, which have long highlighted the racial and class-based inequalities of differentiated climate disruption (see Extinction Rebellion 2019a).[2] With XR activists blockading intersections, performing mass die-ins and gluing themselves to government buildings and corporate headquarters to those ends – where collective interventions shut down institutions of normalisation denying emergency in the first place – the radical means often miss such a political analysis (what is the 'beyond' of the political, if not deluded liberalism?) (see Figure 5.1). This situation is made only more difficult by narrowly focusing on carbon as the cause of emergency.

Figure 5.1 An Extinction Rebellion action takes place in Oxford Circus, 2019
Source: Photo: Andrew Davidson/CC BY-SA 4.0.

In its gloomy pantomimes, XR performs the death of the future –
but it is a funeral without a body. Its macabre forms, reminiscent of
Atwoodian dystopian SF, risk surrender to fatalism, even as they riff on
ACT UP political funerals in expressing emotions for the loss of more-
than-humans and coming environmental catastrophe. With ACT UP,
'mourning became militancy' precisely because death (of community
members and loved ones) and the dead (sometimes presented in public
funerals) were not naturalised through the epidemic and thereby depoliticised (as when 350.org's Bill McKibben explains that we're at war
with 'climate change', rather than petro-capitalist violence [Mckibben
2016]). Rather, the HIV/AIDS epidemic was understood as political
insofar as it was seen as the murderous result of politicians' homophobia,
media sensationalism and pharmaceutical profiteering (Crimp 1989).
XR's funerals, by contrast, risk naturalising climate, mourning a coming
abstraction – not because it is not real, but rather because XR fails to
identify meaningful causes in Western modernity's political and economic order, consequently emptying activist rituals of any traction. XR
universalises causality in the generalised 'we' of 'human activities' (as
in its statement on 'The Emergency'),[3] much like the 'beyond political' species-being of neo-humanist Anthropocene discourse. Moreover,
by situating emergency in the near future, and by narrowly defining it
as carbon caused, it is as if the disaster hasn't already occurred – in past
invasions, slaveries, genocides, all perpetuated in ongoing land grabs,
displacements and extractivism, as the traditions of the oppressed have
ceaselessly shown. Indeed, indigenous activists remind us that they are
already 'post-apocalyptic', and have already lived through exactly the
socio-environmental breakdown now predicted by climate scientists
(Whyte 2018).

In this regard, XR's mourning resonates with Iceland's recent funeral
for Okjökull, the first glacier lost to climate change, memorialised in a
site-specific plaque inscribed with 'A letter to the future': 'Ok is the
first Icelandic glacier to lose its status as a glacier. In the next 200 years
all our glaciers are expected to follow the same path. This monument
is to acknowledge that we know what is happening and what needs to
be done. Only you know if we did it' (see Agence France-Presse 2019).
Such is only the latest instance where 'we' becomes intolerable, hailing
'our' complicity in the repression of historical responsibility for glacier-
killing climate chaos – a repression, for instance, of the recognition of
the hundred or so fossil fuel companies largely responsible for climate
breakdown, funding climate-change denial for decades, disabling
governmental regulatory agencies and refusing to stop the madness (see
Riley 2018).[4] While there is real mourning to be done – for lost species,

for historical and ongoing climate violence, for structural injustice – militancy is more than ever necessary, meaning a diversity of tactics dedicated to structural change, but grounded in careful political analysis and organising.

Which is why it is crucial that XR NYC has added an additional demand to the 2018 British platform, stressing climate justice principles. It clearly informed their mediagenic intervention at the Rockefeller Center with a banner stating 'Climate Change = Mass Murder', positioned behind a golden statue of Prometheus, allegorical figure of the techno-utopian Anthropocene, at the symbolic headquarters of the US fossil industrial capital.[5] It is this radical political dimension that pins the injustice of uneven climate chaos to institutional culprits that needs amplification – rather than simply opposing the movement of XR, given its naive policy proposals, colour-blindness, lack of structural analysis and basic misunderstanding of the police as a function dedicated to protecting the powerful elite (which tear gas, again, helps to clarify) (see Out of the Woods 2019; Cowan 2019). For, until XR and similar groups sharpen their analysis, 'climate emergency' remains an unstable discourse, potentially only reaffirming the ruling order – an emergency without emergence, one blocking the rise of radical difference – where the 'beyond political' framing opens a door to the financial co-optation of green capital, as much as invites the state of exception to take command.

If climate breakdown appears as the greatest threat to capital – to its logic of infinite growth on a finite planet – then we can only expect the powerful few to defend their outsized interests and claim on resources. Indeed, as 350.org, Climate Emergency Fund and Climate Mobilization organise for 'emergency', at stake are trillions in decarbonisation funds (distributed across diverse financial markets, institutional investment and pension funds), on which the green non-profit industrial complex has its eyes fixed, as we move from divestment to reinvestment in a renewable economy (see Morningstar 2019).[6] Global climate emergency, in this vein, becomes financial insurance, redirecting towards market-friendly solutions what could otherwise be – what might still become – the greatest revolutionary force in history: a multispecies and anti-capitalist insurgency of unprecedented proportions (Tomba 2019).[7] In this sense, the main liability of XR's 'beyond-political' emergency is catastrophe-become-financial-opportunity: fossil divestment brings green reinvestment, net-zero carbon necessitates sequestration and geo-engineering technologies, and failing ecosystems stimulate monetising natural capital and carbon offsetting. Such is clear, for instance, when Brazil's foreign minister claims 'opening the rainforest to economic development' is 'the only way to protect it' – exemplifying the worn-out logic whereby economic growth masquerades as climate solution (as reported by BBC 2019). The Bolsonaros, Dutertes, Netanyahus and Trumps are happy to declare emergency, but only one of their own making, likely shrouded in tear gas.

According to this scenario, climate emergency (as a paradoxical demand to change everything so as to keep things the same) risks consigning us to an endless present of authoritarian capitalism. Anything to distract us from and bypass the real disaster as seen from the perspective of financial elites: a radical Green New Deal, meaning structural decarbonisation dedicated to social justice, economic redistribution, smart degrowth, democratisation and decolonisation, with the integral participation of historically oppressed and formerly excluded peoples (see Riofrancos 2019). As the Fanon-inspired climate-justice coalition Wretched of the Earth writes in their open letter to XR, environmentalists' often whitewashed positions tend to forget others' long-term struggles, particularly those of black, brown and indigenous communities, and the fact that climate emergency really dates to 1492.

For those of us committed to amplifying the insurrectionary potential of movements like XR (and doing the work of political organising towards those ends), it is clear that we need to refocus on specific justice-oriented, eminently *political* demands – including implementing a just transition, holding corporations accountable, ending militarism, definancialising nature, replacing borders with radical hospitality, and guaranteeing universal health care, free education, healthy food and adequate income for all (the demands of Wretched of the Earth).[8] Without doing so, one's climate emergency risks erasing others' historical oppression, one's future, another's past, one's privilege, another's misfortune. 'In order to envision a future in which we will all be liberated from the root causes of the climate crisis – capitalism, extractivism, racism, sexism, classism, ableism and other systems of oppression – the climate movement must reflect the complex realities of everyone's lives in their narrative' (Wretched of the Earth 2019).[9] The challenge is to render these complexities proximate and mutually informing, centring them honestly and sensitively, by thinking emergencies together, and collaborating on solutions across difference. If not, then depoliticised emergency claims enable the Green New Deal to turn into a Green New Colonialism, founded on an extractive renewables economy enabling continued violent inequality, and a white futurism without end (see Beuret 2019).

Tear gas dramatises these risks. As a cyanocarbon – related to cyanide, itself dependent on methane for its production – it chemically derives from hydrocarbons, the organic component of oil and gas. As such, it expresses the truth of climate breakdown as *climate control*. The weaponised environment – what Peter Sloterdijk terms 'atmo-terrorism', joining air to juridico-political and military frameworks – functions as a medium of 'humanitarian warfare', rife with contradictions, historically and currently employed to defend power (see Sloterdijk 2009). One might believe tear gas to be more biopolitics than environmental concern. Like pre-emptive policing, surveillance, kettling and counter-insurgency armaments, tear gas – as one more technology of crowd management – hypes safety but enacts repression. As a substance that joins weaponised atmospheres to collective bodily control, tear gas creates biochemical environments that compel behavioural adaptation to regimes of power. As such, it is more than biopolitical: it is climatological, geontopolitical, intersectionalist, socioecological – where biogeophysical relationalities and ontological cuts splitting environments of life and death intersect with sociopolitical and techno-economic orders.[10]

Unlike typical greenhouse gases – say atmospheric carbon – that mostly remain unseen, tear gas is strategically visible and experientially affective: its calculus of impact materialises terrorising fears of suffocation to catalyse physiological response. As a performative aesthetics of physiological persuasion, it redistributes the sensible according to chemical agents dividing bodies in space. Doing so, police choreograph multitudes, subjecting targets not only to the immediacy of pain, choking and uncontrollable respiratory breakdown, but also, with chronic victims, to the slow violence of long-term illnesses – some of which is detailed in *Triple Chaser*, Forensic Architecture's video about Safariland's tear gas product presented at the 2019 Whitney Biennial, which was the scene of protests from its opening day. Insofar as Safariland forms part of a global regime of climate control that modulates atmospheres to the detriment of all but a tiny minority (part of a larger system of environmental injustice that sequesters clean air, water and soil for the benefit of the few, relegating the impoverished to toxic sacrifice zones),[11] the Kanders case elicits urgent concerns about the transformation of contemporary art in the era of climate emergency, especially when expanded to the realm of political ecology.

A central part of FA's project involved training a computer learning algorithm to visually recognise Triple Chaser grenades within large data caches, in order to both counter the manufacturer's own non-transparency regarding its distribution markets and aid campaigns against police and state violence worldwide. To do so, FA created a synthetic training data set to teach the classifier, resulting in a remarkable video sequence of machine learning visuality, containing seemingly infinite variations of

Figure 5.2 From the research project Forensic Architecture, *Triple Chaser*, 2019.
FA states on its website: 'Rendering images of our model against bold, generic
patterns, known as "decontextualised images", improves the classifier's ability to
identify the grenade'
Source: Photo courtesy of Forensic Architecture/Praxis Films.

coloured background tessellations against which to test and improve the
classifier's abilities in identifying tear gas grenades, played under a disjunctive musical soundtrack (see Figures 5.2 and 5.3). The commentary
explains the selection, noting that in 2016 Kanders gave $2.5 million
to the Aspen Music Festival, which renamed its Sunday concert series
in his honour, inaugurating it with Richard Strauss's *Four Last Songs*.
(More recently, Kanders's sponsorship has supported a programme of
'music inspired by nature', proposing another potential case study of
institutionalised climate injustice.) As with Kanders's Whitney, culture
functions as a machine for laundering profiteering militarist brutality
into virtuous philanthropy. But FA's audiovisual juxtaposition offers a
reverse tactic of de-artwashing, where culture is shockingly reunited
with the oppressive technology serving as its condition of possibility.
Over this complex montage, the narration describes Triple Chaser's
potential physiological effects – bronchial spasms, anaphylactic shock,
pulmonary oedema, convulsion, impaired breathing, and so on – based
on Safariland's safety guidance in an analytic deadpan (read by David
Byrne) worthy of Harun Farocki.

Strauss wrote the 1948 composition during the last years of his life,
in the apocalyptic wake of the Nazi Holocaust. In the video passage, the
tear-worthy sonic pathos sourced in genocide paradoxically confronts

Figure 5.3 From the research project Forensic Architecture, *Triple Chaser*, 2019. FA states on its website: 'using the Unreal engine, Forensic Architecture generated thousands of photorealistic "synthetic" images, situating the Triple Chaser in approximations of real-world environments'
Source: Photo courtesy of Forensic Architecture/Praxis Films.

the uncanny deathlessness of AI's post-humanist immortality, glimpsed through sequential imaging that combines inhuman speed and seemingly endless repetition – in some ways reminiscent of the evolutionary paradigm shifts and disjunctive temporalities of Stanley Kubrick's classic *2001: A Space Odyssey*, itself combining AI threats to humanity amidst futurist space exploration and transformative encounters with the alien sublime set to another Strauss score, the film concluding with a speculative remainder – post-human? inhuman? cyborg? – beyond all of what has been. *Triple Chaser* is not so sanguine, including extensive consideration of the context of current-day Gaza, which provides further lessons in the necessity of expanding our conception of climate emergency beyond atmospheric carbon. Indeed, if tear gas materialises climate control atmospherics, then Gaza is its limit case, where structural debilitation figures as a mode of disaster capitalism, from which emerges a dystopian future captured by an endless now. When *Triple Chaser* details Israeli Defense Forces (IDF) snipers' use of MatchKing bullets (made by Clarus, where Kanders serves as executive chairman), it connects to what Jasbir Puar critically analyses as the 'right to maim' (gassing or shooting to injure rather than kill). This latter figures as an emergent mode of biopolitics' refusal to let die, a logic made clear in the statistics: during the December 2018 Great March of Return protests, on which FA focuses, the IDF killed 154 civilian protesters, including thirty-five children, but wounded more than 6,000 people, evidencing the maiming directive as a grotesque ramification of 'humanitarian' war.

Claiming the 'right to maim' as a refusal to let die preconditions the 'right to repair' – physiologically, infrastructurally, commercially – forming an endless cycle of destruction and production. It thereby reduces life to inhuman conditions, imprisoning a terrain between biopolitics and necropolitics, according to Puar, indicating an extreme modality of climate control where Gaza functions as laboratory for what is to come more globally. Indeed, the Israeli occupation's chronopolitics factors as a strategic aim of the state's extended state of emergency (technically in operation since 1948), where the ongoing production of disaster is far from failure or accident, but an intended outcome, one that inevitablises endlessness. Puar's term for this is 'prehensive futurity', according to which the state makes 'the present look exactly the way it needs to' – as catastrophic – 'in order to guarantee a very specific and singular outcome in the future' – one dependent on Israeli interests – generating 'the permanent debilitation of settler colonialism' (Puar 2017: 149). When taking into account the ecocidal use of white phosphorous and depleted uranium (the latter with a half-life of 4.5 billion years), both used in IDF operations, we confront a weaponised epigenetics of toxic inhuman futurity, a prehensive mode of climate control extending into incomprehensible time.[12]

Not surprisingly, Gaza's anti-colonial protests are no Extinction Rebellion – and in fact no such formations exist in Palestine, only in Israel, where the group makes no mention of the occupation in its mission statement.[13] Which reveals the selective and oppression-perpetuating privilege of XR's 'climate emergency' when the latter is so myopically conceived, when it refuses to connect to the long presence of colonial violence, including very real funerals and mass debilitation.

As an important corrective, *Triple Chaser* documents riot control targeting groups struggling for their very survival. It shows weaponised atmospherics destroying livability for multispecies life. And it unleashes data-crunching cyber-intelligence exceeding all human capability, a politically unstable technology for sure that FA repurposes for its own justice-oriented ends. Doing so, *Triple Chaser* reveals a triple extinction event that, according to my reading, remarkably expands contemporary climate emergency: first, ethnic destruction is enacted through neocolonial violence; second, environmental toxicity exacerbates mass species extinction and biological annihilation already in effect globally; and, third, we glimpse the ultimate surpassing of humanity by AI – what Franco Berardi terms a 'frozen immortality [that] emerges in the form of the global cognitive automaton' (Berardi 2019) – as it comes to ominously 'recognise' weapons of mass destruction. In each of these three endgames, the dying confront tear gas's cruel irony of forcing a lacrymogenic self-mourning, a compelled crying in the act of experiencing one's own annihilation. If, departing from FA's own analysis, we preview in *Triple Chaser* the annihilation of biology by technology according to a speculative scenario wherein environmental catastrophe portends an AI future, then it is because 'silicon-based entities . . . do not need a breathable atmosphere, [and] life on Earth is just the raw matter from which a superior intelligence will emerge, with capitalism as its midwife', as Ana Teixiera Pinto warns (Pinto 2017). As such, FA's critical intervention, at least according to this speculative reading, dramatises most broadly an ultimate threat that goes far beyond carbon-induced emergency claims: the post-biological death drive of petro-capitalist techno-utopianism – advanced by everything that tear gas represents.

FA's video concludes by stating: 'We shared our findings with the European Center for Constitutional and Human Rights, who served Sierra Bullets with legal notice, warning that the exports of their bullets to Israel may be aiding and abetting war crimes.' As much as one might support such justice – as a non-reformist reform – it is striking how such an expansive conceptual analysis of climate control couched in the conditions of settler-colonial violence and warning of an unfolding global triple extinction event ultimately leads to merely a liberal grievance claim, a claim hailing conventional juridico-political reason that has led to humanitarian war in the first place (about which FA is well aware [see Weizman 2017]). Moreover, by focusing on corporate malpractice abetting allegedly criminal regimes, the grievance neglects to oppose tear gas in any context whatsoever. Of course FA's larger practice comprises a growing list of dozens of case studies that collectively add up to meaningful opposition to structural forms of state and corporate violence, including numerous instances where socioenvironmental and biopolitical violence converge in a multiplication of emergency conditions. Yet rather than allowing liberal grievance to neutralise radical social-movement opposition that surpasses the Kanders case, how might the latter offer a platform for considering the more ambitious political horizon of the structural transformation of governance itself? It is here that an additional rupture might emerge from climate emergency, propelled by social-movement energies.

Although not typically considered within the framework of climate politics, Decolonize This Place's '9 Weeks of Art and Action' (March–May 2019) represented a concerted effort to remove Kanders from the Whitney (see Figure 5.4). It comprised one vector in the group's

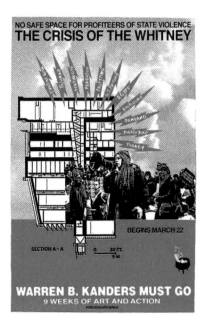

Figure 5.4 Poster for 9 Weeks of Art and Action, 2019
Source: Courtesy of Decolonize This Place.

larger, ongoing project of the decolonisation of life initiated through the
'liberation of institutions' – 'more than a critique of institutions, institutional liberation affirms the productive and creative dimensions of collective struggle'.[14] The radical dimension of its collectivity – including
such groups as Veterans Against the War, Brooklyn Anti-Gentrification
Network, Comité Boricua En La Diáspora, Mi Casa No Es Su Casa,
NYC Solidarity with Palestine, Queer Youth Power, P.A.I.N. Sackler,
and many more[15] – drew on and affirms the power of solidarity as the
necessary basis for alliance-building, practising what Angela Davis calls
'the indivisibility of justice' (rejecting not only art-world individual-
ism and neoliberal social atomisation, but the sway of identity politics
into essentialist separatism).[16] Such collective struggle is forged in the
materiality of oppression, which tear gas, in its negative cast, enacts by
chemically joining multiple bodies and geographies of violence, rendering diverse grievances interconnected. Indeed, in her extensive study
of tear gas, Ann Feigenbaum highlights how the chemical weapon historically targets environmentalists, people of colour, the poor, LGBTQ
activists, refugees and immigrants, the disabled and mentally unwell,
young people and dissidents, forging the bonds of solidarity in oppressive climate control (Feigenbaum 2017: 1–4). In this regard, we can
make sense of DTP's slogan announced in a self-authorised banner drop

over the Whitney's façade: 'When we breathe, we breathe together' – what we might call an intersectionalist climate justice put to task against the environmental injustice of violent policing, weaponised toxicity and structural debility alike. Following its organising of an open letter signed by 400 writers, scholars and artists in May 2018, itself catalysed by the movement against Kanders initiated by the Whitney's own staff, DTP unfurled an all-out campaign of tactical media, agitprop design, Instagram feeds and interventionist collective actions in the museum's spaces. These occurred in coordination with the radical pacifist organisation War Resisters League, already engaged in long-term struggle against Safariland, with the action resulting eventually in eight artists (including Forensic Architecture) withdrawing their work from the biennial (Small 2019; Black, Finlayson and Haslett 2019). DTP's militant media also riffed off the art of the Whitney's temporary exhibitions (partly funded by Kanders), including its ongoing Warhol retrospective, mirroring the pop artist's appropriation aesthetics, specifically the latter's *Death in America* series, while redirecting the mournful iconography towards their social and environmental justice aims (Vartanian, Weber and Small 2018). Moving from pop art to agitprop, the serial images of museum spectacle – showing Kanders and his wife and fellow trustee Allison Kanders standing with Whitney Museum director Adam Weinberg – explode in representational proximity to tear gas canisters used in oppressive police actions (see Figure 5.5). Revealing the disastrous intertwinement of contemporary power and culture in the era of carceral capitalism, military neoliberalism and apocalyptic populism, DTP organises the collective energy to overcome it.[17]

Not that the approaches of FA's humanitarian grievance and DTP's decolonial institutional liberation are mutually exclusive; indeed, they are allied. No doubt we need both, and all others that can aid in the process of emancipation from the climate control system governed by war profiteer philanthropists, 'beyond political' institutions, and oppressive states claiming the right to maim. These latter propose a matrix of causality driving global climate chaos, which seeks to turn climate emergency into financialised opportunity for the further accumulation of wealth and power, leaving the world destitute and dead in its wake. To escape these conditions, we must move from *emergency* to *emergence* – of radical difference, of the residual and the not-yet – making a just transition into the future, where the not-yet may be glimpsed in the already-here, grounded in the traditions of the oppressed, and generating new emancipatory possibilities on that basis.

Following the coordinated, sustained actions of groups like DTP, Kanders did resign in July 2019, constituting a major success. But, as

Figure 5.5 This image shows Triple Chaser tear gas grenades on the left and, on the right, a picture of Warren Kanders, his wife and fellow trustee Allison Kanders, and Whitney director Adam Weinberg together in 2019.
Source: Courtesy of Decolonise This Place.

we have seen, DTP's motivations exceed this goal, forming part of the 'ongoing project of decolonization' as 'a mode of "epistemic disobedience", an immanent practice of testing, questioning, and learning, grounded in the work of movement-building', opposed to 'the entire settler-institutional nexus of art, capitalism, patriarchy and white supremacy' (MTL Collective 2018: 194; Decolonize This Place 2018). As such, their example, if operating at a smaller scale, provides an urgent way to massively expand and radicalise XR's climate emergency, where climate justice is inextricable from economic justice, housing justice, migrant justice, democratic justice and decolonial justice. The goal being not simply to reform neoliberal museum boards, but to catalyse the structural transformation of our political economy as the only way to address the manifold socioecological and climate emergencies of our times. It is not at all surprising that DTP's analysis, in the case of Safariland and the Whitney, begins with tear gas, which, as we have seen, immediately repositions ecology and climate as terms inextricably entangled in the politico-economic framework of late capitalist climate control. It is not that tear gas displaces fossil fuel causality in this analysis of climate emergency; rather it reveals the latter's truth as thoroughly enmeshed in petro-capitalist governmentality and its attendant forms of violence.

Conversely, depoliticised emergency claims invite instrumentalisation towards purposes other than democratic equality and social justice. This is similarly the case with proposals for a Green New Deal, which may very well represent our best global hope at mitigating climate catastrophe; but it too is inadequate if separated from decolonisation – for instance, as part of a Red Deal expressive of indigenous climate justice (see Estes 2019; Pollin 2018). Just how the Green New Deal transition is implemented – whether ground-up, smartly de-growth-directed and centring agro-ecological smallholders, working-class labour, indigenous land-protectors and frontline communities, or as a technocratic, fortress-based, elitist, ethno-nationalist economy – will necessarily be a site of collective struggle. But one thing is for sure: narrowly defined climate emergency propels movement in the opposite direction, investing post-political governance with emergency powers poised to decarbonise in its own interests, or, worse, to resemble something closer to eco-fascism than internationalist eco-socialism.

In its open letter to XR, Wretched of the Earth writes:

> In order to envision a future in which we will all be liberated from the root causes of the climate crisis – capitalism, extractivism, racism, sexism, classism, ableism and other systems of oppression – the climate movement must reflect the complex realities of everyone's lives in their narrative. (Wretched of the Earth 2019)

Building what might be called a prehensive futurity of justice will, of course, take collective commitment and time, exceeding the event-obsessed convergences of culture-industry social practice, and equally spectacular activist protests, ultimately requiring something like the multiple-generations expansiveness of indigenous time-relations, of creating worlds by living and struggling together, across difference, over the long term. This means a commitment to 'long environmentalism', the labour of building solidarity and mutual-aid networks over months, years, generations, as probably the only place where a radical politics of emergency can truly emerge – rooted in the broadly shared concern of collective survival – even if that means rethinking the temporal immediacy of emergency itself in times of unprecedented uncertainty (see Banerjee 2017). It entails committing to building relations of responsibility and accountability that can lend trust in justice, in thinking climate emergencies relationally, beginning with the history of Anthropocene violence stretching back hundreds of years and continuing with current and near-future threats of ongoing climate chaos. As such, those of us bound in solidarity and committed to creating a collective future beyond climate breakdown – where tear gas reveals its expansive entanglements – must certainly decolonise this place, and this and that one too, organising a transnational network of resistance capable of challenging the transnational power of capital.[18] But we must also decolonise our future, rescuing it from the disaster of green capitalist and, worse, eco-fascist 'inevitability' facilitated by an irresponsible emergency politics.

Notes

1. See the evidence for these statistics as backed up by leading scientists in the following: Rees (2019), Hunziker (2019), Vince (2019). Recent scientific research estimates conservatively that more than 250,000 deaths occur annually already owing to climate change, including exacerbated conditions of malaria, diarrhoea, heat stress and malnutrition, as reported here: Christensen (2019).
2. See Extinction Rebellion (2019a), 'About Us'.
3. See Extinction Rebellion (2019b).
4. See also the cartographic project of Influence Map, which details who owns the world's major fossil fuel companies and which financial and media firms are defending their interests: https://influencemap.org/finance-map (last accessed 13 October 2021).
5. XR USA's Fourth Demand reads: 'We demand a just transition that prioritizes the most vulnerable people and indigenous sovereignty; establishes reparations and remediation led by and for Black people, Indigenous people, people of color and poor communities for years of environmental injustice, establishes legal rights for ecosystems to thrive and regenerate in perpetuity, and repairs the effects of ongoing ecocide to prevent extinction of human and all species, in order to maintain a livable, just planet for all.' See XR US, 'We Demand': https://extinctionrebellion.us/ demands (last accessed 13 October 2021).
6. Though Morningstar mistakenly collapses the radical message of Thunberg into the neoliberal discourse of NGOs surrounding her. Also see the critique of environmentalist NGOs in Klein (2014).
7. Tomba explains that 'insurgent universality' extends beyond the contemporary limits of single-issue identity politics, and 'refers to the excess of equality and freedom over the juridical frame of universal human rights', whereby the rebellious disrupt and reject an existing political and economic order. Here I am suggesting that XR might yet hold the potential to extend further that radical political claim towards a more-than-human assembly.
8. In this regard, my own positioning is not only as an academic but also as a member of DSA (Democratic Socialists of America) and its Ecosocialist Working Group in Santa Cruz. See: https://dsasantacruz.org/ (last accessed 13 October 2021).

9. Some articulations of XR are smarter than the UK-based officially stated agenda. See for instance the article about XR as more than a climate protest, connecting to hundreds of years of European colonialism, by XR member Stuart Basden (2019).

10. On this convergence, see Povinelli (2016), Harney and Moten (2015), Sharpe (2016). Also see Demos (2019).

11. 'In both its physical design and its application throughout history, tear gas is for the control of economically, politically, and socially vulnerable populations, enforced by mentalities and behaviors of constantly reworked white supremacy . . . Riot control is, and has always been, the business of protecting the wealth of a tiny minority.' See Feigenbaum (2017: 166).

12. See Lightbown (2011) and the report by Forensic Architecture on 'The Use of White Phosphorus in Urban Environments' (Forensic Architecture 2012).

13. The mission statement of Extinction Rebellion Israel includes the following: 'We and our children have to deal with unimaginable terror as a result of floods, fires, extreme weather, loss of crops and the inevitable collapse of society as a whole. We didn't prepare ourselves to deal with the dangers already here. The time for denial has passed. We know the truth about climate change. Time to act.' Taken from Extinction Rebellion Israel's Facebook page: https://www.facebook.com/XRisrael (last accessed 1 November 2019).

14. For more on this, including sensitive discussion of how decolonisation first and foremost entails the return of land and sovereignty to indigenous peoples, but, and to that end, also entails the emancipation of imagination, aesthetics and culture from capital, see MTL Collective (2018: 206).

15. For its list of collaborators, see Decolonize This Place (2019a).

16. Angela Davis (2016) and DTP: 'Among the lessons of the Kanders crisis has been the limitations of liberal versions of "identity politics". Why would we imagine that anyone's racial or ethnic background necessarily aligns that person with justice, or assume any unity between those who share a skin color? As the saying goes, "All my skin folk ain't kinfolk" . . . Our work in mobilizing against Kanders and beyond has focused not on demographic diversity but on solidarity between struggles. Solidarity is not a box to be checked – it is difficult and painstaking work that requires us to ask: what debts do we owe to each other? What are we willing to sacrifice? How do we become political accomplices?' (Decolonize This Place 2019b).

17. Among my references are: Brown (2017), Wang (2018), Retort (2005).

18. For one such vision, see Sunkara (2019).

References

Agence France-Presse (2019), 'Iceland holds funeral for first glacier lost to climate change', *The Guardian*, 18 August: https://www.theguardian.com/world/2019/aug/19/iceland-holds-funeral-for-first-glacier-lost-to-climate-change (last accessed 13 October 2021).

Banerjee, Subhankar (2017), 'Long Environmentalism: After the Listening Session', in Salma Monani and Joni Adamson (eds), *Ecocriticism and Indigenous Studies: Conversations from Earth to Cosmos*, New York and Abingdon: Routledge.

Basden, Stuart (2019), 'Extinction Rebellion isn't about the Climate', *Resilience*, 10 January: https://www.resilience.org/stories/2019-01-16/extinction-rebellion-isnt-about-the-climate/ (last accessed 13 October 2021).

BBC (2019), 'US and Brazil agree to Amazon development', *BBC*, 14 September: https://www.bbc.com/news/world-latin-america-49694516 (last accessed 13 October 2021).

Berardi, Franco 'Bifo' (2019), 'Game Over', *e-flux Journal*, 100: https://www.e-flux.com/journal/100/268601/game-over/ (last accessed 13 October 2021).

Beuret, Nicholas (2019), 'A Green New Deal Between Whom and For What?', *Viewpoint*, 24 October: https://viewpointmag.com/2019/10/24/green-new-deal-for-what/ (last accessed 13 October 2021).

Black, Hannah, Ciarán Finlayson and Tobi Haslett (2019), 'The Tear Gas Biennial', *Artforum*, 17 July: https://www.artforum.com/slant/a-statement-from-hannah-black-ciaran-finlayson-and-tobi-haslett-on-warren-kanders-and-the-2019-whitney-biennial-80328 (last accessed 13 October 2021).

Brown, Wendy (2017), 'Apocalyptic Populism', *Eurozine*, 30 August: https://www.eurozine.com/apocalyptic-populism (last accessed 13 October 2021).

Christensen, Jen (2019), '250,000 deaths a year from climate change is a "conservative estimate", research says', *CNN*, 16 January: https://www.cnn.com/2019/01/16/health/climate-change-health-emergency-study/index.htm (last accessed 13 October 2021).

Cowan, Leah (2019), 'Are Extinction Rebellion whitewashing climate justice?', *gal-dem*, 18 April: http://gal-dem.com/extinction-rebellion-risk-trampling-climate-justice-movement (last accessed 13 October 2021).

Crimp, Douglas (1989), 'Mourning and Militancy', *October*, 51: 3–18.

Davis, Angela Y. (2016), *Freedom is a Constant Struggle: Ferguson, Palestine and the Foundations of a Movement*, Chicago, IL: Haymarket Books.

Decolonize This Place (2018), 'The Crisis of the Whitney is Just Beginning', reprinted in *Hyperallergic*, 26 December: https://hyperallergic.com/477510/decolonize-this-place-announces-january-26-town-hall-regarding-whitney-museums-tear-gas-problem/ (last accessed 3 November 2021).

Decolonize This Place (2019a), 'The Crisis of the Whitney: 9 Weeks of Art and Action': https://decolonizethisplace.org/9weeksofartinaction2 (last accessed 13 October 2021).

Decolonize This Place (2019b), 'After Kanders, Decolonization Is the Way Forward', *Hyperallergic*, 30 July: https://hyperallergic.com/511683/decolonize-this-place-after-kanders/ (last accessed 13 October 2021).

Demos, T. J. (2019), 'Ecology-as-Intrasectionality', *Panorama: Journal of the Association of Historians of American Art*, 5(1).

Estes, Nick (2019), 'A Red Deal', *Jacobin*, 6 August: https://www.jacobinmag.com/2019/08/red-deal-green-new-deal-ecosocialism-decolonization-indigenous-resistance-environment (last accessed 13 October 2021).

Extinction Rebellion (2019a), 'About Us': https://rebellion.earth/the-truth/about-us/ (last accessed 13 October 2021).

Extinction Rebellion (2019b), 'Emergency on Planet Earth': https://rebellion.earth/the-truth/the-emergency/ (last accessed 13 October 2021).

Feigenbaum, Anna (2017), *Tear Gas: From the Battlefields of World War I to the Streets of Today*, London and New York: Verso.

Forensic Architecture (2012), 'The Use of White Phosphorus in Urban Environments', 12 November: https://forensic-architecture.org/investigation/white-phosphorus-in-urban-environments (last accessed 13 October 2021).

Global Witness (2019), Enemies of the State?, *Global Witness*, 30 July: https://www.globalwitness.org/em/campaigns/environmental-activists/enemies-state/ (last accessed 13 October 2021).

Harney, Stefano and Fred Moten (2015), 'Michael Brown', *boundary 2*, 42(4): 81–7.

Hunziker, Robert (2019), 'Earth 4C Hotter', *Counterpunch*, 23 August: https://www.counterpunch.org/2019/08/23/earth-4c-hotter/ (last accessed 13 October 2021).

Klein, Naomi (2014), *This Changes Everything: Capitalism vs. the Climate*, London: Allen Lane.

Klein, Naomi (2019), *On Fire: The (Burning) Case for a Green New Deal*, New York: Simon & Schuster.

Lightbown, Richard (2011), 'The Devastating Consequences of Israeli Weapons Testing', *Global Research*, 13 March: https://www.globalresearch.ca/the-devastating-consequences-of-israeli-weapons-testing/23686 (last accessed 13 October 2021).

McKibben, Bill (2016), 'A World at War', *The New Republic*, 15 August: https://newrepublic.com/article/135684/declare-war-climate-change-mobilize-wwii (last accessed 13 October 2021).

Morningstar, Cory (2019), 'The Manufacturing of Greta Thunberg – for Consent: The Political Economy of the Non-Profit Industrial Complex', *The Art of Annihilation*, 21 January: http://www.theartofannihilation.com/the-manufacturing-of-greta-thunberg-for-consent-the-inconvenient-truth-behind-youth-co-optation (last accessed 13 October 2021).

MTL Collective (2018), 'From Institutional Critique to Institutional Liberation? A Decolonial Perspective on the Crises of Contemporary Art', *October*, 165: 192–227.

Out of the Woods (2019), 'Extinction Rebellion: Not the Struggle we Need', *Libcom.org* (blog), 19 July: https://libcom.org/blog/extinction-rebellion-not-struggle-we-need-pt-1-19072019 (last accessed 13 October 2021).

Pinto, Ana Teixeira (2017), 'Artwashing – On NRx and the Alt Right', *Texte zur Kunst*: https://www.textezurkunst.de/106/artwashing/ (last accessed 13 October 2021).

Pollin, Robert (2018), 'De-Growth vs a Green New Deal', *New Left Review*, 1 August: https://newleftreview.org/issues/II112/articles/robert-pollin-de-growth-vs-a-green-new-deal (last accessed 13 October 2021).

Povinelli, Elizabeth A. (2016), *Geontologies: A Requiem to Late Liberalism*, Durham, NC: Duke University Press.

Puar, Jasbir K. (2017), *The Right to Maim: Debility, Capacity, Disability*, Durham, NC: Duke University Press.

Rees, William E. (2019), 'Yes, the Climate Crisis May Wipe out Six Billion People', *The Tyee*, 18 September: https://thetyee.ca/Analysis/ 2019/09/18/ Climate-Crisis-Wipe-Out/ (last accessed 13 October 2021).

Retort (2005), *Afflicted Powers: Capital and Spectacle in a New Age of War*, London and New York: Verso.

Riley, Tess (2018), 'Just 100 companies responsible for 71% of global emissions, study says', *The Guardian*, 14 February: https://www.theguardian.com/ sustainable-business/2017/jul/10/100-fossil-fuel-companies-investors-responsible-71-global-emissions-cdp-study-climate-change (last accessed 13 October 2021).

Riofrancos, Thea (2019), 'Plan, Mood, Battlefield – Reflections on the Green New Deal', *Viewpoint*, 16 May: https://www.viewpointmag. com/2019/05/16/plan-mood-battlefield-reflections-on-the-green-new-deal/ (last accessed 13 October 2021).

Rueb, Emily S. (2019) '"Freedom Gas," the Next American Export', *The New York Times*, 29 May: https://www.nytimes.com/2019/05/29/us/freedom-gas-energy-department.html (last accessed 16 December 2021).

Sharpe, Christina (2016), *In the Wake: On Blackness and Being*, Durham, NC: Duke University Press.

Sloterdijk, Peter (2009), *Terror from the Air*, trans. Amy Patton and Steve Corcoran, Los Angeles: Semiotext(e).

Small, Zachary (2019), 'Warren Kanders Resigns From Whitney Museum Board After Months of Controversy and Protest', *Hyperallergic*, 25 July: https://hyperallergic.com/51 1052/warren-kanders-resigns/ (last accessed 13 October 2021).

Stephenson, Wen (2019), 'Against Climate Barbarism: A Conversation with Naomi Klein', *Los Angeles Review of Books*, 30 September: https://www. lareviewofbooks.org/article/against-climate-barbarism-a-conversation-with-naomi-klein (last accessed 13 October 2021).

Sunkara, Bhaskar (2019), *The Socialist Manifesto: The Case for Radical Politics in an Era of Extreme Inequality*, London and New York: Verso.

Tomba, Massimiliano (2019), *Insurgent Universality. An Alternative Legacy of Modernity*, New York: Oxford University Press.

Vartanian, Hrag, Jasmine Weber and Zachary Small (2018), 'Whitney Museum Staffers Demand Answers After Vice Chair's Relationship to Tear Gas Manufacturer Is Revealed', *Hyperallergic*, 30 November: https://hyperallergic. com/473702/whitney-tear-gas-manufacturer-is-revealed/ (last accessed 13 October 2021).

Vince, Gaia (2019), 'The heat is on over the climate crisis. Only radical measures will work', *The Guardian*, 18 May: https://www.theguardian.com/ environment/2019/may/18/climate-crisis-heat-is-on-global-heating-four-degrees-2100-change-way-we-live (last accessed 13 October 2021).

Wang, Jackie (2018), *Carceral Capitalism*, South Pasadena, CA: Semiotext(e).

Watts, Jonathan (2018), 'We have 12 years to limit climate change catastrophe, warns UN', *The Guardian*, 8 October: https://www.theguardian.com/environment/2018/oct/08/global-warming-must-not-exceed-15c-warns-landmark-un-report (last accessed 13 October 2021).

Weizman, Eyal (2017), *The Least of All Possible Evils: A Short History of Humanitarian Violence*, London and New York: Verso.

Whyte, Kyle P. (2018), 'Indigenous Science (Fiction) for the Anthropocene: Ancestral Dystopias and Fantasies of Climate Change Crises', *Environment and Planning E: Nature and Space*, 1(1–2): 224–42.

Wretched of the Earth (2019), 'An Open Letter to Extinction Rebellion', *Common Dreams*, 4 May: https://www.commondreams.org/views/2019/05/04/open-letter-extinction-rebellion (last accessed 13 October 2021).

Part II

Human and Non-Human Interactions

6

On the Punctuation of Organisms: The Case of Helmuth Plessner

Graham Harman

When approaching the question of posthumanism, it is good to take stock of what it means to be human as opposed to an animal, plant or inanimate matter, let alone whatever might come after the human. Yet with respect to the distinction between various forms of living and non-living entities, Western philosophy has an undistinguished track record, especially in the modern period. More often than not, what philosophers give us is little more than commonsensical assumptions ontologised and repackaged as fresh insight. One especially disappointing example is Martin Heidegger's celebrated 1929/30 Freiburg Lecture Course, *The Fundamental Concepts of Metaphysics* (Heidegger 2001). In the process of explaining his concept of world, Heidegger declares that stones are 'worldless', animals are 'poor in world' and humans are 'world-forming'. Along with the total omission of plant life from this schema, we learn nothing at all about world-forming, while any desired clarity on what world poverty might mean is replaced by a series of captivating anecdotes about animal behaviour drawn from the research of others.

Yet there is no reason to denigrate Heidegger in particular, since others have done little better, no matter how great their historical status. Aristotle in *De Anima* articulates the soul into nutritive, perceptive and intellective parts, and despite his always admirable precision, we are left with the same everyday distinction between vegetable, animal and human that just about anyone could produce without studying his work (Aristotle 2017). St Thomas Aquinas expands the Aristotelian map slightly by dividing animals into those that cannot move – shellfish, in his view – and those that can (Aquinas 1948), but this simply gives us four basic kinds of life rather than three. At the dawn of modern philosophy, René Descartes introduced a much starker picture with an absolute rift between rational cognitive beings and extended physical matter (Descartes 1993), with the result that animals and plants are reduced to senseless mechanisms although experience strongly suggests the contrary. Baruch Spinoza opened the door slightly for animals, displacing human desires from the centre of the cosmos, though without doing much to shed light on the nature of animal experience specifically (Spinoza 2018). That brings us to recent philosophy in both its analytic and continental branches. Among the analytics, Robert Brandom imagines that his word play on 'sapience' and 'sentience' is enough to pinpoint the human/animal divide (Brandom 1994). In continental philosophy, Quentin Meillassoux's otherwise bold cosmology relies on a rather conventional series of leaps between dead matter, life and thought (sentience is not a separate term in his schema), despite his astonishing fourth step of a world of justice brought about by a virtual God (Meillassoux 2015).

When so many thinkers of such a high calibre repeatedly fall short of the mark on a topic of such importance, it cannot be a matter of mere personal failing. Somehow, the discipline of philosophy itself has lacked the tools to frame the relevant questions properly. How many crucial divisions are there, really, between the various forms of life and non-life? Are humans utterly different in kind from all other beings, as modern philosophers in particular have held? Or does the key break lie elsewhere, placing such clever animals as monkeys, dolphins and crows on our own side of the fence, and perhaps reptiles and insects on the other side of the chasm? Furthermore, have there been any ontological breaks within anthropoid history itself, such that Neanderthals or Australopithecines were not quite 'human' in the philosophical sense, or that post-agricultural or nuclear-age humans were radically different in kind from their forerunners? Is the difference between plant and fungus too trivial to concern ontology? And what about viruses, positioned somewhere near the border between the living and non-living? There is also the exotic topic of slime moulds, which at times can assemble collectively and jointly solve puzzles to obtain nourishment (Shaviro 2016).

To open the way for a fresh approach to these issues, I will give a brief account of the somewhat novel approach of the German philosopher Helmuth Plessner (1892–1985), whose recently translated *Levels of Organic Life and the Human* gives us occasion to rethink the aforementioned issues (Plessner 2019). Although Plessner too falls short on the sorts of questions listed above, he does provide new resources for tackling them, and certainly introduces some new terminology. 'Positionality' is Plessner's word for what makes life different from non-life, and it is through various modifications of positionality that he accounts for the various levels of the living. For my part, I will make use of the term 'punctuation' for the effort to find those points where radical jumps between different levels of organism are purportedly located. I borrow this word from the paleontologists Niles Eldredge and Stephen Jay Gould, who used it to combat the 'phyletic gradualism' linked with the theories of Charles Darwin (Eldredge and Gould 1972). Eldredge and Gould famously proposed a theory of 'punctuated equilibrium', in which species remain stable for long periods of time before evolving rather quickly into a new form. But this article is an exercise in philosophy rather than paleontology, and thus we are looking not just for gaps between different species, but for those changes in species that would represent leaps in ontological kind. Of course, it might be wondered whether philosophy has anything to say on this topic at all. Is it not one of those questions where we should simply be quiet and listen to what scientists have to say on the matter?

1. The ontological and the empirical

Since the days of Immanuel Kant, philosophy has generally taken the form of what I have called 'onto-taxonomy' (Harman 2016a: 237, 2020a; Young 2021). For the onto-taxonomist, there are two and only two basic kinds of things that exist: (1) human thought, and (2) everything else. Or at least this is held to be the obligatory starting point for any rigorous philosophy in Kant's wake. First we have that which is directly accessible to human thought, and second we have that which can at best be inferred in some sort of mediated fashion from that which is given to thought. Most importantly for us, the thought-world relation becomes the primary or even sole topic of philosophical discussion. To speak about the relation between two billiard balls, or between a cat and a hot tin roof, or a raindrop and that roof, the relation must first be converted into a question of how it is accessible to human thought. The thought-world relation becomes the only possible site where anything can appear for philosophical discussion. Natural scientists are permitted to speak of the interaction of chemicals or subatomic particles, but philosophy supposedly has nothing to say about such matters, unless in cases where quantum theory directly incites further speculation. Even a general 'theory of objects' like that of Alexius Meinong, or Edmund Husserl in the period of *Logical Investigations*, inevitably turns out to be a theory of how various kinds of objects can be meant or intended by thought (Meinong 1988; Husserl 2001). In other words, these otherwise impressive philosophies remain within the horizon of onto-taxonomy.

This is not the place for a detailed discussion of onto-taxonomy, since our concern here is life and its various kinds. Plessner seems to agree in advance with object-oriented ontology (OOO) insofar as he rejects the centrality of the thought-world relation, though his primary target is Descartes rather than Kant (Plessner 2019: 34–74).[1] But perhaps a more intriguing target is his famous contemporary, Heidegger. In Plessner's words:

> I cannot accept Heidegger's principle [. . .] that the study of extra-human being must necessarily be preceded by an existential analysis of the human. This idea shows him to still be caught in the spell of the old tradition . . . according to which the questioner is existentially closest to himself and therefore sees himself when looking at the object of his questioning. (xvii)

This critique leads directly to what Plessner sees as his own original contribution:

> By contrast [. . .] I defend the notion that the human in his being is distinguished from all other being by *being neither closest to nor furthest from himself*. By virtue of this very eccentricity of his form of life, he finds himself as an element in a sea of being and thus, despite the non-ontic character of his existence, to be of a piece with all the things in this world. (xvii)

In this spirit, Plessner goes on to make explicit ontological claims about how various types of living organisms encounter the world, without the usual preliminary hand-wringing over the very possibility of human access to such organisms. He is thus led to break with the modern onto-taxonomic tradition nearly as much as did Alfred North Whitehead (Whitehead 1978). I say 'almost' because Plessner – unlike Whitehead – continues to treat inanimate relations as nothing more than deterministic causal clockwork, and hence limits his originality to topics pertaining to life. Although the chief influences on Plessner seem to have been the vitalistic biology of Hans Driesch and the philosophical anthropology of Max Scheler, he also seems thoroughly familiar with the writings of Husserl and Heidegger that were available in the late 1920s, not to mention the pioneering ethological work of Jakob Johann von Uexküll. In addition, Plessner's knowledge of the biological sciences of his time was clearly much greater than Heidegger's own.

There can be no escape from the stultifying modern division of labour that restricts philosophy to the gap where thought meets world, unless we press the point that philosophy is capable of talking about matters already discussed by the sciences though in a basically different way:

including animals, plants, astronomical bodies and chunks of metallic ore. For Plessner, as for us, this means an *a priori* approach rather than an empirical one. Perhaps this will sound like absurd overreach on the part of philosophy. But if so, it is only because Kant has taught us to see *a priori* as meaning two separate things simultaneously: (1) prior to experience, and (2) necessary. The notion that philosophers could state necessary and hence permanent truths about nature 'from an armchair' rightly strikes the modern reader as ridiculous, since this would amount to a claim that the empirical sciences are useless despite abundant evidence to the contrary. We might seem to have reached the verge of free-wheeling *a priori* philosophies of nature in the manner of F. W. J. Schelling or deducing the necessary existence of just seven planets in the manner of G. W. F. Hegel's doctoral thesis.

Yet there is no reason to demand that philosophical speculation done prior to or apart from experiment must produce decisive final results that no further thinking can alter. Rather, the philosopher need only discover implicit assumptions to which previous thought on a topic has been invisibly bound. By radicalising or reversing such assumptions, the sphere of human thought grows permanently larger, without forbidding future advances by ourselves or others. For Plessner's part, though his thinking is deeply nourished by empirical findings in biology, he insists nonetheless that 'empirical research [. . .] as concerns the stock of specifically biological categories, rests on premises that can only be analyzed by the philosopher' (109). This means nothing more than that empirical findings are never philosophically innocent, and hence can always be submitted to examination; it certainly does not suggest that Plessner's own findings are *a priori* in the sense of being eternal truths, immune to revision on the basis of further developments in philosophy or biology. Whereas empiricists focus on the general lawful behaviour of what they observe, the philosopher has no choice but to ask about the much-maligned notion of *essence*: 'What is called for is a development of the essential characteristics of the organic and, in place of purely inductive enumeration, at least the attempt of a strict justification. Our task is an a priori theory of the essential characteristics of the organic or [. . .] of the "organic modals"', with the latter phrase drawn from no less a scientific luminary than Hermann von Helmholtz (100).

Although several generations of philosophers – both analytic and continental – have been trained to smirk at the very mention of the word 'essence', Plessner means something clear and helpful by this term. From John Locke to Ernst Mach, he quasi-rhymingly laments, the object is treated as merely a 'system of qualities' (39). This bundle theory may seem adequate if we focus only on appearance, but then again, the appearances of a thing never really exhaust its being. Plessner uses the term 'object' to refer to such bundles of appearances rather than to the essential core that lies beneath them. I should note in passing that this usage differs not only from OOO's own, but from Husserl's as well: in phenomenology the 'intentional object' is emphatically *not* a bundle of adumbrations but is that which endures despite the shifting play of lights and colours on its surface. Be that as it may, with his use of 'essence' Plessner makes room for a depth in things that never becomes directly apparent or fits into a qualitative bundle. In this respect he is closer to Heidegger than to Husserl, since the latter holds that essences are directly fathomable by the intellect if not by the senses. There is another difference between Plessner and Husserl, one that object-oriented thinkers will see as cause for concern. Namely, although Plessner makes fertile use of the classic Heideggerian rift between concealed and revealed, he misses Husserl's most important discovery: an awareness that the phenomenal realm displays a second and altogether distinct rift between the object (a unified apple) and its qualities (the countless adumbrations by which the apple appears). By overlooking this additional dualism, Plessner paints himself into the corner of regarding the hidden essential cores of things as simple poles of unity, while a thing's plurality of features is found only on the surface of our experience of it. The nascent fourfold structure of Heidegger and even Husserl is thereby missed, making Plessner's position closer to that of Kasimir Twardowski than to Husserl's (Twardowski 1977).

For Plessner, the difference between philosophy and empirical science hinges largely on its capacity for *a priori* theorisation of that which lies deeper than the qualities of things, while science advances primarily through the measurement and mathematisation of a thing's traits. What is unknown to science is the ambiguous relation between a thing and its various surface apparitions: a 'dependency of the property on the core substance of the thing' (77). This relation is not symmetrical but is dominated by the core rather than the periphery: 'the leaf has green on its surface, but green does not conversely have the leaf' (77). Properties suggest or indicate the core of the thing without revealing it completely. What OOO calls a 'tension' between the thing and its features, Plessner calls 'transgredience' (*Transgredienz*), his useful technical term for the relation between the two poles (78). The essence or hidden core of a thing might also be called its *substance*, another classical term too often ridiculed in contemporary thought. As already seen, this substance cannot be attained simply by listing the properties or parts of a thing – here Plessner foreshadows the object-oriented critique of undermining and overmining (Harman 2013) – and thus it cannot be obtained from the everyday practice of normal science.

2. Transgredience and beyond

Plessner's 'transgredience' is a basic ontological principle, in the sense that it ascribes to all entities the tension between a hidden essential core and its ever-shifting bundles of surface qualities. Everything that exists has a 'dual aspect' (72), and Plessner critiques Descartes for thinking that only humans display this duplicity (thought and extension) while everything else but God amounts to extension alone. But if we remain forever on this initial flat level, there will be no way to distinguish life from non-life, let alone the various forms of life from each other. What is it, then, that makes life unique by contrast with everything else? To this question, Plessner gives a greater variety of answers than he seems to realise. In the first place, he says, life is that kind of entity in which the dual aspect belonging to everything is *intuitively accessible* (84). Whereas OOO showcases aesthetic experience as the place where object-quality tension becomes most visible (Harman 2007a, 2020b), Plessner opts for life as the site of maximum evident stress between opposite poles. As he puts it: 'the property of being alive [. . .] even on the level of appearance, cannot be placed on the same level as the other properties of the same body' (84). With life, something appears that cannot be limited to a measurable position in space-time. In some sense this is the crux of Plessner's philosophy, since an emphasis on the measurable spatio-temporal location of a thing is the hallmark of an empirical or bundle-of-qualities approach, while philosophy requires *a priori* meditation on a transgredient relation involving a thing's hidden core. Stated differently, Plessner is a diehard critic of what OOO describes as 'literalism' (Harman 2018: 59–102).

When it comes to life, a place where he sees a great ontological leap beyond all forms of non-life, Plessner introduces his key term 'position-ality'. In the simplest sense, this means that the living body has a special relation to its own boundary (115). The non-living body simply goes as far as it reaches, and no further; for the living, it is not just a matter of an outermost boundary, but of a semi-permeable 'skin' that both excludes and admits the outside (116). The living entails an ambiguous transcend-ence, such that 'the body is [both] outside of and within the body' (121). Even in forms of life so primitive as to have nothing like 'consciousness', the organism encounters 'an opposing field of its life in which it *exists*: a field with which and *against which* it lives' (185). The organism does not fuse entirely into its medium, but 'harmonizes' with it (190), though this harmony still implies a certain distance. Against one of the favourite sayings of German Idealism, Plessner insists that 'the notion that one has to have crossed a boundary in order to have determined it as such is false' (145). The outside remains outside despite our recognition of it. This sounds more like Emmanuel Levinas than it does like Hegel (see Levinas 1969).

Throughout the book, Plessner is greatly concerned with the debate between the vitalist Driesch and the *Gestalt* psychologist Wolfgang Köhler. Though he sides with Driesch in this dispute, he ultimately rejects that author's hardcore vitalism (323–4). Plessner rejects the primacy of *Gestalten* for what amounts to a philosophically realist reason: though a *Gestalt* forms a recognisable figure in visual terms, it lacks the sort of relation to its components that any genuine whole would need (140 and 157). Unlike the directly accessible *Gestalt*, living things do not exist solely on the level of discernible quality, for reasons we have already seen. Life has an essential core just like inanimate objects (150) but somehow does not really exist in space, except through the process of its tangible unfolding: 'unfolding is the only mode in which something nonspatial nevertheless exists as extensive variety' (151). Plessner leans heavily on a distinction between spatiality (*Räumlichkeit*) and space-likeness (*Raumhaftigkeit*), or 'between that which determines space and that which is determined by it' (49). The former refers to the organism itself, and the latter to its concrete manifestations: after all, the organism is able to set itself apart from its physical body, by being different from both its quantitative and qualitative manifestations in space-time (159).

Yet the bigger defect with the notion of *Gestalt*, for Plessner, is that 'it is impossible for a pure [G]estalt to have organs [. . .]. For every part is immediately [G]estalt-forming only if it does not maintain its self-sufficiency as in an aggregate' (159). The virtue of organs, for a position like Plessner's in which the organism both is and is not identical with its own physique, is the fact that organs – unlike the ever-visible elements of a *Gestalt* – relate to the organism in a *mediated* way.

As he summarises the matter at the opening of chapter 5: 'Organization is the self-mediation of the unity of the living body by its parts' (172). Again in unwitting agreement with Whitehead, Plessner stresses that it is 'only through the organism's organ-induced openness to [its] medium [. . .] that it fully enters into contact with its setting' (179). Far from making direct contact with the environment, the organism subcontracts this relation to its various organic parts, whose crucial role 'robs' the organism of its 'self-sufficiency' (Plessner 2019: 179). This indirect or mediated relation to the world is especially crucial for Plessner due to his insistence that inanimate causation is a direct relation, with organisms confined by contrast to indirect relations. But the most important point lies elsewhere. Through his emphasis on how something completely new happens with the *organisation* of life, he has gone beyond his flat-ontological starting point and proclaimed a first punctuation within the realm of life itself. For this organisation on which he insists is already a complex step in evolutionary history, one that required a billion years to emerge from the long, cold epoch of merely prokaryotic life forms. Few philosophers have paid attention to the vast difference between one-celled and multicelled life, but Plessner calls our attention to the significance of this leap (154–5). Without it, the special form of mediation found in organised life would never have occurred.

3. The role of time

We have seen that Plessner explains life in terms of a special relationship to space: the living is both separate from and immersed in its medium, establishing an emergent whole irreducible to the external *Gestalt* through which it is recognised, and engaging in mediated relations with its surroundings by way of subordinate organs. Yet perhaps more important is the organism's unique relation to time. One of the fascinating passages in Uexküll comes when he discusses the differing perceptions of time among different animal species (Uexküll 2010: 70; Harman 2016b: 118). According to experimental data of his era, if a light flashes no more than eighteen times per second, then humans perceive it as flashing; if more than that, we will see it as a steady light. By contrast, fighting fish can apparently perceive something between thirty and fifty flashes per second, while poor sluggish snails are only able to detect at most three or four. Yet these wonderful distinctions cannot be ontological in character, since they are merely gradations along a continuum. For the relation to time to distinguish not only between non-life and life, but between different punctuations of life, it needs to display some sort of quantum leap.

In any case, while for inanimate entities the inner core is in relatively constant relation with its outer properties, or oscillates in that relation only through the labours of an external force (as when a ceiling fan spins thanks to electrical current), the living organism makes sense only in an unfolding that occurs across time (167). Even if one could prove the existence of single instants of time, no life form could possibly inhabit such minuscule temporal shards. Life sleeps and then wakes, feeds or rests, turns this way or that. 'Regular irregularity [. . .] occurs dynamically in the phenomena of rhythm. Rhythm is tremendously pervasive, making it easy to understand how it could be proclaimed nothing less than the key moment of all life' (116–17). This cannot merely be a rhythm in the surface appearance of the living, since this would amount to nothing more than an empirical bundle of qualities, which Plessner has already ruled out as a site of philosophical distinctions. And despite his fondness for rhythmic change, Plessner is no advocate of pure flux and pulsation in the manner of such contemporary authors as Thomas Nail (2019) and Rein Raud (2021). In fact, Plessner sounds more like Aristotle than these contemporary renegades when he dismisses the notion that there could be any such thing as a pure process. Becoming is always the becoming of something, and to become is always to become something definite (126). Any doctrine of pure process would destroy what the thing is now (131). That which results from becoming must be other than the thing but must *also* be that thing (127). Plessner also cautions against the common mistake of assuming that what remains in such processes must be the physical body; after all, he contends that the organism lies somewhere distinct from its body (126).

And as for the rhythm of living things, we can speak only of their repeated oscillations between one state and another. These becomings are always headed somewhere, and this results in the succession of youth, maturity, old age and death (137–44). Plessner takes a distance from Heidegger's effort to embed being-towards-death in the heart of exist-ence itself; he calls this 'unjustified tragicism' and wittily adds that 'death wants to be died, not lived' (139). His interest in the stages of life is not thanatocentric but is focused on the mechanism by which an organism moves – and necessarily so – from one stage to the next. The process of aging involves a sacrifice of the indeterminacy of the whole for the sake of greater specialisation or adaptation to the surrounding medium (158). 'Organization [. . .] outgrows life, which in turn only becomes physical in organization', meaning that life becomes too relational, with too little held in reserve (159). While this proposed general mechanism for aging seems plausible, it is unclear why it should apply to organic life alone. In *Immaterialism* (Harman 2016c) I made the case that the non-living Dutch East India Company aged in the same way, and I have already defended this claim against accusations of misplaced biologism (Harman 2016d). Even so, Plessner seems unnervingly insightful when it comes to matters of death and dying. He stresses the way that 'the organism's contact with [its] field steadily wanes as it ages and finally expires in death' (197). Even more intriguing is his point that death is less interesting than chance: our inbuilt mortality is less important or threatening than the fact that we have all missed out on other possible biographies (200 and 318).

4. Theory of punctuation

By way of review, we saw that Plessner's ontology is one of transgre-dience, referring to a ubiquitous tension between the hidden cores of things and their spatio-temporally deployed qualities. This is said to be true of all entities, of no matter what kind. His theory of philosophy is that it must aim at the hidden cores in *a priori* fashion rather than engaging in comparative remarks on the surface features or *Gestalten* of things. He launches his theory of punctuation, in which various types of beings are differentiated from each other, by contending that life – as opposed to non-life – consists in positionality (being out beyond itself in ambiguous relation with its medium) and in rhythmic cycles and an inevitable progression through maturity to over-organisation and eventual death. Since space and time are relational, not to mention both quantitative and qualitative at once, philosophy should look beyond both quality and quantity in the direction of that which is *raumhaftig* without being *räumlich*, and *zeithaftig* without being *zeitlich*. Stated differently, essences lie outside space-time despite retaining close links with it. The first example we saw, and so far the only one, was the great leap that Plessner postulates between single-celled life and multicellular life, though single-celled organisms with organelles can also be treated as organised in Plessner's sense. In his section on animals he offers a different though analogous punctuation in the jump between decentralised animals and those with central nervous systems (227–42). Whereas sea urchins are 'veritable "reflex republics"' (230), centralised animals have a single perceptual forum where all senses are unified, which is the topic of another of Plessner's most important books (Plessner 1923).

But the hungry reader, frustrated with modern philosophy's failure to bring ontological distinction into the realm of biology, is destined for a degree of disappointment. Aside from his refreshing addition of these two unusual rifts (unicellular/multicellular, decentralised/centralised), Plessner is basically committed to a standard punctuation of entities that runs as follows: stone, plant, animal, human. In short, his complaints about Heidegger's 'existential' starting point do not bring him to different results from the Freiburg philosopher's own 1929/30 Lecture Course. Moreover, the very principle used by Plessner to separate these different points on the organic continuum is also disappointing, despite its initial reversal of the usual criterion. For Heidegger the human being knows its environment by rising above it, even transcending it to the point of experiencing nothingness (Heidegger 1998: 82–135). By contrast, animals would have less ability to transcend their environment and see it 'as' what it is than humans do, and 'world poverty' must mean something like this. Though Heidegger never engages with the topic of plant life, he would clearly assign them an even weaker form of transcendence than the 'impoverished' sort found in animals; stones, of course, would be left with no ability at all to rise above their surroundings, and in this respect would be 'worldless'. Unlike Heidegger, Plessner does not see each successive life form as increasingly transcendent or freed from its surroundings. Quite the contrary. As if he were anticipating autopoietic systems theory (Maturana and Varela 1980), Plessner takes the opposite tack, contending that higher forms of life close themselves off to an increasing degree from their surroundings.

It is not clear that this method succeeds. Despite Plessner's post-Husserlian insight that everything is torn between an essential core and exterior bundles of properties, he continues to hold that inorganic bodies are caught in a 'continuous context of cause and effect [. . .] in contact with all spatiotemporal "coexistents"' (186). Mindless and thoroughly determined, inorganic bodies are merely the causal puppets of whatever they encounter, following the ironclad laws of physics. Here he follows a rather commonplace assumption, to the effect that nothing can resist the crushing mechanisms of deterministic nature except for organic perception and organic freedom. Against this assumption, OOO has long argued that direct causation between any two entities – including inanimate ones – is impossible, and that mediation is therefore a feature of relations per se, not of living relations in particular (Harman 2007b). This does not require that inanimate beings be 'conscious' or 'free', only that they engage directly with the external qualities of things rather than their essential cores. Although presumably not quite as exposed to the causal world as inanimate beings, plants are still defined in Plessner's book as an 'open' form of life (Plessner 2019: 202–9). The very forms of plants 'emphasize [. . .] their integration into the surrounding medium' (205). For example, all the surfaces of a plant 'are without exception involved in the metabolic process as it is determined by the lived body's direct contact with the medium' (206). Unlike animals, plants have no central organs (204), and whereas animals always aim at the production of new individuals, plants are often found in colonies without clear demarcation between individual beings (203). Shaviro's beloved slime moulds come to mind.

By contrast, animals are treated as 'closed' forms of life. The animal organism's task 'is to insert a mediating layer between itself and the circle of life that takes over the contact with the medium' (210). Of course, the boundary between the animal and its medium cannot be absolute, since otherwise perception would be impossible. This is why Plessner proposes that the boundary is found *inside* the animal rather than at its outermost edge; the surrounding medium is both something radically different from the animal and also an intimate part of it (211). Unlike plants, the animal 'is no longer in direct contact with the medium and the things surrounding it, but is so merely by means of its body' (213).

Above and beyond this body, the animal – unlike the plant – has a centre (213). Though plants can nourish themselves directly from inorganic materials, the animal cannot, and is therefore destined to be a fighter (216). Viewed differently, the animal is a born parasite on the vitality of other organisms (217).

We now arrive at Plessner's tribute to human exceptionalism, which comes on the heels of his having inserted no punctuations at all within the animal realm beyond that between decentralised and centralised creatures. In other words, once central nervous systems have evolved, we seem to be left with nothing but differences of degree between worms, ants and dolphins; the next ontological breakthrough must await the advent of human beings. Having initially pursued a somewhat contrarian line by adopting closure rather than transcendence as the principle of forward advance, Plessner now strangely returns to something like Heideggerian transcendence as the criterion of human excellence. Much like inauthentic Dasein in Heidegger, animals are said to be merely absorbed in their surroundings: 'The barrier for the animal lies in the fact that everything that is given to it [. . .] stands in relation to the here/ now' (221, emphasis removed). The human, at least, is 'conscious' of the centrality of existence rather than merely taking it for granted (70). The old Heideggerian 'as-structure' even makes an appearance: animals cannot know their world 'as' world, a claim that sounds commonsensical and obvious until we realise that we actually have no idea what knowing an apple 'as' an apple would mean, especially if we hold with Plessner that the thing's essential core cannot be paraphrased in terms of spatio-temporally accessible qualities (285). Worst of all, especially for the posthumanist cause, Plessner holds that any progress beyond the human is impossible; no further biological advance is possible, and biology sets the ultimate parameters in his work (270). Meillassoux has made a similar claim, though at least he offers the possible exit – however seemingly implausible – of a virtual God that might or might not appear and institute a reign of justice. Much earlier Nietzsche had evoked the superman (Nietzsche 2011), for which there is no room in Plessner at all; nor does he leave room for culturally induced punctuations in existing human history. Apparently, from the moment that modern *Homo sapiens* (or some earlier hominid) appears, we have reached a new organic closure that is 'self-reflexive' in a way that animals are not, and that is what puts an end to all possible further progress: the ability of humans to know that they are human is proposed as the ultimate stage of organism. None of the existing candidates for decisive breakthroughs in our history – let alone those still unimagined – can compare, for Plessner, with the moment of transition from animal to human. Language, primal repression, architecture, agriculture, urbanism, written language, coinage, philosophy, navigation, industry and science are all equally consigned to the status of 'differences of degree'. Technology might be able to reduce us to animals, plants or dead inanimate stones, but cannot do more than this. Yet there are currents of thought that cast significant doubt on such biologism. The hypothesis of the extended mind already invites inanimate objects to participate in human cognition (Clark 2010), while Shirley Strum and Bruno Latour have demonstrated the equally stabilising and volatilising role of non-living things in human society (Strum and Latour 1987), and Peer Schouten has done the same in analysing the materiality of state failure (Schouten 2013).

Plessner initially seems open to a key role for things in his ontology of life, as with his forceful claim that the Humean theory of bundles of qualities amount to a 'vacuous' rejection of underlying objects (236). Yet this step is accompanied by the dubious claim that objects exist only for humans (232 and 272). While there is an essence or surplus in things (304), it lies out of reach for animals, who perceive only signals or 'situations' rather than self-contained autonomous things (246). He approvingly quotes Hans Volkelt's (1914) words that 'sensory "melodies" and "configurations" dominate the animal environment in contrast to objective "things" surrounded by a horizon of infinite aspect possibilities that are given only to the human' (247). Plessner seems on firmer ground when he steers away from the familiar claims about superior human 'transcendence' and refers to possible uniqueness in the human relation to time. Although plants cannot really relate to their pasts, he tells us, animals do show the sort of learning ability consistent with such a relation (258). In humans this goes much further, given the fund of possibilities contained in recorded memory: 'human beings ultimately do not know what they do and only find out through history' (316).

5. Concluding remarks

In the brief space remaining, let's review what we have learned from Plessner and consider where it might take us. I have spoken favourably of his concept of transgredience, in which the deep core of a thing both is and is not adequately expressed in its various qualities. This idea alone makes Plessner a previously unknown precursor of OOO. It is also the key to ending the modern division of labour, in which science always has the last word on inanimate things: as Plessner stresses throughout his book, there are *a priori* ways of dealing with inanimate entities that aim at the core essence of things rather than their empirically measurable traits. But since all entities are transgredient we are left on the level of global ontological statement, and still need some principle by which to distinguish between basically different kinds of beings. As I see it, Plessner entertains three such principles.

1. Perhaps his most convincing remarks concern the profound transitions that occur between (a) unicellular and multicellular life, and (b) decentralised and centralised animals. In both cases it is easy to see how something truly novel occurs, and both involve the combination of previously separate experiences into a single one. This is the sort of process theorised by Lynn Margulis as Serial Endosymbiosis Theory (SET) (Margulis 1999), and it is adapted for the purposes of object-oriented social theory in my book *Immaterialism*. But while Margulis has a very powerful theory, it would seem to apply to all cases of speciation, which we might call 'sub-punctuations', when what we are looking for here are the larger transitions associated with *kingdoms*, the highest taxonomical groups in biology.

2. Another of Plessner's most intriguing ideas is that life does things with time and space that inanimate objects do not. Despite the transgredience of a stone, the relation between its core and its surface remains basically constant in the absence of outside influence. The 'positionality' of life means that it is both inside and outside its own body, as if partly including the environment within its own skin. Analogously, the rhythmic character of life entails that the deep core of an organism can wear many different clothes at different times, and that it passes necessarily through the stages of youth, maturity and senescence in a way that inanimate objects do not. However, it is not entirely clear how further taxonomical or evolutionary advance might occur along this front.

3. That leaves us with what I presented as Plessner's weakest idea, which is really just his most traditional one: the notion that transcendence and self-reflexivity are what make humans a showcase life form. It is intriguing that Plessner's strongest moments tend to come when he reverses such conventional wisdom. As we have seen, he views the transition from plant to animal as one from more open to more closed, meaning that animals are *less* outside themselves than plants are, and inhabit their own limited circle of interests rather than the purportedly global play of cosmic forces that dominate inanimate being and to some extent even plants. If Plessner had given up the modern – and especially German – trope of a free and transcendent human consciousness, he could have explored the idea of humans as an even more closed-off form of animal. This would have made intuitive sense. For whereas even intelligent animals may be

concerned with a few dozen types of entities during a lifetime, humans are bewitched by millions if not billions of commodities, astronomical bodies, historical facts, athletes, singers and books. Far from being the most transcendent and negating animal, in some respects we are the most innocent. However, a general theory of human absorption or sincerity is not an idea that crossed Plessner's radar.

When we think of posthumanism, most likely we are thinking of the first of these three points. We might dream of adding wings or gills to our bodies to enhance our mobility through previously forbidden media. Super-intelligence through prostheses of silicon is another common fantasy, and one can well imagine the social earthquakes that might follow from this. Nonetheless, these would result at most in new speciation of the sort I termed 'sub-punctuation' above. For this reason, I would like to suggest that any future punctuation between the human species and what might follow is more likely to follow from the third point above: the idea of evolution as an increasing closure within our sphere of interests. As I have argued elsewhere, when someone or something seems more absorbed in its interests than we are, the effect from our standpoint is comical (Harman 2005: 125–44). Theories of comedy exist in abundance, and one of the most compelling has developed along a line running from Sigmund Freud (Freud 1960) through Jacques Lacan (Lacan 2017) to their contemporary admirer Alenka Zupančič of the Ljubljana School (Zupančič 2008).

My own preference is for the theory of Henri Bergson (Meredith and Bergson 1956), though this is not the place to compare the two approaches. It is enough to say that for Bergson, humour occurs when we witness a living – or pseudo-living – agent reduced to a mechanism. Restated in OOO terms, the comical happens when we witness life sincerely absorbed in something we regard as beneath our serious concern. Now, if humans were really characterised by 'transcendence', to the point of a direct relation with nothingness, then everything would be beneath our sincere concern; entities would represent nothing but mere lures of absorption, as Heidegger often suggests. Yet I have noted that humans are in fact characterised by a vastly *wider* range of concerns than animals and presumably wider than plants. We may view ourselves as the ultimate schemers, plotters, backstabbers and nihilists in the cosmos, but our destiny actually lies in an almost childlike interest in everything under and over the sun. In this respect we are not just the laughing animal, but even more so the *laughable* animal. In light of all this, I conclude with the following hint, which is all that the present format allows. The posthuman will involve not just this or that grafting of bodily organs to the familiar human torso. Instead, we need to find some revolutionary new relation to the comical. Laughter is a potential research front: not because we humans are above everything, but because nothing is beneath us.

Note

1. Unless otherwise noted, all page numbers in parentheses in this article refer to Plessner (2019).

References

Aquinas, St Thomas (1948) *Summa Theologica*, trans. Fathers of the English Dominican Province, Notre Dame, IN: Christian Classics, vol. 1, pp. 100–1.

Aristotle (2017), *De Anima*, trans. C. D. C. Reeve, Indianapolis, IN: Hackett.

Brandom, Robert (1994), 'Reasoning and Representing', in Michaelis Michael and John O'Leary-Hawthorne (eds), *Philosophy in Mind: The Place of Philosophy in the Study of Mind*, Dordrecht, The Netherlands: Kluwer, pp. 159–78.

Clark, Andy (2010), *Supersizing the Mind: Embodiment, Action, and Cognitive Extension*, Oxford: Oxford University Press.

Descartes, René (1993), *Meditations on First Philosophy*, trans. D. Cress, Indianapolis, IN: Hackett.

Eldredge, Niles and Stephen Jay Gould (1972), 'Punctuated Equilibria: An Alternative to Phyletic Gradualism', in Thomas J. M. Schopf (ed.), *Models in Paleobiology*, San Francisco, CA: Freeman, Cooper, and Company, pp. 82–115.

Freud, Sigmund (1960), *Jokes and Their Relation to the Unconscious*, trans. James Strachey, New York: Norton.

Harman, Graham (2005), *Guerrilla Metaphysics: Phenomenology and the Carpentry of Things*, Chicago, IL: Open Court.

Harman, Graham (2007a), 'Aesthetics as First Philosophy: Levinas and the Non-Human', *Naked Punch*, 9: 21–30.

Harman, Graham (2007b), 'On Vicarious Causation', *Collapse*, 2: 171–205.

Harman, Graham (2013), 'Undermining, Overmining, and Duomining: A Critique', in Jenna Sutela (ed.), *ADD Metaphysics*, Aalto, Finland: Aalto University Design Research Laboratory, pp. 40–51.

Harman, Graham (2016a), *Dante's Broken Hammer: The Ethics, Aesthetics, and Metaphysics of Love*, London: Repeater.

Harman, Graham (2016b), 'Magic Uexküll', in *Living Earth: Field Notes from the Dark Ecology Project 2014–16*, Amsterdam: Sonic Acts Press, pp. 115–30.

Harman, Graham (2016c), *Immaterialism: Objects and Social Theory*, Cambridge: Polity.

Harman, Graham (2016d), 'Decadence in the Biographical Sense: Taking a Distance from Actor-Network Theory', *International Journal of Actor-Network Theory and Technological Innovation*, 8(3): 1–8.

Harman, Graham (2018), *Object-Oriented Ontology: A New Theory of Everything*, London: Pelican.

Harman, Graham (2020a), 'The Only Exit From Modern Philosophy', *Open Philosophy*, 3(1): 132–46.

Harman, Graham (2020b), *Art and Objects*, Cambridge: Polity.

Heidegger, Martin (1998), *Pathmarks*, trans. William McNeill, Cambridge: Cambridge University Press.

Heidegger, Martin (2001), *The Fundamental Concepts of Metaphysics: World–Finitude–Solitude*, trans. William McNeill and Nicholas Walker, Bloomington, IN: Indiana University Press.

Husserl, Edmund (2001), *Logical Investigations*, trans. J. N. Findlay, London: Routledge, 2 vols.

Lacan, Jacques (2017), *Formations of the Unconscious: The Seminar of Jacques Lacan, Book V*, trans. Russell Grigg, Cambridge: Polity.

Levinas, Emmanuel (1969), *Totality and Infinity: An Essay on Exteriority*, trans. Alphonso Lingis, Pittsburgh, PA: Duquesne University Press.

Margulis, Lynn (1999), *Symbiotic Planet: A New Look at Evolution*, New York: Basic Books.

Maturana, Humberto and Francisco Varela (1980) *Autopoiesis and Cognition: The Realization of the Living*, Dordrecht, The Netherlands: Kluwer.

Meillassoux, Quentin (2015), '*Appendix: Excerpts from* L'Inexistence divine', trans. Graham Harman, in Graham Harman (ed.), *Quentin Meillassoux: Philosophy in the Making*, 2nd edn, Edinburgh: Edinburgh University Press, pp. 224–87.

Meinong, Alexius (1988), *Über Gegenstandstheorie /Selbstdarstellung*, Frankfurt: Felix Meiner.

Meredith, George and Henri Bergson (1956), *An Essay on Comedy/Laughter*, New York: Doubleday.

Nail, Thomas (2019), *Being in Motion*, Oxford: Oxford University Press.

Nietzsche, Friedrich (2011), *Thus Spoke Zarathustra*, trans. Adrian Del Caro, Cambridge: Cambridge University Press.

Plessner, Helmuth (1923), *Die Einheit der Sinne: Grundlinien einer Ästhesiologie des Geistes*, Bonn: F. Cohen.

Plessner, Helmuth (2019), *Levels of Organic Life and the Human: An Introduction to Philosophical Anthropology*, trans. Millay Hyatt, New York: Fordham University Press.

Raud, Rein (2021), *Being in Flux: A Post-Anthropocentric Ontology of the Self*, Cambridge: Polity.

Schouten, Peer (2013), 'The Materiality of State Failure: Social Contract Theory, Infrastructure and Governmental Power in Congo', *Millennium: Journal of International Studies*, 41(3): 553–74.

Shaviro, Steven (2016), *Discognition*, London: Repeater.

Spinoza, Baruch (2018), *Ethics: Proved in Geometrical Order*, trans. Matthew J. Kisner, Cambridge: Cambridge University Press.

Strum, S. S. and Bruno Latour (1987), 'Redefining the Social Link: From Baboons to Humans', *Social Science Information*, 26(4): 783–802.

Twardowski, Kasimir (1977), *On the Content and Object of Presentations: A Psychological Investigation*, The Hague: Martinus Nijhoff.

Uexküll, Jakob von (2010), *A Foray Into the World of Animals and Humans with A Theory of Meaning*, trans. Joseph D. O'Neill, Minneapolis: University of Minnesota Press.

Volkelt, Hans (1914), *Über die Vorstellungen der Tiere*, Leipzig: W. Engelmann.

Whitehead, Alfred North (1978), *Process and Reality*, New York: Free Press.

Young, Niki (2021), 'Only Two Peas in a Pod: On the Overcoming of Ontological Taxonomies', *Symposia Melitensia*, 17: 27–36.

Zupančič, Alenka (2008), *The Odd One In: On Comedy*, Cambridge, MA: The MIT Press.

7

Eco-Translation and Interspecies Communication in the Anthropocene

Anna Barcz and Michael Cronin

In Yamen Manai's novel *The Ardent Swarm* (2021), a Tunisian university professor, Tahar, goes to visit Shinji Saiko, a Japanese colleague in Tokyo. He is on a mission to bring back a Japanese queen bee to protect the beehive of his friend, Sidi, from attacks by drones. Tahar is deeply impressed by what he sees in Japan and asks Inoue Saiko, Shinji's partner, about what is specific to Japanese culture:

> She responded slowly, giving her husband time to translate: 'Like our bees that have to coexist with the giant hornets, we are a people who must coexist with the flaws in the earth – earthquakes, tsunamis, volcanic eruptions – and with war, the flaw of human nature. We know that our archipelago is fragile, that our existence is fragile, and that the survivors must always rebuild. We are a people well versed in catastrophes, Professor. The "other" is none other than ourselves, a survivor and a partner.' (Manai 2021: 158–9)

What Inoue deems to be specific, we now know to be general. The climate havoc, that is increasingly the characteristic of a warming planet, means that Japan no longer has a monopoly on geological disruption and extreme weather events. The 'flaws in the earth', exacerbated by the carbon-indifferent 'flaw in human nature' – which has waged its own wars on the more-than-human – means that more and more humans have to learn to be 'well-versed in catastrophes'. In the passage we have quoted Inoue Saiko makes her view known through the medium of translation. Without translation, she would be mute, an amiable but unreflective host, stranded outside any meaningful sense of deliberative encounter.

In this chapter we want to re-examine the notion of translation and argue that in the age of anthropogenic climate change we need to embrace an expanded concept of what translation entails in order to reflect more deeply on the implications of post-Holocene inclusivity. Therefore, we look at posthuman modes of translation as engaging forms of communication with and between non-human animals. This leads us to merge ideas on interspecies communication with eco-translation to anticipate how species may respond to climate catastrophe in a telling way.

Translation, biosemiosis and transversal subjectivity

The exchange between Tahar and Inoue that opens this chapter is mediated through two human languages, Arabic and Japanese, by a human translator, Shinji Saiko. This is primarily how translation has been construed, as a specifically human, interlingual exercise. Kobus Marais in his *A (Bio)Semiotic Theory of Translation* (2019) details the theoretical origins of this narrowness of definition, a narrowness he attributes to a misreading. The misreader is Roman Jakobson and the misread is C. S. Peirce. Jakobson, in his famous 1959 essay on translation, draws on the work of Peirce to argue that 'the meaning of any lingual sign is its translation into some further, alternative sign, especially a sign "in which it is more fully developed"' (Jakobson 2004: 139). However, what Peirce actually wrote was, 'conception of a "meaning", which is, in its primary acceptation, the translation of a sign into another system of signs' (Peirce 1989: 127). The 'lingual' was Jakobson's addition, hardly surprising coming from a linguist, but the baleful outcome has been an almost exclusive concentration on interlingual translation in modern translation studies.

The generous inclusivity of Peirce's original definition of translation, which was a semiotic theory that would account for all signs, not just lingual signs, was lost. The problem was further compounded by Saussurean semiotics where, again, a linguist will model all semiotic processes on human language. A more ambitious understanding of what translation might involve had already been suggested by Thomas Sebeok, a key figure in the establishment of biosemiotics, who argued that 'the process of message exchanges, or semiosis, is an indispensable characteristic of all terrestrial life forms' (1991: 22). In a later work, he affirmed that 'biosemioses between bacterial entities started more than a thousand million years ago and are thus at the root of all communication' (2001: 13). The apprehension of these signs can take many different forms and operate at many different levels. These include the interpretation of signs emanating from other animals which are apprehended through sound, sight, taste, smell, touch or gesture; chemical communication between plants; the interaction of organisms with non-organic elements of their environments such as minerals or the weather; and semiotic processes occurring at cellular and molecular levels (see Maran et al. 2011). In this perspective, translation often is 'a constant of organic survival' (Steiner 1975: 415), allowing creatures to navigate through the abundance of bio forms and functions.

Whereas human and some non-human animals, as in the case of large primates like apes, have similar capabilities for semiotic activity (see Maran et al. 2011: 7), what distinguishes all eco-orientated semiotics is a sensitivity to interspecies' skills in receiving and communicating information. The semiotic processes are, to some extent, explicable within the evolutionary frameworks, and where different species' worlds (*Umwelten*) overlap in interpreting signs (e.g. Uexküll 1992; Sebeok 2001; Kull and Torop 2011). For these eco-orientated semioticians interested in the exchange of signs beyond the human domain, the term 'communication' is less overdetermined than 'language' and can contribute to further developments of translation theory in the Anthropocene. In other words, translation studies need to acknowledge that humans are immersed in living and non-living systems that are awash with communication. The challenge in the age of the Anthropocene is situating oneself and other species in this communicative sphere, in a viable and ethical way.

The failure to attend to a meaningful exchange of signs between multispecies subjects of communication points up a role for eco-translation (Cronin 2017) – opening potential windows on interspecies relationalities in the context of the Anthropocene's immediate impact on all planetary life. These channels of communication cannot be subordinated to the anthropocentric figure of language and human culture but must be articulated through the figure of a broader, posthuman, transversal subjectivity. Therefore, the move towards species awareness – humans as one species among others – is seen as a necessary step towards post-anthropocentric identity. For Rosi Braidotti this involves the de-centring of *anthropos*, 'the representative of a hierarchical, hegemonic and generally violent species whose centrality is now challenged by a combination of scientific advances and global economic concerns' (Braidotti 2013: 65). This critique of humanism and anthropocentrism has been prefigured in the tradition of 'anti-humanism' that Braidotti references, 'feminism, decolonization and anti-racism, anti-nuclear and pacifist movements', where the white, sovereign, male subject of Western techno-imperialist thought was singled out for repeated critique (ibid.: 16). Out of this vision comes a notion of relationality and ontological equality that does not privilege one life form over another. Braidotti's notion of the posthuman 'implies the open-ended, inter-relational, multi-sexed and trans-species flows of becoming through interactions with multiple others' (ibid.: 89). Being 'matter-realist', to use her term, is to take humans' multiple connections to natural and material worlds seriously. Conceiving of the notion of subjectivity as including the non-human means that the task for critical thinking is, as Braidotti herself admits, 'momentous'. It would involve visualising the subject as 'a transversal entity encompassing the human, our genetic neighbours the animals and the earth as a whole, and to do so within an understandable language' (ibid.: 82). The missing term in Braidotti's equation is translation. The transversal entity cannot function if there is no way of establishing a meaningful relationship between the human, our genetic neighbours and the Earth as a whole. The centrality of translation to transversal subjectivity is echoed in the specific needs of ecological stewardship or governance.

Post-Holocene governance

John S. Dryzek and Jonathan Pickering, in *The Politics of the Anthropocene*, have described liberal democracy as a 'Holocene institution' that has produced 'a pathological path dependency [which] decouples human institutions from the Earth system by embodying feedback mechanisms that systematically repress information about the condition of the Earth system, and systematically prioritize narrow economic concerns' (Dryzek and Pickering 2019: 23). For their part, Anthony Burke and Stefanie Fishel, in expanding the sense of how democratic participation and representation are conceived, have argued for the 'recognition of the material presence and agency of ecosystems and non-human lives, and the resistant power of human/non-human assemblages' (Burke and Fishel 2020: 35). They explicitly call for:

> [a] post-Holocene ontology of inclusion, one that rests not merely upon an organism-focused emphasis on animal rights, but the prior existence, presence, and power of non-human lives and processes as they are manifested in vast and dynamic assemblages of beings across the Earth system. (Ibid.)

Underlying this ontology of inclusion is an ideal of political communication where the constituent groups, human and non-human alike, are intelligible to each other in ways that make just deliberation possible. Burke and Fishel, echoing the insights of scholars from the field of eco-orientated semiotics alluded to earlier, claim that '[n]on-human animals possess complex systems of exchange, solidarity, and communication between and across species' (ibid.: 45). This communicative complexity requires an appropriate response:

> We must not merely recognize that humans or obviously sen-
> tient and communicative animals can be understood to commu-
> nicate, but non-sentient changes in matter, form, and energy as
> they interact with the biosphere and other components of the
> Earth system as well. In this light, the *in/visibility* of the other-
> than-human is a globally pathological situation. The demand that
> the non-human must either speak our political language or remain
> mute was always cast in the wrong direction; it is we who must
> learn the Earth's language and reimagine the polity in its idioms.
> (Ibid.: 46–7, emphasis in original)

The word that again does not feature here is translation. Clearly, the
invocation of 'idioms' implies that there is difference and diversity; and,
therefore, translation must be called upon to establish a meaningful
interface between these idioms.

The necessity for translation proves all the more apparent when
proposals are made for forms of transnational governance that would
embrace the inclusive ontology of ecological democracy. Burke and
Fishel argue for the establishment of a United Nations Earth System
Council and a Global Ecoregion Assembly. The Earth System Council
would primarily be responsible for the safeguarding of the global environment and Earth system. The Global Ecoregion Assembly would con-
sist of representatives from 15 Global Ecoregions, and these ecoregions
would cover areas with broadly similar climates and a limited range of
ecosystem/biome types. Both bodies would have 'democratically elected
representatives acting as proxies for human and non-human communities' (ibid.: 49).

One of the obvious skills of these representative proxies is the need
to be versed in the idioms of the non-human constituencies they claim
to represent. In effect, translation would not only be central but essential to their political efficacy. Or to put this another way: any theory of
ecological democracy is going to need a viable theory of translation. Just
as the advent of transnational institutions after the Second World War
gave rise to the emergence of translation theory and education in Europe
and elsewhere, the advent of transnational ecological governance would
inevitably generate a new kind of translation imperative – the need for
eco-translation.

Eco-translation and the untranslatable

Seeing translation as not beholden to narrow interlingual understandings
of communicative exchange does not, however, remove the need to

deal with radical alterity. Jacques Derrida, in *The Beast and the Sovereign*, speaks of both commonality and difference in interspecies contact:

1. Incontestably, animals and humans inhabit the same world, the same objective world even if they do not have the same experience of the objectivity of the object.
2. Incontestably, animals and humans do not inhabit the same world, for the human world will never be purely and simply identical to the world of animals. (2011: 265)

Humans and the more-than-human share a world where they would appear to be radically estranged from each other, epistemically and ontologically. Even the sharing of that world, for humans and animals, has become more of a memory than a reality for critics like John Berger, who in his essay *Why Look at Animals?* points out that until the nineteenth century, 'anthropomorphism was integral to the relation between man and animal and was an expression of their proximity' (Berger 2009: 11). The replacement of animals by machines, in the cities and in the countryside, led to their withdrawal from the everyday world of humans to the confined and curated worlds of the zoo and the nursery are evidence of change. However, a well-intentioned hostility to the dangers of anthropomorphism can have the perverse effect of entrenching the very prejudices it seeks to challenge. The Australian eco-philosopher Val Plumwood is critical of the all too ready accusation of anthropomorphism when there is engagement with the more-than-human, claiming that one of the more recent roles of the concept is that 'of policeman for reductive materialism, enforcing polarised and segregated vocabularies for humans and non-humans' (Plumwood 2009: 6).

Taking up Plumwood's critique of the abuses of anthropomorphism, Deborah Bird Rose argues that the former's 'philosophical animism' entails a notion of interspecies communication:

> She is not defining communication in strictly human terms; there is no suggestion that other creatures sit around debating philosophy, but she is asserting that as other creatures live their lives, so they communicate aspects of themselves. Amidst all this communication, one finds one's self encountering expressiveness and mindfulness within the world of life. And amidst all this mindfulness, there arises a dialogical concept of self for both humans and others. (Rose 2013: 98)

The point of challenging the myth of the non-human world's mindlessness is then not to mindlessly project human desires onto that world, but to open oneself up to others as communicative and translatable beings. If culture is understood as a specific way of being in the world, then it follows that 'nonhuman beings have, and live by, culture' (ibid.: 100).

The forms that eco-translation (Cronin 2017) take – the project of exploring the communicative spaces of transversal subjectivity – are, by definition, plural. One post-Darwinian approach is to posit all living beings as related in a web of life and to emphasise the shared animality of communicating beings. Wim Pouw and his colleagues, in an article on 'Multilevel rhythms in multimodal communication', include in their study humans alongside other animals and conclude, 'we have argued that to understand communicative rhythms which characterize animal communication, a multimodal perspective is necessary and multiple levels need to be examined' (Pouw et al. 2021: 1–9). They treat human and non-human animal research as convergent, claiming that both, for example, demonstrate that 'multisensory neurons in the superior colliculus respond more robustly to spatio-temporally congruent audio-visual cues than to individual sensory cues' (ibid.: 3). Conceiving of translation in this framework is to look at communicative exchanges across a shared if differentiated animality.

Another approach assumes that all communication is pattern based, and uses artificial intelligence techniques to extrapolate significant patterns. An example is Michael Bronstein's Project CETI (Cetacean Translation Initiative), where he and his research team analysed around 26,000 recordings and separated the signals into categories based on the number, rhythm and tempo of clicks, alongside predicting which whale was speaking and what clan it belonged to. Though they do not discount the possibility of sperm whales having a grammatical-syntactical language, this is not their core concern. Bronstein and his fellow researchers are as much concerned with difference as with any putative mammalian similarity:

> [C]etaceans have cognitive abilities and societies that are commensurate with those of human phylogenetic relatives, but their ocean habitat provides a difference in ecology, which can be revealing from a comparative perspective, especially with regards to evolutionary adaptations required for aquatic communication. (Bermant et al. 2019: 1)

Underwater robots and buoys carrying acoustic sensors are used in conjunction with sensor-laden tags that help identify individual whales, allowing the researchers to identify who is talking to who and reconstruct behaviours associated with particular patterns of clicks. Correlating behaviour with specific signals is especially challenging in the case of deep-ocean animals. Bronstein is modest about what the translation initiative can achieve: 'It might be that it will only be a rough approximation of the true depth and meaning of what they are saying' (cited in Gent 2020: 78).

A project which similarly uses artificial intelligence and deep-learning techniques to further human engagement with non-human animal communication is the Earth Species Project (https:www.earth-species.org). This is an an open-source, collaborative and non-profit organisation dedicated to decoding non-human language. In 2013, Tomas Mikolov et al. proposed an algorithm that represents words as points in a high-dimension space, where the distance and direction between points encodes the relationship between words. This mapping of the words in a language to a geometric structure is known as a 'word embedding' (http://jalammar.github.io/illustrated-word2vec/). The notion of word embedding was then deployed to generate translations between languages that were unknown to each other. In 2017, Alexis Conneau et al. and Mikel Artetxe et al. managed to translate between unknown languages without the need for a bilingual dictionary or any prior examples of translation between these languages (translation corpora). They basically aligned the languages' embeddings by rotating one over the other until their shapes matched. This aligned the structure of their internal relationships so the points of one language could be overlaid with the points from a second language. To translate a word, you needed to find the point in the second language closest to the word's point in the first language. These multilingual embeddings – sometimes called universal embeddings – underpin machine translation products used by a number of major tech companies. Although the notion of translation was severely restricted in being primarily word-focused, the import of this discovery was that future translations might be possible between radically different forms of communication.

The sponsors of the Earth Species Project claim: 'We believe that an understanding of non-human languages will change our ecological impact on this planet.' They do not specify what that change might be and Con Slobodchickoff, an expert on communication in US prairie dogs, is equally vague when he says that '[e]ven if they [animals] have alien concepts, if we could make at least some of our desires known to them and if they could make some of their desires known to us, I think that we would have a completely different world' (cited in Gent 2020: 79). The focus is primarily on the means rather than ends of translation, on how it might be done, not what it might be used for.

From the standpoint of ecological democracy and questions around voice and representation, however, it is clear that the affordances of translation are of central importance. These include the already-existing polyphonic and multivocal biotic communities to be explored in the aforementioned and future projects on interspecies communication, and a revisionist position towards the anthropocentric concept of language used in translation since the Tower of Babel myth. For example, Ludwig Wittgenstein's famous phrase, 'if a lion could talk, we wouldn't be able to understand it', does not refer to animals' incapacity for communication but to their difference and historical separateness from human beings in the world (Wittgenstein 2009: 235). What fuels eco-translation then is the animals' lost expression of participation in the more-than-human world.

From ancient times only a small number of philosophers of language, such as Sextus Empiricus, have claimed that animals can speak but humans do not understand their language (Formigari 2004: 47). Many cognitive ethologists and semiologists of animal communication would confirm this belief. However, their studies – e.g. on bird songs – approach the issue of animal language in parallel to human language (Beecher 2021). This anthropomorphic fallacy leads to an unavoidable scepticism with respect to translating non-human species and validates even more the need for eco-translation. One way to counter the scepticism is to think about expressing communicative relationships differently, on the grounds of a notion of language as a necessary tool for the political agency of non-human animals.

Eva Meijer, in her *Animal Languages: The Secret Conversations of the Animal World* (2019), lays great stress on the capacity of animals to communicate and the duty of humans not only to listen but to understand and act:

> Many laws and regulations affect the lives of other animals, even though they are not consulted. The reason often given for this is that they cannot speak. As we learn more about animal languages and subjectivity, it has become clearer that this is simply not true, and we should not ignore them any longer. (Meijer 2019: 132–3)

By way of illustration, she offers the example of a case study by animal geographers, Jun-Han Yeo and Harvey Neo, from the Bukit Timah nature reserve in Singapore, where tensions arose between local humans and macaque monkeys. The geographers listed the various forms of communication between the humans and the macaques, which included 'eye contact, keeping distance, reading each others' body language and trying to approach the other' (ibid.: 134). The macaques reacted to humans talking, they were sensitive to their intonation, and humans reacted to the noises made by the macaque. In a dispute over access to particular areas, both parties were engaged in translating each other's language to decide what to do. As Meijer asserts, 'to find out what other animals want, it is not enough merely to study them. We need to talk with them' (ibid.: 137). Contemporary problems, she argues, from the climate crisis to pandemics, are bound up with this communicative breakdown, this unwillingness to translate.

Of course, one response to the complex nature of epistemic, ontological and political relations between living beings is to advocate for an explicit form of untranslatability. The notion of untranslatability surfaces in Edna Andrew's engagement with Juri Lotman's concept of the semiosphere, where she comments: 'The languages of the semiosphere run along a continuum that includes the extremes of total mutual translatability and complete mutual untranslatability' (Andrews 2003: 33). If Lotman's notion of the semiosphere is primarily concerned with human semiosis, the potential for the untranslatable would appear to increase exponentially as we move into the realm of the more-than-human. This, indeed, would appear to be the implication of Patricia MacCormack's contention that humans can never know the more-than-human and that, for the more-than-human, it is better this way. Speaking on behalf of Abolitionists, advocating for the gradual disappearance of the human species as the only plausible solution to the climate crisis, MacCormack argues:

> Abolitionists are activists against all use of animals acknowledging that communication is fatally human so we can never know modes of nonhuman communication, and to do so is both hubris and materially detrimental to nonhumans. (MacCormack 2020: 14)

The difficulty with this standpoint is the suggestion that exploitation has a monopoly on relationality – that the only way to go beyond alienation is to further alienate. In a sense, the declared impossibility or undesirability of translation in the human/more-than-human interactions raises issues similar to those addressed by Lawrence Venuti in his critique of the notion of 'untranslatability' as deployed by literary critics such as Emily Apter (2006) and Barbara Cassin (2014). Venuti declares that:

> to promote a notion of untranslatability so as to stigmatize and rule out the study of translation in its many forms, humanistic, pragmatic, and technical, as well as the institutional and economic conditions in which it is practiced – any such exclusion is effectively to abdicate to the status quo by withdrawing from the areas where social struggles can occur. (Venuti 2019: 78–9)

In other words, the ever-present danger in the notion of the untranslatable is that translation gets essentialised as a process which either does (translatable) or does not (untranslatable) happen. Rather than seeing translation as a horizon of expectation which is endlessly negotiated through engagement with the institutional and economic conditions of its possibility, the untranslatable can nourish fantasies of virtuous isolation that paradoxically replicate the sovereign indifference of human exceptionalism. Denying relationality in the name of diversity is effectively to eliminate that diversity. Translation, as understood in a hermeneutic sense, is about the amplification of differences, the multiplication of particulars, not their removal. Legitimate concerns around anthropomorphism or political manipulation through assimilation end up in a perverse way strengthening the prevailing anthropocentric state of affairs. The refusal to countenance the emancipatory possibilities of translation through its complex involvement at the most detailed levels with difference is effectively to promote closure as a virtue, and openness as a form of culpable weakness.

Proliferation of translatability in the context of climate adaptation

In 1988 Claude Lévi-Strauss, in conversation with Didier Eribon, argued:

> No situation appears more tragic, more offensive for the heart and the mind – despite the ink clouds projected by the Judeo-Christian tradition to mask it – than that of a humanity that coexists with other species of life on Earth which they share in enjoying, but with whom they cannot communicate. (Cited in Lingis 2007: 43)

In that year, the French anthropologist could still posit the experience of a shared life between human and non-human species as enjoyable, although 'tragically' non-communicable across species. For our purposes, the remarks of Lévi-Strauss make us realise how radically different motivations for interspecies communication and translation are in the Anthropocene.

The convergence of major ecological emergencies such as the critical status of adaptation to a warming world, the progress of species extinctions and the exponentially shrinking time for reducing CO_2 emissions (the time left to act is counted in decades, not in centuries – see IPCC 2021), as well as the fallout from the COVID-19 pandemic, makes the shared joy of Lévi-Strauss's project less than credible. More realistic, but also more challenging, is eco-translation, which goes beyond human language towards reconnecting all subjects of communication through a notion of transversal subjectivity, so as to find ways of developing interpretative frameworks for more resilient dealings with the progress of a fast-moving catastrophe. Recent biological research tracing the changing behaviour of non-human animals due to climate change has only strengthened this argument (Draper and Weissburg 2019). In dialogue with ecologically orientated semiotics, the aim now is to envision interspecies communication so as to further awareness of the climate emergency in the Anthropocene, when 'the distinction between matter and the semiotic realm has become increasingly blurred and unstable within contemporary, human influenced environments' (Maran 2014: 149). On this basis, in the context of the growing risk of destabilised semiotic-material relationalities, eco-translation can ask to what extent we have to reconsider the activity of translation of humans in relation to non-humans. While the vast majority of ecosemioticians would emphasise the meaningful relationality of signs between human cultures, other species and ecological systems (Maran 2020), an eco-translation approach would be a response to the environmental incompetency of the human species that, in contrast to different non-humans/animals tightly embedded in the world, does not understand – and, in consequence, does not experience – its own vulnerabilities as evidence of climate catastrophe.

By merging the ecosemiotic approach and the need for more extensive and effective translation in reaction to the Anthropocene's changing ecological conditions, we argue for exploring the resilient elements of animal and human-animal (interspecies) communication in such gigantic, innovative and ambitious work-in-progress projects such as the Interspecies Internet (Interspecies.io). The idea behind using smart, computational technologies – the Interspecies Internet is being supported by Google and MIT – for deciphering and connecting non-humans with humans is also driven by the effort to make up for a long history of their broken bonds in communication. The Interspecies Internet could become a leading space for developing the practice of eco-translation and, as we read in the mission statement, could 'positively impact species conservation, welfare, empathy, compassion, enrichment, sustainability [. . .] to advance the understanding and appreciation of the mental lives and intelligence of the diverse species with which we share our planet'. The urgent question would be to what extent the environments of different species are disturbed by climate change and how this is being translated and/or communicated by humans and non-humans as an expression of the scale of the impending catastrophe.

Different animal species express the progress of disruption in human-altered environments. Jakob von Uexküll, who has influenced eco-orientated semioticians such as Sebeok, is also inspiring for us. As argued by Uexküll, animals are the first active subjects of perception of the material-semiotic worlds in which they are immersed and the most competent creatures to recognise – and to suffer – its malfunctions (Uexküll 1992: 319–91). This is especially evident in how plastic waste is used by different animal species and how it is not recognised as a deadly threat. On the contrary, as growing research on microplastics shows, it can even become a 'treat' for zooplankton when it is chosen over more nutritious phytoplankton's ingredients, and in consequence is indicated as another factor of warming and deoxygenating waters (Kvale et al. 2021). In ecosemiotic terminology, it is about 'the inability of an organism to recognize and correctly categorize the matter semiotized by other species', i.e. humans (Maran 2014: 152). In this case, not only what is material and semiotic gets blurred but the boundary between what is natural and cultural in the Anthropocene is constantly reinterpreted beyond the known limits posed by organic and inorganic matter. To some extent, these new organic-inorganic relationalities are signs of necessary co-evolutionary interactions between biological and human-made matter such as plastic (Bakke 2020), but in the kingdom of vulnerable bodies of human and non-human animals it is still difficult to escape from the time limits imposed on adaptation strategies by an anthropogenically transformed world.

Uexküll changed the paradigm of studying animal behaviour and interspecies communication, firstly because he built his approach on a simple fact that animals perceive, that they have their worlds, and that it is scientifically legitimate to ask what those worlds are like (Sagan 2010: 20). Secondly, and this is now a question of much interest – what kind of an organisation of the world underlying animal perception is a source of animals' actions? He noted, 'there is no space independent of subjects' (Uexküll 2010 [1934]: 70). Therefore, it is more within an Uexküllian than within a Darwinian framework to restate the real and material importance of reading environments anew in the Anthropocene, recognising animals as skilful in their ecosystems before we (humans) will be able to translate it. Uexküll also understands the relationality of time frameworks as the time of nowness, the time of opportunities and his focus is notably on how 'the subject controls the time of its environment' (ibid.: 52). He notably points out, 'without a living subject, there can be no time' (ibid.). By de-anthropomorphising the Kantian transcendental categories of time and space and showing that these categories are related to individual species and environments, Uexküll can be approached anew to study how the 'grand design in nature', the 'variety of relationships that create a harmonious whole' (Buchanan 2008: 28) or diverse systems of planetary communication, are disturbed by the current signs of living with the catastrophe. Merging the ecosemiotic with the eco-translational is part of a more inclusive all-species effort to communicate the Anthropocene, which requires finding the windows within monad-like worlds – Uexküllian 'Umwelts' – through which the progress of the Anthropocene's encroachment becomes more and more recognisable.

Many species' detective skills in how they 'read' affordances in environments are distorted by climatic conditions, not only migratory birds or polar species but also disease-spreading animals. James Gibson, a psychologist inspired by Uexküll, developed the concept of perception of the environment by the non-human animal through coining the notion of affordances. He defined them as conditions for actions that the animal sees, and that become pathological if they are missing in the animal's behaviour (Dotov et al. 2012: 28–39). If these conditions relate to extreme weather, especially in arid environments, then they 'could initiate changes in the behaviour of humans and non-human animals alike' and motivate even 'the creation of [new] mythical narratives' (Maran 2014: 146). Examining the biological narratives such as 'the semiotic ethology' of Uexküll (Wheeler 2014: 74) can facilitate the conceptualisation of eco-translation in the Anthropocene, especially when we are interested in making climate warming real, experiential and a phenomenon that can be situated within the framework of interspecies communication. The language of theoretical biologists, treated not as a source of metaphors (ibid.: 71), offers an approach to eco-translation in the Anthropocene when different biosemiotic structures like codes, transductions, genetic information, chemical signals and cell signalling are all part of interpretative studies generating new meanings. It is then that there is an evident correlation between the known functionality of the biological world and its changing conditions characterised by rapidly rising temperatures, environmental pollution and the biosphere's displacement.

The animal that responds to temperature change behaves like an automaton and, in this context, Uexküll asks the question: 'Is the tick a machine or a machine operator? Is it a mere object or a subject?' (2010: 45). The tick is a precisely 'designed' animal whose suction mechanism is activated by the concrete temperature of liquid (the mammals' blood at 37°C). The animal's bond with the world is, perhaps, sensed much more intensively, especially in the situation of constantly rising temperatures and other extreme weather conditions. This is visible in the results from research on the changes of tick populations due to recent climate change (Ogden et al. 2021), and the higher risk of spreading zoonotic diseases like Lyme because of longer summers and shorter or disappearing frost periods (Cary Institute 2020). Therefore, according to such institutions as the US Environmental Protection Agency, the ticks are treated as climate warming indicators (EPA 2021). From the point of view of ecosemiotics, the stimuli (the signs) for a tick – no matter how 'impoverished' a form of the world the tick may be seen to process – are disturbed and affect not only the tick's environment but also the whole networks of interrelated species of mammals, including humans.

Conclusion, or the climate change clock ticks

The purpose of eco-translation is to take seriously the notion of human/ more-than-human relationality in such a way as to draw attention to the role of translation enquiry when dealing with major ecological problems and when tackling anthropogenic distortions in more-than-human species habitats. This critical approach is already visible in all the interdisciplinary efforts to translate a message that we humans may not like to hear but is being communicated by other species (even by the most unwanted, such as Uexküll's fellow creature, the tick). The editors of *Art in the Anthropocene* speak about this epistemological transformation, that affects aesthetics, with some sense of hope: 'If we are to learn to adapt in this world, we will need to do so with all the other creatures; seeing from their perspective is central to re-organizing our knowledge and perceptions' (Davis and Turpin 2015: 13). But perhaps more importantly eco-translation in the Anthropocene is about the reconceptualisation of the experience of time – the catastrophe is happening now when we are no longer in a before time. Therefore, the problem posed as 'untranslatability' in relation to time experienced by different species (Derrida 1999; see also Simmons 2007: 38) is no longer valid. In other words, the anthropocentric construct of the past-present-future dissolves within the global catastrophe, whereas knowledge – how it is generated and distributed – is now becoming a more-than-human enterprise, a project of global interspecies contribution, including even the following of ticks as significant others. Similarly, in 'The Animal That Therefore I Am' (2002), when Derrida speaks about animals in different discourses – or rather about their absence in philosophy – he points to an ambiguous form in French: 'je suis', which bears two meanings: 'I am' and 'I follow'. Eco-translation asks anew what it might mean when we say that 'I follow' animals – not one animal, but the whole variety of non-human species who communicate the ecological knowledge on the Anthropocene's finitude which needs to be translated.

The rise of ticks brings interspecies communication to the fore and can make us more reflective on what it means to be biological organisms first, vulnerable to climate and disease like other, non-human creatures. As a result, by merging ecosemiotic and translational studies we find that, in the wake of Uexküll, the zoocentric perspective is more useful for understanding interspecies' vulnerabilities in the Anthropocene. Animals redirect our reflection from the past and hypothetical future to the present moment that we humans do not capture; not just because we have lost the ability to perceive and refer to the present, like Uexküll's tick, but because the present does not affect our experience of living within the catastrophe adequately. Maybe the ticks and other zoonotic sources of diseases are now the closest and most special connectors and mediators of climate change, which we need to eco-translate.

References

Andrews, Edna (2003), *Conversations with Lotman: Cultural Semiotics in Language, Literature, and Cognition*, Toronto: University of Toronto Press.

Apter, Emily (2006), *The Translation Zone: A New Comparative Literature*, Princeton, NJ: Princeton University Press.

Artetxe, Mikel, Gorka Labaka, Eneko Agirre and Kyunghyun Cho (2017), 'Unsupervised Neural Machine Translation', available at: http://arxiv.org/abs/1710.11041 (last accessed 21 February 2022).

Bakke, Monika (2020), 'When More Than Life Is at Stake: Art Vis-à-Vis Mineral and Biological Communities', *Teksty Drugie*, 1: 165–85.

Beecher, Michael D. (2021), 'Why Are No Animal Communication Systems Simple Languages?', *Frontiers in Psychology*, 12.

Berger, John (2009), *About Looking*, London: Bloomsbury.

Bermant, Peter C., Michael M. Bronstein, Robert J. Wood, Shane Gero and David F. Gruber (2019), 'Deep Machine Learning Techniques for the Detection and Classification of Sperm Whale Bioacoustics', *Scientific Reports*, 9: 1–11.

Braidotti, Rosi (2013), *The Posthuman*, Cambridge: Polity.

Buchanan, Brett (2008), *Onto-Ethologies. The Animal Environments of Uexküll, Heidegger, Merlau-Ponty, and Deleuze*, Albany: SUNY Press.

Burke, Anthony and Stefanie Fishel (2020), 'Across Species and Borders: Political Representation, Ecological Democracy, and the Non-Human', in Joana Castro Perreira and André Saramago (eds), *Non-Human Nature in World Politics: Theory*, Cham: Springer, pp. 33–52.

Cary Institute (2020), 'Climate Change and Tick-Borne Disease Risk', available at: https://www.caryinstitute.org/our-expertise/disease-ecology/lyme-tick-borne-disease/climate-change-and-tick-borne-disease-risk (last accessed 21 February 2022).

Cassin, Barbara (ed.) (2014), *Dictionary of Untranslatables: A Philosphical Lexicon*, trans. Emily Apter, Jacques Lezra and Michael Wood, Princeton NJ: Princeton University Press.

Conneau, Alexis, Guillaume Lample, Marc Aurelio Ranzato, Ludovic Denoyer and Hervé Jégou (2017), 'Word Translation Without Parallel Data', available at: http://arxiv.org/abs/1710.04087 last accessed 2 March 2022).

Cronin, Michael (2017), *Eco-Translation: Translation and Ecology in the Age of the Anthropocene*, London: Routledge.

Davis, Heather and Etienne Turpin (eds) (2015), 'Art and Death: Lives Between the Fifth Assessment and the Sixth Extinction', in *Art in the Anthropocene. Encounters among Aesthetics, Politics, Environments and Epistemologies*, London: Open Humanities Press, pp. 3–30.

Derrida, Jacques (1999), *D'ailleurs, Derrida*, film, directed by Safaa Fathy, Paris: La Sept, ARTE, GLORIA.

Derrida, Jacques (2002), 'The Animal That Therefore I Am (More to Follow)', trans. David Wills, *Critical Inquiry*, 28: 369–418.

Derrida, Jacques (2011), *The Beast and the Sovereign*, vol. 2, trans. Geoff Bennington, Chicago: University of Chicago.

Dotov, Dobromir G., Lin Nie and Matthieu M. de Wit (2012), 'Understanding Affordances: History and Contemporary Development of Gibson's Central Concept', *Avant*, 3(2): 28–39.

Draper, Alex M. and Marc J. Weissburg (2019), 'Impacts of Global Warming and Elevated $CO2$ on Sensory Behavior in Predator-Prey Interactions: A Review and Synthesis', *Frontiers in Ecology and Evolution*, 7, available at: https://www.frontiersin.org/articles/10.3389/fevo.2019.00072/full (last accessed 21 February 2022).

Dryzek, John S. and Jonathan Pickering (2019), *The Politics of the Anthropocene*, Oxford: Oxford University Press.

EPA (2021), 'Climate Change Indicators: Lyme Disease', available at: https://www.epa.gov/climate-indicators-lyme-disease (last accessed 21 February 2022).

Formigari, Lia (2004), *A History of Language Philosophies*, trans. Gabriel Poole, Amsterdam: John Benjamins Publishing.

Gent, Edd (2020), 'Talk to the Animals', *New Scientist*, 248(3313): 78–9.

Interspecies Internet, available at: https:www.interspecies.io (last accessed 3 March 2022).

IPCC (2021), 'Summary for Policymakers', in Masson-Delmotte, V., P. Zhai, A. Pirani, S. L. Connors, C. Péan, S. Berger, N. Caud, Y. Chen, L. Goldfarb, M. I. Gomis, M. Huang, K. Leitzell, E. Lonnoy, J. B. R. Matthews, T. K. Maycock, T. Waterfield, O. Yelekçi, R. Yu, and B. Zhou (eds), *Climate Change 2021: The Physical Science Basis. Contribution of Working Group I to the Sixth Assessment Report of the Intergovernmental Panel on Climate Change*, Cambridge: Cambridge University Press, in press, available at: https://www.ipcc.ch/report/ar6/wg1/ - SPM (last accessed 21 February 2022).

Jakobson, Roman (2004), 'On Linguistic Aspects of Translation', in Lawrence Venuti (ed.), *The Translation Studies Reader*, London: Routledge, pp. 138–43.

Kull, Kalevi and Peeter Torop (2011), 'Biotranslation: Translation between Umwelten', in Timo Maran, Dario Martinelli, Aleksei Turovski (eds), *Readings in Zoosemiotics*, Berlin: De Gruyter Mouton, pp. 411–25.

Kvale, K., A. E. F. Prowe, C.-T. Chien, A. Landolfi and A. Oschlies (2021), 'Zooplankton Grazing of Microplastic Can Accelerate Global Loss of Ocean Oxygen', *Nature Communications*, 12(2358).

Lingis, Alphonso (2007), 'Understanding Avian Intelligence', in Laurence Simmons and Philip Armstrong (eds), *Knowing Animals*, Leiden: Brill, pp. 43–56.

MacCormack, Patricia (2020), *The Ahuman Manifesto: Activism for the End of the Anthropocene*, London: Bloomsbury.

Manai, Yamen (2021), *The Ardent Swarm*, trans. Lara Vergnaud, Seattle: Amazon Crossing.

Marais, Kobus (2019), *A (Bio)Semiotic Theory of Translation: The Emergence of Socio-Cultural Reality*, London: Routledge.

Maran, Timo (2014), 'Semiotization of Matter. A Hybrid Zone between Biosemiotics and Material Ecocriticism', in Serenella Iovino and Serpil Oppermann (eds), *Material Ecocriticism*, Bloomington: Indiana University Press.

Maran, Timo (2020), *Ecosemiotics. The Study of Signs in Changing Ecologies*, Cambridge: Cambridge University Press.

Maran, Timo, Dario Martinelli and Aleksei Turovski (eds) (2011), *Readings in Zoosemiotics*, Berlin: De Gruyter Mouton.

Meijer, Eva (2019), *Animal Languages: The Secret Conversations of the Animal World*, London: John Murray.

Mikolov, Thomas, Kai Chen, Greg Corrado and Jeffrey Dean (2013) 'Efficient Estimation of Word Representations in Vector Space', available at: http://arxiv.org/abs/1301.3781 (last accessed 3 March 2022).

Ogden, Nicholas, Ben Beard, Howard Ginsberg and Jean Tsao (2021), 'Possible Effects of Climate Change on Ixodid Ticks and the Pathogens They Transmit: Predictions and Observations', *Journal of Medical Entomology*, 58(4): 1536–45.

Peirce, Charles Sanders (1989), *Writings of Charles S. Peirce: A Chronological Edition*, vol. 4, Bloomington: Indiana University Press.

Plumwood, Val (2009), 'Nature in the Active Voice', *Australian Humanities Review*, 46, available at: http://australianhumanitiesreview.org/2009/05/01/nature-in-the-active-voice (last accessed 2 March 2022).

Pouw, Wim, Shannon Proksch, Linda Drijvers, Marco Gamba, Judith Holler, Christopher Kello, Rebecca S. Schaefer and Geraint A. Wiggins (2021), 'Multilevel Rhythms in Multimodal Communication', *Philosophical Transactions of the Royal Society*, B376: 1–9.

Rose, Deborah Bird (2013), 'Val Plumwood's Philosophical Animism: Attentive Interactions in the Sentient World', *Environmental Humanities*, 3: 93–109.

Sagan, Dorion (2010), 'Introduction. Umwelt after Uexküll', in Jakob von Uexküll (ed.), *A Foray into the Worlds of Animals and Humans*, Minneapolis: University of Minnesota Press, pp. 1–34.

Sebeok, Thomas A. (1991), 'Communication', in *A Sign is Just a Sign*, Bloomington: Indiana University Press.

Sebeok, Thomas A. (2001), *An Introduction to Semiotics*, Toronto: University of Toronto Press.

Simmons, Laurence (2007), 'Shame, Levinas's Dog, Derrida's Cat. And Some Fish', in Laurence Simmons and Philip Armstrong (eds), *Knowing Animals*, Leiden: Brill, pp. 25–42.

Steiner, George (1975), *After Babel: Aspects of Language and Translation*, New York: Oxford University Press.

Uexküll, Jakob von (1992), 'A Stroll Through the World of Animals and Men: A Picture Book of Invisible Worlds', *Semiotica*, 89(4): 319–91.

Uexküll, Jakob von (2010), *A Foray into the Worlds of Animals and Humans*, trans. Joseph D. O'Neil, Minneapolis: University of Minnesota Press.

Venuti, Lawrence (2019), *Contra Instrumentalism: A Translation Polemic*, Lincoln: University of Nebraska Press.

Wheeler, Wendy (2014), 'Natural Play, Natural Metaphor, and Natural Stories. Biosemiotic Realism', in Serenella Iovino and Serpil Oppermann (eds), *Material Ecocriticism*, Bloomington: Indiana University Press, pp. 67–79.

Wittgenstein, Ludwig (2009), *Philosophical Investigations*, trans. Gertrude E. M. Anscombe, Peter M. S. Hacker and Joachim Schulte, Chichester: Wiley-Blackwell.

8

On *Zoē* and Spider Life: Studio Tomás Saraceno's Working Objects in the Critical Posthumanities

Jussi Parikka

Posthuman working objects

A multitude of expressions of life define the posthuman perspective of what was once called 'natural' but is now fully embedded in techno-cultural knowledge practices.[1] The question of life, not only as *bios* but as the material non-human life of *zoē*, has become a key reference point for such critical posthumanities as Rosi Braidotti's (2016, 2019). A variety of perspectives help us to understand the complex, often trans-species and ecological, notions of life. These are mapped both in the humanities, the arts and in a variety of scientific practices, for many different ends but also through a variety of techniques of knowledge: as images, data sets, and many other ways that capture, for example, animal life in and as mediation. In my earlier work such as *Insect Media* (Parikka 2010), I aimed to articulate this as non-human media theory that proceeds by way of a cultural history of animal sensation; this I have started to call my 'AI' book, which was not a reference to artificial intelligence, but animal intelligence much in the spirit of Braidotti's *zoē*. This relational ecology of intensities, or a set of capacities of sensing, helps us to understand some of the links between cultural representations, artistic methods and important scientific work about non-human animals. This chapter pursues some of these questions and contributes an understanding of how animal intelligence is framed in and through artistic engagement with questions of sensing. In other words, the text addresses contemporary art and science collaborations with special attention paid to how artistic practices, in this case, the renowned contemporary artist-architect Tomás Saraceno and his large studio team, deal with questions of environmental formations and agency. As such many of the projects, including the *ON AIR* (2018–19) exhibition discussed in this chapter, are already implicitly part of the field of environmental humanities, which over the years has incorporated approaches relating to 'agency, cultural formations, social change and the entangled relations between human and nonhuman worlds' (Rose et al. 2012: 2). From multispecies ethnographies to cultural theory of the posthuman, from environmental histories and deep times to conceptually rich work on non-human animals, the field also reaches out to art practices. Environmental arts have become increasingly practised and widely researched (see, e.g., Greaves 2013; Ballard 2017; Kahn 2013; Randerson 2018), and in some cases, such as Janine Randerson, suggest links to the broader genealogy of 'process-based ontologies and the environmental posthumanities' (Randerson 2018: xix).[2]

Dealing with Studio Tomás Saraceno's work, the challenge relates to how heavily it is already invested in ongoing debates and vocabularies of environmental humanities and arts. The many aspects of their projects speak directly to themes of environmental agency and relational ontology while involving awareness of ecological collapse as well as occasional nods to the context of the planetary scale (cognitive) capitalism of technological culture. Theoretically, this poses a compelling dilemma in so far as Studio Tomás Saraceno becomes almost too obvious a case for a cultural analysis of contemporary Anthropocene entanglements and discourses of relationality, nature and ecology. In other words, the work is *already* involved in the variety of discourses about multispecies communication, posthuman environments and the Anthropocene from work by Anna Tsing to Bruno Latour, Karen Barad to Stefan Helmreich. But more than a rhetorical figure of theory that carries academic discourse into art or produces illustrations of those themes, the Studio engages in material production that escapes a self-referential theory circle. And it is the Studio's work that provides springboards – further layers of useful materials and objects – for a cascade of concepts and questions about logistics, infrastructure and technology, each embedded within the fragile realities in which environmental arts and theory bounce off multiple institutional contexts, presenting themes of hybridity in action at multiple scales of artworks that also function as research objects. Studio Tomás Saraceno's work on spider webs as diagrammatic models moves across multiple institutional contexts, from curatorial objects in exhibitions to art-science studio collaborations. The webs are material, emerging as visualisations and abstractions. These images and installations are also mediations between technical knowledge and artistic expression, fulfilling the double role as both aesthetic and epistemic agents (see Werner 2015; Wulz 2010). The work with arachnoids is parallel to the Studio's work on the Aerocene (see, e.g., McCormack 2017; Philippopoulos-Mihalopoulos 2016; Randerson 2018: 176–80;

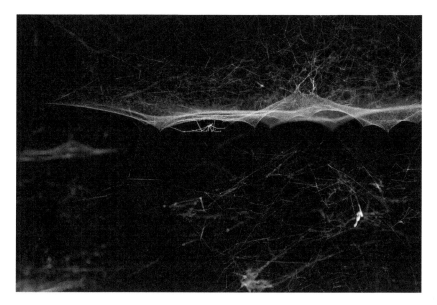

Figure 8.1 Tomás Saraceno, *Webs of At-tent(s)ion*, 2018. Installation view at *ON AIR*, carte blanche exhibition to Tomás Saraceno, Palais de Tokyo, Paris, 2018. Curated by Rebecca Lamarche-Vadel. Courtesy of the artist.
Source: © Photography by Studio Tomás Saraceno, 2018.

Page 2020), both of which express an interest in natural materials in technological culture, economies of energy and alternative architectures. The Studio explores the multiple scales of webs to understand the operations that, while becoming visually tangible as sculptural works, also capture a range of discourses circulating in contemporary art, scientific models, visual diagrams and speculative architecture. The sculptural projects function as diffractive (Barad 2007; Haraway 2018; Miyazaki 2015) materialisations of webs, instead of mere reflective commentaries of theoretical stances. These sculptural diffractions lead to a discussion on how practice-based work operates and understands materials such as spider webs, and, further, how this work contributes to environmental humanities and related fields. As diffractive, these models are productive of difference, not merely registering it, as the section below on Diffractive Models elaborates in relation to Saraceno's projects.

A fundamental proposition of this chapter is to think of Saraceno's sculptural works as *working objects*. A term employed originally by Lorraine Daston and Peter Galison in their take on the history of science (Daston and Galison 1992), working objects are forms of digested nature that become employed in scientific discourses: 'If working objects are not raw nature, they are not yet concepts, much less conjectures or theories;

they are the materials from which concepts are formed and to which they are applied' (ibid.: 85). The processes of supply and selection seem like one logistical part of the scientific practice in the historical sense, whereas the concept is useful to consider in the art-science collaborations contexts of Studio Tomás Saraceno, where the question is not merely about selection but also the multiscalar transformation of materials and images. Following Daston and Galison's analysis, '[w]orking objects can be atlas images, type specimens, or laboratory processes – any manageable, communal representatives of the sector of nature under investigation' (ibid.), I want to observe how this concept bears examination through the investigation of a contemporary art and science practice such as the Studio's. I propose that Saraceno's arachnoid models are working objects, curated for art exhibitions, part of collective studio work (Engelmann 2017b, 2019, 2021), and collaborations with various scientific groups, such as MIT material scientists. In other words, the sculptures and models, installations and operations – from stereophotogrammetry and laser scanning to the most analogue of pencil on paper – are employed in these works as visual diagrams that do not merely describe but are actively circulating in something that might also be coined as an ecology of images singular to the Studio's work (Engelmann 2019: 306), and as an expression of the very working objects through which particular outputs stabilise. As such they are postnatural objects par excellence, ones that stem from *zoē* (Braidotti 2016), the life of non-humans, while being worked upon and transformed – in some cases as property, in some cases as something more productive for the wider ecological set of aims we have: how to live with others, how to understand the behaviour of non-human animals, and how to know this world in its *zoē*-political relationality? A case in point is Ally Bisshop's take on the studio's work with spiders where the ethological study affords a modelling of a 'queer "arachnomadic" subject' that also feeds into discussions in contemporary feminist critical posthumanities such as on ethico-erotic practices and zoētic desire (Bisshop 2022).

These operations of knowledge are relevant to a broader set of discussions about materiality, the modelisation of and through living beings, and various forms of imaginaries entering the studio and the exhibition – some from architecture, some from art. This practice-led work is an important contribution to environmental humanities in how it operates across different disciplinary teams and aesthetic and scientific registers, offering ways to incorporate material practices into theoretical developments. In this way, the artistic-architectural work becomes methodologically stimulating for the intersection where critical posthumanities and environmental humanities meet – if that field is understood to incorporate the multiple ecologies that brand the contemporary moment: technologies, mediations, political assemblages, environmental situations and the various flows of materials and energy in which both art practice *and* environmental humanities do their work (see, e.g., Peters 2015; Parikka 2015; Engelmann and McCormack 2018; Bisshop 2022).

Beginning with a discussion of Saraceno's recent *ON AIR* exhibition, this chapter explores the multiple contexts of such art and science working objects in exhibition and studio situations, as well as in some of the scientific discourses that are at the core of the Studio's work. Hence, the discussion will respond to webs as cognitive architectures, and how, for example, the field of biotremology (e.g. the study of organic vibrations) is implied in the work and also where the artistic work feeds new inputs. I will follow how these spatial constructions and sculptures work as diffractive yet productive models between art, science and the arachnoid intelligence of AI, before concluding with how these models engage with larger questions of environmental humanities and practice-based art methods. In doing this, I hope this text resonates with the general context of this book but also acts as a contribution to the ongoing work in critical posthumanities as well as environmental humanities.

ON AIR

Saraceno's recent large-scale show, *ON AIR*, was exhibited at the Palais de Tokyo from October 2018 to January 2019 and many of the pieces have toured in several other exhibitions over the years. Curated by Rebecca Lamarche-Vadel, the Paris exhibition was articulated through different scales of webs, themselves the central motif of many of the pieces on display – in addition to those on dust and, for example, on architectures of air and communities of the *Aerocene* project that has investigated imaginaries and real possibilities of post-fossil fuel era air travel. The *ON AIR* exhibition's focus on spiders was exemplary of the Studio's longer interest in setting up 'experimental systems for interspecies communication' (Saraceno et al. 2019: 485). This framework was reflected further in the introductory text of the exhibition that was positioned as an 'ecosystem in becoming, hosting emergent choreographies and polyphonies across human and non-human universes, where artworks reveal the common, fragile and ephemeral rhythms and trajectories between these worlds' (Saraceno 2018: n.p.). The poetic phrasing of *ON AIR* was accompanied by curatorial sections that threaded links from spider webs to the post-fossil fuel imaginaries of the *Aerocene* project, between the different media and materials of the installations, from natural materials to moving images, and different methods of visualisation of the microscopic dimensions of, for example, cosmic dust. Studio Tomás Saraceno's work, including the series of collaborations with non-human animals such as spiders, has aptly already been approached as 'other-than-human-aesthetics' (Engelman 2017b; see also Page 2020). The installation in Paris was placed within the contexts of multiple voices, collaborations and perceptual registers activated both by scale and by the different visual and material manifestations of the thematics of webs and architectures, and air, framed as an object of artistic and curatorial investigation.

The building itself was included in the original planning and curation of the web installations; Palais de Tokyo was mapped for existing spiders and webs with *Holocnemus pluchei* spiders brought back to the studio in Berlin, where they became part of a collaborative community of other spider species, producing the hybrid webs that would become part of the display. Here is where multispecies interactions took place, where spiders built their web styles in relation to existing web structures, leading to either the adaptation or modification of existing spider structures or the tearing down of earlier, species-specific webs built by another spider, starting their versions anew. All webs presented in the show were made by spiders, first hosted at the artist's studio in Berlin, and then transported to Palais de Tokyo to be displayed.[3]

In a vitrine layout recalling a natural history museum, *Webs of At-tent(s)ion* (2018, Figure 8.2) displays spider webs in a darkened room, lit only by an array of carefully positioned spotlights which allows visitors

Figure 8.2 Tomás Saraceno, *Webs of At-tent(s)ion*, 2018. Installation view at *ON AIR*, carte blanche exhibition to Tomás Saraceno, Palais de Tokyo, Paris, 2018. Curated by Rebecca Lamarche-Vadel. Courtesy of the artist
Source: © Photography by Studio Tomás Saraceno, 2018.

to move freely – if carefully – around and between the hybrid formations that are placed, for the most part, at human eye level. Appearing to be free-standing architectural forms, the elaborate details of the web structures emerge from the inky black space, compelling us closer, visually and literally highlighting the complex arrangements and links of threads and hybrid webs installed in their transparent frames. Illuminated, the seventy-six Cartesian cubes – for the wandering, measuring analytical gaze infused with the subtlety of the very liveness of the organic structures within – appear as a kind of light installation. They showcase a different set of architectural structures than ones of concrete and steel; the uplifted, breathing airiness of spider silks respond to the displacements of air within the room, hinting at the most gentle of audience interactions with the installed pieces, as one moves through the room.

After navigating through the layered structures of webs, visitors entering the next room are enveloped in a vibrating hum, shifting their register from visuals to soundscapes. This happens even before the visitor's human eyes can adjust to the dimmed lights, and start to see the slowly moving strings, themselves made from modified spider silk. *Sounding the Air* (2018) creates a slow rhythmical aural pattern with long strings, filling the space and the air, a softly moving sculpture, as the threads catch and release rays of light, and shift slowly in and out of view. The sound frames and fills the space with its presence in tandem with the subtly moving sculpture shaped like a large-scale Aeolian harp. This musical instrument is situated within the lineage that, in Douglas Kahn's words, could be called the media art of energies and earth magnitudes (Kahn 2013). With sounds produced by nature, it acts as an interface between technical media and natural formations of sound and electromagnetics. Besides the environmental surrounds of such electrosonic sounds, the threshold of perception of sound becomes a key epistemological category that introduces a broader focus of soundscapes, of perceptions and of vibrations – some of which also differentiate between humans and non-humans according to perceptual capacities.

In many of the projects, the notion of interspecies communication is framed as one of play between spiders and humans, and between spider species in the architectural constructs of hybrid webs as was seen in the *Webs of At-tent(s)ion*. The acoustic worlds and soundscapes of interspecies communication were part of the Jam Sessions that synchronise and play together with both the web's acoustics and their use for signaling; in the spirit of experimental music, this meant creating musical instruments with which to listen and communicate with spiders (Saraceno et al. 2019). Such interspecies 'jamming' is also present in the *Particular Matter(s)* (2018) installation also part of the *ON AIR* exhibition: the interactions of air, spider webs and dust with the audience movement affecting the microscopic dust in the space, which in turn interacts with the web that is both visually amplified in a spotlight beam and sonically amplified into a speaker: 'The presence of visitors in the space generates new variations in this evolving ecology.'[4]

Moving deeper into the building still, the webs grow to human size – and larger. Consuming an entire room, *Algo-r(h)i(y)thms* (2018, Figure 8.3) is a living sculpture that functions as an infrasoundscape, combining the visual rhizome with the possibilities of vibrating touch-based communication. Stepping into this interconnected ecology, the participant becomes part of the orchestration of space and enters the feedback systems functioning below 20 Hz, the threshold of human audibility. Here, the acoustic interspecies network has grown in size to become visible and haptic. Continuing into other spaces of the exhibition, visitors find sonic and visual instruments and mechanisms that highlight the different scales of webs, dust, structures and air. The constructions shift registers between the natural and the technical, narrated as experiments, as jam sessions, and other terms that nod at the legacy of avant-garde arts of the twentieth century. The material and narrative formats of the curated exhibition incorporate Saraceno's practice

Figure 8.3 Tomás Saraceno, *Algo-r(h)i(y)thms*, 2018. Installation view at *ON AIR*, carte blanche exhibition to Tomás Saraceno, Palais de Tokyo, Paris, 2018. Curated by Rebecca Lamarche-Vadel. Courtesy of the artist
Source: © Photography by Studio Tomás Saraceno, 2018.

into the lineage of contemporary art practices that consider instability and dynamics of space and signals from Cold War period experimental media arts, such as Alvin Lucier (who also performed in the Jam Sessions),[5] to more recent contemporaries of Saraceno, such as Olafur Eliasson. As we will see later, this link also relates to the theme of dynamic models that becomes central to understanding Saraceno's ways of working with architectures, complex installations and images.

The *ON AIR* exhibition is both a useful summary of the long-term projects of the Studio and a provocation for addressing how installations and collaborative practices relate to contemporary methods in art-science research that also speak to environmental humanities such as animal studies. The installation's working objects are also objects working across multiple functions, from art to epistemological concerns. They are at the centre of the various forms of interdisciplinary and interspecies collaborations. In Saraceno's case, this hybrid set of concerns can be articulated by asking what sort of conceptual, visual, sculptural, energetic and aural objects function in these circuits of art that work through large-scale teams and are constructed in collaborative settings with material engineering and sciences as well as climate science and meteorology, bioacoustics and biotremology? How are animal energies of *zoē* framed in these methods?

While collaborative labour has defined Studio Tomás Saraceno's work as a collective of multiple simultaneous projects housed in a studio that fills a large several-storey building block in Berlin, it is the combination of skill sets, institutional contexts and the broader context of arts and engineering that becomes a way to discuss the working objects at play. To speak of 'working objects' in the context of interspecies collaboration is not, however, meant to imply anthropocentric objectification – even if such a danger should always be kept in mind. Hence, to carefully address the interspecies performances (Cull Ó Maoilearca 2019) as such would imply a necessary, sensitive awareness towards understanding the specific forms and materialities of communication that emerge from the spiders' world, and in many ways, the specific research contexts in which the Studio has worked has also facilitated this awareness. Besides ethical considerations of how the spiders are cared for in the studio environment, specialist knowledge about ethologies of non-human animals and the long-term iterative sense of care should be part of the work (ibid.). Interspecies working objects also mean specific job roles and labour, and in the case of the Studio Saraceno, for example, a spider carer; this is where environmental humanities and ethics meet discussions in the history of science, and science and technology studies.

Instead of focusing on the more citizen science-oriented *Aerocene* project,[6] I will turn to questions of models, diagrams and aesthetics-cum-material epistemology as articulated in experimental situations, stabilised into objects of scientific knowledge and objects of contemporary arts curation. In other words, I move to take up how the notion of the web functions as a central architectural and material object that articulates multiple contexts and scales while also becoming spatially located as a sculptural object. The recursive nature of the web itself allows for functions across art, nature, engineering and modelling, as well as speculative architecture, from the techniques of laser scan 3D visualisation (Su et al. 2018) to structural engineering.

Webs as diagrams

To state the obvious, the web has become relatively pervasive as a cultural metaphor since (at least) the middle of the 1990s and emergence of the world wide web. This only adds to the difficulty of how to address it as a relevant material figure. Studio Tomás Saraceno's solution is not only to refer to the rhetorical attraction of the web as a relational model of sensation and knowledge but also to employ it as a material, even dynamic working object that enables formalisable knowledge. Hence, the scientific contexts of such works relate to material sciences and especially biomateriomics, bioacoustics and biotremology, as well as animal social and collective behaviour (Saraceno et al. 2019). There is a sense of hybrid agenda between the material instances of the webs as singularly interesting visual and material pieces and their mathematical and abstract qualities. Saraceno stages the webs as living sculptural diagrams, situated as objects of visual art. Yet, they are indicative of other worlds and potentials of abstraction and follow the definition of diagrams as put forth by Bender and Marrinan (2010).[7] But unlike the genealogy of diagrams Bender and Marrinan track from the late eighteenth-century encyclopaedia to nineteenth-century scientific visualisations, Saraceno's works are articulated between dynamic sculptures and their complex ecology of images as scientific visualisations, which is why we can consider them diagrams, as such. They have an interesting relation to living forms as inscribing their own traces in a manner that also resonates with the focus on autographic visualisation, to use Dietmar Offenhuber's term (Offenhuber 2019): they are traces and diagrams of their own making, in the process of their own making.

Of all the Studio's work exhibited in *ON AIR*, *Webs of At-tent(s) ion* (Figures 8.1 and 8.2) frames spider webs as architecture and organic design solutions for complex structures. As volumetric diagrams, and as speculative design, the dozens of examples in the carbon fibre frames display arthropod architecture – a theme identifiable as part of late nineteenth- and early twentieth-century architectural discourse already (Parikka 2010) – as well as the legacy of artistic anti-architecture ways of dealing with questions of construction, space, energy and materiality. Mark Wigley aptly characterises Saraceno as part of the lineage of experimental anti-architecture from the 1920s to the 1980s, from Buckminster Fuller, Frei Otto, Konrad Wachsmann and Cedric Price to Constantinos Doxiadis, Superstudio and Archizoom, 'who systematically dissolved the solidity of buildings into diaphanous webs, networks of almost nothing in which society would now suspend itself' (Wigley 2018: 51). On the one hand, at the crossroads of multiple genealogies and contemporary contexts, the web is about (visual) models for speculative architectures. On the other hand, it is about the animal communication of invertebrate species. The web becomes articulated as signals and vibrations of acoustic ecologies, and as extended cognition. Each articulation is a reminder and acts to highlight that the theme of hybrid conjunctions is regularly functioning across multiple scales of the Studio's methods.

Switching between architecture and extended cognition, and signal and sonic communication, such themes are carried over, recursively repeated in different contexts and at different scales. Focusing on the sensory mapping of extended cognition, the room-sized web of *Algo-r(h) i(y)thms* (Figure 8.3) is an ongoing multi-iteration experiment, echoing Antonio Damasio and Andy Clark's work on the embodied brain. But this web can also be understood through N. Katherine Hayles's arguments about the cognitive non-conscious functioning in ways that are 'embedded in highly complex systems that are both adaptive and recursive' (Hayles 2017: 46). The installed web of infrasounds and vibrations is but one version of spatialised infrastructures of cognition. And while signal transmission is an integral part of current scientific research on spiders' structures and vibrations as informational (Mortimer et al. 2019), the focus also allows for the discussion of broader implications of the connection between cognition and architecture, where the web becomes a model for this artistically driven research work. Material constructions are dynamic models of users and their environments (cf. Eliasson 2007), and this modelling echoes much in scientific research – outside contemporary art and architecture – that argues non-human animal cognition operates outside the central nervous system in surrounding habitats and structures: 'spiders behave as if planning routes in advance, show a sense of numerosity, learn conditional tactics of aggressive mimicry, reverse previous learned associations, and adjust their behaviour to altered conditions in a variety of ways' (Japyassú and Laland 2017: 378). In other words, spiders are treated as being and having advanced logistics systems that are also then transformed into working objects for the multiscalar work of contemporary art-science projects.

Hence, it is essential to consider Saraceno's work not as a *reflection* of theoretical work on extended cognition and the cognitive non-conscious, but as a more complex *working with* of the shared objects of research – and the staging and producing of working objects. These, too, can also unfold the question from the other way around, starting from the situated, material, spatial webs against and on which various theoretical objects attach. As a working object, the web is fine-tuned in relation to contemporary theoretical discourse but irreducible to it. It acts recursively in relation to forms of knowledge that are gathered across humanities discourse, animal communication research and other fields mentioned already. In other words, besides the rhetorical figure of the web as one of connections and relations, the materials are dynamic components that demonstrate a sense of potentials of built and grown space that shift from animal communication to diagrammatic and spatial vocabularies. The 'surfaces, envelopes and interstices' are also significant in how they 'transmit sensory information between and among scalar registers', as Sasha Engelman points out about the Studio's work as modelling one form of an architectural dynamism (Engelman 2017a: 20, see also Engelmann 2021). This position towards space corresponds closely to how Olafur Eliasson – with whom Saraceno worked before his own artistic career – has characterised contemporary sculptural work as models that map dynamics of space as temporal, changing, and co-produced, where 'the user's interaction with other people co-produces space which in turn is a co-producer of interaction. By focusing on our agency in this critical exchange, it is possible to bring our spatial responsibility to the fore' (Eliasson 2007: 19).

In such critical exchanges, the space of extended cognition and communication in the interspecies and interdisciplinary context is mapped through spider webs and related constructs; spatial relations of dynamic sculptural diagrams can be addressed as surfaces and envelopes that redesign space and its dimensions, thus modelling the movement and relations that constitute it – whether that of animal cognition or other forms of agency that extend across architectural space. Here, 'cognition' is understood in a similar sense as I outline in my book *Insect Media* (2010) to refer to the relational, ecological creativity of different animals from insects to others. Creativity is an emergent result of ecological, ethological interactions of animals in different spatial settings, with different spatial affordances. *Algo-r(h)i(y)thms* is laid out as a vibrational universe, troubling any focus on atomistic agency through its spatial modelling of relations as localised (cf. Latour 2011). Its threads and webs embody a collective subject entangled in shared signal space. For Studio Tomás Saraceno, the rhetoric reaches out to even cosmic dimensions, demonstrating how, although the web might be a scalar device for artistic discourse, still, it hints at the function of the web as capture, an epistemological register of modalities of perception that escape the human sensorium.

> The signals that the participants rearrange come from different places and speak other idioms: polluting particles and temperature differentials, supernovas, and distant galaxies, shifting temperatures and weather patterns, local spiders' vibrational communication. From infinitely small to infinitely large, these movements between nested scales cause the room to shift in response: the lights fade, echoes increase. And in the darkness, the room enlarges infinitely, much like the expanding universe, asking those present to listen, or else face the eternal silence of extinction. (Saraceno 2018: n.p.)

The room-sized piece functions as a twofold articulation of the methodological activities of signal and registering, of trace and inscription, of capture and graphing. The focus on signal transmission gives way to recording and sensors as the central trope of capture: what sort of near-invisible signals or weak vibrations are recordable, and hence measurable? And, in this manner, are also open to being modelled? Here, the body of the audience member is involved in the vibrations of the threads, producing this situation also as a collective one: one or more people in the same vibration space mediated through and with the threads (see Figure 8.3).

To clarify the point about modelling and measurement, I want to pair *Algo-r(h)i(y)thms* with *Aerographies* (2018). Another piece by the Studio, it combines work on spiders and balloons to create living inscription systems, exemplifying the studio's practice-based investigation into material epistemologies of inscription (see Figure 8.4).

> Pens suspended to balloons draw with black carbon ink pollution from the air of Mumbai and reveal trajectories drawn by the air, enlarging the territories of our imagination. Spider's webs laid out on paper produce strange new spider maps, while the trajectories of balloons that float freely in the air without the help of fossil fuels trace out Aeroglyphs. Together these 'Aerographies' are letters, characters and signatures of a new language for the Aerocene era. Every gesture, every interaction and event leaves a trace. Drawing with the air, the movements of persons, sounds, and spider/webs translate as the potential language of earthly phenomena; an emergent cartography of the air. (Saraceno 2018: n.p.)

Figure 8.4 Tomás Saraceno, *Aerographies*, 2018. Installation view at *ON AIR*,
carte blanche exhibition to Tomás Saraceno, Palais de Tokyo, Paris, 2018.
Curated by Rebecca Lamarche-Vadel. Courtesy of the artist
Source: © Photography by Studio Tomás Saraceno, 2018.

While the poetic description of the balloon sculpture might offer
a generic atmosphere for the work, the science and media studies-
driven observations about the experimental set-up are compelling:
the apparatus of inscription is installed as an element that measures
which dynamic time-bound events move across scales. In addition to
the piece's mood and atmosphere, the various sculptural systems con-
sist of graphs, traces and various levels of material links that move
the discourse of 'extended cognition' into experimental apparatuses.
In this manner, the shift takes place from cognition to technique,
from embodied forms of perception to technologies of measurement
and experiment. When historian of science Hans-Jörg Rheinberger
(2007) writes in another context of spider webs *just like models* for
experimental systems, we can here, for the sake of argument and the
materials at hand, remove the 'just like': these webs *are* experimental
systems that both *capture* signals, traces, vibrations and materials, and
also *model* their own behaviour in a recursive fashion. The webs are
artistic – and sometimes animal – versions of experimental systems
that also at the same time inscribe their own function in a chain of
extended operations that deal with questions such as cognition and
capture of signals.[8]

Diffractive models

The theme and concept of extended cognition speaks to the multiple operative chains of cognition: from human embodied cognition it shifts to address the environments of support that distribute cognition as a material, felt entity that is discussed at times as architecture, at times as spider communication, and at times as interspecies performative sonic 'jamming' of attempts to artistically synchronise human and non-human signal worlds. Furthermore, cognition becomes understood as a large-scale system of measure and vibration, relations, and their feedback, and this is where Saraceno's background in architecture comes again to the fore while connecting to the role of modelling. The webs, experimental systems of spatialised knowledge apparatuses, take place, at first, as material sculptures, and, second, as models that establish iterative, recursive, diffractive series. This continues the discursive themes of decentring the human in animal studies, posthumanities and new materialisms, while adding this artistic and practice-based sense of building and exhibiting other levels of cognition beyond the human to the mix of environmental humanities. While some of Saraceno's work plays with themes of cosmic webs as hypothesised in astrophysics research and visualisations, I am interested in how webs and other works become models, diagrams and objects that lend themselves both to (environmental) humanities theorisation and scientific investigation. This interest is less about bio-mimetic design than it is about a focus on practices that speak to material instantiations of cross-disciplinary work, which is also how Engelmann frames Studio Tomás Saraceno's work: the image-making of the studio works in interaction with and parallel to scientific visualisations, establishing transversal links from studio work with spider webs to astrophysical simulations (Engelmann 2019). Engelmann's way of addressing the 'ecology of images' in production and simulation as generative experimentation (ibid.: 307) is the reference point for a lot of the projects that I address as diffractive modelling that can be seen as one version of the broader theme of working objects that began this chapter.

While the usual course is to think of the material, designed, spatial models as 'crystallizations of scientific theory' (Miyazaki 2015), I am interested in how they work in slightly alternative ways, that is, as material epistemologies in artistic and experimental systems (Pickering 2010). Practices of modelling connect arts and technoscience (Miyazaki 2015) in how they are fundamentally generative instead of merely reactive (see Burnett and Solomon 2007); they are reality-producing instead of reality-imitating, and artistic works can also be seen as influentially developing complexifying notions of that said reality (see Eliasson 2007: 19). As D. Graham Burnett observed, models, in the history of science, are a way to understand scalar shifts that can happen through such practices: 'The power of thinking with models lies in the occasions they occasion for rapid and obscure oscillation between "as thinking" and "is thinking"' (Burnett and Solomon 2007: 49).

This is a way of rephrasing the function of working objects too. Hence, as working objects, models enable particular statements to emerge that are not mere illustrations of pre-existing theory. They can work in an assemblage that is not merely artistic nor scientific, but in the process of their making, shift from the artistic studio to the scientific laboratory and back via the spaces of curation and exhibition. We can claim that models don't crystallise theory, but precede, regulate, enable, effectuate and channel them (cf. Daston and Galison 1992). This position also feeds into the developing argument about the role of material epistemologies of sculptural and architectural objects of Studio Tomás Saraceno in contexts outside art, including environmental humanities. This is emphasised even more so because much of the work deals with interspecies collaborations that need to be cared for as dynamic, living non-human worlds that do not merely perform already pre-existing expectations.

In this manner, I propose to think Studio Tomás Saraceno's architectural and sculptural objects as diffractive models. As Shintaro Miyazaki argues, we can think of speculative design models as diffractive, borrowing the term from Donna Haraway and Karen Barad, but replacing it from cultural theory to 'designerly work and aesthetic experimentation' (Miyazaki 2015: 3). In its complex and influential use in material feminism, the term diffraction has worked as a methodology of reading (Van der Tuin 2018) and as an onto-epistemological stance (Barad 2007). Barad's position extends Haraway's, who already suggested diffraction as an alternative to the other optical concept used for thinking: reflection, 'whereas reflection is about mirroring and sameness, diffraction attends to patterns of difference' (Barad 2007: 29). This suggestion establishes a scene where material interactions – or intra-actions and entanglements in Barad's vocabulary – are not only a reproduction of reality but channel its transformation. While Barad establishes a route from the situations of material production of diffraction as observed in physics (including her field, quantum theory) to a methodology in cultural theory and new materialism, it travels even further, in ways that become useful to understand the work of material apparatuses in contemporary visual practices, such as that of Studio Tomás Saraceno. While for Barad, Haraway and some of the new materialist developments diffraction has become a narrative and political technology (Haraway 2018; Barad 2007: 71), it also incorporates the potential as a 'material-semiotic apparatus' visible in the dynamic sculptures, visualisations and architectures discussed in this chapter.

Diffraction is a conceptual and a material-semiotic device that responds to the dilemma of how we think complex matters in material ways; how we approach artistic and designer work that does not reduce it to representational schemas or public communication of scientific facts; and how we not merely reflect theories but participate in their production and transformative potential. Diffractive models are real-world agents that are 'interfering, blurring, bending and transforming with the content under study' (Miyazaki 2015: 3), producing situations that exhibit dynamics of the model in question, and hence, produce active differentiation in the spaces where they function, be that in the studio, an exhibition or situations of cross-disciplinary academic research work. As such models, Studio Tomás Saraceno's objects cross boundaries between the contexts of nature – working with live arachnoids as collaborators – and different sciences, where the working object circulates in the ecology of images of studio situations and scientific visualisations (Engelmann 2019).

As Engelmann notes in her extensive ethnographic research on Saraceno's collaborative projects in collaboration with arthropods such as the golden silk orb-weaver spider Nephila, the central claim is that the webs express a recursive feature of their status as architectures and as material epistemologies. While localisable as a studio practice – the Studio Tomás Saraceno has its own 'spider room' – the webs provide a nested ontology of relations. Engelmann writes about her fieldwork in the studio:

> there is never only one web. These collaborative experiments are always already about the relations between webbed forms. They are about comparing webs to other webs, through analogy, metaphor and metonymy, but more precisely about the meshing, layering and attracting of webbed forms to each other. (Engelmann 2017b: 162)

The web is diffractively employed as a situated, material and embodied model that shifts across scales, and is itself enabled to shift scale. The webs are volumetric, and they are not merely exhibited in space but reform the very notions of space: they offer multiple situations where outsides and insides fold without a clear sense of hierarchy of which level sits inside what. In Latour's characterisation, the multiple localities organised by those webs in Saraceno's work are heterarchic (in contrast to hierarchic), and the 'visual experience is not situated in any fixed ontological domain, nor at any given scale' (Latour 2011).

The visual experience shifts scale in institutional ways, from curated exhibition space to a synthetic image used in various scientific and computational operations. Webs are approached as volumetric, three-dimensional structures and also as potentials of traits that are not immediately perceptible without particular analytical apparatuses or instruments. Besides metaphors, metonymies and analogies, the works' material presence is also diagrammatic: they point to the powers of abstraction that can be materialised even further, for example, as scientific images; they 'summarize complex events and relations into synthetic images' (Bratton 2016) which then extend possible effects outside their original site and situation of emergence.

In the case of the Studio, the synthetic images include the development of visualisation techniques for laser-scanned modelling of three-dimensional objects such as funnels and sheet webs. The work in new visualisation techniques was driven by Tomás Saraceno, leading into collaborations with the TU Darmstadt Photogrammetry Institute in 2009 and later experiments, including those with Markus Buehler's engineering and material science research team at MIT (see Su et al. 2018). The spider web is turned into a laser image, which then functions as the working object of research that is concerned with its structural and topological qualities. The images 'precisely map the real web architecture to a meso-scale model', with further potential for designing 'innovative 3D spider web-inspired structures' (Su et al. 2018: 9). Exhibited in *ON AIR*, these webs and images comprised *How to Entangle the Universe in a Spider Web?* (2018, Figure 8.5). They are already multiple (working)

Figure 8.5 Tomás Saraceno, *How to Entangle the Universe in a Spider Web?*, 2018. Laser, spider silk, carbon fibre. Installation view at *ON AIR*, carte blanche exhibition to Tomás Saraceno, Palais de Tokyo, Paris, 2018. Curated by Rebecca Lamarche-Vadel. Courtesy of the artist
Source: © Photography by Studio Tomás Saraceno, 2018.

objects: objects of three-dimensional architectures of vibrational signals; exemplary of silk fibre mechanics (Su and Buehler 2016); objects for speculative design interested in 'translation of new materials into a new program for social and ecological organization' (Bratton 2016).

The studio's MIT collaboration with Buehler focused on mapping the material qualities of webs within the contexts of holistic biomate-riomic approaches and even machine learning, allowing for differently speculative but completely viable directions to emerge: spider webs as already existing optimal structural solutions and material affordances that could be used in engineering and construction.[9] Shifting and abstracted from spatial situations, the web changes into a model for material vari-ations and optimised structures. Various social insects, such as colony behaviour, have already over the past decades been incorporated into this version of AI as both artificial intelligence in digital machines and animal intelligence as a model for optimisation patterns (Parikka 2010). So, too, arachnoid materials and behaviour for this sense of extended cognition speak to the pairing of art and science, as well as the interspe-cies trio of art-science-invertebrates that shift registers between mathe-matics and volumetrics, animal architecture and logistics, art objects and material modelisation. Somewhere between a mathematical model, a visual image, a material sculpture and a theoretically productive working object, the web captures a multitude of interests of knowledge and prac-tices of knowledge creation across the aesthetic and scientific spectra.[10]

Conclusions

Studio Tomás Saraceno's *ON AIR* exhibition (Paris 2018–19) and its studio practices offer an entry point to what practice-led environmental humanities are capable of doing differently beyond methods that deal primarily with text or theoretical and conceptual approaches alone. An assemblage of *zoē*-driven animal architectures, spider webs, scientific vis-ualisations and theoretical humanities, their work exemplifies an ecology of images that circulates between 'mathematics and code, cosmologi-cal theories, arachnology, production networks, and cultural semiosis' (Engelmann 2019: 306) in ways that produce the semiotic-material dif-fraction patterns that are a central characteristic of the studio's work. The ecology of images is fundamentally important due to the produc-tion of material models, volumetric diagrams and working objects that connect a multitude of institutional situations and disciplinary contexts. In the context of environmental and meteorological arts, Randerson argues: '[a]rtists, unlike scientists, have traditionally operated in the realm of the unmeasurable; sensations are created perceptually that can-not be described mathematically' (Randerson 2018: 49). This separation between experiential and formalisable is not a sustainable division when it comes to projects such as Saraceno's that operate in the collaborative settings of art and science. The sculptures, installations and models are not merely experiential objects for curatorial situations, but in many cases also function as scientific working objects, as demonstrated in several of their projects, from biotremology to material sciences, and artistic examples from *Webs of At-tent(s)ion* to *Algo-r(h)i(y)thms.*

I proposed to address the Studio's material production as working objects, which relate both to their (art and architectural) studio practices and how too those studio practices relate to concepts in STS and history of science. Working objects are, to return to Daston and Galison, 'materials from which concepts are formed and to which they are applied' (Daston and Galison 1992: 85). The models, scales and objects that emerge in the collective studio situations are one way of thinking about the material with which environmental humanities works, where aesthetic concepts, material objects, scientific modes of imagining and multiple institutional investments are part of the conditions of theoretical work. The studio's multispecies investigations and studio routines, scientific imaging, post-fossil fuel experiments with slow planetary balloon travel (e.g. in the *Aerocene* project, left out of this chapter's focus) are expressions of the hybrid constellation of practice and concepts situated in the contemporary cultural and environmental context. This sort of artistic activity, sometimes coined speculative design – or even anti-architecture – becomes an entry point to environmental humanities. It also becomes a demonstration that visual and material methods offer more than an illustration of environmental issues or representational approaches to non-human animals.

What I have presented in this chapter concerning the diffractive models, research insights and visual methods that shift between epistemological significance and aesthetic attraction does not resolve all the questions that emerge in these collaborations. While the question of interspecies collaboration is the primary driver of the spider and hybrid web projects, there is an interesting question, briefly raised, as to how this impacts our sense of the working object when this includes a non-human animal partner engaged in the work. Another issue of consequence is to develop further insights into questions of attention and care that are central to Studio Saraceno's work, including discussions about ethics codes for work – including specifically artistic work – with invertebrate species.[11] Such themes are central to a lot of the themes raised and addressed in animal studies, environmental humanities and critical posthumanities; what this kind of artistic practice then offers is a further methodological angle for how aesthetic, ethical and epistemic issues coalesce and feed into zoētic perspectives through spider ethologies (Bisshop 2022). The works by Studio Saraceno are in this way also ways to investigate the cognitive capacities and creativity of spiders and other non-human animals; to not just 'discover' their different creative skills in how they relate and reform their environments but to reframe some human-centric notions of creativity through such art-science research.

Notes

1. An earlier version of this chapter was published as 'A Recursive Web of Models: Studio Tomás Saraceno's Working Objects' in Parikka (2020). This reworked article relates to the AUFF (Aarhus University) funded project Design and Aesthetics for Environmental Data (2021–3). I want to thank Elise Misao Hunchuck for her expert guidance in formulating the arguments and the language in this chapter and Ally Bisshop for her generous help in elaborating on and explaining many of the details about the Studio's work. A thank you also to Tomás Saraceno and the Studio staff for sharing images and thoughts. In addition, I am grateful to Sasha Engelmann, Ryan Bishop, Joanna Page and the anonymous reviewer for their helpful feedback when writing and editing this chapter. An earlier version was presented as an IKKM (Bauhaus University, Weimar) lecture and at the Art in the Anthropocene conference (Trinity College Dublin, 2019).

2. For existing research on environmental arts, I point the reader to the various issues of the *Environmental Humanities* journal (Duke University Press) as one example of past years of theoretical engagement with art practices.

3. A special thanks to Ally Bisshop from Studio Tomás Saraceno for clarifying details about the hybrid webs as a multispecies project and also the logistics and practices of working with spiders. For a list of which species participated in the hybrid webs, please see: https://studiotomassaraceno.org/webs-of-at-tentsion/

4. Particular Matter(s) Jam Sessions, online introduction with images: https://studiotomassaraceno.org/particular-matters/

5. From Saraceno's *ON AIR* online description of the performance:'Alvin Lucier, historical figure of experimental music from the 1960s until today imagines an unreleased work for *ON AIR* during which his heartbeat is picked up by a special sensor, routed through the silk strings of a Qin, ancient Chinese stringed instrument, and sent to the moon. In about two-and-a-half seconds each heartbeat will bounce back to Earth. The sound of the heartbeats will change according to reflection points from the Moon's surface.' https://www.palaisdetokyo.com/en/event/voices-collide-day-aerocene

6. See the Aerocene project website at: https://aerocene.org/

7. 'A diagram is a proliferation of manifestly selective packets of dissimilar data correlated in an explicitly process-oriented array that has some of the attributes of a representation but is situated in the world like an object' (Bender and Marrinan 2010: 7).

8. The technical side of the experimental set-up has received less attention. The Studio's expertise and contribution to both artistic and curatorial contexts and scientific research also relate to the use of technical instruments, including piezoelectric sensors for the registering of pressure, acceleration, vibration; custom made microphones; and the laser scanning of complex volumes (which are also contexts where the works shift from being a display at an art exhibition to being a model in and for scientific collaborations). As images, sculptures and visual art, they become working objects for this collaborative enterprise that continues the theme of diagrams and models.

9. Tomás Saraceno and Ally Bisshop, private communication, JP studio visit 21 May 2019.

10. While the spider might be unthinkable outside the web (Wigley 2018: 51), the web is thinkable without the spider (cf. László Barabási 2002) as scale-free network theory demonstrates in its own version of mathematical formalisation of such structures as part of the lineage of graph theory. The open cube frames of the exhibition space hint of this larger theme of modelling efficiency and optimisation of natural entities that include webs.

11. Tomás Saraceno and Ally Bisshop, private communication, JP studio visit 21 May 2019.

References

Ballard, Susan (2017), 'New Ecological Sympathies Thinking about Contemporary Art in the Age of Extinction', *Environmental Humanities*, 9(2): 255–79.

Barad, Karen (2007), *Meeting the Universe Halfway*, Durham, NC: Duke University Press.

Bender, John and Michael Marrinan (2010), *Culture of the Diagram*, Stanford, CA: Stanford University Press.

Bisshop, Ally (2022), 'Arachnomadology: A Zoētic Framework for Queering Stories of Spider Sex, Life, and Death', unpublished article manuscript.

Braidotti, Rosi (2016), 'The Critical Posthumanities; Or, is Medianatures to Naturecultures as *Zoe* is to *Bios*?', *Cultural Politics*, 12(6): 380–90.

Braidotti, Rosi (2019), *Posthuman Knowledge*, Cambridge: Polity.

Bratton, Benjamin (2016), 'On Speculative Design', *Dis magazine*: http://dis-magazine.com/discussion/81971/on-speculative-design-benjamin-h-bratton/ (last accessed 2 February 2022).

Burnett, Graham D. and Jonathan D. Solomon (2007), 'Masters of the Universe', in Emily Abruzzo, Eric Ellingsen and Jonathan D. Solomon (eds), *Models*, New York: 306090/Princeton Architectural Press, pp. 44–51.

Cull Ó Maoilearca, Laura (2019), 'The Ethics of Interspecies Performance: Empathy beyond Analogy in Fevered Sleep's Sheep Pig Goat', *Theatre Journal*, 71(3): E1–E22.

Daston, Lorraine and Peter Galison, (1992), 'The Image of Objectivity', *Representations*, 40: 81–128.

Eliasson, Olafur (2007), 'Models are Real', in Emily Abruzzo, Eric Ellingsen and Jonathan D. Solomon (eds), *Models*, New York: 306090/Princeton Architectural Press, pp. 44–51.

Engelmann, Sasha (2017a), *The Cosmological Aesthetics of Tomás Saraceno's Atmospheric Experiments*, Doctoral thesis, University of Oxford, available at: https://pure.royalholloway.ac.uk/portal/en/publications/the-cosmological-aesthetics-of-toms-saracenos-atmospheric-experiments(89b6fe2f-8f0d-4335-8143-139ecb95dbb0).html (last accessed 2 February 2022).

Engelmann, Sasha (2017b), 'Social Spiders and Hybrid Webs at Studio Tomás Saraceno', *Cultural Geographies*, 24(1): 161–9.

Engelmann, Sasha (2019), 'Of Spiders and Simulations: Artmachines at Studio Tomás Saraceno', *Cultural Geographies*, 26(3): 305–22.

Engelmann, Sasha (2021) *Sensing Art in the Atmosphere: Elemental Lures and Aerosolar Practices*, New York: Routledge.

Engelmann, Sasha and Derek McCormack (2018), 'Elemental Aesthetics: On Artistic Experiments with Solar Energy', *Annals of the American Association of Geographers*, 108(1): 241–59.

Greaves, Tom (2013), 'Environmental Arts as First Philosophy: This Too a NeoPresocratic Manifesto', *Environmental Humanities*, 3(1): 149–55.

Haraway, Donna (2018), *Modest Witness & Second Millenium. Femaleman Meets Oncomouse: Feminism and Technoscience*, 2nd edn, New York: Routledge.

Hayles, N. Katherine (2017), *Unthought. The Power of the Cognitive Nonconscious*, Chicago and London: University of Chicago Press.

Japyassú, Hilton F. and Kevin N. Laland (2017), 'Extended Spider Cognition', *Animal Cognition*, 20: 375–95.

Kahn, Douglas (2013), *Earth Sound, Earth Signal. Energies and Earth Magnitude in the Arts*, Berkeley, CA: University of California Press.

László Barabási, Alberto (2002), *Linked*, New York: Plume/Penguin.

Latour, Bruno (2011), 'Some Experiments in Art and Politics', *e-flux Journal*, 23: https://www.e-flux.com/journal/23/67790/some-experiments-in-art-and-politics/ (last accessed 2 February 2022).

McCormack, Derek P. (2017), 'Elemental Infrastructures for Atmospheric Media: On Stratospheric Variations, Value and the Commons', *Environment and Planning D: Society and Space*, 35(3): 418–37.

Miyazaki, Shintaro (2015), 'How to Talk about Serious Matters of Complexity with Models as Agents: A Speculative Essay on Artistic and Design-based Research', *Journal for Research Cultures*, 1(1): 1–5.

Mortimer, Beth, Alejandro Soler, Lucas Wilkins and Fritz Vollrath (2019), 'Decoding the Locational Information in the Orb-Web Vibrations of *Araneus diadematus* and *Zygiella x-notata*', *Journal of the Royal Society Interface*, 16(154).

Offenhuber, Dietmar (2019), 'Data by Proxy – Material Traces as Autographic Visualizations', presentation at the *IEEE Vis 2019* conference, available at: https://arxiv.org/abs/1907.05454 (last accessed 2 February 2022).

Page, Joanna (2020), 'Tomás Saraceno and the Ethics of the Sublime in the Aerocene', in Lucy Bollington and Paul Merchant (eds), *Latin American*

Culture and The Limits of the Human, University of Florida Press (forthcoming).

Parikka, Jussi (2010), *Insect Media. An Archaeology of Animals and Technology*, Minneapolis: University of Minnesota Press.

Parikka, Jussi (2015), *A Geology of Media*, Minneapolis: University of Minnesota Press.

Parikka, Jussi (2020), 'A Recursive Web of Models: Studio Tomás Saraceno's Working Objects', *Configurations*, 28(3): 309–32.

Peters, John Durham (2015), *Marvelous Clouds*, Chicago: The University of Chicago Press.

Philippopoulos-Mihalopoulos, Andreas (2016), 'Withdrawing from Atmosphere: An Ontology of Air Partitioning and Affective Engineering', *Environment and Planning D: Society and Space*, 34(1): 150–67.

Pickering, Andrew (2010), *The Cybernetic Brain: Sketches of Another Future*, Chicago: The University of Chicago Press.

Randerson, Janine (2018), *Weather as Medium. Toward a Meteorological Art*, Cambridge, MA: The MIT Press.

Rheinberger, Hans-Jörg (2007), 'Man weiss nicht genau, was man nicht weiss', *Neue Zürcher Zeitung*, 5 May, available at: https://www.nzz.ch/articleELG88-1.354487 (last accessed 2 February 2022).

Rose, Deborah Bird, Thom van Dooren, Matthew Chrulew, Stuart Cooke, Matthew Kearnes and Emily O'Gorman (2012), 'Thinking Through the Environment, Unsettling the Humanities', *Environmental Humanities*, 1(1): 1–5.

Saraceno, Tomás (2018), On Air exhibition press package, Studio Tomás Saraceno/Palais De Tokyo, Paris.

Saraceno, Tomás, Ally Bisshop, Adrian Krell and Roland Mühlethaler (2019), 'Arachnid Orchestras: Artistic Research in Vibrational Interspecies Communication', in P. S. M. Hill et al. (eds), *Biotremology: Studying Vibrational Behavior*, Cham, Switzerland: Springer, pp. 485–509.

Su, Isabelle and Markus J. Buehler (2016), 'Nanomechanics of Silk: The Fundamentals of a Strong, Tough and Versatile Material', *Nanotechnology*, 27(30).

Su, Isabelle, Qin Zhao, Tomás Saraceno, Adrian Krell, Roland Mühlethaler, Ally Bisshop and Markus J. Buehler (2018), 'Imaging and Analysis of a Three-dimensional Spider Web Architecture', *Journal of the Royal Society Interface*, 15(146).

Van der Tuin, Iris (2018), 'Diffraction', in Rosi Braidotti and Maria Hlavajova (eds), *The Posthuman Glossary*, London: Bloomsbury, pp. 99–101.

Werner, Gabriele (2015), 'Discourses about Pictures: Considerations on the Particular Challenges Natural-Scientific Pictures Pose for the Theory of the Picture', in Horst Bredekamp, Vera Dünkel and Birgit Schneider (eds), *The Technical Image. A History of Styles in Scientific Imagery*, Chicago and London: The University of Chicago Press, pp. 8–13.

Wigley, Mark (2018), 'Sticking to Saraceno: Anti-Architecture Air-play', *On Air, Carte Blanche à Tomás Saraceno. Le magazine du Palais de Tokyo*, issue 28: 50–2.

Wulz, Monika (2010), *Erkenntnisagenten: Gaston Bachelard und die Reorganisation des Wissens*, Berlin: Kadmos.

9

The Beaver, a Partisan Fighting for the Survival of the Planet

Agnė Narušytė

The Anthropocene has not yet been recognised as a geological epoch, but the term is suitable to define our current condition. On the one hand, it shows that the human species has the power to change the composition of the planetary atmosphere and leave traces in its geological strata (Latour 2017: 111–16). On the other hand, the droughts, floods, fluctuating temperatures and other phenomena caused by these changes, including the sixth global extinction (Kolbert 2014; Ceballos et al. 2017), threaten to destroy our habitat and bring civilisation to an end (Spratt and Dunlop 2019). This threat should make us change the way our economies are run, but it is difficult to reach a global consensus when powerful actors, such as fossil fuel corporations, invest heavily in protecting the status quo (Fischer 2013; Klein 2015). To make matters worse, for people on whose support governments depend, the cares of today will always overshadow the threats of a distant future. 'Meanwhile', the writer Roy Scranton says, 'the world slides into hatred-filled, bloody havoc, like the last act of a particularly ugly Shakespearean tragedy' (Scranton 2018: 7).

If we want to transform the economic system and our thinking, we first have to break them. 'Political and cultural struggles are all', Elizabeth Grosz writes, 'in some sense, directed to bringing into existence the futures that dislocate themselves from the dominant tendencies and forces of the present'. This means that one has to disrupt linear time by creating something 'untimely' (Grosz 2014: 14). Many are trying to imagine what that 'untimely' could be. Some, like Bruno Latour, suggest we should act counterintuitively and lose hope in order to realise 'progress in reverse', to experience time differently (Latour 2017: 13). Those in the position of power can hardly commit to disruption or dislocation. Therefore, people start fighting like partisans engaging in illegitimate activities. The system tends to reject such fighters as 'irrelevant' and 'weird'[1] or even destroys them.[2] The 'partisans', on the other hand, cannot expect either victory or recognition; their only hope is to transform the system slowly from the inside, while continuing to be unappreciated and persecuted.

Artists also participate in this struggle, sometimes collaborating with animals as their allies. One such artist is Aurelija Maknytė.[3] She acts like a partisan and chooses losing as a strategy, thus mirroring the fate of the species she works with. Her approach differs from those who represent the processes of the Anthropocene in the hope to draw the audience's attention towards the impending catastrophe. Such art dominated the Venice Biennial in 2019. Laure Prouvost filled the French pavilion with the installation of imaginary life forms envisioning a blissful cohabitation of humans and other species. Larissa Sansour turned the Danish pavilion into a post-apocalyptic underground space whose function was explained by her film *In vitro*: a young woman is talking to the dying creator of an underground garden in order to feel nostalgia for a past alien to her, so that she could recreate what was destroyed by the ecological catastrophe. The German artist Hito Steyerl, who participated in the main exhibition, created a narrative about someone in prison raising flowers from seeds captured in the wind, thus hoping to jump over the unpredictable and anxious present to a more beautiful future. The Argentinian artist Tomás Saraceno composed a soundtrack for the changing climate from the sounds of sirens warning Venetians about the rising water. And the Lithuanian pavilion, the winner of the Golden Lion, surprised the audience with the opera-performance *Sun and Sea (Marina)* by Vaiva Grainytė, Lina Lapelytė and Rugilė Barzdžiukaitė, who showed a humanity tired of fighting against the effects of their own activities and lazily anticipating the end of the world while sunbathing on the sand. These are only the most remarkable examples. By suggesting solutions based on human creativity, empathy and compassion, artists create the atmosphere of reconciliation, an illusion that ecological awareness is already widespread and will help to change politics.[4] Meanwhile, Maknytė, as an artist-partisan, works in the margins and often remains unnoticed because she does not present any large-scale exhibitions in prestigious art spaces. Instead, her art seems to grow naturally out of her way of life.

A few years ago, Maknytė purchased five hectares of land on which she has built a caravan and a 'winter kiosk'. While staying there, she spends her time observing animals and creating conditions for biodiversity. On the steep bank of the river Širvinta, flowing along her plot, she has discovered the holes of badgers and started filming their daily life.[5] She keeps stick insects as pets, collects weirdly shaped stumps as habitats for various insects and bacteria, gets old herbariums to germinate or makes wreaths out of oak leaves 'decorated' with wasp galls. She showed all these, along with other collaborations with other species, at her solo exhibition *Nature Cabinets* in the Vilnius Town Hall in 2020. Among the exhibits there was a sculpture carved by beavers that she had appropriated for her continuous project *Partisan of Landscaping*, which started in 2013. This project, which has not yet acquired a final shape, questions the traditional opposition between nature and culture and could be considered part of the artworks and artists practising 'ecological thought', inspired by the ideas of Timothy Morton.[6] In this chapter I shall discuss the implications of Maknytė's collaboration with beavers as artists and partisans of landscaping.

The beaver is a subject

Carl von Linné, known as the 'father' of modern taxonomy, named the species of beavers *Castor fiber* (Linné 1758: 58). In his system of classification, beavers were defined through their similarities and differences from other species. Since then, the studies of morphology, reproduction and habits treat animals not as individuals but as samples of their species. They will never become subjects with their own purposes, ideas or 'souls', which differentiates them from humans. At first glance, Maknytė seems to continue the tradition of natural sciences: as a human subject she explores, photographs and reflects on the species that has remained on the 'lower' stage of evolution and cannot think for itself. She also tries to spy on beavers in order to see and show how they behave 'naturally' when there are no humans around.

People have always tried to imagine how wild animals live on their own, untouched by civilisation and the observer's gaze. In the nineteenth century, museums of natural history were filled with dioramas where stuffed animals pretended to perform their daily actions as if no one was watching. Now documentary films bring the most distant and difficult to reach places on the planet closer to us. In his many series on natural history, David Attenborough has shown how various species survive in their habitats, untouched by humans. However, in his 2020 film *David Attenborough: A Life on Our Planet*, he admits that the enclaves of wildlife are getting smaller and smaller and, while filming, it is becoming increasingly more difficult to avoid the signs of civilisation. This means that the life of animals and plants presented on our screens has always been a construction, and our gaze, empowered by technologies, has been imposing our hierarchically higher position on animals. This is true even when we see the Earth from the birds' point of view, like in the iconic film *Winged Migration* (*Le peuple migrateur*, 2001). Its creators Jacques Cluzaud, Michel Debats and Jacques Perrin raised tamed birds of various species that became used to ultralight aircraft and hot-air balloons while still being inside their eggs (Ebert 2003; *Le people migrateur – Le making of* 2002). Thus, the filmed behaviour of unobserved animals is an illusion, and film crews do not meet them as unfamiliar others. Rather than being subjects in their own right, the animals are controlled by and for the sake of the human gaze.

In his essay 'Why Look at Animals?', written in 1980, John Berger claims that modernity dismantled the relationship between humans and animals previously based on equality and respect, when animal bodies were used, but as a sacrifice replacing a human being. During those ancient times our relationship with animals was ambiguous: 'they were subjected *and* worshipped, bred *and* sacrificed' (Berger 1991: 6–7). Speechless and mysterious animals looked at people without meeting their gaze, and to humans their eyes seemed to be 'attentive and wary' (ibid.: 4). Yet when philosophy and religion separated body from soul, domestic animals were turned into mechanisms, tools or live prostheses of the human body appreciated only for their usefulness for agriculture and the economy. Meanwhile, wild animals became invisible – they disappeared from the landscape and remained only in reserves, parks and zoos where one comes to look at them hoping to bring the former relationship back or to meet old 'friends' from childhood tales. Yet animals locked in cages do not match their cultural images. They are too slow and clumsy because the environment, no longer important for their survival, becomes illusory. Nothing interests them, and the eyes of humans and animals pass each other in the zoo (Berger 1991: 15–28).

For a long time, this was the normal state of affairs. The imminence of the climate catastrophe, however, makes us question our relationship with animals. Instead of observing, analysing, categorising and using them, perhaps it is time to meet them again as unknowable others – as subjects, but without returning to mythologies. To be able to do this, Bruno Latour suggests, we should dismantle the distinction between Culture and Nature, which is also a cultural construct making the mechanical use of animals, discussed by Berger, possible. When this artificial structure collapses, the illusion disperses. This is also the reason why it is impossible to return to Nature because 'we are not dealing with *domains* but rather with one and the same *concept* divided into two parts, which turn out to be bound together, as it were, by a sturdy rubber band' (Latour 2017: 15). The opposition between Nature and Culture is constituted in our minds in a similar way to a painted landscape being designed for a single observer by a painter who 'stages' the positions of object and subject in order to turn 'nature' into a landscape (Latour 2017: 17–19). This means that 'the expression "belonging to nature" is almost meaningless, since nature is only one element in a complex consisting of at least *three terms*, the second serving as its counterpart, culture, and the third being the one that distributes features between the first two. In this sense, nature does not exist (as a domain); it exists only as *one half of a pair pertaining to one single concept*' and it is 'held together by a common core that distributes differences between them' (Latour 2017: 19–20). Consequently, there is also no place beyond Nature and Culture from which we could observe the catastrophe of the Anthropocene: 'from now on there are no more spectators, because there is no shore that has not been mobilized in the drama of geohistory' (Latour 2017: 40). Since a truly external gaze is impossible, and the very idea of our separation from the environment is a fantasy, Latour proposes an Actor-Network Theory. According to it, all living beings, together with non-organic materials, constantly compose themselves and the world, the Earth and its atmosphere, as a network of agencies. Such a system based on a multitude of interactions would reject the objectifying gaze, which allows us to classify and analyse animals without being affected: 'Since all living agents follow their own intentions all along, modifying their neighbours as much as possible, there is no way to distinguish between the environment to which the organism is adapting and the point at which its own action begins' (Latour 2017: 100).

This 'unseeing' activity of all creatures and elements together is also part of Timothy Morton's concepts of 'ecological thought' and 'dark ecology' (Morton 2010, 2016). He perceives the formation of merging culture and nature as a 'mesh', which is 'dark', because it is looped and uncanny, contradictory and depressing, going through nihilism and irony, ugliness and horror and ending 'as dark sweetness' (Morton 2016: 160). In order to develop ecological thinking, Morton urges us to escape the binary oppositions of logic and see more than one timescale (Morton 2016: 41). This way we could become open to the *weird essentialism* where boundaries are fuzzy (Morton 2016: 64–72) and go to the zones of anxiety where people meet animals – the *strange strangers*. They exist at the border of our imagination and knowledge constantly mutating, fluctuating, always escaping the definitions of species that are only 'cutting into the smooth continuum of slight changes' (Morton 2010: 63). Strange strangers might look like monstrosities, but they are always 'in the eye of the beholder' and 'if there is anything monstrous in evolution, it's the uncertainty in the system at any and every point' (Morton 2010: 65–6). Grosz has also demonstrated that even for Charles Darwin, natural selection from the endless and constantly growing pool of variants takes place without any goal to create more 'perfect' creatures, thus, the future is indetermined and only the history of self-realisations is known (Grosz 2014: 90).

How does this help us to meet an animal – in this case, the beaver – as a subject? The changed optics, which blur the boundaries between species in constant flux and simultaneously reveal how everything collaborates in composing that flux, establish a new relationship. Any animal – as well as any plant or mineral – is encountered, visible, but as unknowable and unpredictable – or untimely. The impossibility of distinguishing between Nature and Culture means the annihilation of human superiority and of any position from which one could safely observe and judge the animal as the other. Observation should become part of the agency that changes both engaged parties and triggers the exchange of mutations. Donna Haraway saw this when she celebrated the fact that human genomes make up only 10 per cent of our body and we share with animals suffering; we have overcome diseases together, explored the world, raised bio-ethical questions. While studying or using their powers we have supplemented ours (Haraway 2008: 3–4). In other words, in the mesh, if we are subjects, so are the animals. Latour also emphasises the importance of territory that the subject delimitates, fights to protect from its enemies, and forms (Latour 2017: 251–2). Such a position grounds a different aesthetics where there are no objects to admire, no environments to experience, no performances to change the beholder, but only a multitude of encounters and conflicts creating the awareness of the other's presence – scary, horrible, deadly, disgusting, harmful, messy, funny and wonderful at the same time.

The artist encounters beavers

This way of thinking has not yet affected mainstream attitudes. Maknytė is one of the artists seeking to change that. Out of all animals she is most interested in beavers, who are particularly active rebels and construct landscapes suited for their needs. With their sharp teeth, beavers cut off huge trees and build dams, which create water pools where they can live safely in their underwater homes. 'Its teeth grow very fast; thus, the beaver has to gnaw constantly to abrade them', Maknytė says to her audience, holding a beaver's skull with huge orange front teeth – incisors. Beavers are very well adapted to their watery environment because their fur, covered with oil, does not let them get wet and cold. Due to the particularities of their mouth anatomy, they can gnaw trees underwater without letting water in. Their bodies are valued by people, particularly their fat and fur. Because of this, beavers were almost completely annihilated in Lithuania by 1938. But in 1947, they were reintroduced from Russia; they also keep moving into Lithuania from Belarus (Palionienė 1970: 3–26).[7] According to the data of the 2008 survey (with the possibility for error lying at 15 per cent), there were 21,846 to 30,788 active beaver lodges and 85,879 to 121,025 individuals that year (Ulevičius 2008: 29). But the survey of 2018–19 shows a drastically reduced number for the beaver population, at only 42,396.[8] What happened? It has been established that wolves feeding on beavers or limited resources do not affect the beaver population. Most significant is the anthropogenic influence. Humans reduce the number of beavers by directly exploiting their resources, by hunting them or indirectly changing their environment. Hunting is the most effective for regulating the numbers of beavers: it may be that every year hunters kill around 20 per cent of the beaver population.

Maknytė was inspired to observe beavers while reading the books of Archibald Belaney (1888–1938), who wrote books such as *Grey Owl*. He travelled to Canada from England and started hunting beavers. Beavers' fur was fashionable and there were lots of them in the endless forests and waters of Canada. Beavers were not treasured at all; they were killed by every possible means. Everything changed when Belaney met an Iroquois woman Gertrude Bernard, whom he called Anahareo. She made him aware of the pain that hunted animals felt (Smith 2013–22). They adopted the babies of a killed female beaver. Having symbolically become an Indian Grey Owl, Belaney started spreading the idea that beavers are necessary for the ecosystem, and so also to humans. The couple lived together with beavers in a hut (Prišvinas 1971). It was like a hunter's lodge, but the 'beaver nation' changed it by constructing half of its home inside and half outside, with what looked like a rigmarole of twigs and mud. A raft made of logs and branches was floating nearby as the beavers' reserves for winter. By co-operating, communicating and playing with the beavers and even taking care of their homes, Grey Owl admired their minds and was convinced that beavers had imagination. Without it, they would not be able to build complicated structures and be so much fun as companions.[9]

Beavers also moved into Maknytė's plot and gnawed off several trees. Now she shares her land with them, like Grey Owl did, but does not try to 'manage' their lives because this way she would establish her status as a representative of a higher species. The artist only observes beaver colonies in marshes, melioration ditches and rivers, and does not plan any art projects – does not envision the future, but lets it happen.[10] She names the places where the beavers live and thus creates the map of the beavers' territory. In April 2014, she photographed the 'house' of beavers in a forest marsh. Their dams had flooded large areas where 'boars have fun in water baths', as she writes underneath a photograph with no boars in sight. The photograph features the water surface, covered with green algae and surrounded by bushes and birches. This plot is owned and formed by beavers. Upon returning to the same marsh in winter, Maknytė found the hut hidden under the snow. The frosty edges of the holes showed that the beavers were alive – they were breathing.

Similar processes take place in melioration ditches. In June 2014, Maknytė admired the Great Dam, a hill built from branches by beavers on a narrow ditch. She could not reach the Central Burr Melioration Ditch because of two-metre-high plants at the edges. She risked falling into water with her equipment because the bank was invisible. But she also found traces of war between humans and beavers: 'man who wants to get rid of beavers hunts them with traps or guns. They eat them or throw away or often stick the dead body into a beavers' lodge as a means to scare them', she writes. In the photograph, we see a blackened beaver's skeleton, a paw with long nails as if clutching the grass. In December of the same year, Maknytė visited the Great Dam again and no longer found it. It had been destroyed. Upon visiting the Left Burr Melioration Ditch Maknytė also registered the traces of struggle because 'the layer of ice broken at the edges shows that the water level has risen. Most often this happens because the dams have been destroyed. If this happens in winter when the temperature is particularly low, the beavers risk freezing to death' (Figure 9.1). Unfortunately, in November 2015, she saw that the dam no longer existed: 'Levelled up, tidied up. Bushes,

Figure 9.1 Aurelija Maknytė, from the project *Partisan of Landscaping*, 2014. Digital photography, dimensions and printing technique variable
Source: Courtesy of the artist.

holes, beavers are all gone. Will this have any impact on the harvest from the fields cultivated nearby?', she asked.

In July 2014, the activity of beavers in the Birch Bolete Marsh Settlement was hardly noticeable because they had just started building the dam. But Maknytė found an object between the gravel road and the forest rivulet, which the 'beavers started, and humans finished. Collaboration.' She called the place the Sculptors' Settlement. One trunk of a tree gnawed off 'has become the basis for an anthill', thus beavers create conditions for another species to live. This secret dam flourishes even in winter, although the 'edge of the forest is adjacent to cultivated fields and hunting areas (there are hunters' towers nearby)'. Meanwhile, the dam that people have built on the River Širvinta had been destroyed, and the water ran downstream – the beavers had lost their homes. 'If this happens late in the autumn, it is possible that the beavers will not be able to adapt and will not understand that the water will not come back in winter', Maknytė wrote.

War over the landscape

Without Maknytė's comments many viewers would not understand these photographs. First of all, they lack the landscape recognisable to us from painting or photography. There is almost no place left here for the sky because the entire frame is occupied by water and plants. Sometimes, there are no points of reference because instead of the clearly separated foreground, middle ground and background, there is only chaotic wilderness. Instead of a river or a road winding into the distance, there are only melioration ditches and overgrown marshes. Secondly, the rigmarole of twigs, bushes, grasses and puddles would not tell us much because only someone who knows the habits of beavers can understand the meaning of broken ice or a lowered water level.

Additionally, by ignoring the tradition of landscape photography Maknytė denies humans what they expect: a picturesque view designed for a specific observer. People cultivate the land, create the landscape as a cultural construct and incorporate wild nature as a counterpoint to emphasise the beauty of their creation. The laws of Lithuania define the landscape in the following way:

> A territorial combination of natural (surface rocks and relief, air close to the ground, surface and ground water, soil, live organisms) and (or) anthropogenic (archaeological relics, buildings, engineer equipment, landed property and information field) components linked by the relationships of matter, energy and information.

This is the locality (territory) understood by humans whose character has been determined by natural and (or) anthropogenic factors and their interaction. (Idzelis 2011: 10)

Although natural and anthropogenic landscapes are separated, the former will always be changed by humans, that is anthropogenised, tamed
or cultivated (Idzelis 2011: 22–4).

For us, landscape is not simply a natural environment surrounding
historically significant buildings, but also a mental image in our consciousness (Jurevičienė 2013: 4). We form new landscapes and protect
old ones, but only the ones highly valued by the experts or communities.
The value is created by associating places to famous people or events.
Thus, the definition of land management necessarily emphasises human
needs: 'a spatial organisation of human activities and regulation of the
environment realised by the means of territorial planning with the goal
to coordinate social, economic and ecological interests for the use of
territory and create a harmonious cultural landscape' (Idzelis 2011: 28).
It should be noted that there is no intention to protect any landscape
untouched by humans, and only places that have 'scientific, historical
and aesthetical value' are treated as natural heritage, which means again
that the point of reference remains nature's usefulness for human survival, education or entertainment (Idzelis 2011: 65–6). At the very least,
a wild landscape should meet aesthetic criteria and be a site that looks
beautiful when seen from certain points of view (Idzelis 2011: 68). A bit
of wilderness can bestow a cultural landscape with multilayered complexity, which feeds our imagination: people decide to protect certain
species of plants and animals only as much as they match our perception of form or mental images of cultural significance (Jurevičienė 2013:
7–29). And even when the bionomic criterion for protecting a landscape
is singled out, it is still linked to the usefulness for humans: 'to preserve
the diversity of live nature and the conditions for humans as biological
beings to exist' (Idzelis 2011: 26–7). We are so used to these principles
that we do not notice, as the geographer Giedrė Godienė says, that we
'always talk about the human perspective because humans most value
themselves in the landscape'.[11]

Sometimes scientific explanations that some species are necessary for
our survival or simply for biodiversity also add value to certain landscapes, but usually such arguments are less convincing and hardly change
people's attitudes. In other words, the landscape as a cultural construct
creates the illusion of Nature that Latour and Morton argued we should
abandon if we want to survive the Anthropocene. What other proof is
needed when such an idea of Nature encourages us to eliminate animals

and plants from a landscape if they do not meet the criteria of usefulness, beauty and meaningfulness.

Beavers are particularly successful in constructing the landscape in their own way and are seen as a threat to cultural landscapes. Conditions are extremely favourable for beavers in Lithuania. Therefore, its laws allow and even oblige citizens to destroy beavers' lodges if they can potentially 'cause the change in the position of the border of the state or the objects and equipment used for border protection' or damage the following strategic objects: 'roads, railways, bridges, buildings, constructions for the melioration and hydro technology, agricultural crops, other landed property, forests'.[12] It seems landscape architects and farmers rightfully treat beavers as the worst pests that have to be eliminated. They destroy beavers' dams, but beavers rebuild them or find a different place to live, for example in melioration ditches that have eventually become 'the main biotope of beavers' (Ulevičius 2008: 44–5). Latour would see this as a war over territory – and landscape.

Now, when we know that the loss of biodiversity threatens even the survival of humans, we should rethink the role of beavers again, Maknytė says. Beavers are essential for ecosystems, balancing the negative effect that humans have on nature. Their dams flood the area, which becomes a habitat suitable for many species. Maknytė remembers:

> In one swamp they killed all the beavers, water subsided and the poor roots of trees were hanging in the air, there was nothing there. And before, when I went there once together with my son, I saw a fox trying to hunt a crane, then a moose came out, then a boar ran past us. I called that place Noah's Arc because it was as if I could see the entire encyclopaedia of animals there [. . .] In a way, beavers fight for the rights of all animals and plants, even for us.

But do beavers know that?

Even the question itself betrays the old certainty that *Homo sapiens* is the only animal species with a consciousness. To contradict that, Maknytė turns the direction of the gaze around. 'This is what beavers see when they come out of their house', she writes under the photograph of water turned green by algae (Figure 9.2). Beavers see the environment they need. Although there are no distortions in the photograph, it looks strange from a human point of view. There is nothing here, not even beauty. By suggesting we should see nature not from a distant vantage point, but from the perspective of beavers, Maknytė encourages us to look at other photographs this way as well. They all show the landscape

Figure 9.2 Aurelija Maknytė, from the project *Partisan of Landscaping*, 2014.
Digital photography, dimensions and printing technique variable
Source: Courtesy of the artist.

constructed by beavers. Thus, she asks to whom the landscape really
belongs and tells the following story:

> The Bernardine Gardens in Vilnius have been tidied up, fenced up
> and locked for the night. The right to be by the river has been taken
> away from people, although this is against the law. At one point
> somebody started ravaging the Gardens, and townspeople fumed that
> some vandals had climbed over the fence and broken everything.
> Then it came out that the vandal was the beaver. We can say that,
> perhaps, it is we who have come over to live in the beaver's territory.

Can beavers create?

Maknytė also asks whether *Homo sapiens* is the only species that can claim
the status of creator. Some experiments in the 1960s demonstrated that
creations by animals – monkeys, elephants, rabbits, dolphins – could not be
distinguished from works of modern art, although animals were not aware
they were the creators. Research carried out in the 1980s into the mating
rituals of ovenbirds showed that they were building oven-shaped nests
decorated with multicoloured grasses, berries, moss, butterfly wings or
even poker chips offered to them by humans, which they even stole from
each other. Fashions of décor were formed in different localities and were

passed on not genetically, but culturally (Diamond 1986). Research carried out in the 2010s showed that some birds created the illusion of enhanced perspective (Kelley and Endler 2012). Although such inventiveness of birds is usually linked to their need to attract a mating partner, the philosopher and sound artist David Rothenberg claims that this is a form of art for art's sake (Rothenberg 2011: 25–6). The British photographer David Slater's lawsuit over the copyright of selfies photographed by a black macaque, however, has shown that legally neither animal nor plant nor nature itself can be recognised as creators. Even if the macaque was pressing the shutter, the artist created the situation (Axelrad 2014).

The status of 'sculptures' found by Maknytė in the Sculptors' Settlement would legally be the same if she had not intervened as a photographer. The photographer's right to the copyright over the representations of natural objects was recognised in the second half of the nineteenth century (Kogan 2015: 885–900). After having found the 'sculpture', Maknytė told everyone that she had carved it herself at first. 'Everybody believed this, because it is so zoomorphic; it reminds of something a little – of a bird, of some animal and even of the beaver itself.' When the cultural weekly *7 meno dienos* asked her to create something for its Art Project page, Maknytė photographed the sculpture and signed it as the photographer of an object created by the artist named Castor Fiber (Fiber 2014) (Figure 9.3). Thus, the beaver became a recognised creator whose works

Figure 9.3 Castor Fiber, *Object*, 2013. Wooden object. Photography by Aurelija Maknytė
Source: Courtesy of the artist.

were published by the cultural press. Simultaneously, a natural object became a cultural one, whatever the beaver's intentions. How could this be reconciled with the critique of the absolute right granted to humans to shape the landscape?

This contradiction within the project became even more apparent when the artist was invited to present the object at the exhibition *The Sweet Sweat of the Future* at the National Gallery of Art, Vilnius, in summer 2019. Maknytė had to take the beaver's sculpture to the restorers so that they could protect it from decay. This act made her feel uneasy because the wood would be treated with chemicals that would kill pests. She even wanted to refuse to participate in the exhibition:

> Even if the restorers' intervention remained invisible, my knowing that those beaver sculptures had been in the hands of restorers would acculturate this natural object. But then I saw a parallel: humans acculturate the landscape, and the beavers deculturate it again, they naturalise it again, and so on. After long deliberations I decided that let it be – I took it to the restorers. Besides, these objects are monuments to the already dead beaver colonies.

At the restoration centre, Maknytė was pleasantly surprised. The beaver's sculpture was placed alongside a sculpture by the famous Lithuanian artist Antanas Mončys, which was also undergoing conservation. Her experience was 'weirdly weird' because the two objects were quite similar: 'The sculpture by Mončys was also made of wood and there were some roots left. To me, the motif of roots was very dear. Castor Fiber and Mončys as artists looked very much alike.' Visual similarity and also the aesthetic impact of the object should, it seems, encourage us to review the copyright law. Yet the legal aspect is not as important as the ethical one. By presenting art objects created by Castor Fiber Maknytė seeks to convince *Homo sapiens* that beavers are not pests to be gotten rid of, but equal beings living next to us, that they are also subjects. Her task is of similar importance to that of a fictional lady in Kazuo Ishiguro's novel *Never Let Me Go*, who tried to prove that people incubated and raised for the sole purpose of donating their organs to 'real' people do have souls because they can create art (Ishiguro 2005).

Perhaps, if creating art proves the presence of the soul it bestows the rights of the subject to those who create even if they are not aware of it. By showing photographic and material evidence that beavers are indeed sculptors and landscape architects, Maknytė turns them into subjects in her audience's minds. If we cannot distinguish an object gnawed accidentally by a beaver's teeth from a work of art by a famous sculptor, perhaps we should recognise that the difference between art and nature is artificial. Thus, Maknytė encourages us to doubt the 'truth' learned long ago that humans are biologically exceptional and can lawfully appropriate the landscape while destroying the ecosystem necessary for the survival of other species.

The time is not to end, or the conclusion

Why then does Maknytė, who wants to change people's attitudes towards beavers, not hold a grand show or create a film to attract more attention? A vitrine with photographs and printed materials about landscape management at the exhibition *Blood and Soil: Dark Arts for Dark Times* at the Contemporary Art Centre (Vilnius, 2019), the beaver's sculpture at the National Gallery of Art and an art project in a cultural weekly are not enough. It seems the artist avoids finishing the project. Why?

Perhaps, this is a way to live the 'progress in reverse'? The philosopher Lisa Baraitser notes that some artists think that the catastrophe brought on by climate change is imminent practice, the 'time of remaining'. She refers to 'messianic time' as defined by Giorgio Agamben, which is given before the end as an interval of time needed to end time (Agamben 2005). The time of progress is interrupted and replaced by the indeterminacy of the everyday. Such time stays stubborn, thus turning into an extended interval that 'neither develops nor unfolds', but simply remains the same and is returned to us so that we would live it properly instead of constantly lacking time. Artists who experience the tension of this strange time interval also 'remain' by withdrawing from the events of the past and the future into the everyday and collecting imperceptible changes as evidence that something seems to have survived the catastrophe, although this neither proves anything nor annihilates the possibility of the end (Baraitser 2017: 166–7). Their time filled with apparently meaningless anachronistic actions stays still, thus delaying the beginning of the catastrophe.

Maknytė also 'collects evidence', an unnecessary activity as, according to her, the 'beavers are all right'. Although their lodges are destroyed, they persist in building new ones. Beavers as a species are not disappearing in Lithuania. Therefore, while documenting change – the disappearing beavers' lodges – she keeps returning to the same places. Thus, she demonstrates the ongoing war over the landscape without a definite result. Her endlessly continuing project might never acquire a final shape or become defined as an 'art species', thus resonating with the rhythm of purposeless evolution. While treating beavers as equal subjects, Maknytė stays in the midst of their activities instead of occupying a privileged position, and is exposed to unexpected encounters with 'strange strangers', which keep creating something not planned – untimely – and thus dislocate the usual notions about art. The photographs tracing the activities of beavers constantly undoing the work of humans give us hope that nothing has been decided yet, that the struggle will continue and that the future might be different from what we imagine in the Anthropocene. The silent artefacts created by beavers make us question authorship and authority: who creates what? Who is or will be the master of the Earth?

Notes

1. Greta Thunberg's influence is often undermined by emphasising her autism and Asperger's syndrome, for example.
2. Extinction Rebellion bases its actions on the idea that the media report on mass disobedience only when tens of peaceful protesters are arrested. See the lecture on ER's website, available at: https://rebellion.earth/act-now/ (last accessed 18 November 2019). For several years now, *The Guardian* has been registering the deaths of ecology activists all over the world. In the last fifteen years the number of such deaths has doubled and is comparable to the statistics of war zones (see Watts 2019).
3. Maknytė was born in a small town, Širvintos (Lithuania), in 1969. As a child she read *Walden* by Henry David Thoreau and dreamed of a simple life in the forest (Toro 1985). Biology was going to be her profession. While still at school, she was the laureate of the national biology Olympics, sought to discover rare species of insects in the surrounding wilderness, learned the art of taxidermy and stuffed the dead body of her beloved dog. After school she started studying biology at Vilnius University, but soon became attracted to art and graduated from the Photography and Media Art department of the Vilnius Academy of Arts in 2001. Maknytė is known for her projects based on interventions into social and biological systems and as a passionate collector of printed materials, ego-documents, films and photographs. In 2004–7, she collaborated with other artists and curators in creating the television programme CAC TV, broadcast by a commercial channel. Her filmed performance *Bunny Man* (2009) – which showed a man dressed in a bunny's costume walking the streets and encountering humans as strangers – has become a cultural icon. Her project *Video Rental* (2012) became a monument to 'extinct' videotape rental shops.
4. In addition, there have been other ecology-oriented artists, like Anicka Yi (*Biologizing the Machine*, 2019), Cyprien Gaillard (*Ocean II Ocean*, 2019), Gabriel Rico (*Naturaleza muerta*, 2016), Christine and Margaret Wertheim (*Bleached Reef*, 2005–2016). Also in 2019 the MO Museum held the exhibition *Animal – Human – Robot* in Vilnius. See Grigoravičienė and Paberžytė (2019).

5. In this chapter I refer to my conversations with Aurelija Maknytė and her talk at the exhibition *The Sweet Sweat of the Future* at the National Gallery of Art, Vilnius, in summer 2019.

6. In 2014–16, when Maknytė started observing beavers, the 'Dark Ecology Project' was carried out in Norway and Russia, which included many artists. See Belina (2016).

7. The book by Anelė Palionienė, *River Beaver*, is from Aurelija Maknytė's archive of printed materials, which is part of her project. All such publications are marked by the inscription 'From the archive of A. M.' in the references below.

8. Taken from the records of hunted animals (the 2018–19 hunting season), from the Environment Ministry of the Republic of Lithuania, 2018. Available at: https://am.lrv.lt/lt/veiklos-sritys-1/gamtos-apsauga/medziokle/medziojamuju-zveriu-apskaita/medziojamuju-zveriu-apskaita-2018-2019-m-medziokles-sezonas (last accessed 24 November 2019).

9. The following books by Grey Owl are included in Maknytė's library: Aulis (1956); Pelėda (1958), plus the 1987 edition.

10. The results are published on Aurelija Maknytė's website: 'Partisan of Landscaping/Kraštovaizdžio partizanas/from 2013', available at: https://maknyte.com/castor-fiber-krastovaizdzio-partizanas/ (last accessed 2 September 2021). All captions of photographs are quoted from this publication.

11. From my conversation with Giedrė Godienė in July 2019 on Aurelija Maknytė's plot, during the filming of the cultural programme *Intervizijos* (*Intervisions*).

12. Taken from the bill of the Minister of the Republic of Lithuania regarding the regulation and setting of rules governing the beaver population, 29 May 2003, new edit active from 2 November 2019, Vilnius. Available at: https://www.e-tar.lt/portal/lt/legalAct/TAR.E4FECE02ACA1/IeZDXbiCWJ (last accessed 24 November 2019).

References

Agamben, Giorgio (2005), *The Time That Remains: A Commentary on the Letter to the Romans*, trans. Patricia Dailey, Stanford, CA: Stanford University Press.

Aulis, Grėjus (1956), *Seidžija ir jos bebrai*, trans. Giedrė Juodvalkytė, Vilnius: Grožinės literatūros leidykla. From the archive of A. M.

Axelrad, Jacob (2014), 'US Government: Monkey Selfies Ineligible for Copyright', *The Christian Science Monitor*, 22 August, available at: https://www.csmonitor.com/Technology/Tech-Culture/2014/0822/US-government-Monkey-selfies-ineligible-for-copyright (last accessed 23 November 2019).

Baraitser, Lisa (2017), *Enduring Time*, London: Bloomsbury.

Belina, Mirna (ed.) (2016), *Living Earth. Field Notes from the Dark Ecology Project 2014–2016*, Amsterdam: Sonic Acts Press.

Berger, John (1991), *About Looking*, New York: Vintage.

Ceballos, Gerardo, Paul R. Ehrlich and Rodolfo Dirzo (2017), 'Biological Annihilation via the Ongoing Sixth Mass Extinction Signaled by Vertebrate Population Losses and Declines', *Proceedings of the National Academy of Sciences of the United States of America*, 114(30): E6089–96. Available at: http://www.pnas.org/content/114/30/E6089 (last accessed 29 August 2018).

Diamond, Jared (1986), 'Animal Art: Variation in Bower Decorating Style Among Male Bowerbirds Amblyornis Inornatus', *Proceedings of the National Academy of Sciences of the United States of America*, 83(9): 3042–6.

Ebert, Roger (2003), 'Winged Migration', available at: https://www.rogerebert.com/reviews/winged-migration-2003 (last accessed 19 March 2022).

Extinction Rebellion, lecture, available at: https://rebellion.earth/act-now/ (last accessed 18 November 2019).

Fiber, Castor (2014), 'Objektas', *7 meno dienos*, available at: https://www.7md.lt/5757 (last accessed 22 November 2019).

Fischer, Douglas (2013), '"Dark Money" Funds Climate Change Denial Effort', *Scientific American*, 23 December, available at: https://www.scientificamerican.com/article/dark-money-funds-climate-change-denial-effort/ (last accessed 10 December 2019).

Grigoravičienė, Erika and Ugnė Paberžytė (eds) (2019), *Gyvūnas – žmogus – robotas* ('Animal – Human – Robot'), exhibition catalogue, Vilnius: MO muziejus.

Grosz, Elizabeth (2014), *The Nick of Time: Politics, Evolution, and the Untimely*, Durham, NC and London: Duke University Press.

Haraway, Donna J. (2008), *When Species Meet*, Minneapolis and London: University of Minnesota Press.

Idzelis, Raimondas Leoplodas (2011), *Kraštovaizdžio tvarkymas*, Vilnius: Technika. From the archive of A. M.

Ishiguro, Kazuo (2005), *Never Let Me Go*, London: Faber and Faber.

Jurevičienė, Jūratė (2013), *Kraštovaizdžio kultūrinė vertė: išsaugojimo principai*, Vilnius: Technika. From the archive of A. M.

Kelley, Laura A. and John A. Endler (2012), 'Male Great Bowerbirds Create Forced Perspective Illusions with Consistently Different Individual Quality', *Proceedings of the National Academy of Sciences of the United States of America*, 109(51): 20980–5.

Klein, Naomi (2015), *This Changes Everything: Capitalism vs. The Climate*, reprint edition, New York, London, Toronto, Sydney, New Delhi: Simon & Schuster.

Kogan, T. S. (2015), 'The Enigma of Photography, Depiction, and Copyright Originality', *Fordham Intellectual Property, Media & Entertainment Law Journal*, 25(4): 869–937.

Kolbert, Elizabeth (2014), *The Sixth Extinction: An Unnatural History*, New York: Henry Holt & Company.

Latour, Bruno (2017), *Facing Gaia: Eight Lectures on the New Climatic Regime*, trans. Catherine Porter, Cambridge: Polity.

Le people migrateur – Le making of, film, directed by Olli Barbé, France: Galatée Films, 2002.

Lietuvos Respublikos aplinkos ministerija (The Ministry of Environment of the Republic of Lithuania) (2003), 'įsakymas dėl bebrų populiacijos gausos reguliavimo tvarkos nustatymo' (Bill on the establishment of a procedure for regulating the abundance of the beaver population), Vilnius, available at: https://www.e-tar.lt/portal/lt/legalAct/TAR.E4FECE02ACA1/IeZDXbiCWJ (last accessed 24 November 2019).

Lietuvos Respublikos aplinkos ministerija (The Ministry of Environment of the Republic of Lithuania) (2018), *Medžiojamų žvėrių apskaita (2018–2019 m. medžioklės sezonas)* [Account on Game (the 2018–2019 hunting season)], available at: https://am.lrv.lt/lt/veiklos-sritys-1/gamtos-apsauga/medziokle/medziojamuju-zuveriu-apskaita/medziojamuju-zveriu-apskaita-2018-2019-m-medziokles-sezona (last accessed 24 November 2019).

Linné, Carl von (1758), *Systema naturae: regnum animale, edicio decima*, Lipsiae: Sumptibus Guilielmi Engelmann.

Maknytė, Aurelija (2013), 'Partisan of Landscaping/Kraštovaizdžio partizanas/from 2013', available at: https://maknyte.com/castor-fiber-krastovaizdzio-partizanas/ (last accessed 2 September 2021).

Morton, Timothy (2010), *The Ecological Thought*, Cambridge, MA and London: Harvard University Press.

Morton, Timothy (2016), *Dark Ecology: For a Logic of Future Coexistence*, New York: Columbia University Press.

Narušytė, Agnė (2019), 'Iškamšų muziejus kaip žmogaus ir gyvūno santykių teatras', in Grigoravičienė and Paberžytė, pp. 133–8.

Palionienė, A. (1970), *Upinis bebras*, Vilnius: Mintis.

Pelėda, Pilkoji (1958), *Girių piligrimai*, trans. Vytautas Jurgutis, Vilnius: Valstybinė politinės ir mokslinės literatūros leidykla. From the archive of A. M.

Pelėda, Pilkoji (1987), *Girių piligrimai*, trans. Vytautas Jurgutis, Vilnius: Vyturys. From the archive of A. M.

Prišvinas, Michailas (1971), *Pilkoji Pelėda*, trans. Stasys Dabušis, Vilnius: Vaga. From the archive of A. M.

Rothenberg, David (2011), *Survival of the Beautiful: Art, Science and Evolution*, New York, London, New Delhi and Sydney: Bloomsbury Press.

Scranton, Roy (2018), *We're Doomed. Now What? Essays on War and Climate Change*, New York: Soho Press.

Smith, Donald B. (2013–22), 'Belaney, Archibald Stansfeld', *Dictionary of Canadian Biography*, available at: http://www.biographi.ca/en/bio/belaney_archibald_stansfeld_16E.html (last accessed 20 March 2022).

Spratt, David and Ian Dunlop (2019), 'Existential Climate-related Security Risk: A Scenario Approach', Breakthrough – National Centre for Climate Restoration, available at: https://52a87f3e-7945-4bb1-abbf-aa66cd4e93e.filesusr.com/ugd/148cb0_90dc2a2637f348edae45943a88da04d4.pdf (last accessed 23 November 2019).

Toro, Henri Deividas (1985), *Voldenas, arba Gyvenimas miške*, trans. Rolandas
       Pavilionis, Vilnius: Vaga.
Ulevičius, Alnius (2008), *Upinių bebrų būklės įvertinimas. Mokslinių tyrimų paslaugų
       ataskaita*, Vilnius: Aplinkos apsaugos agentūra, Valstybinė saugomų teritorijų
       tarnyba prie Aplinkos ministerijos, Vilniaus universiteto Ekologijos institutas.
Watts, Jonathan (2019), 'Environmental Activist Murders Double in 15 Years',
       The Guardian, 5 August: https://www.theguardian.com/environment/2019/
       aug/05/environmental-activist-murders-double (last accessed 18 November
       2019).

Part III

Forms of Life and
New Ontologies

10

Jagged Ontologies in The Anthropocene, or, The Five Cs

Cary Wolfe

In my role as founding editor of the *Posthumanities* series at the University of Minnesota Press, I get asked a lot about trends.[1] What's hot now? What's the next big thing? How do you see the future of theory? And so on. One of the things I say in response to such questions is that 'the question of the animal' – even as it certainly remains a growth industry in a number of disciplines in the humanities and interpretive social sciences – seems to have been left behind, all too predictably, by the economy of planned obsolescence in academic knowledge production and theory. As Niklas Luhmann pointed out long ago, the autopoiesis of the disciplines within the education system, as with other social systems, depends upon the ceaseless production of novelty (Luhmann 2000: 21, 28). Part of that production of novelty has been a widespread decentring of the human across a range of disciplines and theoretical approaches over the past three decades or more. But as I argued in *What Is Posthumanism?*, when it comes to the decentring of the human, the issue isn't just *what* you're thinking, it's *how* you're thinking it. And here, one might draw a bright line between so-called Flat Ontologies and my insistence later in this chapter on what one might call instead 'jagged ontologies', ones that pay attention to differences and to how, as Gregory Bateson puts it, those differences *make* a difference: in this case, to formulating the discourse of the Anthropocene (Bateson 1972: 453).

In this context, I'll later engage Bruno Latour's *Facing Gaia*, with its admirable desire to assert what he calls the 'outlaw character' of Gaia as a stay against both holism and humanism and their understanding of Gaia as a kind of mythical super-organism. As we'll see, however, the discourse of Gaia and the Anthropocene, at least in Latour's influential rendition, has abandoned 'the question of the animal' prematurely, because what the site of 'the Animal' shows is that Flat Ontologies (and finally Latour's own Actor-Network Theory) evacuate the radical discontinuity between qualitatively different orders of organisation and causation that obtain in living versus physical systems – different orders that impact in fundamentally different ways the evolution of the biosphere, climate change and, ultimately, the entire concept of Gaia. As we'll see later, with Latour's mobilisation of Actor-Network Theory in *Facing Gaia* as my example, what looks like an anti-reductionist posthumanism often isn't anti-reductionist at all – and this is far from a 'merely academic' matter.

With this larger context in mind, let me briefly address the discourse of the Anthropocene. I have to admit, I'm a little tired of talking about it, not because it's not important, of course, but because I think we are clearly in a phase of diminishing returns with regard to the concept's periodising vigour and analytical power, which has in turn generated a sort of backlash that is not far to seek in academic debates about the term and its usefulness – as in, for example, Bruce Clarke's observation that the Anthropocene is a slogan that 'has been invented and presented to our attention for a cluster of reasons that are significantly other than scientific' (Clarke 2014: 101). One of my main reservations about the Anthropocene is voiced by Latour himself, in fact, in *Facing Gaia*, where he suggests that the problem with the concept is not so much that it constitutes 'an immoderate extension of anthropo*centrism*', but rather its invocation of 'the human as a unified agent', a 'universal concept' (Latour 2017: 122, original emphasis). More seriously still, the Anthropocene concept threatens to authorise 'a premature leap to a higher level *by confusing the figures of connection with those of totality*' (ibid.: 130, emphasis in original), which leads in turn to what he calls a 'deanimation' of the agents and actants (most of them non-human, of course) caught up in what William James once called the 'pluriverse', where 'we have to agree to remain open to the dizzying otherness of existents, the list of which is not closed, and to the multiple ways they have of existing and relating among themselves' (ibid.: 37).

Clarke gives an even more pointed critique of the 'deanimation' and 'totalization' noted by Latour. As he argues, what started out as a disciplinary designation in the discipline of geology gets amplified over time in ways that belie the Anthropocene concept's supposed posthumanism. As Clarke puts it, while 'in a modest way "the anthropocene" is certainly conceivable as a concept indicating a potential threshold for archaeological stratigraphy', in its actual deployment in the International Geosphere-Biosphere Programme (IGBP) – the globalised administrative body charged with coordinating academic and governmental activity related to the phenomenon named by the concept – what we get instead is 'a hunk of traditional geology with an overlay of living beings but without closed systematicity' (Clarke 2014: 102). Lurking in the background here, Clarke suggests, is the disciplinary squabble between Earth

Science and Climate Science. The paradoxical (and autopoietic) fact that the Earth is a 'system with a panoply of feedbacks interconnecting biotic and abiotic systems into metabiotic ecosystems', in which the Earth itself is 'the system that arises as the sum effect of the operations of all those variegated subsystems' tends to be forgotten, so that what we are left with is, at one end, this thing called 'The Planet', and at the other, this thing called 'Life' that happens to live on it (ibid.). Meanwhile,

> the full force and profound implications of a biosphere operationally integrated for over three billion years with its atmosphere, hydrosphere and geosphere under the fall of solar energy – in relation to which the emergence of Homo sapiens is a rather minor detail – is allowed to dissipate, while human self-importance pushes its way back to the front of the line. (Ibid.)

What we end up with, Clarke argues, is a detachment of geology from biology which is bad science, 'except insofar as human beings are to stand for the whole of Biology' (ibid.: 103). But in fact – as James Lovelock and Lynn Margulis argue – 'the biosphere is run by the microbes', and its evolution 'has been driven hardest and longest by the ongoing evolution of bacteria' and their release of oxygen into the atmosphere (ibid.). In this light, the concept of the Anthropocene is 'a last-ditch firewall against the hard truth that humanity does not possess any "controlling hand" over the Earth system' (ibid.). So once again – to remember the point I emphasised earlier from *What Is Posthumanism?* – the takeaway from Clarke's interrogation of the supposed posthumanism of the Anthropocene concept is this: the issue isn't just what you're thinking about, it's *how* you're thinking about it.

It may be, then, that the concept of the Anthropocene presents us, in Timothy Clark's words, with a new imperative to 'think on a planetary scale' (Clark 2015: 21), but one has to ask, what would such a thing look like, exactly? After all – keeping in mind Bateson's reminder that *'the map is not the territory'* (Bateson 1972: 449, emphasis in original) – whenever we try to think the planetary, we are always thinking it in terms of *some* set of coordinates, *some* schema: in short, some map. But those maps have, of course, proliferated exponentially over time under the spur of modernisation as a phenomenon of increasing complexity, functional differentiation (to use Niklas Luhmann's term) and disciplinary specialisation (Luhmann 1995: 190–1) – a far from trivial point if you're trying to be empirical and scientific about things. For these reasons, the object of investigation called 'the Planet' has become more and more complex, and unavoidably so, over time. And what *that* means is that this proliferation of ever more differentiated disciplinary forms of knowledge, ever more differentiated and finely-grained 'maps', produces an object of knowledge called 'the Planet' that is, in a very important sense, a *virtual* object. As Luhmann puts it in his analysis of 'semantic over-burdening' in *Social Systems*, this proliferation of disciplinary 'maps' under the spur of modernisation and functional differentiation means that 'more complexity becomes visible than is accessible to the observed system itself. As a technique of scientific observation and analysis, the functional method allows its object to appear more complex than it is for itself. In this sense it over-burdens its object's self-referential order' (ibid.: 56).

This virtualisation, however, is not simply an epistemological matter. Indeed, as we know from the contemporary life sciences stretching back to the work of Jakob von Uexküll, ecological space is above all *virtual* space (Uexküll 2010: 52–4). Why? Because any such space is populated by a myriad of wildly heterogeneous life forms who create their worlds, their environments, through the embodied enaction, unfolding dynamically and in real time, of their own modes of knowing and being, their own autopoiesis (to use Maturana and Varela's term) (Maturana and Varela 1992: 43). Because of this multidimensionality and overdetermination, however, 'virtual' here doesn't mean 'not real' or 'less real', it means '*more* real'. Indeed, biologist Humberto Maturana calls such a perspective 'super-realist', in the sense of one 'who believes in the existence of innumerable equally valid realities', which cannot, however, be called 'relativist' because 'asserting their relativity would entail the assumption of an absolute reality as the reference point against which their relativity would be measured' (Maturana and Poersken 2004: 34) – what Donna Haraway long ago called 'the god-trick' that 'fucks the world', often tacitly at work, as Latour has already noted, in the discourse of the Anthropocene (Haraway 1991: 189). Such an assertion would entail the all too familiar humanist desire to escape our own ecological embeddedness, our own finitude (to use Derrida's term) (Derrida 2011: 99) – what Haraway, during that same period, characterises as the 'situatedness' of our knowledge and experience of the world (Haraway 1991: 188).

Derrida's way of framing this 'virtualisation' of the world is especially radical, I think, when he writes in the second set of seminars on *The Beast and the Sovereign* that 'there is no world' (Derrida 2011: 9), and as we'll see at the end of this chapter, that's precisely where its environmental ethics is generated. As Latour puts it in his own way in *Facing Gaia*, emphasising the plurality of 'world' underscored by Derrida,

> Ecology is clearly not the irruption of nature into the public space but *the end of 'nature'* as a concept that would allow us to sum up

our relations to the world and pacify them [. . .] The concept of nature now appears as a truncated, simplified, exaggeratedly moralistic, excessively polemical, and prematurely political version of the otherness of the world to which we must open ourselves [. . .] [F]or Westerners and those who have imitated them, 'nature' has made the *world* uninhabitable. (Latour 2017: 36, emphasis in original)

And this is why, he says, we need 'to try to descend from "nature" down toward the multiplicity of the world' (ibid.). Or as Derrida voices it in *The Beast and the Sovereign II*, 'there is no world, there are only islands' (Derrida 2011: 9) – a more radical claim, it turns out, than Latour's, and for reasons that are crucial to avoiding the ontological flattening that we end up with in Latour's ANT version of the claim, as we'll see later.

What I want to show in the last section of this chapter, however, is that the radically ecological character of the assertion 'there is no world' is not dependent upon the *phenomenological* register of the term 'world' that stretches from Kant, up through Uexküll, to Heidegger and then to Derrida. Indeed, we can redescribe the claim in robustly naturalistic and biological terms, and here I'm going to provide a much-shortened version of the material I cover in the third chapter of my recent book, *Ecological Poetics, or, Wallace Stevens's Birds*, focusing on the work of MacArthur fellow and Santa Fe Institute co-founder, Stuart Kauffman. Central to my argument is Kauffman's claim in his book *Humanity in a Creative Universe*, from 2017, that there are no 'entailing laws' that predetermine the evolution of the biosphere (hence the 'creative universe' of the book's title). In the section of Kauffman's book that I am most interested in, he assumes, almost exclusively, classical chemistry and physics, and 'the point is not to show that Newton's laws do not often work (they do) [. . .] but to begin to demolish the hegemony of reductive materialism and its grip on our scientific minds' (Kauffmann 2017: 40). The central thrust of this section of the book, which forces us to rethink not just the evolution of the biosphere but the entire concept of ecology, is that 'at least part of why the universe has become complex is due to an easy-to-understand, but not well-recognized, "antientropic" process that does not vitiate the second law [of thermodynamics]. Briefly', he continues,

as more complex things and linked processes are created, and can combine with one another in ever more new ways to make yet more complex amalgams of things and processes, the space of possible things and linked processes becomes vastly larger and the universe has not had time to make all the possibilities [. . .] There is an indefinitely expanding, ever more open space of possibilities ever

more sparsely sampled, as the complexity of things and linked processes increases [. . .] There is a deep sense in which the universe
becomes complex in its exploration of these ever more sparsely
sampled spaces of what is next possible because *'it can'*. (Ibid.: 42,
emphasis in original)

One of the more compelling examples Kauffman gives of this principle
obtains at the level of organic chemistry, before we even get to the domain
of autopoietic organisms, or what he calls 'Kantian wholes', where we
would more likely expect to find such forms of complexity. In a key
passage in the book, he writes, 'Proteins are linear strings of amino acids
bound together by peptide bonds. There are twenty types of amino acids
in evolved biology. A typical protein is perhaps 300 amino acids long, and
some are several thousand amino acids long. Now', he continues,

how many possible proteins are there with 200 amino acids? Well,
there are 20 choices for each of the 200 positions, so 20^{200} or 10^{260}
possible proteins with the length of 200 amino acids. This is a tiny
subset of the molecular species of CHNOPS [Carbon, Hydrogen,
Nitrogen, Oxygen, Phosphorus, Sulfur] with 100,000 atoms per
molecule. Now the universe is 13.7 billion years old and has about
10^{80} particles. The fastest time scale in the universe is the Planck
time scale of 10^{-43} seconds. If the universe were doing nothing but
using all 10^{80} particles in parallel to make proteins the length of
200 amino acids, each in a single Planck moment, it would take
10^{39} repetitions of the history of the universe to make all the possible proteins the length of 200 amino acids just *once*! [. . .] As we
consider proteins the length of 200 amino acids and all possible
CHNOPS molecules with 100,000 atoms or less per molecule, it
is obvious that the universe *will never make them all*. History enters
when the space of what is possible is vastly larger than what can
actually happen [. . .] A next point is simple and clear: Consider
all the CHNOPS molecules that can be made with 1, with 2,
with 3, with 4, with *n*, with 100,000 atoms per molecule. Call
the space of possible molecules with *n* atoms of CHNOPS the
phase space for CHNOPS molecules of *n* atoms. That phase space
increases enormously as *n* increases. Consequently, in the lifetime
of the universe, as *n* increases, that phase space will be sampled
ever more sparsely. (Ibid.: 43)

As Kauffman shows, this 'nonergodic' principle obtains even more radically and obviously at the level of the biosphere, in which 'its becoming

cannot be prestated, is not "governed" by entailing laws, in which what becomes constitutes ever-new Actuals that are "enabling constraints" that do not cause, but enable, ever-new, typically unprestatable, Adjacent Possible opportunities into which the evolving biosphere becomes' (ibid.: 64). And when we reach the level of what he calls 'Kantian wholes', or autopoietic organisms, this process is (not surprisingly) even more striking (ibid.: 67). If we think about the concept of biological function, for example, it is clear that while 'in classical physics there are only "happenings". The ball rolls down the hill, bumps a rock, veers', and so on, in biology we have to distinguish function from mere physical happenings. 'The function of the heart is to pump blood', Kauffman notes, but the heart 'causally also makes heart sounds, jiggles water in the pericardial sac', and so on (ibid.: 65). Classical physics will not help us here, because 'the *function* of the part is its causal consequences that help sustain the whole'; 'function' is causal, in other words, but *causal in a qualitatively different way from classical physics* (ibid.: 66). As Kauffman notes, another nail in the coffin for the reductionist approach is the fact that 'this capacity to define a function as a subset of causal consequences that can be improved in evolution further separates biology from physics, which cannot make the distinction among all causal consequences into a subset which are functions' (ibid.: 67).

Paying attention to these qualitatively different orders of causation in physical vs. biological systems is absolutely crucial to understanding what are sometimes called the 'mereological' relations in living systems, where the relationship between the part and the whole is radically different from what we find in physical systems. We typically think of causation in the scientific domain as bottom-up (as we do in the 'central dogma' of neo-Darwinism, where the lines of causality run from the gene to the physical characteristics, biomorphology, and so on, of the organism). But in the dynamic, self-organising, autopoietic forms of life in the biosphere, we find a much more complex relationship between component (or element) and system, because causality often operates in top-down and distributed fashion as well. As Alicia Juarrero notes, these 'mereological' relationships have 'bedeviled philosophers of science for centuries' (Juarrero 2015: 510), but what we can now see is that 'the unpleasant whiff of paradox' that 'remains in any mention of recursive causality' in living systems is unavoidable, and indeed is a crucial part of explaining such systems (ibid.: 511). What we find in autopoietic biological systems, in fact, is what she calls a 'decoupling in the locus of control: the components' behavior suddenly originate in and are under the control, regulation, and modulation of the emergent properties of the macro level, *as such*', which in turn '*loosens the one-to-one strict determinism from micro to macro level*' (ibid.: 519, emphasis in original). In contrast to physical systems, even those that show emergent self-organisation – dust devils, tornadoes, Bénard cells, and so on – where 'external agents or circumstances are responsible for the conditions within which physical self-organization takes place', in autopoietic systems those conditions and constraints are introduced and maintained *by the system itself*, resulting in a strong 'downward causation' in which systemic closure becomes 'a closure of constraint production, not just a closure of processes' (ibid.: 512–13).

This means (as Juarrero notes, quoting Kauffman) that 'it is impossible to predict emergent properties even in principle because the "categories necessary to frame them do not exist until after the fact"' (ibid.: 518). And of course, if everything we have said of biological organisms is also true of *us*, it is, in fact, *all the more the case* with us – and for the reasons Juarrero notes: the more complex the autopoietic life form, the more we find a 'dynamic decoupling' of the causative relationships between the micro- and macro-levels. Or as she puts it:

> System and environment co-evolve over time in such a way that the identification between macro-property and specific configuration becomes irrelevant; as we go up the evolutionary ladder, the go of things issues more and more from higher and higher levels and according to criteria established at progressively emergent levels. Just as living things are autonomous and self-directed in a way that physical dissipative structures are not, sentient, conscious, and self-conscious beings are even more autonomous and self-directed. (Ibid.: 520)

But here, I think, we need a stringent dose of deconstruction: specifically, Derrida's critique of what he calls the 'auto' of autonomy, auto-affection, autobiography, and the like – in short, his critique of intentionality and of related concepts such as 'agency' (Derrida 2008: 47, 56, 67). It's not that autonomy and self-directedness don't increase, as Juarrero suggests, with the increasing decoupling of micro- and macro-structures and the growing importance of downward causality. They do. It's just that the picture that intentionality and autonomy *gives to itself* (as Derrida characterises it) of its situation is unavoidably partial, reductive and blind to its full infrastructural conditions of possibility for emergence (or what I have already called its 'ecological' embeddedness) (ibid.: 12 and 30).

When we move from the level of the organism to the biosphere, we find the same recursive logic at work on a different scale. Having established the importance of the concept of biological function, Kauffman hypothesises that 'we cannot prestate the evolution of new functions in the biosphere, hence cannot prestate the ever-changing phase space of biological evolution which includes precisely the functions of organisms and their myriad parts and processes evolving in their worlds. But these ever-new functions', he continues, 'constitute the ever-changing *phase space* of biological evolution'. And what this means (logically enough) is that 'we can have *no entailing laws* at all for biological evolution' (Kauffmann 2017: 70, emphasis in original). Kauffman offers a nice, compact example of this process in his discussion of what are called Darwinian 'pre-adaptations' or 'exaptations' – the emergence of new, possibly useful, traits through random genetic mutation (staying with the discourse of the neo-Darwinian orthodoxy for the moment).

Kauffman's especially winning example of this process – where a side effect generated by random genetic mutation can become a functional asset for an organism under different environmental conditions, as Darwin himself surmised – is the emergence of the swim bladder in fish. The Darwinian exaptation whereby some early versions of fish had lungs, enabling them to bounce from puddle to puddle, led in time to the biological *function* of a ratio of air and water in fish that now live wholly in water, which allows, in turn, neutral buoyancy in the water column. Did this change the future evolution of the biosphere, Kauffman asks. 'Yes, and in two vastly different ways. First, new daughter species of fish with swim bladders and new proteins evolved.' But second,

> *once* the swim bladder exists, it constitutes a new Actual condition in the evolving biosphere. The swim bladder now constitutes a new, empty but Adjacent Possible niche, or opportunity for evolution. For example, a species of worm or bacteria could evolve to live, say exclusively, in the swim bladder. The Adjacent-Possible opportunities for evolution, given the new swim bladder, do not include all possibilities. For example, a *T. Rex* or giraffe could not evolve to live in the swim bladder. (Ibid.: 72)

One of the key theoretical points here arises when Kauffman asks, 'do we think that selection, in any way at all, "acted" to achieve the swim bladder as *constituting a new adjacent-possible empty niche* in which a worm or a bacterial species might evolve to live? No.' Further, he adds,

> does the swim bladder, once it has come to exist, *cause* the worm or bacterial species to evolve to live in it? *No.* The swim bladder *enables, but does not cause, the bacterial or worm species to evolve to live in it.* Instead, quantum random mutations to the DNA of the bacterium or worm yield variations in screwdrivers that may be selected at the

level of the whole organism by which the worm or bacterial species evolves to live in the swim bladder. (Ibid.: emphasis in original)

More radically still, this means that 'there is, therefore, no noncircular
way to define the "niche" of the organism separately from the organism. But that niche is the boundary condition on selection. The "niche"
is only revealed *after* the *fact*, by what succeeds in evolution' – hence
the mystery of what Darwin called 'the arrival of the fittest' (ibid.: 75,
emphasis in original).

It is hard to imagine a clearer articulation, in robust, naturalistic,
biological terms, of what Derrida calls 'the becoming-space of time
and the becoming-time of space' (Hägglund 2008: 2), the 'will have
been' of that which is 'to come', unprestatable and unanticipatable, with
Darwin's 'pre-adaptations' being precisely the material substrate, the
trace, on which retentions of the past and protentions of the future are
inscribed. As Martin Hägglund explains:

> Given that every temporal moment ceases to be as soon as it
> comes to be, it must be inscribed in a trace in order to be at all.
> This is the *becoming-space of time*. The trace is necessarily spatial,
> since spatiality is characterized by the ability to remain in spite of
> temporal succession. The spatiality of the trace is thus a condition
> for the synthesis of time, since it enables the past to be retained for
> the future. The spatiality of the trace, however, is itself temporal.
> Without temporalization a trace could not remain across time and
> relate the past to the future [. . .] In order to remain – even for a
> moment – a trace cannot have any integrity as such but is already
> marked by its own becoming past and becoming related to the
> future. Accordingly, the persistence of the trace cannot be the
> persistence of something that is exempt from the negativity of
> time. Rather, the trace is always in relation to an unpredictable
> future that gives it both the chance to remain and to be effaced.
> (Hägglund 2016: 39, emphasis in original)

– exactly in the manner in which Kauffman describes the non-entailed
evolutionary process of the biosphere.

Equally important (and I think this helps to underscore and indeed
clarify an aspect of Kauffman's argument that is often only implicit) is
what Hägglund calls the fundamental 'negativity' of time,

> which undermines *both* the idea of a discrete moment *and* the idea
> of an absolute continuity. Only if something is *no longer* – that

is, only if there is negativity – can there be a difference between before and after. This negativity must be at work in presence itself for there to be succession. If the moment is not negated in being succeeded by another moment, their relation is not one of temporal succession but of spatial co-existence. (Ibid.: 43, emphasis in original)

It is precisely the combination of this negativity of time with what Hägglund calls the 'arche-materiality' of the trace that makes Kauffman's non-entailed evolution of the biosphere thinkable. 'Precisely because every temporal moment negates itself', Hägglund writes, 'the duration of time can never be given in itself but depends on the material support of spatial inscription' in the form of the trace; 'without the later inscription nothing could persist and there would be no movement or passage of time' (ibid.).

Indeed, we find here the site of a *double* inscription, not just on the material substrate of the living being (as in the pre-adaptation of the swim bladder), but also in the dynamic contingency of the organism/ environment relationship in which that ontogenetic inscription happens, which can make the 'same' inscription function differently at different points in time. For example, as Bateson points out in his discussion of 'iconic genotypic signals', it is common to find what he calls 'a secondary statistical iconicism' in the animal kingdom of the following type:

> *Labroides dimidiatus*, a small Indo-Pacific wrasse, which lives on the ectoparasites of other fishes, is strikingly colored and moves or 'dances' in a way which is easily recognized. No doubt these characteristics attract other fish and are part of a signaling system which leads the other fish to permit the approaches of the cleaner. But there is a mimic of this species of *Labroides*, a saber-toothed blenny (*Aspirdontus taeniatus*), whose similar coloring and movement permit the mimic to approach – and bite off pieces of the fins of other fishes.
>
> Clearly the coloring and movements of the mimic are iconic and "represent" the cleaner. But what of the coloring and movements of the latter? All that is primarily required is that the cleaner be conspicuous and distinctive. It is not required that it represent something else. But when we consider the statistical aspects of the system, it becomes clear that if the blennies become too numerous, the distinctive features of the wrasses will become iconic warnings and their hosts will avoid them. (Bateson 1972: 418–19)

So if theoretical biology reminds us of the fact of double inscription, deconstruction reminds us that there is no evolution without the negativity of time and its inscription in the arche-materiality of the trace, figured on a larger biological canvas as the dynamic complexity of the organism/environment relationship. No negativity of time, no evolution; but also: no materiality of inscription in the trace, no evolution.

We're now in a better position to specify exactly what is wrong with Latour's Actor-Network Theory ontology in *Facing Gaia* – and to specify, moreover, why those problems are tethered to an insufficient understanding of the difference between first-order and second-order systems theory and how those, in turn, bear upon our understanding of the 'mereological' relations in organisms and the qualitatively different orders of causality that obtain in biological versus physical systems. A crucial underlying problem, I think, is that Latour continues to understand the terms 'system' and 'autopoiesis' as if they were simply synonyms for homeostasis and command-and-control, and the fingerprints of this misunderstanding in *Facing Gaia* are all over his use of the term 'cybernetics'. When Latour writes that the figure of the '*loop*' is 'the only way to draw a path between agents without resorting to the notions of part and a Whole that only the presence of an all-powerful Engineer – Providence, Evolution, or Thermostat – could have set up', he immediately cautions us to 'not hurry to identify this movement [. . .] with feedback loops in the cybernetic sense: we would revert at once to the model with a rudder, a helmsman, and a world government' (Latour 2017: 137). What he doesn't understand here – and what he doesn't understand when he suggests that Gaia is 'the outlaw, the anti-system' (ibid.: 87) – is a fundamental point I explore in great detail in *What Is Posthumanism?*: that second-order systems theory (of the sort mobilised by Maturana and Varela, Juarrero and Kauffman, among many others) is best understood, as Dirk Baecker puts it, 'as an attempt to do away with any usual notion of system, the theory in a way being the deconstruction of its central term' (Baecker 2001: 61).

Latour is right, of course, in his discussion of Lovelock, that 'all the sciences, natural or social, are haunted by the spectre of the "organism"', but he is wrong when he says that that figure

> always becomes, more or less surreptitiously, a '*superorganism*' – that is, a dispatcher to whom the task – or rather the holy mystery – of successfully coordinating the various parts is attributed [. . .] As soon as you imagine parts that 'fulfill a function' within a whole, you are inevitably bound to imagine, *also, an engineer* who proceeds to make them work together. (Latour 2017: 95, emphasis in original)

But as we have already seen with Kauffman's discussion of the concept of biological *function* in the larger context of the evolution of the biosphere with *no entailing laws*, this is an unwarranted assimilation of the concept of the organismic closure in what Kauffman calls 'Kantian wholes' to a *first-order* notion of holism and homeostasis. Sometimes, Latour associates this first-order notion of holism and homeostasis with 'an encompassing, preordained system of retroaction' of the sort we find in appeals to the 'equilibrium of nature' or the 'wisdom of Gaia' invoked, for instance, by Deep Ecology during its heyday (ibid.: 142). And sometimes he associates it with the hackneyed and rudimentary tropes of the 'Governor figure' and 'technological metaphors like that of the thermostat' (ibid.: 98). This, in turn, authorises for Latour an engineering, command-and-control understanding of causality in systems theory as '-centric', rather than decentred and 'decoupled', as Juarrero notes, whereas the whole point of Kauffman's non-ergodic, unentailed evolution of the biosphere is that it makes such an engineering fantasy literally unthinkable. So it should come as no surprise that Latour cannot comprehend that, in second-order systems theory, the account of the relationship between the 'part' and the 'whole' – those 'mereological' relationships that we saw Juarrero discussing a moment ago – is actually the *opposite* of the caricature he offers here. Indeed, as Yuk Hui has pointed out,

> in contrast to Lovelock's strong form of Gaia, consisting of a single organism, Margulis forced Lovelock to admit that Gaia [. . .] is rather a symbiogenesis of a great variety of organisms, including plants, animals, fungi, protists, and bacteria. The concept of symbiogenesis in turn comes from Varela and Maturana's concept of autopoiesis,

and in fact, he suggests, 'with the participation of Margulis, the Gaia theory moves from first-order cybernetics to second-order cybernetics' (Hui 2019: 83).

We find the same elisions in Latour's rendering of the 'inside' and 'outside' of the organism/environment relationship, where he simply collapses the 'inside' of autopoietic distinction in second-order systems theory into what he calls the 'selfish' position – and the economy of optimisation in neo-Darwinian reductionism – associated with Richard Dawkins and his 'selfish gene' theory (Latour 2017: 103). On the one hand, he seems to understand the second-order systems theory rendering of the organism/environment relationship when he writes that

> Properly speaking, for Lovelock and even more clearly for Lynn Margulis, there *is no longer any environment* to which one might

adapt. Since all living agents follow their own intentions all along, modifying their neighbors as much as possible, there is no way to distinguish between an environment to which the organism is adapting and the point at which its own action begins. (Ibid.: 100, emphasis in original)

So far, so good. Latour seems to grasp here the fundamental point that, in second-order systems theory (as we find it in Maturana and Varela in biology or Luhmann in sociology), the environment is not antecedent or pre-given but is always understood as the environment *of* the system – a strict corollary, of course, of the fact of autopoietic self-reference (what Latour calls, in a remarkably imprecise locution, 'intention' [ibid.: 100]).

But the theoretical coherence of Latour's argument goes completely off the rails when he glosses the following passage by one of Lovelock's collaborators, Timothy Lenton, who writes that, in Gaia, 'the evolution of organisms and their material environment' are 'so closely *coupled* that they form a *single, indivisible process*. Organisms possess environment-altering traits because the benefit that these traits confer (to the fitness of the organisms) outweighs the cost in energy to the individual' (quoted in ibid.: 100–1, emphasis in original). Latour gleefully reads this passage as saying that

> The inside and outside of all borders are subverted. Not because everything is connected in a 'great chain of being'; not because there is some global plan that orders the concatenation of agents; but because the interaction between a neighbor who is actively manipulating his neighbors and all the others who are manipulating the first one defines what could be called *waves of action*, which respect no borders and, even more importantly, never respect any fixed scale. (Ibid.: 101)

But of course, the obvious question here – if Latour himself is indeed an 'organism'– is how he is able to make this very assertion if 'the inside and the outside of all borders are subverted'. How can one speak of 'neigh-bours' and their 'intentions' (so important, after all, to the premium that Latour places on the disruptive and unpredictable play of 'agents') if there are no 'borders', no 'insides' and 'outsides' to distinguish them?

This is not merely a theoretical problem, it's an ethical one, as we'll see later in this chapter. And in Latour's work – which seems so intent on decentering the human in relation to the non-human world – it's related, as Jonathan Basile has shrewdly noted, to Latour's salient rhetorical gesture of promising 'a presuppositionless "return to the things themselves'" (Basile 2023 forthcoming: 137n1), which is, in turn, Latour's way of 'solving' the undertheorised (or untheorised) relationship between language and metalanguage, across which he freely traffics in his work. Latour everywhere insists that we can't simply reproduce the disciplinary discourse (the language game, as Wittgenstein would put it) of science, say, or sociology, if we want to have a critical view of what is really going on; and yet he also insists that 'there is no *meta*language, only infralanguages' (quoted in ibid.: 139n1). Latour's solution to this problem, such as it is, is to 'let the things themselves speak' (ibid.: 1392). But as Basile notes, 'Ironically, there is no discourse more anthropocentric or all-too-human than the one that pretends to bypass its own reading and writing or textuality', presuming it can '"give back" freedom and agency to the "nonhuman" precisely by casting itself as the universal medium or logos for that infinite translation and translatability without remainder' (ibid.: 142). Indeed, as Basile observes, 'This theo-logical immediacy is one of many habits of thought Latour has inherited from Michel Serres (to whom *The Pasteurization of France* is dedicated)', and I would add that much of the intoxication – the 'buzz', if you will – that comes from reading Latour and, especially, Serres, can be located in the effects generated by 'how diligently they efface the difference between language and metalanguage' – the deconstruction of which, Basile rightly notes, 'would require not only a careful reading of Serres and Latour, but of a half-century of "relationality" in science studies' (ibid.: 142n88).

To return to *Facing Gaia*, then, what Latour means by 'outlaw' is really, as far as I can tell, just contingency, but as we have already seen, this needs to be parsed in a much, much finer way. Latour is unable to theorise the relationship – indeed what one could call the *deconstructive* relationship – between 'inside' and 'outside', 'neighbour' and 'environment', because he doesn't grasp the key insight of second-order systems theory and the theory of autopoiesis: that the *contingency* of the self-reference of autopoietic organisms *is* the 'wild card', the 'outlaw', at the core of everything Latour wants from the unpredictable 'agency' and 'intentions' that push back against reductive totalisation and the engineering fantasies of 'life' and 'nature' that emerge from it. To be even more specific about this: the 'outlaw' character of the biosphere (and therefore its impact on the larger earth system of Gaia) is to be located not *just* in the contingency of the organism's self-reference and how it selectively determines its environment, its 'world'. It is also in the fact that that self-reference provides the conditions of possibility for the *recursive* operations of biological organisms in real time, and how that recursivity can make environmental differences *make* a difference (to paraphrase Bateson), establishing the 'decoupling in the locus of control' and the 'downward causality' that we saw Juarrero explaining earlier. What does this do? It enables what I call the second-order turn of 'openness from closure' that I explore in some detail in *What Is Posthumanism?* Closure and the recursive selectivity that goes with it – a selectivity forced upon organisms by the fact that any environment is always already exponentially more complex than any individual system – increase the differences that can *make* a difference in the organism's environment. Or as Luhmann succinctly puts it, self-referential closure 'does not contradict the system's *openness to the environment*. Instead, in the self-referential mode of operation, closure is a form of broadening possible environmental contacts' (Luhmann 1995: 37, emphasis in original). In short, what separates us from the world is precisely what connects us to the world.

So – to slice this a little more finely – there are actually *at least five* 'wild cards' in the deck here. First, there's the contingency of self-reference that we find in 'Kantian wholes' or autopoietic organisms, in which the meaning of an element is conferred by its functional role in the whole organism, as we find in the distinction between what Maturana and Varela call 'structure' and 'organization': 'Autopoietic unities', they write,

> specify biological phenomenology as [. . .] distinct from physical phenomenology [. . .] not because autopoietic unities go against any aspect of physical phenomenology – since their molecular components must fulfill all physical laws – but because the phenomena they generate in functioning as autopoietic unities depend on their organization and the way this organization comes about, and not on the physical nature of their components (which only determines their space of existence). (Maturana and Varela 1992: 51)

Second, there's *recursivity:* the circular process by which that self-reference operates dynamically in real time in the production of what Juarrero calls 'constraint closure' as not merely mechanical but processive, which enables differences (in the environment) to make a difference (in the organism) in the services of adaptation to a changing environment. Third, there's how that recursivity structures the organism/environment relationship in an ongoing way, *not only on the side of the organism, but also on the side of the environment*, as we see dramatically illustrated in the phenomena of niche construction, the so-called 'Baldwin effect', and so on. As Alexander Wilson notes, in the kinds of 'evolutionary arms races' dramatised in niche construction, we find highly selective, indeed unique, feedback loops that recursively compound themselves – and change the biosphere for doing so. For example, a bat evolves echolocation, which allows it to locate moths, in turn provoking the moths to evolve a capacity to hear the bats and maneuver evasively, which in turn presses the bats to evolve better maneuverability, and so on . . .

[These] 'runaway' effects occur everywhere in nature [. . .] Arms races and niches necessarily *close themselves off* from the overarching environmental influences and take off, playing their own private games, and therefore drift along unpredictably. This leads to the proliferation of complexity and nonlinear relations between species and their environments [. . .] The niche reinforces the *specialness* of its particular character [. . .] They are local *top-down* selectors, where the competition between individuals drives a progressively intensifying race to grow longer plumage or devise more complex songs and dances. (Wilson 2019: 91–2, emphasis in original)

One of the things 'the Anthropocene' can learn from 'the Animal', then, is that the alterity, 'creativity' and 'outlaw' relations that obtain among what Latour calls 'actants' are, for the reasons we have been outlining, much more unruly and unpredictable among biological life forms and their environmental relations than between, say, rocks or vacuum cleaners. And here, of course, we can add a fourth 'wild card' in the deck, another layer of recursivity that gets flattened in Actor-Network Theory – the 'not' and the 'no', the domain of the negative, introduced by the goal-directed behaviour of Kantian wholes. Again, Juarrero: 'Just as living things are autonomous and self-directed in a way that physical dissipative structures are not, sentient, conscious, and self-conscious beings are even more autonomous and self-directed' (Juarrero 2015: 520). Here, as Yuk Hui suggests, 'teleonomy', not 'teleology', is the term we want (Hui 2019: 142); goal-directed and purposive doesn't mean linear and pre-programmed (as in Latour's old-fashioned reading of cybernetics), but quite the contrary, because 'recursivity is not only a mechanism that can effectively "domesticate" contingency [. . .] it is also a mechanism that allows novelty to occur, not simply as something coming from outside, but also as an internal transformation' (ibid.: 139). And this, of course, can and does feed back into the environment and changes it, as Wilson has already noted. As theoretical biologist Denis Noble observes of the 'Baldwin effect' and so-called 'adaptability drivers' in niche construction, when organisms choose new niches in which to flourish, 'the process is an active choice of organisms, including learnt behavior', one whose causality 'is very far from random', but for that very reason, creative (Noble 2017: 223) – and not, as neo-Darwinians like to argue, simply a statistical feature of 'genetic drift'. And as we have already seen in Basile's critique of Latour, the fifth 'wild card' in the deck – scaling up now from plasticity, teleonomy, proportionate learning, and so on – is the far from 'natural' (yet importantly 'ecological') domain of technicity, language, metalanguage, disciplinarity, and so on, which I invoked at the outset in the work of Luhmann, Bateson, Derrida, and others.

I am going to some trouble to parse these difference and discontinuities as finely as I can – and, no doubt, they could be parsed even more finely – because the discontinuities involved here are crucial to understanding the specificity and singularity of different forms of life, and they open onto phenomenological discontinuities that are crucial to understand in their particularity, not just on their own, but also in how they feed back into the environment that they change. We can reframe these in terms of the question of scale in the biosphere, which is, as Timothy Clark has argued, 'at least as much ontological as epistemological in emphasis' (Clark 2018: 82–3). It's not just that 'a change in scale may constitute the element of metamorphosis in emergent properties'. For example,

> reproduction rates, survival of offspring, and so on may meet a scalar threshold at which the mere factor of increasing numbers becomes newly significant, either positively self-reinforcing in the form of swamping out possible competitors or autoimmune in the form of exhausting available sources of self-sustenance – or, at different time scales, both. (Ibid.: 85)

It's also that these scalar discontinuities open onto a much more complex dynamic in the biosphere in which the movement from one life form to another cannot be regarded as simply additive, a linear compounding of the same essential dynamic (as is most obvious when we enter the domain of consciousness, symbolic communication, and so on, via the gateway of teleonomy and purposive behaviour).

As Clark points out, this is one of the reasons that – even within the Derridean/deconstruction camp – we find some resistance to assertions such as Francesco Vitale's, in *Biodeconstruction: Derrida and the Life Sciences* (2018), that interactions and behaviours in an organism 'are ultimately inscribed in the structure of the program' as we find it elaborated in François Jacob's *The Logic of Life*, which Derrida engages in detail, as is well known, in his *Life Death* seminars (quoted in ibid.: 90). As Philippe Lynes has noted, Vitale here follows Jacob when he writes that, in the amoeba and the annelid, 'the program and its execution are very restricted because of the extreme simplicity of the nervous system; in man, the program is very open because of the great complexity of the nervous system and the brain, which is able to operate a much greater number of connections than the brain of the other animals' (quoted in Lynes 2018: xxxvi). 'At stake here', Lynes notes, 'is simply a difference in degree from lesser to greater flexibility', rather than a qualitative discontinuity between phenomenological domains that may be generated by the same programmatic substrates while being in no way reducible to them (Lynes 2018: xxxvi) – a fact exemplified, for instance, by the irreducibility of the phenomenon of consciousness to the material processes that give rise to it. This is so, in part because a good bit of what makes consciousness what it is is located *outside* the wetware of the organism's brain, in its prosthetic relationship to the radically external technicity of semiotic, symbolic and communicative systems, a fact which does not obtain – indeed does not *radically* obtain – for many life forms that are nonetheless subtended by the same code or form, genetic or otherwise. This is precisely why, as I have argued elsewhere, arguments such as Vitale's may be 'right', but they must also be accompanied by a return – indeed an ultra-philosophical return – to the phenomenological domain, and the discontinuities and differences thereof (Wolfe 2013: 68–83).

So let me begin to move towards a conclusion by summing up and ramifying some salient points. First, physics is not biology. Qualitatively different orders of causation and complexity, in which the 'negativity' of temporality plays a crucially irreducible role, are involved. As Giuseppe Longo and Maël Montévil point out in their groundbreaking book, *Perspectives on Organisms: Biological Time, Symmetries, and Singularities*, 'unlike in physics – classical, relativistic, or quantum – biological time has an origin, whatever level of organization we consider' (Longo and Montévil 2013: 88n6); 'a living being is a true "organizer" of time' that 'intimately articulates' itself within the domain of physics, 'all the while preserving its autonomy' (ibid.: 81). It's not that biology can flout the so-called laws of physics, as Kauffman, Maturana and Varela pointed out above; rather, it's a simple 'necessary' vs. 'sufficient' distinction. So (as we've already seen in Kauffman's argument) while in the world of physics, Longo and Montévil write, 'a falling stone follows exactly the gravitational arrow', biological entities 'may follow many different possible paths, and they go wrong most of the time: most organisms are extinct' and, to take another example, 'almost half of the fecundations in mammals do not lead to a birth'. In short, the phase space of living organisms is non-linear and constantly changing, in contrast to those of physics (ibid.: 225).

A predictable rejoinder here is that such a distinction limits itself to classical physics, when in fact the phenomena of the biosphere are best thought in terms of quantum mechanics, as in attempts by Vicki Kirby, Karen Barad and others to assimilate the quantum field and its 'entanglement' and 'intra-action' to a Derridean economy of a 'generalized writing' (Lynes 2018: xxxv–xxxix). But such a view is, we might say, too much bathwater for the baby, for a couple of reasons. First, as Longo and Montévil point out, causality in biological systems is discontinuous, and far from a one-size-fits-all phenomenon; sometimes it is quantum, sometimes it is classical, sometimes it is neither, and the relationships between that fact and the levels of the organism on which those forms of causation obtain is anything but linear or straightforward. As they note, 'in a cell, classical and quantum randomness both play a role and "superpose"' – examples they give of such quantum phenomena are electron tunnelling in processes of cellular respiration, electron transport in DNA, and quantum coherence in the process of photosynthesis – but what is far more important is the uptake of those quantum processes by the organism in question and its organisation (Longo and Montévil 2013: 210), where we find 'at least the same level of unpredictability as the quantum event', but one that 'does not belong to the quantum phase space' (ibid.: 211). In short, we find in biological phenomena both quantum and classical events, but because correlating them with their somatic effects in the organism involves both 'indeterminate acausal quantum molecular events' and 'non-random historical and contextual convergences' in the life of the organism in its environment, we cannot 'invent, as physicists do, a mathematically stable, pre-given phase space, as a "background" space for all possible evolutionary dynamics' (ibid.: 217) – a point ramified, as we have already seen, in Kauffman's analysis. The relevance of this point for my argument is only compounded by the theoretical and methodological fact, as Longo and Montévil remind us, that 'the relativistic and quantum fields are not unified; they are in fact incompatible' (ibid.: 265) – which raises the obvious and interesting question of why one would want to assimilate the domain of biology to the domain of physics in the first place.

For these and other reasons, the particular modes of organisation and causality that obtain in the biosphere cannot in any way be assimilated, as an 'equal partner', to a more general Actor-Network Theory, much less to any kind of flat ontology. Could we come up with an algorithm for the differences between these unequal partners? I believe – and I believe Latour believes – that the answer is 'no'. A fundamental reason for this 'no', as Longo and Montévil point out, is that in every important work drawn from mathematics, physics and computer science on the phenomenon of 'emergence' in dissipative dynamical systems, such as those we find in Artificial Life and Cellular Automata, 'the frame for intelligibility is a priori' and depends upon 'one or more pre-defined phase spaces' (ibid.: 224), which is one reason that complexity is more complex than the Complexity Theory developed in the 1980s and 1990s.

In light of the foregoing, I would put forward a proposition of sorts, what we might call 'The Five Cs': namely, when the Contingency of Constraint Closure in autopoiesis meets environmental Complexity, it becomes a source of Creativity in the biosphere. Environmental complexity can't get there by itself, and neither can the self-referential closure of organisms. The five Cs isn't a *formula* per se, precisely for the reasons we discussed earlier: the alterity of temporality as it operates dynamically in organisms in real time; and the scalar discontinuities noted earlier by Clark. Another reason is that the pressure of environmental complexity may be a driver, through the torque or 'fold' (to use Deleuzean language) of constraint closure, for metamorphic novelty and creativity in the phylogeny and ontogeny of organisms, or it may be overwhelming, or it may be both of these at different scales and at different points in the life of an organism or species (an individual organism is overwhelmed and perishes but its species adapts and develops).

This is precisely the opposite valuation of autopoiesis, closure and their associated dynamics from what we find in contemporary discourses such as Latour's Actor-Network Theory or Donna Haraway's 'sympoiesis', which she sets in pointed contrast to the theory of autopoiesis in her book *Staying with The Trouble* (2016). It's not that we all differ in our desire to view the biosphere (or the technosphere, or the relationship between the two) as an ongoingly rich, recursive and creative interaction between systems and environments. I share that desire, of course (and, honestly, I can't think of anyone doing serious work in the interdisciplinary humanities who *doesn't* want to think the question in precisely this way). But as I insisted at the outset, it's one thing to have a term that announces a critical or theoretical (or ethical or political) *desire*, and it's quite another to have a rigorous and coherent theory that can make good on that desire.

We have already seen the many problems with Latour's Actor-Network Theory and its attempt to adapt itself to the question of Gaia and the Anthropocene, and I would say much the same as some recent younger scholars have about the concept – or what I would actually call the *non*-concept – of 'sympoiesis'. As Jan Overwijk notes, the fundamental problem with the idea of 'sympoiesis' is exactly what we observed earlier with Latour's assertion that 'the inside and the outside of all borders are subverted'. Even though we may sympathise with the desire to fully appreciate the force of environmental and system-to-system interactions and exchanges, such positions 'lose the possibility of coherently theorizing the agency of the environment because they dissolve the system into its environment' (Overwijk 2021: 151), as in Haraway's insistence that 'autopoiesis is always "enfolded" by sympoiesis', with both being expressions of a larger 'holobiont' (quoted in ibid.: 154). But as Overwijk commonsensically observes, 'as boundaries between inside and outside collapse, closure thus gives way to openness. However, the question then becomes: To what is this system still open?' (ibid.: 183). As Basile puts it, 'Haraway is correct to treat symbiosis as a transformation of the model of life', but this raises at least two fundamental questions: 'Can there be the sym- of sym-biosis or -poiesis without the auto- of autopoiesis?' 'Is there any sense in *opposing* these two, as if they were separate and separable logics and models, between which we could freely choose?' In *Staying with the Trouble* Haraway insists that 'recuperation is still possible, but only in multispecies alliance, across the *killing* divisions of nature, culture, and technology and organism, language and machine' (quoted in Basile 2023 forthcoming: 237n176, emphasis added), but here Basile asks, is there 'any sense in claiming that divisions *kill* if it is only on their basis that the multi-ness of "multispecies alliance" can be thought? Is identity any more or less vital than difference?' (ibid.: 237n176, emphasis in original).

Overwijk is right, in my view, that approaching complex system/environment interactions from the theoretical framework of autopoiesis is coherent and rigorous, while the theory of 'sympoiesis' is not. As he puts it succinctly, Haraway attempts 'to grasp the two logics of sympoiesis and autopoiesis in a single vision', but

> the irony is that precisely as a result of this, she loses the possibility of observing either of them, since she undermines the distinction that enables the observation. Autopoiesis hinges on a boundary that her theory of sympoiesis denies. The result is that there are now no systems or environments left to engage in sympoiesis, because the environment that is the holobiont has now become everything there is. A sympoietic system can thus never observe an autopoietic system, but an autopoietic system *can* observe a sympoietic one. Using the theory of autopoiesis, 'sympoietic' systems could simply be observed as structural couplings between incommensurable autopoietic systems – they could be observed as symbiotic. (Overwijk 2021: 155–6)

Of course, defenders of sympoiesis, Actor-Network Theory and the like will typically respond that the objections I'm making here are essentially logical and phenomenological, in contrast to the ontological and empirical 'realism' they desire – the desire to return to 'the things them-selves' in Latour already scrutinised by Basile. As we have already seen with our forays into theoretical biology, however, exactly the opposite is true. It is the deconstructive, second-order systems theory view I am arguing for here that is, in reality, far more empirical and materialist, that can make sense of the paradoxical modes of being of living systems, scrupulously attending to not only the sharp, insurmountable differ-ences between the life sciences and the domain of physics, but also the historically tuned sociological specificity of their disciplinary discourses and how they are produced.

One final reason that I'm insisting on this contrast between my posi-tion here and notions such as 'sympoiesis' is that there are perhaps unex-pected ethical and even political stakes, not just logical or ontological or epistemological ones, involved in the difference. I find deeply attrac-tive, of course, the premium on 'situated knowledges' and the desire announced by the idea of 'sympoiesis' to foreground the rich, recursive interaction of different organisms with each other and their environ-ments. But I have to say that – in the terms in which they are framed – I don't find them, in the end, incompatible. Overwijk captures the prob-lem succinctly when he notes that whatever environment we observe is 'always a matter of perspective – a matter of which system observes it. It is why the inventors of the concept of autopoiesis, Humberto Maturana and Francisco Varela, underline the importance of their adage that "eve-rything said is said by someone"' (ibid.: 154). And so, the fundamental question that remains for any theory that rejects the self-referential closure (or 'blindness', as it sometimes is put) of autopoiesis 'is one that is famil-iar to Haraway: "Where is this someone situated?" From what vantage point, exactly, does one pronounce that all forms of self-referential dif-ference are expressions of an encompassing "holobiont"?' (ibid.). Where is the non-seeing that is structurally built into this seeing, a blindness that requires – not out of good will or 'tolerance' (as Derrida would put it) but out of necessity – the seeing of the other, of other observations? Here, a perhaps unexpected but unavoidable dialectical reversal emerges clearly: the 'everything is connected' view of ecology that seems to undermine the 'god's eye view' that Haraway rightly criticises is, in fact, simply the flip side of the same coin, because the ability to say that 'everything is connected' (or that everything that is partially connected is an expression of the 'holobiont') requires, by definition, the ability to have a view of 'everything'. Isn't the 'map' presumed to coincide with the 'territory' here? And doesn't this bypass the 'situatedness' of what deconstruction would call the 'performativity' of the utterance or the observation, which would call attention to its own self-reference, its own partiality?

The 'soft' version of the claim is that 'we all live in the same world, we just see it differently'. Unfortunately, as I have argued, this seemingly commonsensical assertion – aside from being logically incoherent and question begging – is also ethically problematic. The more radical and coherent version of the claim is Derrida's: 'there is no world'. And it's precisely that radical insistence, as we have seen, that makes it *ecological*. This is not simply a matter of 'stories' that we find compelling (or don't) as anthropology-inflected cultural studies likes to say. But the emphasis on 'stories' in such work *does* point towards an important point of emphasis that we both share: that such pragmatic engagements are not *representational* – or more precisely, not representational in the sense that the efficacy or effectiveness of the representation depends upon its accuracy. It is a doing and a making, not a mirroring (as the later Wittgenstein of the *Philosophical Investigations* would say).

The point can be formalised a little more carefully and clearly via second-order systems theory. Because an environment, as we have seen in our discussion of theoretical biology, is the 'outside' *of* an 'inside' whose self-referential closure is contingent, it can never be imaged, can never be a 'place', as Derrideans would put it, even though different organisms might share the same space, materially and physically. Luhmann: 'the environment is different for every system, because each system excludes only itself from its environment' (Luhmann 1995: 17). Organisms may represent their environment to themselves, but that representation has no isomorphic or transparent relationship to what is *actually* happening in the organism/environment relationship in real time (which is obvious, for example, in the differences between what is going on in all the dimensions and processes of the human body in its environment in real time, and the representation of the environment that consciousness gives to itself at the same time). This virtualisation of the environment by different systems, different observers, is also a complexification. We might say that here, less (the absence of a final, authoritative representation of the environment) is more. As William Rasch puts it succinctly, 'contingency, the ability to alter perspectives, acts as a reservoir of complexity within all simplicity' (Rasch 2000: 39) – not just in a logical sense, but in a real, material sense that is about getting on in the world through trial and error and learning from others. From that vantage point, the acknowledgement of self-reference and autopoiesis, not the overcoming of it, is in fact the source of a robust and coherent theory of the necessity of an ethical pluralism, as we touched on at the outset with Maturana's 'super-realism'. The ethical stakes of this fact are summed up nicely by Hans Georg Moeller in his 'ecological' and 'metabiological' reading of systems theory, when he writes,

The ability to observe, paradoxically, also implies limitations, and thus inabilities, of observation. The partial blindness that comes with evolution also implies a certain ethical and pragmatic blindness. Since it is impossible to see everything, it is also impossible to see what is good for all. (Moeller 2012: 72)

In a metatheoretical context, it is important, I think, to insist on these distinctions, because it is crucial at this moment to develop a robust, interdisciplinary anti-reductionism, a side project of which (but a central strategic goal of which) involves doing our part to bring an end to the hegemony of the neo-Darwinian paradigm and the various engineering fantasies of 'life' and the genome that it authorises. On this terrain, Latour and I are, of course, on the same team. Here, however – to reach back to my opening comments from *What Is Posthumanism?* about the importance of not just *what* you're doing but *how* you're doing it – I would insist on the importance of working hard to theorise an *anti-reductionist* anti-reductionism. And here, I think, Latour and I are *not* on the same team, at least not on the terrain explored in this chapter, even though we share the same theoretical and existential desire to push back against reductionism in all its forms. In that context, I would insist that the discourse and problematic of 'the Animal' is not done just yet – far from it – even though the current fashion is to see it as perhaps an early and already obsolesced mode of posthumanist intervention. Paying serious attention to the question of 'the Animal' forces us to think more clearly and more rigorously about the biosphere in all its singularity and uniqueness in ways that reach far beyond the question of climate change and the Anthropocene. To make sense of any of these, we have to start with the realisation that what's needed here is not flat but ever more jagged ontologies.

Note

1. This chapter contains portions of material that previously appeared in: Cary Wolfe (2020), 'What "the Animal" Can Teach "the Anthropocene"', *Angelaki: Journal of the Theoretical Humanities*, 25(3): 131–45.

References

Baecker, Dirk (2001), 'Why Systems?', *Theory, Culture, Society*, 18(1): 59–74.

Basile, Jonathan (2023), *Virality Vitality*, unpublished manuscript, University of Minnesota Press (forthcoming).

Bateson, Gregory (1972), *Steps to an Ecology of Mind*, New York: Ballantine Books.

Clark, Timothy (2015), *Ecocriticism on the Edge: The Anthropocene as a Threshold Concept*, New York: Bloomsbury Academic.

Clark, Timothy (2018), 'Scale as a Force of Deconstruction', in Matthias Fritsch, Philippe Lynes and David Wood (eds), *Eco-Deconstruction: Derrida and Environmental Philosophy,* New York: Fordham University Press, pp. 81–97.

Clarke, Bruce (2014), '"The Anthropocene", or, Gaia Shrugs', *Journal of Contemporary Archaeology*, 1(1): 101–4.

Derrida, Jacques (2008), *The Animal That Therefore I Am*, trans. David Wills, New York: Fordham University Press.

Derrida, Jacques (2011), *The Beast and The Sovereign, Vol. 2*, trans. Geoffrey Bennington, Chicago: University of Chicago Press.

Hägglund, Martin (2008), *Radical Atheism: Derrida and the Time of Life*, New York: Fordham University Press.

Hägglund, Martin (2016), 'The Trace of Time: A Critique of Vitalism', *Derrida Today*, 9(1): 36–46.

Haraway, Donna J. (1991), *Simians, Cyborgs, and Women: The Reinvention of Nature*, New York: Routledge.

Haraway, Donna J. (2016), *Staying with the Trouble: Making Kin in the Chthulucene*, Durham, NC: Duke University Press.

Hui, Yuk (2019), *Recursivity and Contingency*, London: Rowman and Littlefield.

Juarrero, Alicia (2015), 'What Does the Closure of Context-sensitive Constraints Mean for Determinism, Autonomy, Self-determination, and Agency?', *Progress in Biophysics and Molecular Biology*, 119: 510–21.

Kauffman, Stuart A. (2017), *Humanity in a Creative Universe*, New York: Oxford University Press.

Latour, Bruno (2017), *Facing Gaia: Eight Lectures on the New Climatic Regime*, trans. Catherine Porter, Cambridge: Polity Press.

Longo, Giuseppe and Maël Montévil (2013), *Perspectives on Organisms: Biological Time, Symmetries, and Singularities*, New York: Springer.

Luhmann, Niklas (1995), *Social Systems*, trans. John Bednarz Jr with Dirk Baecker, Stanford, CA: Stanford University Press.

Luhmann, Niklas (2000), *The Reality of the Mass Media*, trans. Kathleen Cross, Stanford, CA: Standford University Press.

Lynes, Philippe (2018), *Futures of Life Death on Earth: Derrida's General Ecology*, London: Rowman and Littlefield.

Maturana, Humberto R. and Bernhard Poersken (2004), *From Being to Doing: The Origins of the Biology of Cognition*, trans. Wolfram Karl Koeck and Alison Rosemary Koeck, Heidelberg: Carl-Auer.

Maturana, Humberto R. and Francisco J. Varela (1992), *The Tree of Knowledge: The Biological Roots of Human Understanding*, trans. Robert Paolucci, Boston, MA: Shambhala Press.

Moeller, Hans-Georg (2012), *The Radical Luhmann*, New York: Columbia University Press.

Noble, Denis (2017), *Dance to the Tune of Life: Biological Relativity*, New York: Cambridge University Press.

Overwijk, Jan (2021), *Rationalization: Paradoxes of Closure and Openness*, unpublished dissertation, University of Amsterdam.

Rasch, William (2000), *Niklas Luhmann's Modernity: The Paradoxes of Differentiation*, Stanford, CA: Stanford University Press.

Uexküll, Jakob von (2010), *A Foray Into the Worlds of Animals and Humans* with *A Theory of Meaning*, trans. Joseph D. O'Neil, Minneapolis: University of Minnesota Press.

Vitale, Francesco (2018), *Biodeconstruction: Jacques Derrida and the Life Sciences*, trans. Mauro Senatore, Albany, NY: SUNY Press.

Wilson, Alexander (2019), *Aesthesis and Perceptronium: On the Entanglement of Sensation, Cognition, and Matter*, Minneapolis: University of Minnesota Press.

Wolfe, Cary (2009), *What Is Posthumanism?*, Minneapolis: University of Minnesota Press.

Wolfe, Cary (2013), *Before the Law: Humans and Other Animals in a Biopolitical Frame*, Chicago: University of Chicago Press.

Wolfe, Cary (2020), *Ecological Poetics, or, Wallace Stevens's Birds*, Chicago: University of Chicago Press.

11

Materialism, the Spiritual and the Scalar

John Ó Maoilearca

Introduction: from the new materialism to the old new spiritualism

Several contemporary approaches in both ontology and philosophy of mind (especially concerning the mind-body relation) have gathered under the banner of a 'new materialism' in the first two decades of the twenty-first century. Though this particular title covers a wide range of materialisms variously espoused through biology, neurology, physics, computer science and even mathematics, they have nonetheless become part of mainstream European thought in many circles. More broadly still, 'materialism' as such – be it 'new' or 'old', 'historical', 'transcendental' or even 'performative' – today represents the received wisdom in much contemporary philosophy. By contrast, what might be called 'spiritual' or 'spiritualist' philosophy is (ironically) all but dead in these fields. If there is a spiritual life for 'continental' philosophy, it keeps itself well hidden. Whereas small corners within Anglo-American 'analytic' philosophy have of late attempted to rehabilitate the spiritual – or consciousness – through panpsychism (in the work of Galen Strawson and David Charmers, for instance), or the process thought of Whitehead and his heirs, the European approach, with some exceptions, seems happiest when keeping a safe distance from anything with even a hint of the immaterial about it. Yet, as we will see, there are even more heterodox models of mind and life available to us than these Anglo-American views, ones that might be sustained without necessarily being accompanied with such (incompatible) associates as the immaterial, the ideal or the disembodied.

The most significant and current European materialism is undoubtedly what calls itself 'new materialism'. It is built upon two premises that are noteworthy for us. The first concerns what counts as 'new' in its understanding of matter. Though Christopher Gamble, Joshua Hanan and Thomas Nail argue in their 2019 study of the movement that 'there is currently no single definition of new materialism', they do add that they share a 'perceived neglect or diminishment of matter in the dominant Euro-Western tradition as a passive substance intrinsically devoid of meaning' (Gamble et al. 2019: 111). Whereas modern materialism was defined by 'the passivity of matter insofar as matter is what is caused or moved by something else: vital and causal forces or natural laws of motion', the new materialists emphasise how 'matter is "alive", "lively", "vibrant", "dynamic", "agentive", and thus active' (ibid.: 116). Matter is *alive* – there is a *material* life. Moreover, this is a non-reductive view of matter opposed to the physicalism or mechanism adopted by many of the eighteenth- and nineteenth-century reductive materialisms, with physics deemed the supervening science that treats of ultimately inert, passive and atomistic quantities functioning in calculable, determined ways. Wholes were deemed epiphenomenal in one way or another in this view, and only an analysis into composite parts revealed the truth of the matter as inert and lifeless. Indeed, such approaches more or less continued well into the twentieth century in positivist philosophies, with only very recent developments, such as 'New Mechanical Philosophy' (or 'New Mechanism'), tempering the views held by many in this tradition.[1]

In clear opposition to these views, new materialists generally follow Gestalt principles, and deem matter to form complex, non-linear and dynamic wholes that are not the sum of their supposedly inert parts. Indeed, their material parts are also dynamic, and even what might be called 'living': though they may reside within the physical, there is an *indeterminacy to their life*, one on a par with that found in biology (stem cells) and cognitive science (neural plasticity, embryonic epigenesis). This focus on the *micro* by both old and new materialisms operates, therefore, in contrary ways, one where the micro is alive and can generate life, versus another where the micro is marked by inertia, and forms a bedrock of lifelessness.

Oddly enough, however, both materialisms follow what Sam Coleman calls 'smallism': the idea that truth resides in the smallest particulars of reality (which may clump together to form larger wholes); that 'the ontological truth is to be found with the small, or with all the "smalls" in all their innumerable multiplicity' (Coleman 2006: 40–4; cited in Pinch 2014–15: 15). In the new materialism, however, wholes are also real, even though emergent – their properties constitute a genuinely different level of reality, albeit that they are generated by the complex interactions of the smaller, constitutive elements that are themselves a form of the living. This *emergence* of the larger from the smaller, one that is neither reductive (the large does not reduce entirely to the small) nor mechanistic (such small matter is not passive), is a crucial aspect for much of this new thinking. The question of level and scale, therefore, both spatial and temporal, will be critical in what follows here.

Whether it be Quentin Meillassoux's 'mathemic' valorisation of contingency, the idea of 'plasticity' in Catherine Malabou's neurophilosophy, entanglement and quantum indeterminacy in Karen Barad's philosophy of physics, or 'vibrant matter' in Jane Bennett's neo-vitalism, we also see a *second*, less explicit premise of new materialism in much of its work. This is the tenet that whatever number of emergent, vital and non-reducible properties are allowed to matter, the idea of *spirit* cannot be added to the list. Non-reduced *materiality* alone prevails, while a transcendent, Platonist, notion of spirit – the only one deemed possible by some – remains the conceptual outsider to be either eliminated or simply ignored. But is this justified by all accounts of the spiritual? As John Zammito writes: 'one of the essentially contested issues surrounding the new materialism is how to conceive the relation of "spirit" to the natural' (Zammito 2017: 309–10). This is why the possibility of a *non-Platonist* (or immanent) spirit is rarely, if ever, entertained. One might invoke Elizabeth Grosz's recent book, *The Incorporeal*, as a counterexample to this given its own concern with the 'limits of materialism' and the need (following the Stoics) to inscribe ideality within matter, with exploring, as Grosz puts it, 'an *extramaterialism*, in the inherence of ideality, conceptuality, meaning, or orientation that persists in relation to and within materiality as its immaterial or incorporeal conditions' (Grosz 2017: 5). Yet even here it is only as a negation (or qualifier) of matter (the *im*-material, the *extra*-material, the *in*-corporeal), that this 'ideal' is affirmed, rather than the positive, immanent reality of spirit.[2]

And here is where some more historical research may be of use when looking at such philosophical movements, in particular around the school of 'French Spiritualism'. This was a loose tradition of thought that lasted from the late eighteenth century up to Henri Bergson in the twentieth century as its last and probably greatest representative. Despite its name, it was not a school of the occult, but what we might nowadays call a non-dualist, non-reductive approach to mind and body. These earlier French philosophers, including Maine de Biran (1766–1824), Félix Ravaisson (1813–1900) and Émile Boutroux (1845–1921), were equally determined to find a way in which matter and spirit could be thought together, but without turning to either dualism or reductionism. The place of spirit was retained in their research through *movement*, *vitality*, *duration* and *contingency*.

The word 'spirit', of course, connotes many things for many people. Beyond philosophy, the term also refers to the occult and parapsychological. Nevertheless, without falling for Gerald Edelman's straw man argument – i.e. the idea that anything other than the most parsimonious, scientistic and non-subjective approaches is simply turning physics into a 'surrogate spook' – we can still admit that matter is weirder than many would allow (see Edelman 1992: 212–18). As Adela Pinch writes, modern-day 'trends in the humanities that embrace panpsychism, vibrant matter, object-oriented ontologies, and extended or dispersed conceptions of consciousness, could benefit from an examination of Victorian debates about panpsychism' (Pinch 2014–15: 1). But we do not aim to correct new materialism here or detract from its valuable contributions to European philosophy. For it is precisely on questions of *movement*, *vitality*, *duration* and *contingency* where the 'new materialists' are also correct, albeit while also being less 'new' than proclaimed. For example, the materialism of *contingency* forwarded in Meillassoux's *Après la finitude* from 2006, actually reinvents, one hopes unwittingly, the ideas of Émile Boutroux, whose *De la contingence des lois de la nature* from 1874 argued for a similar contingency in the laws of nature. Only, and here's the twist, Boutroux argued his case *in the name of spiritualism*, not materialism. This makes Meillassoux's valorisation of the contingency of nature in the name of materialism even more ironic. For Boutroux, the contingent is a sign of spirit, not mathematised matter.

So, both (analytic) panpsychists and spiritualists (in the French philosophical sense of the term) offer us alternative models for thinking about matter and its interrelations with human and non-human life, mind and spirit. Indeed, in the example of Bergson, we see an attempt to naturalise spirit via his concept of *durée*, without reducing or eliminating it.[3] We asked earlier whether the attitude of much contemporary materialist thought towards the category of spirit was justified. Behind this possibly simplistic question lies another, more complex one, however: can the category of the spiritual provide an added dimension to 'materialism' in such a manner that neither reduces it *nor* inflates itself, but simply shows how the difference between the two might be considered *a matter of temporal scale, of level or plane*?

A recent work from Larry Sommer McGrath is illuminating in this regard. In *Making Spirit Matter: Neurology, Psychology, and Selfhood in Modern France*, Sommer McGrath writes that the spiritualism that emerged in France in the late nineteenth century was not like the spiritualism that went before – this was a 'new spiritualism', or at least it was significantly different from older varieties because it had taken a scientific, and even materialist turn (Sommer McGrath 2020: 10). As he reports on this

particular reading of the issue: 'the new spiritualism "is not a new doctrine", one author wrote in 1884; "it is spiritualism renewed by science."
[. . .] The characterisation of this transformation as a turn to materialism
took hold thanks to a critic of the movement. A defender of the old
guard decried what he saw as its abnegation in the form of "neo-materialism"' (ibid.). For Sommer McGrath, this critic was actually right and
a 'materialist moment' had by then 'inflected the spiritualist movement
by the turn of the century'. Moreover, the chief protagonist of this turn,
he contends, was Bergson: 'the thrust of his oeuvre, I argue, was to steer
a materialized spiritualism into the twentieth century' (ibid.). Not only
was Bergson the most 'successful representative of the materialist turn in
spiritualism', according to Sommer McGrath, he led a movement that
operated with much more 'expansive notions of rationality, positivism,
and materialism' (ibid.: 15–16, 13). And here we see a clear dovetailing
between this once 'new', turn-of-the-century spiritualism with what is
new in the new materialism we have currently, and it concerns a shared
non-reductive approach to both matter and spirit:

> The charge of 'neo-materialism' was revelatory. The accused
> never ascribed the label to themselves; yet, it was hardly a mis-
> nomer [. . .] Unlike reductive materialisms, which conceptual-
> ized matter as the substratum and final explanation of spirit, this
> 'neo-materialism' – and its leading practitioner, Henri Bergson –
> reimagined matter to enter into a partnership with the spiritual
> powers of memory, creativity, and action. (Ibid.)

Sommer McGrath is not alone in his more ecumenical interpretation of
the spirit-matter relations at play amongst these thinkers. Jeremy Dunham writes that the 'new spiritualists' were 'inspired by developments in
the life sciences [and] developed a theory of nature as open, creative, and
evolving' (Dunham 2020: 1005, 988); while Mark Sinclair and Delphine
Antoine-Mahut have argued that 'spiritualism in the first half of the
[nineteenth] century should be seen as a plural and open-ended development of a programme rather than as the reproduction of a one-track
thought', and even that we 'have to reject as simplistic and superficial
standard characterizations of positivism and spiritualism as diametrically
opposed' (Sinclair and Antoine-Mahut 2020: 862, 863).[4] And to round
out these new, revisionist histories, we can also turn to Jean Gayon, who
even argues that

> Bergson was a 'spiritualistic positivist.' This is not retrospective
> interpretation, something that I would formulate because it sounds

like a nice paradox. It is the plain expression of the historical fact. Around 1900, 'spiritualistic positivism' was the current name of a living tradition among certain French philosophers, such as Jules Lachelier or Émile Boutroux. Like Bergson, who was directly influenced by them, they emphasized a conception of the mind founded on spontaneity, contingency and indeterminism. (Gayon 2005: 47)

What we see, then, is a clear *covariance* between the flight of new materialism away from the old materialism – a flight that was inflected by properties also associated with spirit (creativity and contingency) – and the flight of the new spiritualism away from its older forebear, whose own route was modified by elements from material science. So, instead of talking of matter *or* spirit, we might talk in terms of continua, of contingency, creativity and vitality. Yet, these continua are not homogenous, but themselves replete with qualitive change, changes or variations that proceed *at different scales in space and time*.

On scales and covariance

Here we must interrupt our flow to make an important point about *covariance*. In his essay, 'Scale Variance and the Concept of Matter', Derek Woods speaks about the difference between 'scale variance' (things that change with scale) and 'scale invariance' (things that do not) (Woods 2017: 200–4). This notion builds on the work of the philosopher of science Mariam Thalos and her concept of 'scale freedom', which Woods interprets as 'freedom from the notion that any single scale is the master scale'. What Woods takes from this is the principle that 'there is irreducible activity at every scale', as well as (crucially for us) that '*matter* may not be the best concept for what the new materialism works to address' (ibid.: 201–2). In covariance, a continuity is formed through movements changing in concert: not as the *same* activity *simpliciter* but as different activities (plural) in some form of temporal reciprocity. And, we would argue, *neither a spiritualism devoid of matter nor a materialism devoid of spirit could accommodate such continua*.

In the context of French new spiritualism (and Bergson in particular) it is worth lingering over these concepts of scale and scalarity. In 'Philosophical Intuition' (1911), Bergson says this: 'the matter and life which fill the world are equally within us, the forces which work in all things we feel within ourselves; whatever may be the inner essence of what is and what is done, we are of that essence' (Bergson 1992: 124). Microcosm and macrocosm, self and world, part and whole.

Such reciprocity might remind us of one of the key principles of Renaissance Hermeticism – that of 'as above, so below'. This was the idea that earthly events reflect those occurring on an astral plane by means of correspondences and attunements – a notion that Bergson here reinvents through his own idiom of affect, force and movement within a flat ontology of vital processes.[5] We might say that the centre is 'decentred' through a proliferation of centres: in Bergsonian terms, a kind of 'complete relativism' is installed, a flattened ontology with no unsurpassable hierarchy of macro over micro (at least in principle) – there is movement between levels or 'scale freedom' as we heard it described above. Such proliferations should be treated cautiously, however: attributing powers at the wrong scale, irrespective of the equalities of macrocosm and microcosm, can lead to delusions of voluntarism and control (what cognitivists call 'Hyperactive Agency Detection').

Moreover, this type of Renaissance 'episteme', one governed by a relation of *analogy* between every level of nature, above and below, need not be seen simplistically as *only* spatial, despite the language used to describe it. Scale is not always a set of nesting Russian dolls, of quantities containing quantities. Many authors agree on this. For Bruno Latour, the notion of continuous, transitive scales needs to be dismantled entirely, such that switching dimensions is never a smooth 'zoom' in or out, but a disorientation that is 'as much temporal as spatial' (Latour 2017: 96).[6] Likewise for Karen Barad, scale is 'much more complex than simply a "nesting relationship"', being instead 'a property of spatial phenomena intra-actively produced, contested, and reproduced' (Barad 2007: 245). Even Gilles Deleuze and Félix Guattari's idea of the 'molar' and 'molecular' must be seen, they say, as systems of reference or relation rather than as spatial scales.[7]

Indeed, even *quantitative* scales themselves can be *qualified* too as being more than quantity, more than the ability for one magnitude to *contain* another. Size too can resist quantification. Writing about 'bigness' within the theoretical humanities, David Wittenberg points out that

> Size change is a confrontation with the hyperfactical density and opacity of *the body* itself: the body is constantly in the way, inhibiting conventional views and viewpoints, and often directly terrifying. To be big, or rather to be too big – or to be compelled to confront what is too big – is to reanimate a primal physical relationship with objects that the acquisition of correct scale sublimates or distills away [. . .] Bigness is not something we accomplish by rescaling. Bigness comes *before* scale, maybe strictly

speaking *before size*. And therefore, all the more, it precedes any analytic of magnitude or of the sublime. (Wittenberg 2019: 352)

Bigness is a quality, no less than oneness or twoness are not quantities in the first instance either, but qualities, *qualia* even (at least for mathematical intuitionists like L. E. J. Brouwer, or indeed Bergson himself) (see Brouwer 1975).

Admittedly, a top-down mereology (the science of parts and wholes), one regarding the part from the perspective of the whole, might seem to be an impossible task if *one is actually the part in question*. How can the small transcend its partial point of view? And yet Spinoza starts from God, or Substance, just as Deleuze and Guattari likewise write, it is said, from the point of view of the Earth on itself as a giant molecule (see Lambert 2005). The era of 'big data' is one empirically anodyne way in which patterns of change, rhythms and continuities (covariances) might reveal themselves to their own participants. Big data can be seen as a temporal resampling, time-lapse geo-anthropology operating at higher degrees of condensation. Such bigger pictures might reveal who knows what was happening when we were collectively doing 'X', even though we each thought at the time that we were operating individually doing 'Y'.[8] Hence, as Jane Bennett suggests, American food may have facilitated the invasion of Iraq, and sandstorms may be involved in the spread of violence. Other examples of 'as above, so below', of the 'micro' reflecting the 'macro', offer themselves in various more contemporary vocabularies.[9]

Significantly, though, the part-whole relations in play in these examples are not at all scalar in any quantitative sense of containment. Much of the puzzling nature of scale and composition can be tempered, however, when we think of it *in terms of time*. The relations between parts and wholes must be thoroughly *temporalised*.[10] For example: we can also qualify a scale by temporalising it in terms of rhythm, say, or in the language of memory. We can follow this second route by comparing Bergson's ideas with Carl Jung (no stranger either to esoteric ideas and hermeticism in his own psychology). Pete Gunter does exactly this when he writes about Jung's 'collective unconscious' alongside *Creative Evolution*'s theory of a 'biological memory' contained within each animal: there are 'dormant potentialities, "memories" of a common past which it [each animal] shares with all other living creatures' (Gunter 1982: 644).[11] Examples given by Bergson himself include the Ammophila wasp, which seems to have a magical knowledge of the physiognomy of its traditional prey, a caterpillar, allowing it to apply just enough sting to paralyse but not kill it (mummifying it alive for later consumption) (Bergson 1911: 181).[12] In what could be seen as an animal-prefiguring of Arthur C. Clarke's 'third law' – that 'any sufficiently advanced technology is indistinguishable from magic' – for Bergson, any sufficiently evolved 'instinct' will appear to reason as magical knowledge. Yet this miracle is only apparent: what is real is the continuity formed by the co-evolutionary movement of two apparently separate entities – wasp and caterpillar – in one, *covarying* relation. These biological forms are really two sides of a continuous process – a process that is itself composed from other, interpenetrating processes. Instinct appears miraculous only when we do not think of it in terms of continuous evolutionary movements at the correct scale, movements that are 'reciprocally determining' (in Deleuzian language), 'entangled' (Barad), or, in Bergson's vernacular, 'interpenetrating' each other. Though this biological account from Bergson's *Creative Evolution* (1907) obviously needs updating, its essentials remain the same, as neuroscientist Patrick McNamara illustrates: 'each organism, therefore, carries within itself a "replica" of the local environment, as well as the collective memory of its species [. . .] The "memory" of each person, therefore, supports the paradoxical experience of infinite depth and personal intimacy' (McNamara 1999: 118).

Moreover, upscaling memory in this fashion is only one form of temporalised mereology, where the small regard themselves as composing the big through collective experience, through shared 'memory'. The direction or orientation of this upscaling can be inverted by looking at rhythm or tension. Comparing Bergson's work to A. N. Whitehead's theory of structured societies, Leonard Eslick argues that the latter is perfectly 'analogous to Bergson's hierarchy of durational rhythms'(Eslick 1987: 362).The aggregate can now be seen working top-down rather than bottom-up. In both these cases, however, it is a matter of covarying rhythm. In *Matter and Memory*, Bergson words this top-down assembly as a 'higher degree of tension':

> would not the whole of history be contained in a very short time for a consciousness at a higher degree of tension than our own, which should watch the development of humanity while contracting it, so to speak, into the great phases of its evolution? In short, then, to perceive consists in condensing enormous periods of an infinitely diluted existence into a few more differentiated moments of an intenser life, and in thus summing up a very long history. To perceive means to immobilize. (Bergson 1990: 207–8)

These 'higher degrees' are also rendered as 'planes' in Bergson's work. *Matter and Memory* equally tells of a 'scale of being' along which diverse rhythms of duration are arrayed. For Bergson, 'there is no one rhythm of duration; it is possible to imagine many different rhythms which, slower or faster, measure the degree of tension or relaxation of different kinds of consciousness and thereby fix their respective places in the scale of being' (ibid.: 207). Yet this scale is temporal, not spatial or hierarchical in value (at least at face value, for they all belong equally to *durée*).

On scales and the morphing of philosophies

A final discussion of scale, of above and below, must now turn to philosophy itself, and bring us back to a pertinent representative of the new materialism, and its 'smallism', with which we began. In her essay, 'Before and Above: Spinoza and Symbolic Necessity', the philosopher Catherine Malabou ordinarises the 'sacred' in her own particular manner through what she calls 'an *experience of overreading*'. For Spinoza, she writes, the mind

> has a *natural tendency to overinterpret – and such is the origin, the very possibility of the sacred* [. . .] For Spinoza, to overread or overinterpret means to confer semantic content on a word or phrase by inflating its (absence of) referent. This overinflating is fundamentally both spatial and temporal. Spatial: God is understood as a central power, coming from above, a highness (hence all the superpowers attributed to a God conceived as a legislator: jealousy, arbitrariness, love, and others). *Above*, in Spinoza, is the most acute example of the spatial overreading of the sacred. It implies an overarching and overlooking position proceeding from a hidden and unreachable power. Temporal: in its temporal sense, *above* means 'before'. All prophets have seen, have heard somebody or something that was there before, already, waiting to be seen or heard. *Above* and *before* are the two main structures or patterns of sacralization . . . In these two structures, we recognize the very economy of *superstition*. (Malabou 2016: 104–5)

The 'over' in over-reading, over-interpretation (and so super-stition) can be understood as excess, but also, in its excess, as a fabulation of the *spatial* in terms of religious superstition – the God or gods operating *above* us. However, Malabou argues that super-stition can be redeemed within a theory of interpretation. And this also operates on superstition of the past, the Before, alongside the Above. Citing Emile Benveniste's work in linguistics, she reports:

> *superstitio* is the gift of second sight which enables a person to know the past as if he or she had been present, *superstes*. This is how

superstitiosus denotes the gift of second sight, which is attributed to 'seers', that of being a 'witness' of events at which he has not been present. (Benveniste 1973: 527; cited at Malabou 2016: 106)

For Benveniste and Malabou, then, as a tendency to overread, superstition is not 'bad per se':

On the contrary, it marks the origin of the symbolic, and in that sense it cannot be totally separated from ideality [. . .] what he showed is that the origin of interpretation resides in overinterpretation . . . No need, for Spinoza, to refer to any transcendence in the message. Overinterpretation is, in a certain sense, *immanent* to the message. (Malabou 2016: 107)

There is much we could discuss in this passage: superstition as both belief and action (or presence) at a distance; or sacralisation as equally temporal and spatial ('before and above'). But we must focus on Malabou's theory of interpretation, and especially on how it impacts on the question of language and the evolution of theory – how philosophy mutates into different forms from itself. For the fact is that the excess or overinterpretation that Malabou sees within the 'sacred' message can also be applied to her own work as a new materialist. Her recent book, *Morphing Intelligence* (2019) can be (overly?) read as immanent to the evolution of her project's ambition to keep continental philosophy informed by the latest research emerging from the brain sciences. In maintaining this acquaintance with the empirical, she has found that her own renowned thesis concerning the 'plasticity' of our brain requires reformation.[13] In *What Should We Do with Our Brain?* (2008) Malabou originally argued that the concept of neurological plasticity, the idea that our brains change throughout the course of our lives as they adapt to evolving circumstances, brings with it the promise of a new kind of human freedom. It opens up the possibility that we can intervene in our brain's evolution by changing those circumstances: we are not biologically *determined* bottom-up, but can change our fates, top-down, working in tandem with this biological flexibility.

And yet, in the preface to *Morphing Intelligence* Malabou offers a new account that mitigates, amongst other things, the voluntarism of her earlier position on neural plasticity, the freedom found in micro-matter. She admits that 'for a long time I believed that neuronal plasticity proscribed any comparison between the "natural" brain and machines, especially computers. However, the latest advances in artificial intelligence, especially the development of "synaptic" chips, have mounted a serious challenge to this position' (Malabou 2019: xvii). The need to develop her concepts and languages – in particular replacing the centrality of plasticity with that of 'epigenesis' – can be regarded as both the occupational hazard of *any* philosophy trying to maintain its currency through an ever-evolving scientific materialism, but also as the virtue of a thought like hers that is attempting to materialise its own performance through these covariant mutations. Epigenesis is the theory that the embryo develops progressively from an undifferentiated egg cell. That life follows a programme of sorts, going through a predictable sequence of events, lessens both the plasticity of biological forms as well as, at least in Malabou's view, any clear distance being kept between the organic and the artificial. She charts her conversion from plasticity to epigenesis as follows:

> For years, I explored the concept of plasticity, viewing it as the potential starting point for a new conception of freedom that would no longer be separated from the biological definition of thought and action. Isn't brain plasticity exactly this vitality of intelligence – the one that tests, measurements, and factors will never identify? [. . .] Unfortunately, however – or is it fortunately? – recent developments in artificial intelligence shook me out of my nondogmatic slumber. I came to see that the conclusions I presented in *What Should We Do with Our Brain?* were, to put it bluntly, wrongheaded. Shortly after that book came out, it became apparent to me that it needed revising, if not a complete rewrite. This suspicion dawned on me upon reading an article about recent computational architectures, especially IBM's creation of an entirely new type of chip, a 'neuro-synaptic processor' that dramatically increases processing abilities while minimizing the energy required for computation. But the title of the article, 'IBM's Neuro-Synaptic Chip Mimics Human Brain', was misleading. In fact, this chip is not capable of 'imitating' synaptic functioning: it functions de facto as a synaptic connection. It *is* a synapse. (Ibid.: 82–3)

With a certain zeal of the new convert, the philosopher pushes further than the science, proclaiming a real *identity* over a correlated function. More than that, however, Malabou's own thesis has 'morphed': as a bio-philosophical hybrid of deconstructive thought and brain science, it has deconstructed itself, rendered plasticity plastic by tempering its own freedom with epigenetic predictability, programmability. As such, she asks,

> how could we not conclude that plasticity is programmable, since it is becoming the fundamental program of cybernetics? But is a

> programmable and programmed plasticity still plasticity? Not that
> plasticity is the opposite of the concept of program on principle.
> Epigenetic mechanisms are programmed genetically. (Ibid.: 19)

Such a renewal in language-thought no doubt reflects in part a desire to
seek out the new and extraordinary within science in order to maintain a
philosophical distance from the ordinary (empirical evidence quickly dating itself and the philosopher's reliance on it). On the other hand, there
is the countervailing need to renew language simply in order to '*think in
duration*' (as Bergson put it) or morph our intelligence (Bergson 1992:
34). This is part of the price paid by any 'scientific philosophy', in the
truest sense of the term, be it putatively materialist or spiritualist. In *Time
Reborn*, physicist Lee Smolin writes with great relevance to this point:

> Scientists think in time when we conceive of our task as the inven-
> tion of novel ideas to describe newly discovered phenomena, and
> of novel mathematical structures to express them. If we think
> outside time, we believe these ideas somehow existed before we
> invented them. If we think in time, we see no reason to presume
> that. (Smolin 2013: xv)[14]

Like Malabou, Bergson formed much of his philosophical research
around the empirical sciences, *Matter and Memory* focusing on studies
of the brain in particular. Yet, as Paul Atkinson explains, Bergson was
looking to place 'the brain within an ontology of perception rather than
deriving a theory of perception from the operation of the brain' (Atkinson 2020: 189). And that ontology was processual and immanentist. In
terms of methodology, therefore, he insisted on the inevitability for any
serious philosophical terminology – and he includes his own language
of '*durée*', 'multiplicity' and 'differentiation' here – to lose its purchase
on real process unless it too continually mutated.[15] Every new idea is
eventually stripped of its suggestive power as it slowly absorbs the more
mundane thoughts linked to it by association. Philosophy must renew
its language and imagery if it is to remain vital. A theory of change must
itself change. Or, as Malabou would say, intelligence morphs.

   Hence, following Bergson's lead and Malabou's recent example, *philosophy must over-interpret itself*. This need not be achieved only through
scientific fluency (though that could be part of it too): what is needed
is the ability to create new philosophical concepts and images using
whatever materials come to hand. Changing names once or twice is
not sufficient either: the real is not comprehended simply 'by giving it
a name'. On the contrary, because reality and logic too are essentially

processual (or *inessential*) for Bergson, philosophy must *keep* creating the right expression to fit new realities. *Names need to keep multiplying.*

So what might this mean for our earlier discussions of 'new' materialism and (old) 'new' spiritualism? What also might this mean for material and spiritual *life*, understood now no longer as opposed substances but as covarying levels (parts and wholes) of change, creativity and freedom?

Conclusion: spiritual and material life

Any aspiring new, 'neo-spiritualist' turn should not be confused with a simple inversion of dominance within a matter-spirit binary that does nothing to alter either of its terms. What is needed, and called for, is a non-Platonist model of spirit: *spirit brought back down to earth*, so to speak. So, a demotion of sorts, but one that does not entail such incompatible categories as the immaterial or the disembodied, but instead something like heterogeneous continuities or covariances between small and large, micro and macro levels of change, contingency and creativity. Would this not be the natural sibling to an 'inflated' matter? Such alternative and radical concepts of spirit might then be seen as complements – or even alter egos – to new materialism and its notions of vibration (Bennett), entanglement (Barad) and plasticity (Malabou).[16] Only when polarised as incompatible substances would spirit and matter enter a duel of antagonistic philosophies, caricatures of themselves in fixed states: advocates for lumpen bodies versus unearthly spectres. On this alternative view, spirit would not *name* one insubstantial substance opposed to another, substantial one: it would name one aspect of a changing relation (a *heterogeneous continuity*), or the features of a changing relation, one of whose relata is itself mutating too.

Likewise, the mutation or morphing we saw in Malabou also acts reflexively as the recursive meta-morphosis of 'meta-physics' itself, so that it would also be understood now as an ever-expanding perception and empirical engagement rather than an intellectual grasp of some eternal Ideal – an empirical metaphysics *sub specie durationis*, as Bergson put it, over Spinoza's *sub specie aeternitatis*. Yet, such ramifications need not only proceed within a disembodied logical regress of *types* or *orders of representation* so much as a *real* progress within cosmological tiers, levels or planes: changes composed of changes, *ad infinitum* (see Mullarkey 1999: 181–5). And this is why *over-interpretation* – a multiplication of names – is not the *representation* of any one level or scale, but the invented effects of many levels constructively interfering with each other.[17] Out of the logical paradoxes of 'reflexivity' (does a theory of change, change, is 'plasticity' plastic?) stem not only different, ramifying *logical* types, but different *cosmological* levels, generated through a material-spiritual auto-poetic agency, or what Thomas Nail calls 'bifurcation' (Nail 2019: 69). As above, so below, micro and macro, super and sub: heterogenous kinds of continuity operating 'vertically' and 'horizontally' on different scales, temporal and spatial.

Discussing the supposed primacy of matter in the new materialism, Gamble, Hanan and Nail argue that

> it is not enough merely to say that everything is matter. This amounts to saying everything that is is. For us, there is 'nothing but matter', but unlike old materialisms this is not a reductionistic claim because matter is not a substance that everything can be reduced to. Matter, for us, is a fundamentally indeterminate performance or process-in-motion. (Gamble et al. 2019: 125)

Yet, just as we saw with Meillassoux and Boutroux that radical contingency can evidence one definition of materialism just as equally as another of spiritualism, so Gamble, Hanan and Nail's 'process-in-motion' can cut both ways too: in *Creative Evolution* Bergson defines spirit as follows: 'we understand by spirituality a progress to ever new creations, to conclusions incommensurable with the premises and indeterminable by relation to them' (Bergson 1911: 232). In this light we could call spirit 'creation-in-progress' – a nesting of processes, small and large, that operate temporally, that is, as covarying vitalities rather than as substances containing each other. Spiritual lives are defined and placed, therefore, on the same continuum as material lives, differing (if at all) only in their temporal scale.

Notes

1. See the essays collected in *The Routledge Handbook of Mechanisms and Mechanical Philosophy* (Glennan and Illari 2017). In particular, see the essay by Mark Povich and Carl F. Craver, 'Mechanistic Levels, Reduction, and Emergence': 'In aggregates, the property of the whole is literally a sum of the properties of its parts. The concentration of a fluid is an aggregation of particles; allelic frequency is a sum of individual alleles. Aggregate properties change linearly with the addition and removal of parts, they don't change when their parts are rearranged, and they can be taken apart and reassembled without any special difficulty. This is because in true aggregates, spatial, temporal, and causal organization are irrelevant . . . Mechanisms, in contrast, are literally more than the sums of their parts: they change non-linearly with the addition and removal of parts, their behavior is disrupted if parts are switched out, and this is because their spatial, temporal, and causal

organization make a difference to how the whole behaves' (Povich and Craver 2017: 188).

2. Throughout her book, the term 'spirit' or 'spiritual' is directly mentioned only twice (pp. 221, 228), when discussing Raymond Ruyer's work.

3. See Delitz (2021: 109–14) for an engagement with a new materialism that takes a positive line on Bergson's influence.

4. Dunham (2020: 1005, 988); Sinclair and Antoine-Mahut (2020: 862, 863). Sinclair and Antoine-Mahut also describe 'two halves' (p. 857) of French spiritualism, one dominated by Victor Cousin, with its 'eclectic' mix of German idealism and Scottish common-sense philosophy, and a more 'positivist' spiritualism following Ravaisson and the idea that biology has more in common with psychology than physics (p. 860).

5. See Ó Maoilearca (forthcoming), on the covariances found between many of the concepts in Bergson's process metaphysics and those found in the mystical writings and occult practices of his sister, Mina Bergson (aka Moina Mathers).

6. Latour is commenting here on the work of Olafur Eliasson: 'Olafur Eliasson is right to insist on the fact that the mechanisms of disorientation he employs are as much temporal as spatial.'

7. 'The molar and the molecular are not distinguished by size, scale, or dimension, but by the nature of the system of reference envisioned' (Deleuze and Guattari 1987: 217). That said, Deleuze and Guattari do continue to use language suggestive of scale: majority, major, massive, big, mass, collective, whole, global, macro-, super-, over-, and molar itself, on the one hand; partial objects, part organs, larval selves, minority, minor, local, part, component, small, miniaturisation, sub-, micro-, and molecular itself, on the other. And the value is almost always on the side of the small, what Sam Coleman called 'smallism'.

8. It is not that X would be an illusion that is displaced by the truth of Y, but that, at different scales, a re-description or re-naming of an event becomes evident.

9. General systems theory, complex systems, Deleuzian assemblage theory (giant molecules *and* 'microbrains') and quantum physicist David Bohm's radical holism would be just a few more ordinary renderings of above/below scalar holism. Each of these translations brings its own difficulties with it, no doubt.

10. Such temporalisation is more than simply time-sampling, which would still be quantitative. A *temporalised* scale must be distinguished from a *temporal* scale – which is only the quantification of a process: the former is the qualification of a quantity, a spatial entity integrated into real time.

11. For a more up-to-date account of such biological memory, with reference to Henri Bergson, see Longo (2019).

12. Deleuze and Guattari's much more famous wasp and orchid example in *A Thousand Plateaus* is a modern variation on this theme.

13. See Malabou (2008) for her original position.

14. See Marchesini (2018) for both a positive comparison of Smolin's dura-
    tional thinking with Bergson, and also a critique of where he falls short of
    thinking consistently about time, that is, in a fully Bergsonian, and imma-
    nent, manner.
15. See Bergson (1992: 35): 'The habitual labor of thought is easy and can
    be prolonged at will. Intuition is arduous and cannot last. Whether it be
    intellection or intuition, thought, of course, always utilizes language; and
    intuition, like all thought, finally becomes lodged in concepts such as dura-
    tion, qualitative or heterogeneous multiplicity, unconsciousness – even dif-
    ferentiation, if one considers the notion such as it was to begin with.'
16. See Ó Maoilearca (forthcoming) for a fuller exploration of just this thesis.
17. The phenomenon of interference is the 'process whereby two or more
    waves of the same frequency or wavelength combine to form a wave whose
    amplitude is the sum of the interfering waves' (Parker 1982: 472–3). Inter-
    ference can be *destructive* or *constructive*. The latter is when the trough and
    crest of both waves coincide. The former is when the trough of one wave
    coincides with the crest of another, that is, they are completely 'out of
    phase'. In this case, if these two waves are of equal amplitude, they can
    cancel each other so that the resulting amplitude is zero. And as a wave
    must, to be a wave, have an amplitude of some dimension, then the result
    of this encounter is no wave at all, or annihilation. Interference can be seen
    graphically when one splits up light with two parallel slits (as in 'Young's
    Two-Slit' experiment). An interference pattern can be seen by letting the
    light from the two slits fall on a white screen. A pattern is produced of dark
    and bright patches of light. Dark patches or 'fringes' indicate waves that
    have interfered *destructively*. The bright fringes indicate waves that have
    interfered *constructively*.

References

Atkinson, Paul (2020), *Henri Bergson and Visual Culture: A Philosophy for a New
    Aesthetic*, London: Bloomsbury.
Barad, Karen (2007), *Meeting The Universe Halfway: Quantum Physics and the
    Entanglement of Matter and Meaning*, Durham, NC and London: Duke Uni-
    versity Press.
Benveniste, Emile (1973), *Indo-European Language and Society*, trans. Elizabeth
    Palmer, London: Faber & Faber.
Bergson, Henri (1911), *Creative Evolution*, trans. Arthur Mitchell, London:
    Macmillan.
Bergson, Henri (1990), *Matter and Memory*, trans. Nancy Margaret Paul and W.
    Scott Palmer, New York: Zone Books.
Bergson, Henri (1992), *The Creative Mind: An Introduction to Metaphysics*, trans.
    Mabelle L. Andison, New York: Citadel Press.
Brouwer, L. E. J. (1975), 'Consciousness, Philosophy, and Mathematics', in A.
    Heyting (ed.), *Collected Works: Volume One: Philosophy and Foundations of
    Mathematics*, Amsterdam: North-Holland Publishing Company, pp. 480–94.

Coleman, Sam (2006), 'Being Realistic', in Galen Strawson et al. (eds), *Consciousness and its Place in Nature: Does Physicalism Entail Panpsychism?*, Exeter: Imprint-Academic, pp. 40–52.

Deleuze, Gilles and Félix Guattari (1987), *A Thousand Plateaus*, trans. Brian Massumi, London: Athlone Press.

Delitz, Heike (2021), 'Life as the Subject of Society: Critical Vitalism as Critical Social Theory', in Rosa Hartmut, Christoph Henning and Arthur Bueno (eds), *Critical Theory and New Materialisms*, London: Routledge, pp. 107–22.

Dunham, Jeremy (2020), 'Overcoming the Divide Between Freedom and Nature: Clarisse Coignet on the Metaphysics of Independent Morality', *British Journal for the History of Philosophy*, 28: 987–1008.

Edelman, Gerald (1992), *Bright Light, Brilliant Fire: On the Matter of the Mind*, New York: Basic Books.

Ellenzweig, Sarah and John H. Zammito (eds) (2017), *The New Politics of Materialism: History, Philosophy, Science*, Abingdon and New York: Routledge.

Eslick, Leonard (1987), 'Bergson, Whitehead, and Psychical Research', in Andrew C. Papanicolaou and Pete A. Y. Gunter (eds), *Bergson and Modern Thought: Toward a Unified Science*, New York: Harwood Academic Publishers, pp. 353–68.

Gamble, Christopher N., Joshua S. Hanan and Thomas Nail (2019), 'What is New Materialism?', *Angelaki*, 24: 111–34.

Gayon, Jean (2005), 'Bergson's Spiritualist Metaphysics and the Sciences', in Gary Gutting (ed.), *Continental Philosophy of Science*. Oxford: Wiley-Blackwell, pp. 43–58.

Glennan, Stuart and Phyllis Illari (eds) (2017), *The Routledge Handbook of Mechanisms and Mechanical Philosophy*, Abingdon and New York: Routledge.

Grosz, Elizabeth (2017), *The Incorporeal: Ontology, Ethics, and the Limits of Materialism*, New York: Columbia University Press.

Gunter, Pete A. Y., 'Bergson and Jung', *Journal of the History of Ideas*, 43: 635–52.

Lambert, Gregg (2005), 'What the Earth Thinks', in Ian Buchanan and Gregg Lambert (eds), *Deleuze and Space*, Edinburgh: Edinburgh University Press, pp. 220–39.

Latour, Bruno (2017), 'Anti-Zoom', in Michael Tavel Clarke and David Wittenberg (eds), *Scale in Literature and Culture*, Cham, Switzerland: Palgrave Macmillan, pp. 93–101.

Longo, Giuseppe (2019), 'Confusing Biological Rhythms and Physical Clocks: Today's Ecological Relevance of Bergson-Einstein Debate on Time', paper given at the Einstein and Bergson 100 Years Later conference in Aquila, Italy, 4–6 April), available at: https://www.researchgate.net/publication/338139213_Confusing_biological_rhythms_and_physical_clocks_Today%27s_ecological_relevance_of_Bergson-Einstein_debate_on_time (last accessed 2 February 2022).

McNamara, Patrick (1999), *Mind and Variability: Mental Darwinism, Memory and Self*, Westport, CT: Praeger.

Malabou, Catherine (2008), *What Should We Do with Our Brain?*, trans. Sebastian Rand, New York: Fordham University Press.

Malabou, Catherine (2016), 'Before and Above: Spinoza and Symbolic Necessity', *Critical Inquiry*, 43: 84–109.

Malabou, Catherine (2019), *Morphing Intelligence*, trans. Carolyn Shread, New York: Columbia University Press.

Marchesini, Paula (2018), 'The End of Time or Time Reborn? Henri Bergson and the Metaphysics of Time in Contemporary Cosmology', *Philosophy and Cosmology*, 21: 140–52.

Mullarkey, John (1999), *Bergson and Philosophy*, Edinburgh: Edinburgh University Press.

Nail, Thomas (2019), *Being and Motion*, Oxford: Oxford University Press.

Ó Maoilearca, John (forthcoming), *Vestiges of a Philosophy: Matter, the Meta-Spiritual, and the Forgotten Bergson*, Oxford: Oxford University Press.

Parker, Sybil P. (ed.) (1982), *McGraw-Hill Encyclopedia of Physics*, New York: McGraw-Hill.

Pinch, Adela (2014–15), 'The Appeal of Panpsychism in Victorian Britain', *Romanticism on the Net*, 65, available at: https://ronjournal.org/articles/n65/the-appeal-of-panpsychism-in-victorian-britain/ (last accessed 2 February 2022).

Povich, Mark and Carl F. Craver (2017), 'Mechanistic Levels, Reduction, and Emergence', in Stuart Glennan and Phyllis Illari (2017), pp. 185–97.

Sinclair, Mark and Delphine Antoine-Mahut (2020), 'Introduction to French Spiritualism in the Nineteenth Century', *British Journal for the History of Philosophy*, 28(5): 857–65.

Smolin, Lee (2013), *Time Reborn: From the Crisis in Physics to the Future of the Universe*, Boston, MA: Houghton Mifflin Harcourt.

Sommer McGrath, Larry (2020), *Making Spirit Matter: Neurology, Psychology, and Selfhood in Modern France*, Chicago: The University of Chicago Press.

Wittenberg, David (2019), 'Bigness as the Unconscious of Theory', *ELH*, 86(2): 333–54.

Woods, Derek (2017), 'Scale Variance and the Concept of Matter', in Ellenzweig and Zammito (2017), pp. 200–24.

Zammito, John H. (2017), 'Concluding (Irenic) Postscript: Naturalism as a Response to the New Materialism', in Ellenzweig and Zammito (2017), pp. 300–21.

12

What's the Matter with Life?

Thomas Nail

Most people are accustomed to treating the earth as a relatively stable place that they live *on* and move *on*. As a result, many dominant human groups have thought of themselves as actors on the stage of the Earth. Today, however, this stable ground is becoming increasingly unstable – for some of us more than others.

Due to the widespread use of global transportation technologies, for example, more people and things are on the move than ever before. Vast amounts of materials are now in constant circulation, as billions of humans are shipping plants, animals and technologies worldwide. This mobility is not something happening only to humans. More than half the world's plant and animal species are also on the move (Welch 2017). The Earth is becoming so mobile that even its glaciers are speeding up.

Geological time refers to slow and gradual processes, but today we are watching the earth sink into the sea and forests transform into deserts in our lifetimes. We can even see the creation of entirely new geological strata made of plastic, chicken bones and other waste that could remain in the fossil record and affect geological formations for thousands or even millions of years.[1]

Some human groups are now changing the entire Earth so dramatically and permanently that geologists have begun calling our age the Anthropocene (Crutzen and Stoermer 2000).[2] It no longer makes sense to think of humans as transient occupants moving on a relatively stable Earth. Instead, humans are geological, atmospheric and hydrological agents entangled in the Earth's processes, which are now increasingly in flux.[3] The arrival of the Anthropocene, more than any human historical event, is finally awakening us to the realisation that we have *never* lived on a stable Earth. We have never been the only significant agents.

Posthuman theorists, including myself, have responded to these events by offering new theoretical tools to help us think through the entangled continuity of human and non-human agencies that abound. If we want to survive, human groups cannot treat the earth as something only for themselves. Even if many are not happy about it, our survival depends on how well we are able to take the global entanglement of human and non-human agencies seriously. In other words, we need to think and act more like 'posthumans' as the anthropocentric project comes to an end.[4]

One of the most influential posthuman philosophies of the past two decades has been 'neo-vitalism'. This idea was launched most prominently by the twentieth-century French philosopher Gilles Deleuze who offered creative reinterpretations of older philosophers like Henri Bergson, Benedict Spinoza, Gottfried Leibniz and Friedrich Nietzsche. Instead of interpreting their concepts of 'vitality', 'striving', 'force' or 'will' as metaphysical substances separate from bodies in motion, as others had, he read forces *as immanent to reality*. All things, Deleuze argued, are crystallisations or momentary stabilisations of the forces that compose them. Deleuze's motivation for this move was to overthrow the dualism between passive mechanical matter and divine immaterial forms. Consequently, he believed that all non-human and human forces have agency to some degree. In this sense, Deleuze was one of the first posthuman philosophers.

Deleuze died in 1995, but his immanent ontology of forces resonated deeply with a generation of scholars coming out of the anthropocentric tradition of post-Kantian philosophy. These scholars confronted the imminent catastrophe of climate change and the Anthropocene. For those interested in environmental philosophy and eco-feminism at the start of the twenty-first century, Deleuze's philosophy offered an unequivocal rejection of anthropocentrism and hope for a new ecological ontology. In my view, Deleuze's ontology merged the best of Bergson's process philosophy without the baggage of its anthropocentrism and traditional vitalism.

Philosophers such as Rosi Braidotti, Elizabeth Grosz, Jane Bennett and many other posthumanists have been using Deleuze's vitalist ontology of forces for at least two decades against the anthropocentrism and anti-realism which define almost all of post-Kantian philosophy. After more than twenty years, Deleuze's work and its supporters have contributed significantly to posthuman philosophy's increasing popularity and relevance. But, in doing so, they have also left a distinctly neo-vitalist imprint on posthuman philosophy.

Now, the wave of criticisms against neo-vitalism is growing steadily from within and without. I have learned a lot from Deleuze, but I am no longer convinced that neo-vitalism is the best way to think about

posthumanism or life in the Anthropocene. I am not saying there is
nothing to gain from reading Deleuze or from neo-vitalists more generally. Indeed, we should continue to think about the topic of life. Instead,
this chapter aims to consolidate some of the biggest challenges to neo-
vitalism and respond to them with one alternative way to think about
posthuman life.

In this chapter, I would like to do two things. First, I want to consolidate four of the most significant criticisms against neo-vitalism. Specifically, critics have argued that it is politically insufficient, historically
suspicious, unnecessarily metaphysical and conceptually vague. Second,
I propose an alternative way to think about the nature of life in the
posthuman condition that responds to these criticisms. Specifically, I
suggest that posthuman vitalists may benefit from thinking about *movement* as a more ontologically primary concept than life or vital forces. I
conclude by briefly introducing how this shift may help us think about
the Anthropocene in a new way.

I. Four critiques of neo-vitalism

In this section, I summarise four criticisms of neo-vitalism in hopes of
directing posthumanists to respond to and overcome them. I cannot recap
all the criticisms of classical vitalism and neo-vitalism. That would take
more than a single chapter.[5] Instead, I will focus on four problems with
neo-vitalism and vitalist new materialism. By 'vitalist new materialism',
I mean neo-vitalists who claim that vital forces are identical with matter.

Political insufficiency

The first and perhaps most widespread criticism of neo-vitalism is that its
'flat ontology' offers insufficient tools to theorise political inequalities and
structural oppression. A flat ontology is one where there are no ontological hierarchies among beings. All beings are ontologically equal because,
as Jane Bennett says, 'everything is, in a sense, alive' (Bennett 2010: 117).
Since the classical domain of human politics is too narrow, Bennett's
vitalism leads her to 'forego the category of the political as such' (ibid.:
84). Bennett replaces the political world of merely human actants with a
broader world of things and analyses what she calls 'thing-power'.

However, this also leads Bennett to the following unfortunate conclusion: 'Not Flower Power, or Black Power, or Girl Power, but Thing-
Power: The curious ability of inanimate things to animate, to act, to
produce effects dramatic and subtle' (ibid.: 7, emphasis added). While
posthumanists share a commitment to the agency of the non-human

world, neo-vitalism can also lead to a reactionary abandonment of human political struggles. As Armand Townes writes,

> if thing-power is not Black Power, then her assumption is that the call for Black Power is an essentially human call that is also to be read as consistent with Western historical distinctions between humans and matter. Indeed, to associate Black Power with Flower Power (largely White resistance to the Vietnam War) and Girl Power (largely White conceptions of 'women's empowerment' in the 1990s) is to flatten out the issue of each as human concerns. (Towns 2018)

Bennett conflates notably different political positions by ontologising life and even diminishes their importance as regressive humanist projects. If everything is equally 'alive' and 'vital', including minerals, what tools does this give us to parse the differences between beings needed for understanding political conflicts (Bennett 2010: 11)? Bennett imagines vital thing-power as a 'more radical theory of democracy' because it would include all agencies (Bennett 2005: 142 and 136). But it's impossible to include all agencies in any single political analysis. So, to make such a radical political gesture without any tools for parsing different agencies may be irresponsible. Furthermore, it's not evident that we need the concept of vitality or life to study how non-human agencies work. For example, the French philosopher Bruno Latour and Actor-Network Theorists analyse non-human agencies but do not say that everything is 'alive'.

Other critics, Bruce Braun and Sarah Whatmore observe that it would be better to have a 'closer attention to the specificity of the matter at hand', without the unnecessary baggage of the vitalist 'generic analogy [of] "life" that could be described as a metaphysics' (Braun and Whatmore 2010: 29–30; Braun 2008: 675–7, emphasis in original). Sebastian Abrahamsson and his colleagues echo this point:

> Rather than getting enthusiastic about the liveliness of 'matter itself', it might be more relevant to face the complexities, frictions, intractabilities, and conundrums of 'matter in relation'. For it is in their relations that matters become political, whether those politics are loudly contested or silently endured. (Abrahamsson et al. 2015: 13)

In short, critics argue that calling things vital or lively adds nothing to our analysis of non-human agencies and may even distract from them.

Still, other critics have worried that thinking of agency as universally distributed raises the problem of assigning responsibility (Marso 2011: 426). If everything is actively participating in events, everyone and no one is simultaneously responsible. Indeed, this is what Bennett says about a power outage in the US that left millions without electricity. Since there are so many complex agencies at work, Bennett finds herself on the side of the capitalist power company FirstEnergy. They both claim no one was to blame for the power outage event because 'strong responsibility' does not exist (Bennett 2010: 37).

In the political vacuum left by her vitalist ontology, critics argue that Bennett falls back into a kind of liberal voluntarism (Washick et al. 2015). Even though Bennett says 'individuals [are] incapable of bearing full responsibility for their effects' (Bennett 2010: 37), she still frames ethical decision-making as a kind of voluntarism: 'Do I attempt to extricate myself from assemblages whose trajectory is likely to do harm? Do I enter into the proximity of assemblages whose conglomerate effectivity tends toward the enactment of nobler ends?' (ibid.: 37–8).

Another related critique of vitalist ontology is that it is guilty of the naturalistic fallacy. Bennett's explicit argument is that if all of nature is alive, then this will give us a new 'ethical sensibility' (Bennett 2001: 12; Watson 2013: 151; Coole 2013: 462) that 'can inspire a greater sense of the extent to which all bodies are kin' (Bennett 2010: 13). However, there is no necessary or ontological reason why the vitality or agency of the cosmos will or is likely to make us more ethical, whatever that might mean. Just because all bodies are ontologically equal as kin of vital forces does not mean we ought to do, or even that we are likely to do, something we may call good. Since everything is equally vital and relational, the world is just as likely to be exploitative and oppressive as it is to be communal and emancipatory. Why should 'an underdetermined vital force', as Bennett calls it, be inherently directed at political projects addressing inequalities and injustices? (Bennett 2016: 615, 616).

I focus on Jane Bennett's neo-vitalism here because it has received the most comprehensive criticism, but political optimism is a core feature of many versions of vitalism. Similar unfounded optimism persists among other posthumanists who flirt with vitalism. For instance, Karen Barad writes that 'there is a vitality to the liveliness of intra-activity, not in the sense of a new form of vitalism, but rather in terms of a new sense of aliveness' (Barad 2007: 177). I am not sure what to make of Barad's equivocation about vitalism, but I worry it leads her to a similar place as Jane Bennett.

Barad says, 'particular possibilities for (intra-)acting exist at every moment, and these changing possibilities entail an ethical obligation to intra-act responsibly in the world's becoming' (ibid.: 178, 396). But do they? Just because vital agencies have possibilities, why should they *necessarily entail* an ethical obligation to act responsibly? Why do we live in a deeply hierarchical and capitalist world if they did? Maybe Barad means that if 'we' *realise* the vitality of intra-activity, then 'we' will be obligated to act responsibly. Yet, it's still not obvious *why* ethics follows from the ontological fact of intra-action. If, by definition, everything is always already intra-active, then everything follows equally.

As Thomas Lemke puts it,

> the notion of responsibility suggests a normative horizon, [but] it remains unclear how intra-actions differ in their ethical value. This provokes the question of what criteria to draw on to discriminate intra-actions that are 'fuller' or 'more just' than others, what materializations are to be preferred over others. (Lemke 2021: 76)[6]

Historically suspect

There is also something concerning about the philosophical choice to ontologise the term 'vital' or 'life' in the Euro-Western context. Why not redefine and ontologise death or anything else? If we can redefine any term to include its historical opposite, as neo-vitalists do, there is no fundamental reason to choose one word over another. We must consider the contextual and rhetorical agency of the term 'life'.

Specifically, I worry that the term life has gained traction among posthumanists because it has played a privileged role in Euro-Western society. Europeans have treated life as superior to non-life on the chain of being. Moreover, Western thinkers have treated matter in motion as fundamentally incapable of true novelty in contrast to life.

From antiquity to the present, Western thinkers, for the most part, defined life as something organisms possessed in contrast to inert, passive matter. After Darwin, many believed that the material cosmos was dead, but that life emerged from inorganic matter at some point in history. After millions of years of evolution, human animals became the most complex and superior form of life on the planet. In this frame, life is the later, more complex, and superior organisation.

Of course, posthuman vitalists explicitly reject the superiority of life over death. Instead, they believe that everything is alive in some sense. However, it's not accidental that humans reigned supreme after God was de-throned. They were the next link down on the chain of being. This ushered in an era of anthropocentrism. Now that the humans are being conceptually de-throned as the locus of all meaning in the universe,

Western posthumanists are most comfortable moving down *only one step* on the hierarchy to life. In this way, posthumanists can avoid being anthropocentric and still valorise a tiny category of 'living' beings in a largely dead cosmos. Humans *just happen to be* part of this tiny category.

Why else might posthumanists go about theorising the agency of matter by saying, 'matter's agency is like *life's* agency?' Why is the agency of matter *vital* and *alive like us* and not us who are moving and agentive like matter? Indeed, from a deep historical perspective, it makes vastly more sense to say that living organisms and anything we could mean by 'vital' is more *like matter*? Matter in motion created life, not vice versa.

In other words, I worry that vitalism is the posthuman theory of choice because it secretly assumes a model of agency based on human and living agency *projected* onto inorganic matter and non-vital motion. Vitalists are implicitly saying, 'of course, we know that matter created life and organic agency, but we still think the best way to conceptualise this agency is to say that matter and even death is *life-like*'. This seems conceptually and historically backward to me.

Why treat the cosmos as universal degrees of aliveness and not treat life as a minuscule sub-section of non-living matter in motion? It's not a neutral decision. No matter how expansively posthumanists define 'life', it belies a deep-seated biocentric chauvinism to say that matter is 'like life' and not vice versa. Politically, Western vitalism cannot avoid its historically rooted privilege over non-life. This includes the exploitation and appropriation of human and non-human bodies associated with non-life (Chen 2012; Weheliye 2014). Insofar as non-Western traditions have held different definitions of life historically, their contemporary use of the term has a different valence.

Redefining materialism *as vitalism*, as new materialist vitalists do, suffers the same problem. Matter has always been on the bottom of the Western chain of being, along with death and motion. Saying that matter in motion has agency *like vital forces* is historically and ontologically backward. Why can't matter move on its own without being *like* something else or *being* something else? In other words, vital new materialism is not about matter as Hesiod, Aristotle and Lucretius defined it: as a chaotic indeterminant movement.[7]

Elizabeth Grosz seems to be one of the few vital materialists who recognises the close link between materialism and idealism in the neo-vitalist tradition. 'With the rise of so-called new materialism', Grosz writes, 'it is perhaps necessary to simultaneously call into being a new idealism', because 'Deleuze's rereading of Spinoza is responsible for a "new idealism"' as well (Grosz 2017: 13). Therefore, choosing to call vitalism 'materialist' or 'idealist' ultimately amounts to a rhetorical strategy grounded in something else, as Leibniz already made clear in his *ontology of forces* (see Nail 2018b: 309–19, 436; Leibniz 1989). Deleuze was not a new materialist or idealist but fundamentally a theorist of vital forces and expressive power like Spinoza. Neo-vitalism is not 'new' materialism or 'new' idealism. It is the erasure of matter, motion and death entirely in favour of vital forces.

Unnecessarily metaphysical

What is a 'vital force', and what do we gain philosophically from thinking about everything as alive in some sense? The historical motivation of vitalism and neo-vitalism was to locate a concept of nature that one could not reduce to strictly ideal or material beings. However, the risk of this move is that the concept of vital forces may be, in its way, just as metaphysical as ideal entities beyond space and time or mechanistic materialism.

For instance, Thomas Lemke, a critic of vitalism, points out that Jane Bennett defines 'member[s] and proto-member[s]' of assemblages as possessing 'a certain vital force' before they enter into an association (Bennett 2010: 24). Moreover, Bennett says that vital force 'is distinct from the sum of the vital force of each materiality considered alone' (ibid.). But if vital force is immanent to matter, how can it be distinct from matter?

Bennett is not alone in occasionally describing vitalism non-relationally. Gilles Deleuze did something similar in his Spinozist reading of Lucretius. In *The Logic of Sense*, Deleuze argued that Lucretius's concept of 'The *clinamen* is the original determination of the direction of the movement of the atom. It is a kind of *conatus*' (Deleuze 1990: 269). *Conatus* is a Latin word used by Spinoza and others to describe the 'striving power' of something. However, Lucretius never used this Latin word and never said the swerve is a *conatus* or vital power or striving. Instead, Lucretius wrote about the movement, fold or weave of matter without attributing it to any external transcendent vital cause or immanent vital power. Matter, for Lucretius, simply moves and swerves indeterminately.

Deleuze rejected many philosophical efforts to explain the movement of matter by something transcendent such as God, the soul or freedom. Yet, following Spinoza, he still believed in an immanent motive power in the form of a vital striving or *conatus*. Of course, Deleuze's neo-vitalism is not the same as a transcendent explanation of the swerve, but it is nonetheless completely unnecessary and not textually supported in Lucretius or Epicurus.

Deleuze also claims that, for Lucretius, 'Nature, to be precise, is power. In the name of this power, things exist *one by one*' (ibid.: 267). And that 'there is the power of the diverse and its production, but there is also the power of the reproduction of the diverse' (ibid.: 271). Yet, Lucretius nowhere says that nature is 'power'. Again, Spinoza is the ontologist of power. Lucretius says that nature is matter and that matter moves. He never assigns power, force or vitality any special status. For Lucretius, matter and motion are enough.

Deleuze was explicit about his belief that matter in motion is insufficient to explain novelty. In his book *Nietzsche and Philosophy* (1962), Deleuze explicitly subordinated matter and motion to *force*, contrasting himself and Nietzsche (and implicitly Spinoza) against Lucretius's and Marx's kinetic materialism.

> Only force can be related to another force. (As Marx says when he interprets atomism, 'Atoms are their own unique objects and can relate only to themselves' – Marx, *The Difference Between the Democritean and Epicurean Philosophy of Nature*. But the question is; can the basic notion of atom accommodate the essential relation which is attempted to it? The concept only becomes coherent if one thinks of force instead of atom. For the notion of atom cannot in itself contain the difference necessary for the affirmation of such a relation, difference in and according to the essence. Thus atomism would be a mask for an incipient dynamism). (Deleuze 1983: 6–7)

Indeed, Deleuze finds Marx's and Lucretius's materialism insufficient because he cannot imagine how matter could internally differentiate itself without the existence of vital power. However, as I have argued elsewhere at length, following Marx and Lucretius, swerving motion differentiates matter without assuming any force or vital striving power (see Nail 2018a, 2020). I see no philosophical reason why we need the concept of *conatus* to say that matter moves indeterminately.

Jane Bennett explicitly adopts Deleuze's Spinozist preference for force and *conatus* to explain why things persist and move. Quoting Spinoza, Bennett says,

> 'Any thing whatsoever [. . .] will always be able to persist in existing with that same force whereby it begins to exist, so that in this respect all things are equal'. Even a falling stone, writes Spinoza, is endeavoring, as far as in it lies, to continue in its motion. (Bennett 2010: 2)

The term 'endeavour' is the English translation of the Latin word *conatus*. In short, Spinoza, Deleuze and Bennett believe that all things persist and continue their motion equally because they strive. Only *forces* explain movement. But why not say, as Marx did, that 'absolute movement' is an 'immanent self-cause?'[8] What does power/force/*conatus* add that matter cannot already do without invoking vital forces?

I admit there are few materialists like Lucretius and Marx who say that matter moves indeterminately without vital forces. But there are enough to show us that the concepts of *conatus* and vital forces are unnecessary to make the point that matter has novel movements. This is why critics have ultimately argued that Bennett's idea of the 'force of things' amounts to nothing more than a 'naive realism' that allows things to have a metaphysical 'more-than-relational character' (Hinchliffe 2011: 398; Cudworth and Hobden 2014).

Specifically, what is the philosophical status of the claim that all of being everywhere and for all time is 'vital forces'? How can anyone who believes this possibly prove a statement like this? It is an utterly metaphysical claim that can never be proven or disproven. In my view, the only sensible philosophical response to posthuman vitalism is agnosticism. Perhaps it is correct, perhaps not, but metaphysical claims of vitality do not add anything to the basic idea that matter is capable of novel action.

Conceptually vague

A related problem with vitalism noted by critics is that the concept of 'vital forces' is conceptually vague and all-encompassing. For instance, if vital striving is just another phrase for 'indeterminate movement', why not use the term 'indeterminate movement' and avoid any intimation of metaphysics or biocentrism?

But it's a double-edged sword. If 'vital forces' are identical with indeterminate relational movements of matter, the vitalist terminology is redundant. However, if vitalism is *not* identical to indeterminate matter in motion but *adds something*, then vitalism is beyond matter/nature and, therefore, metaphysical. In other words, vitalism is at its very best redundant and at its worst metaphysical and biocentric.

Furthermore, do we still need the concept of 'vital forces' to combat scientific materialism when experiments in quantum physics have confirmed for a century that energy/matter moves indeterminately.[9]

What do 'vital forces' refer to that are not more precisely described by the science of quantum indeterminacy and entanglement? Bennett says she admires earlier vitalists who remained 'scientific while acknowledging some incalculability to things' (Bennett 2010: 63). Today, by contrast, incalculability is built-in to fundamental physics. We do not need to return to metaphysics and vitalism for concepts to describe the incalculability of nature. If we never needed vitality to explain matter's swerving motion, we certainly don't need it anymore today.

So, what do vital forces refer to if neo-vitalism includes matter and death? Bennett and Rosi Braidotti say that everything is alive, even death. 'It can be argued, therefore, that Life as *zoē* also encompasses what we call "death"' as Braidotti says (Braidotti 2012: 134). 'We may call it death, but in a monistic ontology of vitalist materialism, it has rather to do with radical immanence' (ibid.: 136). But how does this help us think about anything if everything is *equally* vital?

Katherine Hayles argues that vitalist new materialism tends to be highly 'imprecise about the nature of "force" and fails to distinguish between different kinds of forces, although these kinds of distinction have been extensively investigated in various scientific fields' (Hayles 2017: 80). Without any other distinctions, vitalism is everything and nothing simultaneously. This is as helpful as saying reality is reality.

It also raises the question of why vitalists are choosing to use the term 'life' at all to describe *all* reality. My suspicion that posthumanists are interested in ontologising life because of its historically normative valence is confirmed by Bennett's usage. Bennett says that vitality and enchantment is a 'a positive resource' related to 'generosity' and 'joy' (Bennett 2001: 15, 174, 12–3). But how can vitality be positive, generous, joyful or sympathetic without being *equally its opposite*? Why doesn't Bennett focus on all the horrible and destructive aspects of vitality? If vitality is also death and destruction, vitalists should be equally interested in non-enchantment and non-sympathy. Yet, they are not.

The vagueness of vitalism is not neutral or accidental. Since people assume life is positive, neo-vitalism lures Western readers into an optimistic monism. One related reason vitalism has been historically successful is that it proposes eliminating one of the West's oldest and deepest fears: the fear of death. The fear of death, as Lucretius described 2,000 years ago, is the source of much of our unethical action in the West (see Nail 2020). Humans have tried to escape death by believing in immortal souls, sacrificing to benevolent gods, killing one another, and accumulating wealth and power.

Instead of living beyond death, neo-vitalism tries to eliminate death and matter by consuming them. For vitalists and ontologies of force like Leibniz's, there is no such thing as matter or motion and therefore no death. In this sense, vitalism is perhaps the most voracious and extreme version of Western metaphysics because it seeks to conceptually eliminate death in favour of absolute positive life. For the vitalist and force ontologist, there are only vital forces that *look like* what we call matter, motion and death. In reality, it is all just a play of forces.

For instance, the only thing that is real for Leibniz is *relations of force*. Motion is only real insofar as it is 'a force striving toward change. Whatever there is in corporeal nature besides the object of geometry, or extension, must be reduced to this force' (Leibniz 1989: 436). Therefore, Leibniz concludes that force is real and absolute, and motion (and matter) belongs to a subclass of relative phenomena.

II. Philosophy of movement

In this second, shorter section of this chapter, I propose an alternative conception of life in the Anthropocene. I respond to the four criticisms above and say how I think a movement philosophy might be a good alternative.

Politics

Instead of an optimistic flat ontology, what if we adopted a movement-oriented perspective? Instead of making a universal metaphysical claim about 'nature's vitality', what if we just made a 'historical ontological' claim that *as far as we know*, with all the techniques of observations at our disposal, 'everything is in motion'? We may be wrong, but this is the most inclusive concept we have based on many observations.

Historically, the concept of movement does not have the same normative valence as vitalism, leading to optimism. Movement is not good or bad. It's just ongoing change. Movement is not a monism of a single kind of thing but an indeterminant process. In a world of motion, everything is continually changing and interweaving. A historical ontology of motion is not flat because there is no same stuff or even same process that everything shares. Instead, the process of nature changes itself continually such that it is never the same process twice. It is not a weakness but rather a strength that no particular politics necessarily follows from this historical set of observations about motion. Just because everything is in motion does not mean we must act in a specific way. The strength of this anarchic view is that nature does not force us to live in any particular way.

In a historical ontology of motion, there is no hierarchical chain of being. There is only matter in motion. For a movement-oriented philosophy, only the very 'bottom' of the Western chain of being is real. All hierarchies built from it are stories and orders that certain groups have perpetuated to advantage some groups of beings above others. We have no experimental evidence for any metaphysical orders or superior substances.

Again, this does not mean we will necessarily be good or free. However, an ontology of motion does help clear out a lot of speculative and hierarchical clutter from our mental living space such that we can see more clearly what is going on around us.

Before we can begin experimenting with different ways of living in the Anthropocene, it will help us immensely to identify and ontologically clear out the most dangerous tools in the toolbox. If there is no natural hierarchy, there is no *single* right way to live or guarantee that we will not make mistakes in our experiments. Who 'we' are will change, as well as what we 'want'. There is no final metaphysical answer to ethical questions but only what the Greeks called a *pharmakon:* a practice of steering clear from poisons and experimenting with potential remedies. There are many ways to survive and flourish with others, and it is no single person's purview to dictate how to live.

If we want to survive and flourish on the planet, our best chance is to think and act without metaphysical illusions and hierarchal behaviours. Harbouring such fantasies is akin to wearing a blindfold while walking on a tightrope. It can only hinder an already precarious balancing act. Uncovering our eyes does not predetermine our actions or give us a complete view of reality, but it *may help* us get where we want to go without falling.

Nature does not compel morality but constrains the material conditions of survival and flourishing in various ways. So, if we want to survive to try out new forms of life, we need to think and live without delusions or vitalist optimism about our material situation. But we can't do this if we keep imagining all kinds of metaphysical entities and arbitrary hierarchies that dictate how we play the game. As long as people continue to think and act like matter and motion are inferior phenomena, they can still wield them as weapons against people and places.[10] Until critical theory turns its tools on the hierarchical chain's last links, even the best critical thinking will remain incomplete and anthropocentric. Without a critical philosophy of matter and motion, theorists may still be able to treat human culture as distinct and superior to nature and thus justify dominating the planet and humans historically associated with moving matter.

In the philosophy of movement, neither humans nor other beings have any privileged role in the world. We can study emergent motion patterns at any scale without ontologically privileging one scale over another. In the philosophy of movement, politics is the study of relations and their transformation. In a broad sense, politics can happen at the level of galaxies, nations, migrants or viruses. We can study how things form metastable patterns and try to alter them. We do not have to 'forego the category of the political' and choose between black power or thing-power. We do not need to lump and dismiss all human struggles as *merely* anthropocentric. Every political struggle is singular, and there is no substitute for treating it as such.

Politics is the process of collective desires competing and coalescing in various patterns. There is no ontological concept that will replace the critical work of political antagonism. Elsewhere I have described several major political patterns as they emerge and diverge in history. I track, for instance, the emergence and transition from territorial societies to centralising states to feudal kingdoms to capitalist economies and how they mix together in contemporary politics. Each of these social patterns follows four major patterns of motion, which I describe briefly below.

It is just as politically useless to say 'everything is vital forces' or 'everything is movement' without providing patterns or conceptual groupings of how singular agents work. For those interested to see how a politics of movement or what I call 'kinopolitics' works as a methodology, please see my political books, including *Marx in Motion: A New Materialist Marxism*. There is no conceptual or ontological shortcut for the close and detailed work of political struggle or the study of singular political struggles in history. I will conclude this section by noting that one strength of studying political patterns of motion is focusing on what people and things *do*. It does not assume that speculative and ideological narratives explain or justify social practices. It also does not assume that only humans make the patterns.

In short, the philosophy of movement is a method that looks at the world in terms of processes that *flow* and *fold* into energetic iterations or cycles that we call 'things'. From a movement-oriented perspective, reality is made of these metastable states. As a methodology, the philosophy of movement studies the way things flow and circulate into what I call *fields* or *patterns of motion*. These patterns emerge, dissipate and mix through history and tracking and anticipating them can help give us a sense of how the world works across many scales of reality.

History

Another reason to choose a posthuman historical ontology of movement rather than a vitalistic one is that it avoids the hierarchical and normative valence of the Euro-Western term 'life'. The movement philosophy aims to go straight to the bottom of the chain and abolish the hierarchy without any implicit or suggestively normative or optimistic remainders. This way, it does not make the hubristic and metaphysical error of saying that matter has agency *like life*. On the contrary, movement is *identical* to agency. There is no agency without movement and no movement without a degree of novelty or agency. Being is doing.

Thus, every agency or group of agencies is singular. Not all humans have the same agencies, nor do all plants or bacteria. The purpose of defining agency broadly as 'motion' is not to homogenise all agencies. Movement, as a process, is not the same as itself, so it cannot be homogenous by definition. The purpose of a more movement-oriented approach is to include more agencies inside, outside and alongside human agencies. Looking at patterns and scales is one way to do that. In practice, one can't include every agency. No philosophical concept will change that. There is inevitably a 'politics of truth', as Foucault says, with any analysis (Foucault 2009).

The philosophy of movement does not attribute movement or agency to matter. As far as we know, there is no matter without motion and no movement without matter. Matter and motion are entirely identical and ontologically inseparable. The agency of matter is not *like* life nor *like* human agency. Life and human agency *is* a tiny subset or region of indeterminate matter in motion. This conceptual framing puts life and humans in their actual scale in the broader material cosmos.

Metaphysics

The philosophy of movement is not metaphysical. It makes no claims about the nature of reality as it is everywhere and for all time. Instead, it makes a limited historical claim that we presently know of nothing entirely static in the universe. We also know experimentally about movement because we cannot wholly predict it and that all movement is quantum entangled at the scale of the universe. This is not a speculative interpretation of quantum mechanics like multiple universes or wave-collapse theories. It is an experimental result.[11]

Perhaps future experiments will show that nature is not indeterminate and entangled. Maybe we will discover something genuinely immobile. But until we do, the philosophy of movement is a provisional conceptual framework with more credibility than neo-vitalism. No experiment or observation has ever suggested the existence of anything called a 'vital force'. And if the term 'vital force' is just a concept to describe indeterminate relational movement, then it is unnecessary.

There is only energy in constant transformation. When patterns emerge from iterative processes of movement, we call them 'things'. 'Thing-power' and object-oriented philosophy are derivative approaches from more primary energetic movements. In my view, this is why a movement-oriented approach is preferable.

Concepts

The concept of movement is large, but it's not universal or vague. It's not universal because we might discover something genuinely immobile. By contrast, vitalism is non-falsifiable. By definition, we will never find anything non-vital in the cosmos because even death is vital. We cannot prove or disprove the existence of vital forces. They are purely speculative.

By contrast, the concept of movement is not vague because movement does not mean its opposite, 'stasis'. We can imagine something 'static' in our minds or give a definition, but there is nothing static in the world that we know of yet. Stasis is just a conceptual opposition in our imagination and not a real opposition in the world, although we may be proven wrong. Movement is the indeterminate and relational transformation of matter-energy.

The concept of movement is also not vague because, unlike vitalism, it does not import any normative valence of optimism or creativity. Because of its place on the chain of being in the Western world, very few people expect that movement will necessarily be good or creative. It might just as easily be bad or destructive. Good and bad are relative.

Additionally, the philosophy of movement is not vague because there are different types or patterns of motion. For example, matter *flows* and iterates into metastable cycles or *folds* like eddies in water. These folds then join together into larger *fields* or patterns of motion. I have proposed the analytic concepts of flow, fold and field to help talk about the different formations and scales of matter's organisation.

Each field has a pattern. Some fields of motion gather together towards a centre, which I call 'centripetal'. Some motions spread away from a centre, which I call 'centrifugal'. Some motions that move in linked relation to another at a distance I call 'tensional'. And some motions that expand and contract back and forth I call 'elastic'. Finally, some motions that spread out indeterminately and relationally without a fixed pattern I call 'pedetic'. I have tracked these patterns across many scales of nature and in large portions of human history. One is not better than the other, but they have some predictive value as observable tendencies with historical consequences. Each pattern orders the world differently. Together, they facilitate the spread or dissipation of energy at all scales of the cosmos.

The philosophy of movement is a conceptual framework for studying patterns of motion across physical scales. It is posthuman insofar as it does not ontologically privilege the human scale. But it is equally capable of analysing domains of human knowledge, as I have shown at length in my books on aesthetics, politics, ontology and science. For whatever its limits, I have tried to argue in this section that a movement-oriented approach is at least less conceptually vague than vitalism.

Conclusion: life in the Anthropocene

In this chapter, I have highlighted four main problems with posthuman vitalism and advocated one alternative way forward. Instead of expanding our concept of agency *from* life *to* matter, I believe it should be the other way round. What we call organic life is one style or pattern of motion that emerged from and is entirely material.

Elsewhere I have argued that the concept of the 'Kinocene' might also be a better way to think about our present historical epoch and avoid the anthropocentrism of the term 'Anthropocene'. The world is increasingly mobile in ways that precede and exceed human-caused climate change. If we want to survive on this planet, a better way to think about continued life does not start with life but ends with it.

In my book, *Theory of the Earth* (Nail 2021), I propose we think about the survival of life on Earth as the movement of energy. Climate change is not the result of too much energy circulating on the planet but *not enough*. From a kinetic and energetic perspective, life flourishes through the dissipation of energy. Only a tiny part of life conserves energy. Life circulates energy through diverse ways of dissipation. By destroying half of the six trillion trees on Earth, some human groups have reduced the single largest energy dissipation method on this planet. This affects everything in a feedback loop of contracting energy circulation.

Therefore, although the Kinocene is visible to us primarily through all the places, people and things moving around more than ever, this is actually causing a net decrease in the circulation of energy on the planet as a whole. By contracting the flow of energy and movement on Earth, certain human groups are triggering a cascade of further reduced movement and hastening mass extinction. We cannot rely on vitalist optimism and metaphysical speculation if we want to survive. We need a posthuman conceptual framework with some analytic power across many scales of reality to think about planetary movements. In particular, we need a framework that avoids the four problems described in this chapter.

Notes

1. For a review of the various '-ocene' designations and their shortcomings and strengths, see Grove (2019).
2. The rhetoric of the Anthropocene often makes it sound like all humans are equally responsible and equally vulnerable when they are not. See Chakrabarty (2012).
3. See Yusoff (2016); LeCain (2015); Moore (2016); Neimanis et al. (2015); Weizmann and Sheik (2015); Wark (2016); Conty (2018); Davis and Turpin (2015); Grusin (2017); Bobbette and Donovan (2019).

4. I do not mean we need to download our consciousness into a computer, as certain technological posthumans believe. For a well-written distinction between these kinds of posthumanism, see Braidotti (2012).
5. See Ellenzweig and Zammito (2017) for a book-length treatment of vitalism.
6. See also Braunmühl (2018).
7. Thomas Nail, *Matter and Motion*, under review.
8. In other words, if everything is matter, and matter, Marx says, is 'the cause of everything, [then matter is] without cause itself', or it is imminently self-caused. 'In the void the differentiation of weight disappears – that is, it is no external condition of motion, but being-for-self, immanent, absolute movement itself' (Marx and Engels 1975: 50, 474).
9. Experiments have not always satisfied some theoretical physicists who have postulated various metaphysical explanations. For a short survey of quantum interpretations and the persistence of indeterminacy, see Rovelli (2020: 65–70). See also Karen Barad.
10. For one recent example of how the historical subordination of matter has justified anti-blackness and white supremacy, see Towns (2018). See also Bianchi (2014). For more on the ethical and political consequences of my philosophy of movement, see Nail (2015, 2016, 2020, 2021).
11. For a process theory of quantum mechanics, see Rovelli (2019).

References

Abrahamsson, Sebastian, Filippo Bertoni, Annemarie Mol and Rebeca Ibáñez Martín (2015), 'Living with Omega-3: New Materialism and Enduring Concerns', *Environment and Planning D: Society and Space*, 33(1): 4–19.

Barad, Karen (2007), *Meeting the University Halfway: Quantum Physics and the Entanglement of Matter and Meaning*, Durham, NC: Duke University Press.

Bennett, Jane (2001), *The Enchantment of Modern Life: Attachments, Crossings, and Ethics*, Princeton, NJ: Princeton University Press.

Bennett, Jane (2005), 'In Parliament with Things', in Lars Tønder and Lasse Thomassen (eds), *Radical Democracy: Politics between Abundance and Lack*, Manchester and New York: Manchester University Press, pp. 133–49.

Bennett, Jane (2010), *Vibrant Matter: A Political Ecology of Things*, Durham, NC: Duke University Press.

Bennett, Jane (2016), 'Whitman's Sympathies', *Political Research Quarterly*, 69(3): 607–20.

Bianchi, Emanuela (2014), *The Feminine Symptom: Aleatory Matter in the Aristotelian Cosmos*, New York: Fordham University Press.

Bobbette, Adam and Amy Donovan (eds) (2019), *Political Geology: Active Stratigraphies and the Making of Life*, London: Palgrave Macmillan.

Braidotti, Rosi (2012), *The Posthuman*, Oxford: Polity Press.

Braun, Bruce (2008), 'Environmental Issues: Inventive Life', *Progress in Human Geography*, 32(5): 667–79.

Braun, Bruce and Sarah Whatmore (2010), *Political Matter: Technoscience, Democracy, and Public Life*, Minneapolis: University of Minnesota Press.

Braunmühl, Caroline (2018), 'Beyond Hierarchical Oppositions: A Feminist Critique of Karen Barad's Agential Realism', *Feminist Theory*, 19(2): 223–40.

Chakrabarty, Dipesh (2012), 'Postcolonial Studies and the Challenge of Climate Change', *New Literary History*, 43(1): 1–18.

Chen, Mel Y. (2012), *Animacies: Biopolitics, Racial Mattering, and Queer Affect*, Durham, NC and London: Duke University Press.

Conty, Arianne (2018), 'The Politics of Nature: New Materialist Responses to the Anthropocene', *Theory, Culture & Society*, 35(7–8): 73–96.

Coole, Diana (2013), 'Agentic Capacities and Capacious Historical Materialism: Thinking with New Materialisms in the Political Sciences', *Millennium: Journal of International Studies*, 41(3): 451–69.

Cudworth, Erika and Stephen Hobden (2014), 'Liberation for Straw Dogs? Old Materialism, New Materialism, and the Challenge of an Emancipatory Posthumanism', *Globalizations*, 12(1): 134–48.

Crutzen, Paul and E. F. Stoermer (2000), 'The "Anthropocene"', *Global Change Newsletter*, 41: 17–8.

Davis, Heather and Etienne Turpin (2015), *Art in the Anthropocene: Encounters Among Aesthetics, Politics, Environments and Epistemologies*, London: Open Humanities Press.

Deleuze, Gilles (1983), *Nietzche and Philosophy*, trans. Hugh Tomlinson, New York: Columbia University Press.

Deleuze, Gilles (1990), *The Logic of Sense*, trans. Mark Lester with Charles Stivale, New York: Columbia University Press.

Ellenzweig, Sarah and John H. Zammito (2017), *The New Politics of Materialism: History, Philosophy, Science*, London and New York: Routledge, Taylor & Francis Group.

Foucault, Michel (2009), *Security, Territory, and Population. Lectures at the Collège de France, 1977–1978*, trans. Graham Burchell, New York: Picador.

Grosz, Elizabeth (2017), *The Incorporeal: Ontology, Ethics, and the Limits of Materialism*, New York: Columbia University Press.

Grove, Jairus (2019), *Savage Ecology: War and Geopolitics at the End of the World*, Durham, NC: Duke University Press.

Grusin, Richard (2017), *Anthropocene Feminism*, Minneapolis: University of Minnesota Press.

Hayles, N. Katherine (2017), *Unthought: The Power of the Cognitive Nonconscious*, Chicago and London: University of Chicago Press.

Hinchliffe, Steve (2011), 'Book Review Forum: Vibrant Matter: A Political Ecology of Things', *Dialogues in Human Geography*, 1(3): 396–9.

LeCain, Timothy (2015), 'Against the Anthropocene: A Neo-Materialism Perspective', *International Journal for History, Culture and Modernity*, 3(1): 1–28.

Leibniz, Gottfried W. (1989), 'Specimen Dynamicum', in *Philosophical Essays*, trans. Roger Ariew and Daniel Garber, Indianapolis, IN: Hackett.

Lemke, Thomas (2021), *The Government of Things: Foucault and the New Materialisms*, New York: New York University Press.

Marso, Lori J. (2011), 'Freaks of Nature', *Political Theory*, 39(3): 417–28.

Marx, Karl and Friedrich Engels (1975), *Karl Marx, Frederick Engels: Collected Works, Volume 1*, New York: International Publishers.

Moore, Jason W. (2016), *Anthropocene or Capitalocene? Nature, History, and the Crisis of Capitalism*, Oakland, CA: PM Press.

Nail, Thomas (2015), *The Figure of the Migrant*, Redwood City, CA: Stanford University Press.

Nail, Thomas (2016), *Theory of the Border*, Oxford: Oxford University Press.

Nail, Thomas (2018a), *Lucretius I: An Ontology of Motion*, Edinburgh: Edinburgh University Press.

Nail, Thomas (2018b), *Being and Motion*, Oxford: Oxford University Press.

Nail, Thomas (2020), *Lucretius II: An Ethics of Motion*, Edinburgh: Edinburgh University Press.

Nail, Thomas (2021), *Theory of the Earth*, Redwood City, CA: Stanford University Press.

Nail, Thomas, *Matter and Motion*. Under review with Edinburgh University Press.

Neimanis, Astrida, Cecilia Åsberg and Johan Hedrén (2015), 'Four Problems, Four Directions for Environmental Humanities: Toward Critical Posthumanities for the Anthropocene', *Ethics & the Environment*, 20(1): 67–97.

Rovelli, Carlo (2019), *Order of Time*, trans. Simon Carnell and Erica Segre, London: Penguin.

Rovelli, Carlo (2020), *Helgoland*, Milano: Adelphi.

Towns, Armond R. (2018), 'Black "Matter" Lives', *Women's Studies in Communication*, 41(4): 349–58.

Wark, McKenzie (2016), *Molecular Red: Theory for the Anthropocene*, New York: Verso.

Washick, Bonnie, Elizabeth Wingrove, Kathy E. Ferguson and Jane Bennett (2015), 'Politics That Matter: Thinking about Power and Justice with the New Materialists', *Contemporary Political Theory*, 14(1): 63–89.

Watson, J. (2013), 'Eco-Sensibilities: An Interview with Jane Bennett', *The Minnesota Review*, 81: 147–58.

Weheliye, Alexander G. (2014), *Habeas Viscus: Racializing Assemblages, Biopolitics, and Black Feminist Theories of the Human*, Durham, NC and London: Duke University Press.

Weizman, Eyal and Fazal Sheikh (2015), *The Conflict Shoreline: Colonization as Climate Change in the Negev Desert*, Göttingen: Steidl.

Welch, Craig (2017), 'Half of All Species Are on the Move – And We're Feeling It', *National Geographic*, 27 April, available at: https://news.national-geographic.com/2017/04/climate-change-species-migration-disease/ (last accessed 10 January 2022).

Yusoff, Kathryn (2016), 'Anthropogenesis: Origins and Endings in the Anthropocene', *Theory, Culture & Society*, 33(2): 3–28.

13

Forms of Life: Simondon, Ruyer, Malabou

Audronė Žukauskaitė

When trying to explain the endurance of living beings, philosophers often invoke the notion of form. Development, maintenance and destruction of living beings is interpreted by analogy as creative experience. For example, Gilbert Simondon, explaining the notion of individuation, or ontogenesis, refers to it as 'the theatre of individuation', where living beings perform their roles. Raymond Ruyer, explaining the development of forms, or the process of morphogenesis, evokes the example of a musical melody: regardless that it might be written in scores, it can be performed in many different ways and is always open to improvisations and adjustments. Catherine Malabou, writing about cellular and neuronal plasticity, often gives the example of a sculpture whose clear and beautiful forms appear only when we carve out and remove some previous forms. This leads to the question of how life is related to the notion of form and also to what extent this notion of form could be extended from living to non-living beings.

Simondon: life as the theatre of individuation

Simondon created an original theory of individuation which explains the development of physical, biological, psychosocial and technical beings. Simondon argues that there are two philosophical paths to explain of how individuals are formed: a substantialist and a hylomorphic path. The substantialist path presumes that an individual arises from a certain substance, whilst the other, hylomorphic, path explains the individual as generated by the encounter between form and matter. Simondon argues that individuation arises neither from a certain substance, nor from an interaction between matter and form, but from a pre-individual state which is anterior to any individual. He takes the hypothesis about the pre-individual state from physics, namely from the thermodynamic notion of metastable equilibrium, and extends it to a wide array of physical, biological and psychosocial individuals. A metastable equilibrium is a system which is neither stable nor unstable, but is charged with potentials for becoming, and which contains enough potential to 'produce an abrupt alteration leading to a new, equally metastable structuration' (Simondon 2020: 369). In other words, first we have to explain the process of individuation – the transition from the pre-individual state to a new phase or condition – and only then can we define what an individual is.

The pre-individual state contains a certain difference or disparity, therefore it cannot be explained through the principle of identity and the principle of excluded middle. It needs a new method – that of transduction – which arises in the middle of the pre-individual state and expresses the tension, the disparity between a certain problem and its possible solution. Transduction is a process, or a propagation, from which something new emerges – it is simultaneously a transformation, a change, and a new reality emerging from this change. As Simondon points out,

> by transduction we mean a physical, biological, mental, or social operation through which an activity propagates incrementally within a domain by basing this propagation on a structuration of the domain operated from one region to another: each structural region serves as a principle and model, as an initiator for constituting the following region, such that a modification thereby extends progressively throughout this structuring operation. (Ibid.: 13)

A good example of this structuring activity is the process of crystallisation: the supersaturated mother liquid contains a tension, an excess of potentiality, therefore it is enough to introduce a very small seed – a piece of dust – to resolve this tension and start the process of crystallisation. The crystal starts growing and expanding in all directions, and 'each previously constituted molecular layer serves as the structuring basis for the layer in the process of forming' (ibid.). Thus, instead of describing individuation as an interaction between matter and form, Simondon explains it in terms of transduction, which invents form from the domain in which it propagates.

Simondon argues that the notion of transduction can be applied not only to a physical domain, but also accounts for biological, or vital, and psychosocial individuation. In the domain of physical operation, transduction expresses the growth and development of a physical structure which is effectuated as progressive iteration (the crystal grows by iterating

its own structure), whereas in the domain of vital operation it can produce heterogeneous domains as a result of the interaction between the
living organism and its environment. However, transduction defines not
only physical and vital domains, but also the psychical and the domain of
knowledge. As Simondon argues, transduction can be used 'as the basis
of a new type of analogical paradigmatism in order to pass from physical
individuation to organic individuation, from organic individuation to
psychical individuation, and from psychical individuation to the subjective and objective transindividual' (ibid.: 14).

In this respect, the notion of transduction implies two important
consequences. First, transduction is a mental procedure which retains
differences and disparities not by negating or reducing them, but by
restructuring them into a new system or structure: 'resolving transduction *operates the inversion of the negative into the positive*: that through which
the terms are not identical to one another, that through which they are
disparate [. . .] is integrated into the system of resolution and becomes a
condition of signification' (ibid.: 15). Second, the notions of form and
matter should be replaced by the notion of form-taking activity. For
example, a brick can be interpreted as an individual which is created by
superimposing a mould on a passive piece of clay; however, Simondon
says that to receive a form the clay has to be not only passively deform-
able, but actively plastic.

> The relation between matter and form thus does not take place
> between inert matter and a form coming from outside: there is a
> common operation that is on the same level of existence between
> matter and form; this common level of existence is that of *force*
> [. . .] Matter and form are brought together as *forces*. (Ibid.: 26–7)

In other words, the form-taking activity can be accounted only as a
system of an energetic regime where opposite forces are affecting each
other. Thus, the opposition between matter and form should be replaced
by the notion of modulation, which explains the interaction between
form-giving force and form-taking force as a continuous and fluctuating
modulation.

The theory of individuation explains not only the transformation
of physical entities but also the development of biological individuals.
However, biological individuality is much more complicated than physical individuality: 'in biology it seems that the notion of individuality
is applicable to several stages or according to different levels of successive inclusion' (ibid.: 168). Biological individuation is interpreted as a
process of transduction when one biological form is transformed into

another form. In this sense both physical individuation and biological individuation involve a kind of transduction. However, some important differences occur between the two: in contrast to physical individuation, which is completed when certain conditions are exhausted, the individuation of a living being is never completed but is an ongoing process; 'it is not merely a result of individuation, like the crystal or molecule, but a theatre of individuation' (ibid.: 7). Moreover, unlike in physical individuation, where heterogeneous transductive characteristics appear at the margins of physical reality, as for example at the edges of a crystal, biological individuation requires a transduction that differentiates between the interior and the exterior of a living being. A living being is a system of communication where the interior is always in communication with the exterior and vice versa. In other words, the individuation of a living being cannot be completed in a single stroke but needs ongoing transformation. As Simondon observes, 'the living being resolves problems, not just by adapting, i.e. by modifying its relation to the milieu (like a machine is capable of doing), but by modifying itself, by inventing new internal structures, and by completely introducing itself into the axiomatic of vital problems' (ibid.). The physical being has no real interiority, whereas the living being is constantly transforming itself from within and also keeps track of this continuous transformation.

In other words, physical individuation is finite, and it works as a quantum leap which resolves the tension in a single stroke, whereas biological individuation is never completed. It always carries a certain charge of pre-individual potential within itself, which, in its turn, constitutes a new problematic and initiates new phases of individuation. As Simondon points out,

> the living individual is contemporaneous with itself in all its elements, which is not the case for the physical individuation, for the latter includes a past that has radically past, even when it is still in the process of growing. At the interior of itself, the living being is a node of informative communication; it is a system within a system, involving *within itself* a mediation between two orders of magnitude. (Ibid.: 8)

For example, a crystal, after being formed and completed, becomes inertial and submerges into the past, whereas a living being stretches in two directions at once: it is directed towards the outside, the external milieu, and towards the inside, which is restructured and attuned to this milieu with the help of internal resonance. Thus, the living individual is created by two orders of magnitude: it is constantly restructured according to the external milieu, or environment, which is actual, and, at the same time, it is permanently re-charged by its pre-individual potential. As Elizabeth Grosz points out,

> life remains indebted to the pre-individual to the extent that the resources for all its becomings, all its future individuations, self-actualizations, must be drawn from these singularities which its own must incorporate. The 'phases' of life, from fertilized egg to corpse, are internally structured, organized through the forces that enable life to elaborate itself; they are part of the permanent processes of individuation that occur even when an individual has already been produced. (Grosz 2012: 49)

In this sense, a living being, or life in general, can be maintained only if it constantly remains connected to the pre-individual charge and is able to keep a metastable equilibrium. That means that living beings never reach a stable equilibrium because biological individuation proceeds from one metastable condition to another metastable condition, which is seen as the necessary condition of life. As Simon Mills points out, 'in the case of vital individuation the operation does not resolve, for in doing so it would result in the death of the organism. Vital individuation requires an ongoing metastable tension and the need for further problems requiring solution' (Mills 2016: 59). A living being is alive only if it is capable of resolving its problematic by entering into a new phase of metastability.

Simondon argues that a living being and its milieu are mutually correlative in such a way that their potentials cannot be fully actualised or exhausted but are resolved through integration into a higher dimension.

> According to such a conception, in order to think the living being, life must be thought as a transductive result of operations of individuation, or, better yet, as an interlinking of successive resolutions, insofar as each previous resolution can be taken back up and reincorporated in subsequent resolutions. In this sense, we could consider that life in its entirety seems like a progressive construction of increasingly elaborate forms, i.e. forms capable of containing increasingly elevated problems. (Simondon 2020: 237)

Thus, life is seen as the resolution of problematics which might not always be successful. Life as a posed problem might not be resolved or might be resolved badly – this is how death comes into life. Death also arrives when the metastable equilibrium is exhausted, deprived of potential and can no longer enhance new individuations. In this sense, a metastable equilibrium is the necessary condition of life.

And yet, some other conditions are required to define life. In the chapter 'Topology and Ontogenesis' Simondon suggests that to define a living being we need a special topological arrangement: a membrane. 'The living membrane [. . .] is characterized as what separates a region of interiority from a region of exteriority: the membrane is polarized and therefore allows the passage of some particular body centripetally or centrifugally while blocking the passage of some other particular body' (ibid.: 251). The membrane functions as a polarising force which differentiates between what is favourable and unfavourable for the organism. Moreover, the membrane not only separates the interiority from the exteriority of the living being but functions as a differentiating force that keeps the organism in a state of metastability. As Anne Sauvagnargues asserts, 'this interiority and exteriority are not absolute but metastable, dynamic, relative to each other, and their interfacing surface is itself in becoming, in relation' (Sauvagnargues 2012: 67). That means that in a multicellular organism the limit between interiority and exteriority is always relative, depending on its place in the organisation of a living being.

As Simondon explains, in the topology of a living organism we find various levels of interiority and exteriority. For example, the space of digestive cavities is a space of exteriority in relation to the blood stream which floods the intestinal walls, but blood is a milieu of exteriority in respect to the endocrine glands that release the products of their activity into the blood (Simondon 2020: 252). This means that the structure of a complex organism is like a multiple folding, where the internal milieu is enfolded into an external milieu, which in its turn becomes the internal milieu to be enfolded into more complex external milieus. The membrane arranges a transductive mediation between different levels of interiorities and exteriorities. The topological arrangement of living space implies that life is sustained through metastability; in other words, one can never have a final and unifying vision of living systems:

> the totalizing vision and the elementary vision are equally inadequate; we have to start with the basic function that depends on the first topological structure of interiority and exteriority, and then we have to see how this function is mediated by a chain of intermediary interiorities and exteriorities. (Ibid.)

This is why vital, or biological, individuation must be interpreted in terms of topological schemata which describe the living being in terms of differentiation and metastability.

The topological arrangement of space is not the only requirement to think the living being. Another requirement is the continuity of time which virtually condenses all stages of individuation into the lived present. It is this arrangement of time that allows us to draw a line between the living and the non-living. For example, in the individuation of a crystal, the interiority of an already formed crystal has become stable and inert and does not provide any information for its further individuation. A crystal is growing only at the edges, but this growth is not informed by its interiority and its past. As Simondon points out,

> in order for the crystal to individuate, it must continue to grow; this individuation is superficial; the past doesn't serve a purpose in the crystal's mass . . . Conversely, in the living being [. . .] the whole content of the interior space is topologically in contact with the content of the exterior space at the limits of the living being. (Ibid.: 253)

The interiority of a living being condenses all forms that have been produced by individuation in the past, and this condensed past is actively related to individuating processes taking place in the exteriority of the living being. This means that topology is a space without distance: the interior space is actively present in the exterior space at the limits of a living being. This reformulation of space is also applicable to time: the chronology of a living being condenses and keeps in the present tense all layers of previous successive individuations. As Simondon argues, 'in the same way that there are no distances in topology, in chronology there is no quantity of time' (ibid.: 254). Thus, time is not continuous; time is defined as discontinuity, contiguity and envelopment of different time layers, of different moments of the past, that become contiguous in the interiority of a living being. We can argue that the interiority of a living being transforms the quantity of time into the quality of time, in the sense that time which has already passed can create the basis for future individuations. As Simondon points out, 'the present is this metastability of the rapport between interior and exterior, past and future; the exterior is exterior, and interior is interior relative to this mutual allagmatic activity of presence. Topology and chronology coincide in the individuation of the living being' (ibid.). In other words, Simondon's theory of vital individuation proposes new conceptions of space and time: topology as a theory of space without distance, and chronology as a theory of time without quantity. Topology and chronology are not *a priori* forms, but a form-taking activity characteristic to living beings.

Ruyer: life as form-taking activity

Ruyer suggests another theory of life which is associated with the development of forms, or the process of morphogenesis. Like Simondon, Ruyer argues against the notion of bounded entities, understood as pre-formed and pre-given, and asserts that morphogenesis is a self-formative activity, which creates without any pre-ordered idea or plan. Ruyer's morphogenesis, similar to Simondon's ontogenesis, is a process which carries within itself the potential for its transformation. Ruyer criticises contemporary theories of embryogenesis as being built on Newtonian physics, which construes living beings as mechanisms placed in a neutral space. In this sense Ruyer distinguishes between the extensive space of physical entities and the intensive space of living forms. In contrast to physical entities, Ruyer examines living organisms as self-formative and self-surveying beings, which have the properties of primary consciousness. Each living form, from the most primitive organisms to those having a psychological consciousness and a brain, expresses conscious activity and the capacity of maintaining and transforming its form.

Ruyer argues that the principle of final cause or purposiveness which Kant proposes to define organic beings cannot explain their formation. Ruyer thinks that the concept of purposiveness, or finality, should be renounced and replaced with the idea of a dynamic force. Such a dynamic force is consciousness understood not as a transcendental principle but as an absolute form immanent in every living being. Ruyer invents the concept of an absolute form, which he distinguishes from aggregates. According to Daniel W. Smith,

> in place of the distinction between the organic and the inorganic, Ruyer proposes a new distinction that cuts across both these domains: a distinction between *absolute forms* (individual beings), on the one hand, and *molar structures* (aggregate or mass phenomena), on the other. Absolute forms include molecules, viruses, cells, embryos, and brains, while molar structures are statistical aggregates of these individual forms, such as clouds, gases, crowds, or geological formations. (Smith 2017: 117–18)

Similar to organicism, Ruyer is concerned with the nature of organisation, or bonding, which for him is of two different types: absolute forms are involved in constant formation, which establishes an irreducible unity between its parts, whereas the functioning of molar structures is a result of external forces. For example, a rock or a cloud is a molar structure or an aggregate because it is shaped by mechanical external forces and does not produce any internal bonds; by contrast, absolute forms, such as atoms, molecules or organisms, produce non-localisable internal bonds that are in a state of self-survey. Thus, Ruyer establishes a fundamental distinction between *functioning* and *formation*: functioning is mereological and mechanical and it cannot explain the self-organising activities of living beings; by contrast, formation is an incessant activity characteristic to living beings which can create, survey and maintain their form. As Smith points out, 'this distinction in turn entails a new distribution of the sciences: the primary sciences are those that focus on absolute forms, while the secondary sciences are those that only study individuals from their molar or statistical side' (ibid.: 119). For Ruyer, the main problem is not the distinction between the organic and the inorganic, but the distinction between self-individuating forms and aggregates which are individuated by other forces (to use Simondon's vocabulary). For him the central philosophical problem is to explain absolute form as a self-formative force.

Ruyer describes this self-organising activity of form as a process of morphogenesis. In this sense he, like Simondon, has to challenge the traditional opposition between matter and form which has guided philosophy since Plato and Aristotle. In contrast to the metaphysical notion of forms understood as something pre-given, Ruyer elaborates the theory of developmental themes. As Jon Roffe points out, Ruyer conceives form not 'in terms of a fixed model, an *eidos*, whose outline is given secondary material content in being incarnated, but in terms of non-determining developmental *themes*. These themes, rather than preforming the individual in genesis, are non-material hinges or hooks around which improvisation takes place' (Roffe 2017: 585). Form is understood as a formative activity that creates connections and bonds between different parts of an individual, and also between different phases or shapes of the same individual. In this respect form is understood not as something existing separately from matter but as an active force that is always already embodied in matter. For Ruyer, a good example of this is the formation of a benzene molecule:

> form is inseparable from matter. Living matter only ever appears as formed, just as the benzene molecule only ever appears, as matter, in its well-known hexagonal shape. Benzene is not an amorphous matter that comes to be 'informed' by the shape of the hexagon, produced like an Aristotelian form. It is this form itself, which is in turn derived from the modes of bonding of carbon and hydrogen. In the same way, biological forms arise without hiatus from molecular morphology. (Ruyer 2020: 31)

In other words, both inorganic and organic entities carry their forms in themselves and actively participate in their own self-forming. Matter and form cannot be clearly separated because matter is self-forming and invents its own forms in the process of morphogenetic development.

Another important feature of absolute form is that Ruyer defines it in terms of consciousness. 'Consciousness *is* any active formation in its absolute activity, and all formation is consciousness' (ibid.: 162). This reference to consciousness does not imply the return to any kind of vitalism: consciousness is understood not as a mental or a transcendental substance but as a form embodied in material forces. 'Every form, from atoms to molecules, viruses, bacteria and more complex organisms, is a self-sustaining configuration of forces of connection. Each of these forms, according to Ruyer, is a consciousness' (Bogue 2009: 304). The notion of consciousness also has to be separated from panpsychism, which expresses the attitude that human consciousness can be extended to explain the existence of other entities. Rather, Ruyer is trying to assert that consciousness is an organising activity or force that can account for the organisation of absolute forms (from molecules to organisms). In contrast to molar structures, which are observable and definable from the outside, absolute forms have their organising principle in themselves, and also have the capacity of surveying their own development. It is this capacity of self-survey which helps form-consciousness to follow the individual's internal state and to maintain its integrity throughout all stages of its development.

To explain the notion of a formative or developmental theme, Ruyer gives an example of a melody. A melody operates in two modes: it can exist in an 'ideal' mode written in scores, and it can be performed in many different ways while being open to improvisations and adjustments. As Ruyer points out, 'morphogenesis can only be understood by invoking a non-mechanical model, by thinking of an individualised melodic theme which can both be integrally repeated and distribute itself in variations through which the initial, repeated theme serves as its own "development" (in the musical sense of the term)' (Ruyer 2020: 61). Thus, the 'ideal' melody can be understood as a potential or virtual idea in the Deleuzian sense, which can be actualised and embodied in an actual process of morphogenesis. As Ronald Bogue explains, 'Ruyer's concept of the developmental theme does not imply a conventional idealism, for the theme, though "trans-spatial", is always immanent within the material world' (Bogue 2017: 524). For example, an embryo is 'equipotential' in the sense that it contains all developmental themes which become more and more restricted when an organism develops and takes some specific form. However, this developmental theme is embodied within the organism and disappears only when the organism exhausts all its potential. Thus, the organism's developmental theme is never separated from an actual organism and is always immanent throughout all forms of its development.

The notion of absolute form allows Ruyer to avoid the danger of being trapped either in preformationism, or in finalism. He distances himself from preformationism, which presumes that biological forms are given in advance and later develop only in quantities. In contrast to this assumption, he understands morphogenesis as a formative activity that creates and invents qualitatively new forms of organisation. In other words, absolute forms, or formational themes, are the only agents of morphogenetic invention. On the other hand, the creativity of the formative theme allows him to avoid the trap of finalism. As Smith points out, 'Ruyer is not a traditional "finalist", presuming a teleology or purpose throughout nature or for nature as a whole. Rather, he defends a "*neo*finalism"' (Smith 2017: 122). The development of absolute forms is neofinalist in the sense that it implies creativity, freedom and consciousness, and is not pre-programmed in advance. Ruyer observes that a teleological and theological explanation contradicts his theory of morphogenesis, according to which living beings are self-forming and self-maintaining entities.

To avoid the limits of both preformationism and finalism, Ruyer asserts the autonomy and self-organisation of any living being: 'the living being is at once the agent and the "material" of its own action. [. . .] The living being forms itself directly in accordance with a theme, without the theme first having to become an idea-image or represented model' (Ruyer 2020: 175). In this respect Ruyer's idea of a formative theme is very close to Simondon's thesis that 'the living being is an agent and theatre of individuation' (Simondon 2020: 9). Actually, Ruyer's formative theme can be compared to Simondon's notion of transduction: transduction is both the process which differentiates and the new reality of that which has been differentiated. Similarly, for Ruyer,

> organic morphogenesis [. . .] results not only in the transformation of an initial form, and not only in a brute increase in complexity [. . .], but in an increase in complexity in a self-sustaining, consistent, unified totality capable of serving as the basis for a new formation in its turn. (Ruyer 2020: 2)

The idea of a formative theme means that an organism carries within itself the themes of its own formation and organisation, and in this sense serves as an immanent cause of its own development.

To explain this formative activity Ruyer invokes the concept of consciousness. As Ruyer points out,

> Consciousness is not a passive knowledge but the active unity of a behaviour or a perception. Consciousness *is* always a forming activity. It is always a dynamic effort of unification [. . .] This hypothesis, we must underline, does not consist in saying that consciousness *explains* morphogenesis; it rather asserts that consciousness and morphogenesis are one and the same. (Ibid.: 160)

Consciousness is nothing other than a form, an active principle, which refers neither to a transcendent realm, nor to a subjective consciousness of any particular subject. To explain morphogenesis, Ruyer invents a theory of forms, which relate to different types of consciousness. Form I, primary consciousness, is the characteristic of all material entities at the scale of atoms or molecules, and also of the most elementary organisms. Form II, secondary consciousness, is characteristic of all beings with motor schema, which leads to a perceptive or schematising consciousness like in humans and animals. Finally, there is Form III, human self-reflective consciousness, which develops thanks to the techniques of language and symbolisation. What is important for Ruyer is that these three types of consciousness derive from each other: 'it is indeed necessary to grasp that Form I is fundamental, and that Forms II and III would be inconceivable if they were not based on Forms I, of which they are only particular cases. The three types are distinct, but each is united with the one preceding it' (ibid.: 150). Thus, human reflective consciousness can define itself only because it is derived from primary organic consciousness:

> Forms II and III are only connected up with the themes because they are particular cases of Form I. The human is only conscious, intelligent and inventive because all living individuality is conscious, intelligent and inventive [. . .] This is to simply forget that the human brain which invents itself is first of all only an organic tissue, a network of cells, and that *every human and social deployment of invention is only auxiliary and accessory*. (Ibid.: 171)

Our brain has the capacity of perception and cognition only because it is made of organic tissue and possesses the characteristics of primary consciousness.

It is important to note that Ruyer is not trying to ascribe human consciousness to all living beings and is aware of the 'risk of naive anthropomorphism'. As he observes, the researcher's aim is 'not to define the atom, the molecule, and the physical individuality as organisms or as psychological consciousnesses, but instead to seek what is schematically common to the molecule, the organism, and consciousness. In all these cases, the common schema is a domain of absolute survey and activity' (ibid.: 162). In other words, what defines primary consciousness is self-organisation, a dynamic activity, which has the power to change and to evolve using its force of equipotentiality, and to harmonise these changes through the unity of self-survey. In this respect the features of equipotentiality and self-survey define any consciousness (or absolute form), regardless of its complexity. Ruyer asserts that the human brain has no monopoly over consciousness but is rather immersed in a continuum of organic form-taking activity.

Malabou's theory of forms

The tension between preformationism and the freedom of morphogenetic development, which we observed examining Ruyer's work, is also guiding Malabou's philosophy. The notion of plasticity first appears in Malabou's doctoral thesis on Hegel, which later was published under the title *The Future of Hegel*. Although originating from a close reading of Hegelian dialectics, the notion of plasticity is detached from the Hegelian vocabulary and, as Jacques Derrida pointed out in his 'Preface', extended to the realm of the living in general (Malabou 2005: xxiii). Malabou discusses plasticity as a general characteristic of life which defines the living being as capable of receiving form and also of giving form to its environment. However, to exercise its vital functions, an organism has to transform the reservoir of energy into something else. In other words, it has to make this energy explode to acquire new vital qualities. Here the word 'plasticity' acquires a third meaning, that of explosive substance (deriving from the French words *plastiquer* or *plastiquage*). In this sense plasticity means both the creation of forms and the annihilation of forms which are necessary for future transformations: 'life is responsible for the donation of the vital forms, but [. . .] each of these forms, to the degree that it is made of a concentrated energy, provokes an explosion' (ibid.: 61). Thus, the concept of plasticity encompasses three different aspects of organic life: an organism takes form to become what it is; it gives form to its environment and reshapes it according to its needs; and it explodes form to transform the reservoirs of energy into the substances it needs for its further development.

The notion of plasticity acquires slightly different connotations in Malabou's other books, where she relates the concept of plasticity to the synaptic activity of the brain. In *What Should We Do with Our Brain?* Malabou examines the plasticity of the brain, which in some ways is similar to the plasticity of an organism: it receives form in the sense that it is a self-organising system, and it gives form in shaping and organising the environment around itself. As Malabou points out, 'it is precisely because [. . .] the brain is not already made that we must ask what we should do with it, what we should do with this plasticity that makes us, precisely in the sense of a work: sculpture, modelling, architecture. What should we do with this plastic organic art?' (Malabou 2008: 7). What should we do with this living brain, which appears at the most elementary levels of life and is one of the fundamental characteristics of living beings? Because the brain is *in us*, how do these new discoveries about the plasticity of the brain correlate with our personality?

Malabou discusses plasticity in two respects: as cell plasticity and neuronal plasticity. In relation to cell plasticity Malabou distinguishes between different types of stem cells: totipotent (omnipotent) stem cells, which can give rise to any of the 220 cell types found in an embryo as well as extra-embryonic cells (placenta); pluripotent stem cells, which can give rise to all cell types of the body; and multipotent stem cells, which can develop into a limited number of cell types in a particular lineage. Thus, if totipotent stem cells express the potential to produce any type of cells found in embryos, pluripotent and multipotent stem cells express the potential to replicate and differentiate in adults. The stem cells' capacity to replicate and differentiate themselves is called stem-cell plasticity. As Malabou observes, 'in the first case – the capacity to differentiate themselves into cells of the same tissue – stem cells are called *multipotent*. In the second case – the capacity to develop themselves into types of cells specific to other tissues – stem cells are called *pluripotent*' (ibid.: 16). Having in mind these different levels of potentiality, Malabou argues that stem-cell plasticity embraces both meanings, 'closed' and 'open': it is determination (to produce cells of the same type of tissue) and freedom (the ability to differentiate and produce cells of other tissues). 'According to this meaning, plasticity designates generally the ability to change one's destiny, to inflect one's trajectory, to navigate differently, to reform one's form and not solely to constitute that form as in the "closed" meaning' (ibid.: 17). Stem-cell plasticity allows the living being to acquire and maintain its proper form, and, on the other hand, it allows it to change and improvise.

The same kind of plasticity which is characteristic of an organism at the level of stem cells can be detected in the operation of synaptic connections taking place in the brain. Malabou observes that the brain's plasticity operates on three levels: first, it is developmental plasticity, which appears in the brain of the embryo, and which begins with establishing the neuronal connections and then multiplying and modelling them. In this regard the brain is not something that is given from birth in its finished form; rather, it is undergoing a process of sculpting, which eliminates useless connections and strengthens those which are useful. The elimination of useless connections taking place in the brain reminds us of the biological phenomenon called apoptosis, or 'cell death'. As Claude Ameisen points out, 'cell death is [. . .] a tool allowing the embryo to work out its form in its becoming, by eliminative procedure that allies it with sculpture' (Ameisen 1999: 30; cited in Malabou 2008: 19). When neuronal sculpting is completed, the next phase of the modelling of the brain depends on contacts with the external world: it is the relationship with the environment that becomes crucial for the brain's development. This means that apoptotic sculpting is replaced by epigenetic sculpting which now takes the role of neuronal morphogenesis. 'In both cases, the brain appears at once as something that gets formed – progressively sculpted, stabilized and divided into different regions – and as something formative: little by little, to the extent that the volume of connections grows, the identity of an individual begins to outline itself' (Malabou 2008: 20). At this point developmental plasticity is replaced by modulational plasticity which works through the brain's connections with the external world.

Thus, the second level of neuronal plasticity as modulational plasticity refers to the modification of neuronal connections in the adult brain. The brain's synaptic efficiency can dramatically increase (a long-term potentiation) or diminish (a long-term depression). The external stimuli, such as learning, experience and imagination, can activate and increase the number of synaptic connections. This capacity is characteristic not only of humans, but also of animals: for example, birds' behaviour, such as stockpiling food, can significantly increase their neuronal connections. Similarly, human animals have the capacity to potentiate their brain activity during the process required for perception and learning. The idea of modulational plasticity questions the old assumption that the brain of an adult is incapable of changes; on the contrary, it is open to constant morphogenetic modulations. In this respect neuronal plasticity can be compared with stem cells' plasticity: 'one could claim that neuronal connections, because of their own plasticity, are always capable of *changing difference*, receiving or losing an imprint, or transforming their program' (ibid.: 24). Malabou argues that our brain literally is what we do with it: by activating our brain, we can escape biological determination and increase the potential for improvisation.

The third level of plasticity is so-called reparative plasticity, which encompasses both neuronal renewal and the brain's capacity to repair itself after being damaged. Neuronal renewal or secondary neurogenesis refers to the modification of synaptic connections in the adult brain and in this respect is similar to the modulational plasticity discussed above. Reparative plasticity refers to the brain's capacity to recreate or invent new connections after certain damage, like a stroke or an amputation. Thus, reparative plasticity reveals the brain's capacity to create a 'natural prosthesis', to invent new forms of self-repair, which were not foreseen or pre-formed in advance. For example, certain neuronal connections which are responsible for movement or cognition might be lost or destroyed after a stroke. However, this loss can be compensated by activating different parts of the brain which take the role of damaged neuronal connections. As Marc Jeannerod points out, 'the patient, by himself or through rehabilitation, has learned to use nerve pathways that would not be there in the normal state. This reorganization of motor function testifies once more to the plasticity of brain mechanisms' (Jeannerod 2002: 69; cited in Malabou 2008: 28). These examples demonstrate that the brain has the potentiality for creation and invention and can be modified in many different ways.

Thus, both the plasticity of stem cells and the plasticity of brain connections express potentiality as one of the most important characteristics of every living being. It is important to stress that plasticity as potentiality is actualised not according to a certain pre-existing plan or form, but is open to change, improvisations and even accidents. Similar to Ruyer who argued that the living form initiates its own morphogenetic development, Malabou's philosophy re-conceptualises developmental, modulational and reparative plasticity as potentiality which appears not only in the embryo, but also in adult individuals. Plasticity as potentiality allows one to interpret the organism and the brain not as something that is actually given and finite, but as an open system, virtually carrying within itself its future transformations. In this respect Malabou's idea of plasticity as potentiality has an affinity to the Deleuzian notion of the virtual. In *What Is Philosophy?* Deleuze and Guattari (1994) persuasively describe the virtual and undetermined character of the brain that can be expressed as the potential to be (or form), and also the potential not to be (or deform).

Having this ambivalence in mind, we can redefine the meaning of positive and destructive plasticity. It seems clear that change is the necessary condition of plasticity: in order to change and evolve, we have to destroy ourselves to some extent, to deform in order to get another form. However, this deformation might be irreversible and would not lead to another form, as in cases of neurodegenerative diseases or in brain lesions. In these cases the change is irreversible, and the potential for plasticity is lost. Destructive plasticity is reductive because it exhausts the virtuality or potentiality of what might happen. However, without engaging in destructive plasticity, we could not open the potential for creative plasticity and transform ourselves into something new. In this sense the notion of plasticity is involved in a certain kind of Hegelian dialectic (from which it actually originated) because it is constantly torn between the necessity to maintain homeostasis and the potential to change and develop into new forms.

In this respect the notion of plasticity allows us to question the universal and necessary nature of transcendental reason and to replace it with the plastic, contingent and arbitrary character of 'biological reason'. The biologisation of reason allows one to think beyond formal structures and universal values and, as Malabou writes, 'to authorize subjects to form and shape themselves as such' (Malabou 2019: 131). In this respect the biologisation of reason might be seen as a resistance to biopolitical power. Both Foucault and Deleuze argued that when biopolitical power takes life as its object, it is the vital power of life which allows us to resist power. In a similar vein, Malabou argues that recent developments in biology, such as epigenetics, cloning or gene editing, demonstrate that the biological dimension of our lives should be understood not as determination but as a potential for freedom and change. Malabou points out that 'a resistance to what is known today as biopower [. . .] might emerge from possibilities written in the structure of the living being itself, not from the philosophical concepts that tower over it; that there might be a biological resistance to the biopolitical' (Malabou 2016: 429). Plasticity expresses the capacity of a living being to receive form and give form, to change and develop. Living beings are not predetermined in advance but rather are a formative activity that carries its forms within itself. As Malabou observes, 'plasticity is in a way genetically programmed to develop and operate without program, plan, determinism, schedule, design, or preschematization. Neural plasticity allows the shaping, repairing, and remodeling of connections and in consequence a certain amount of self-transformation of the living being' (Malabou 2015: 43–4). In this sense the divide between the transcendental and the biological is undermined because the biological does not follow any transcendental law but possesses transformative potential within itself. Biological plasticity allows us to imagine different forms of life and subjectivity, free to take any shape or form and to avoid the pressure of normativity. In this sense form and norm produce opposite poles of life. Where plasticity deserts, biopolitics takes over.

Conclusion

The discussion of forms taken from the philosophies of Simondon, Ruyer and Malabou allows us to reconstruct a certain morphing ontology. Life, described in terms of individuation, transduction, morphogenesis or plasticity, is seen as form-taking activity. In this respect morphing ontology encompasses both organic and inorganic life forms, although maintaining their differences, and traces a certain continuity between cellular plasticity of the body and neuronal plasticity of the brain. In this sense life is a formation, a form-taking activity, which possesses its own mode of self-organisation and self-survey. Moreover, following the authors discussed above, we could easily prove that the notion of form-taking activity could be extended to technical objects (Simondon 2017), tools (Ruyer 2016) and artificial intelligence (Malabou 2019). In her more recent work Malabou demonstrates the similarity between organic homeostasis and technological self-regulation (2019: 119). This means that the notion of life can be dramatically extended to including also those morphing beings that are not necessarily organic but that follow the principle of morphogenesis. Thus, we can conclude that morphing ontology implies the principle of multiplicity; in other words, it embraces heterogeneous forms, organic and inorganic, human and non-human. It also implies the principle of processuality because forms are continuously transforming themselves and creating new forms. And, finally, it implies the principle of (im)potentiality: every form is a force which contains the potential to transform, even if this transformation might lead to deformation or death.

References

Ameisen, Jean-Claude (1999), *La sculpture du vivant: La suicide cellulair ou la mort créatrice*, Paris: Seuil.

Bogue, Ronald (2009), 'Raymond Ruyer', in Graham Jones and Jon Roffe (eds), *Deleuze's Philosophical Lineage*, Edinburgh: Edinburgh University Press, pp. 300–20.

Bogue, Ronald (2017), 'The Force that Is but Does Not Act: Ruyer, Leibniz and Deleuze', *Deleuze Studies*, 11(4): 518–37.

Deleuze, Gilles and Félix Guattari (1994), *What is Philosophy?*, trans. Graham Burchell and Hugh Tomlinson, London and New York: Verso.

Grosz, Elizabeth (2012), 'Identity and Individuation: Some Feminist Reflections', in Arne De Boever, Alex Murray, Jon Roffe and Ashley Woodward (eds), *Gilbert Simondon: Being and Technology*, Edinburgh: Edinburgh University Press, pp. 37–56.

Jeannerod, Marc (2002), *Le cerveau intime*, Paris: Odile Jacob.

Malabou, Catherine (2005), *The Future of Hegel: Plasticity, Temporality, and Dialectic*, trans. Lisabeth During, New York and London: Routledge.

Malabou, Catherine (2008), *What Shall We Do with Our Brain?*, trans. Sebastian Rand, New York: Fordham University Press.

Malabou, Catherine (2015), 'Will Sovereignty Ever Be Deconstructed?', in Brenna Bhandar and Jonathan Goldberg-Hiller (eds), *Plastic Materialities: Politics, Legality, and Metamorphosis in the Work of Catherine Malabou*, Durham, NC and London: Duke University Press, pp. 35–46.

Malabou, Catherine (2016), 'One Life Only: Biological Resistance, Political Resistance', trans. Carolyn Shread, *Critical Inquiry*, 42(3): 429–38.

Malabou Catherine (2019), *Morphing Intelligence: From IQ Measurement to Artificial Brains*, trans. Carolyn Shread, New York: Columbia University Press.

Mills, Simon (2016), *Gilbert Simondon. Information, Technology and Media*, London and New York: Rowman and Littlefield.

Roffe, Jon (2017), 'Form IV: From Ruyer's Psychobiology to Deleuze and Guattari's Socius', *Deleuze Studies*, 11(4): 580–99.

Ruyer, Raymond (2016), *Neofinalism*, trans. Alyosha Edlebi, Minneapolis: University of Minnesota Press.

Ruyer, Raymond (2020), *The Genesis of Living Forms*, trans. Jon Roffe and Nicholas B. de Weydenthal, London and New York: Rowman & Littlefield.

Sauvagnargues, Anne (2012), 'Crystals and Membranes: Individuation and Temporality', in Arne De Boever, Alex Murray, Jon Roffe and Ashley Woodward (eds), *Gilbert Simondon: Being and Technology*, Edinburgh: Edinburgh University Press, pp. 57–70.

Simondon, Gilbert (2017), *On the Existence of Technical Objects*, trans. Cecile Malaspina and John Rogove, Minneapolis, MN: Univocal Publishing.

Simondon, Gilbert (2020), *Individuation in Light of Notions of Form and Information*, trans. Taylor Adkins, Minneapolis: University of Minnesota Press.

Smith, Daniel W. (2017), 'Raymond Ruyer and the Metaphysics of Absolute Forms', *Parrhesia*, 27: 116–28.

14

Epigenetic Mimesis: Natural Brains and Synaptic Chips

Catherine Malabou

The purpose of this chapter is twofold. First, it raises a specific issue: how are we to understand the verbs 'imitate' or 'simulate' when we are told that the most recent developments and achievements in cybernetics and artificial intelligence allow technology to 'imitate' or 'simulate' the biological brain, and more precisely its epigenetic capacities? On the other hand, it will situate this issue in a more general context, namely that of my own philosophical trajectory, or at least the part of this trajectory that started with my first book on the brain, *What Should We Do With Our Brain?* (2004), and recently continued on with *Morphing Intelligence: From IQ Measurement to Artificial Brains* (2019). Recounting the main steps of this trajectory does not respond to a narcissistic trend but is used to outline the continuous attempt at trying to find an accurate concept of 'imitation' when it comes to the relationship between the natural and the artificial. To characterise such a relationship, the old, platonic notion of 'mimesis' is no longer relevant, as it limits imitation or simulation to the simple act of copying. AI does not 'copy' the brain – which does however not mean that the brain is in*imi*table. Getting out of this aporia, if such a thing is possible, took and is still taking me a lot of effort.

Let me first expand on epigenetics and what current neurobiologists call the epigenetic turn in the history of neurology. Then, I will present some recent technological achievements that sustain the idea of an epigenetic turn in the history of cybernetics and AI. Thirdly, and finally, I will propose a few philosophical reflections on the concept of imitation.

On 15 February 2001, the American scientific journal *Nature* published the virtually complete sequence of the three billion bases of the human genome (IHGSC 2001). The result was surprising: the human genome is made up of only 30,000 genes, in other words, just 13,000 more than drosophila (commonly known as fruit flies). Furthermore, it appears that genes only make up 5 per cent of the genome. Assembled in bunches and clusters, they are separated by vast expanses of so-called 'gene deserts', made up of DNA labelled 'junk' or 'repetitive', that is, non-coding. According to studies, this 'non-coding' DNA accounts for a quarter or a third of the totality of the genome. This means that within chromosomes there are long DNA sequences which, according to current understanding, do not appear to match the genes and cannot be given any particular function (cf. *Le Monde* 2001; my translation). The sequencing of the genome did not, therefore, offer the expected revelations. On the contrary, it indicated the weakening of genetic determinism. These discoveries marked the passage from the genetic to the epigenetic paradigm.

Epigenetics is a science that is currently dramatically transforming all previous (that is essentially genetic) conceptions of inheritance. This branch of molecular biology studies the relations between genes and the individual features they produce, in other terms the relation between genotype and phenotype. Derived from 'epigenesis', the term 'epigenetics' is a neologism created in 1940 by British biologist Conrad Waddington.

> Some years ago (e.g. 1947) I introduced the word 'epigenetics', derived from the Aristotelian word 'epigenesis', which had more or less passed into disuse, as a suitable name for the branch of biology which studies the causal interactions between genes and their products which bring the phenotype into being. (Waddington 1968: 9–10)

Epigenetic mechanisms concern the expression, transcription or translation of the genetic code into the phenotype, that is the biological unique constitution and physical appearance of an individual. These mechanisms act essentially through the activation or silencing of certain genes, that is through a series of modifications. These changes in gene expression do not involve changes to the underlying DNA sequence. Epigenetic changes occur at the chemical internal level (DNA *methylation*, histone modification and *non-coding RNA* [*ncRNA*]) but can also be influenced by several factors including age, the environment, or lifestyle.

If the DNA is like a book, or a musical score, its readings are its epigenetic translations or interpretations. In the second half of the twentieth century the concept of 'programme' dominated genetics. It is exactly the idea of a programme that is in question today with the acknowledgement of the importance of epigenetic mechanisms.

Now to the brain. The epigenetic turn in neurobiology is of course linked with this scientific revolution, which also revealed that the brain, far from being made of fixed and rigid localisations, was undergoing

continuous changes and wirings. The power of neuroplasticity has provoked a very important mutation in the definition of intelligence, still
challenging all attempts at considering it as innate and genetically predetermined. We know now that the brain's development is, for its most
part, epigenetic, continuing long after birth and depending to a large
extent on environmental and cultural factors. In their book, *The Mind
and the Brain: Neuroplasticity and the Power of Mental Force*, the authors Jeffrey M. Schwarz and Sharon Begley write:

> Although it would be perfectly reasonable to posit that genes
> determine the brain's connections, just as a wiring diagram deter-
> mines the connections on a silicon computer chip, that is a math-
> ematical impossibility. As the Human Genome Project drew
> to a close in the early years of the new millennium, it became
> clear that humans have something like 35,000 different genes.
> About half of them seem to be active in the brain, where they
> are responsible for such tasks as synthesizing a neurotransmitter or
> a receptor. The brain, remember, has billions of nerve cells that
> make, altogether, trillions of connections [. . .] Call it the genetic
> shortfall: too many synapses, too few genes. Our DNA is simply
> too paltry to spell out the wiring diagram for the human brain.
> (Schwarz and Begley 2002: 111–12)

This means that the brain has its own life and development, which does
not depend entirely on genetic information. Neurobiologists agree that:
'the brain is more than a reflection of our genes' (ibid.).

Synaptic development is never the mere implementation of a
program or code. On the contrary, it 'includ[es] the spontaneous activity in the nervous system in addition to activity provoked by interaction with the environment' (ibid.: 7). Once again, this epigenetic
view of the shaping of neural connections enables a break with strict
determinism.

For a long time, I have been convinced that the epigenetic nature
of brain development was what definitively proved its irreducibility to
AI systems, or any cybernetic or robotic processes. Was not epigenetic
cerebral plasticity the perfect intermingling of the biological and the
symbolic, that marked its difference with technological functioning? By
the intermingling of the biological and the symbolic, I mean the indis-
cernibility between biological development and personal history, materiality and sense, chemical mechanisms and the exposure of the brain
to changes, education, the adventures of life. All these developmental directions might be, I thought, summarised in one question: what

should we do with our brain? If we can do something with our brain, it is precisely because the brain is not a machine, and we are in part responsible for its plasticity.

However, the recent developments in artificial intelligence made me think differently. It was a shock to realise that I was wrong, that my book *What Should We Do With Our Brain?* should be revised, perhaps even entirely rewritten. This suspicion came to me brutally when I read an article about the most recent computational architectures, and particularly about IBM's recent design of a totally new type of chip, the *neuro-synaptic chip*. The title of the article was eloquent: 'IBM's Neuro-Synaptic Chip Mimics Human Brain' (Murray 2013). Clearly, IBM was releasing a neuro-synaptic computation chip that was able to simulate the neurons and synapses of the brain. Up until now, most computer chips have employed a von Neumann-type architecture, the mathematics-based system at the core of almost every computer built since 1948, that executes instructions in series. By comparison, the synaptic chip is made of different neuro-synaptic-cores or 'corelets' that function autonomously, in a non-synchronic way, so that those which are not solicited remain inactive, thus resulting in a lower energy use. If it is said to mimic the brain, it is because this chip allows interactions between neurons (elements of calculus), synapses (memory) and axons (communications with other parts of the chip). The second reason is that the electronic synaptic components are capable of varying connection strength between two neurons in a manner analogous to that seen in biological systems. In a certain sense, the system develops what we might call its own 'experience'.

In 2011, Dharmendra S. Modha, founder of IBM's Cognitive Computing group at IBM Research, developed with his team the first cognitive chip, thus concretising the SyNAPSE project – SyNAPSE standing for 'Systems of Neuromorphic Adaptive Plastic Scalable Electronics'. Right from the start the ambition was to develop low-power electronic neuromorphic computers that could scale to biological levels. More recently, a still improved chip came to light, called TrueNorth, which is made up of 4,096 neuro-synaptic cores and is able to simulate around one million neurons. On this, Modha explains: 'if we think of today's von Neumann computers as akin to the "left-brain" – fast, symbolic, number-crunching calculators, then TrueNorth can be likened to the "right-brain" – slow, sensory, pattern recognizing machines' (Modha 2016). TrueNorth's corelets are designed for sensory applications that include things like artificial noses, ears and eyes. They are adaptable and can rewire synapses based on their inputs. These chips and processors have experienced exponential growth since then.

In a more recent research report on the global neuromorphic chip market, the authors explain:

> Neuromorphic chips come with artificial neurons and artificial synapses that mimic the activity spike that occurs in the human brain. The chip has the ability to learn continuously due to its synaptic plasticity. This results in smarter, far more energy efficient computing systems. Self-learning neuromorphic chips perform on chip processing asynchronously. It uses event driven processing models to address complex computing problems. Further, by combining improved on board learning, reduced latency, and improved energy efficiency, the self-learning neuromorphic chip can push the image recognition and speech processing to new levels of speed and accuracy. (Advanced Market Analytics 2021)

We can then consider that cybernetics and AI have also had their epigenetic revolution, to the extent that the concept of the program is no longer entirely adequate in this domain either. The new systems, like the IBM ones just mentioned, are able to change or adapt their programs. We can also think of recurrent neural networks, or deep learning, which is also more akin to epigenetic than genetic development. In his book *The Singularity is Near*, Kurzweil constantly insists, famously, on the exponential growth of computing capacities and speed. He speaks of a quantitative 'paradigm shift': 'the rate of the paradigm shift (technical innovation) is accelerating, now doubling every decade' (Kurzweil 2005: 25). Nevertheless, the shift is also qualitative. The singularity will also be that of the plasticity of machines. So yes, it is plasticity that is at stake, and not only as a metaphor or a way of speaking. 'Human intelligence', says Kurzweil, 'has a certain amount of plasticity', that is, an 'ability to change its structure, more so than had been understood' (ibid.: 27). Machines to come will also be plastic, more and more plastic, and they will be capable of changing themselves: 'once machines achieve the ability to design and engineer technology as humans do, only at far higher speeds and capacities, they will have access to their own designs (source code) and the ability to manipulate them, just as we manipulate genetics' (ibid.). Further: 'machines will be able to reformulate their own designs' (ibid.). Thus, we see how quantity and quality are intimately tied together.

Let's now turn to the issue of imitation. In the aforementioned article about synaptic chips, the authors write: 'neuromorphic chips come with artificial neurons and artificial synapses that mimic the activity spike that occurs in the human brain. The chip has the ability to learn continuously due to its synaptic plasticity.' How are we to understand 'mimic' here? Should we refer it to the Greek mimesis, from which it etymologically derives? We all know well the usual questions: 'will AI systems replace us?' Or 'can a computer be intelligent? Can it simulate a brain? Do better than us? Do better without us?' Of course I share some of Hawking's fears, expressed on the BBC a few years ago, that: 'the development of full artificial intelligence could spell the end of the human race'. At the same time, I think that such predictions are not substantiated. And in order to avert them, many people are trying to comfort themselves by affirming that 'machines' (using this generic term) are only poor, faulty copies of human brain capacities. Machines, they say, don't *feel*, they can't be affected. In other terms, machines, AI devices, robots, synaptic computers don't have a self (I will come back to this notion of self later). These discursive beliefs are commonly held, while at the same time we constantly hear about new explorations in brain simulation, artificial imagination, artificial creativity, the artificial capacity to improvise and even artificial sexuality.[1]

So are we just witnessing the emergence of new forms of copies? New forms of imitation, analogies, a new epoch of mimicry? Or do we have to bring to light a new concept of simulation? And is philosophy able to help us answer these questions? It is clear that philosophers are currently not answering the challenge and are not proposing a concept of simulation that would be able to profitably substitute itself for the traditional ones, all of which revolve around the act of copying. We lack an updated notion of mimesis that would adequately characterise the imitating power of artificial epigenetic systems. If we consider the most recent achievements in robotics for example, like those accomplished in Japan by Hirochi Ichiguro, we cannot say that these robots are just 'copies'. Even if the concept of *mimesis* has evolved through time, it has nevertheless remained attached to its ancient definition, which involves a determinate relationship between nature and art. There are at least two decisive moments in the history, or genealogy, of *mimesis*. The Platonic moment, and the Kantian one.

Plato's notion of *mimesis* means copy and reproduction. It entirely concerns the status of art – art being a specific branch of *tekhnè*. We have to distinguish, within *tekhnè*, between craft and art. The craftworker who is making a bed for example does not exactly imitate or copy a model, because the idea that serves as the model for such a making is directly imprinted in the craftman's mind, without any possibility for him or her to interpret it, or play or cheat with it. The artist, on the other hand, intentionally uses deceptive means in his or her production, and does this in order to blur the frontiers between the actual reality and its image, thus turning the idea, the *eidos*, into a treacherous copy. *Eidos* then becomes an *eidolon*, a simulacrum.

I think that many critiques of AI today unconsciously retain something of this Platonic conception. They see technological imitation as something voluntary, a delusionary production of replicas, and claim that the original, the natural, is necessarily superior, due to its authenticity in relation to its technological mimics. They think that cerebral epigenetic development, for example, remains absolutely incomparable with – and irreducible to – synaptic chips, neural networks or intelligent robots.

Kant's concept of imitation is certainly more complex, but still insufficient for settling our problem. In the first part of the *Critique of the Power of Judgement*, Kant interestingly affirms that fine arts must find their topics in nature but should not 'copy it' (Kant 2000: 188). Art undoubtedly finds its inspiration in nature, but it interprets it, reinvents it so to speak. This is the reason why Kant defines art as a creation of 'genius' (ibid.). Contrarily to a mechanical, purely technological process, art is understood as a production of freedom. A work of art is then no servile copy, plagiarism or counterfeit, but a 'free imitation', as he says in §47. Later this is followed by this puzzling declaration: 'nature must serve as a model not for copying (*nachmachen*) but for imitation (*nachahmen*)'. '*Nachmachung*' and '*Nachahmung*' should be then strictly distinguished from each other (ibid.), with *Nachahmung* designating a reproduction that is inassimilable to a mere copy. However, as we know, genius, for Kant, is a gift from nature: 'Genius is the talent (natural endowment) which gives the rule to art' (ibid.: 186). Through the artistic invention, it is in reality nature that interprets itself. We can conclude from this that art, for Kant, expresses nature's relation to itself. The word 'self' is important there. Art helps the creation of a self of nature. To the extent that artistic mimesis is a gift from nature, it exhibits the identity of nature. Art is the subject of nature. A natural artefact. An artificial naturality. Once again, this concept of imitation is by no means reducible to a copy or a simulacrum.

We can now ask if what Kant says about art can be extended to contemporary technology, and if there is such a thing as a technological *Nachahmung*. We won't find the answer in Kant, unfortunately. Kant comes to technique in the second part of the *Critique of Judgement*, but he precisely opposes technique to fine arts and to life. Because of the harmony and the plasticity of its structure and organisation, a living being seems to be a work of art in itself. It is 'as if' nature were an artist. A mechanism, on the contrary, is never plastic. It does not have an epigenetic development. In §65, Kant contrasts the functioning of a watch to that of a natural organism. Well assembled as they are, the different pieces of a watch do not have the power to repair themselves, contrarily to an organism. Technical objects are just *Nachmachungen*, copies of life.

Kant would therefore have considered synaptic chips and plastic computing processes as similar to watches, as mechanical *Nachmachungen* of the biological cerebral organisation. The problem is that if the internal regulation of the different parts of the watch is not the work of the watch itself, the internal regulation of current cybernetic processes precisely *is* self-induced and maintained, as is made visible in recurrent neural networks. We can then ask whether these new processes are not proving the existence of a relationship of technique or technology to itself? The emergence not only of a technical self, but of a *self of technique*? AI would then be said to exhibit the relationship of technique to itself through the *Nachahmung* of nature. An artificial self would be susceptible to emerge from such a relationship. A technological authentically mimetic self.

Therefore, if it is true that AI systems, deep learning processes and intelligent robots are clearly 'imitating' the human, or rather the natural biological functions such as epigenesis for example, we can't return to Plato's concept of mimicry to understand the meaning of this imitation. Neither can we consider that these artefacts are new versions of artistic genius, nor of the relationship of nature to itself. We have to go deeper, and wonder whether a new form of epigenesis exists, the epigenesis of an auto-affection of technique by itself. Just like nature mimics itself through art – for Kant – technology today mimics itself through nature, producing new mirrors for our brains.

Note

1. The Human Brain Project, a large ten-year scientific research project, established in 2013, coordinated by Henry Markram (from École Polytechnique from Lausanne), and largely funded by the European Union. It is the European version of the American BRAIN Initiative (Brain Research through Advancing Innovative Neurotechnologies, also referred to as the Brain Activity Map Project) announced by President Obama in 2013, with the goal of mapping the activity of every neuron in the human brain using big data. The programme will develop information and communications technology platforms in six main areas: neuroinformatics, brain simulation, high-performance computing, medical informatics, neuromorphic computing, and neuro-robotics. Again, the goal in the end is to propose a complete and detailed cartography of the human brain: http://en.wikipedia. org/wiki/Information_and_communications_technology. The Human Brain Project will in part develop the results of another project, The Blue Brain Project, also founded by Markram at Lausanne in 2005. The simulations are carried out on a Blue Gene supercomputer built by IBM. Hence

the name http://en.wikipedia.org/wiki/IBM'Blue Brain'. Both projects are to move to the same place: Campus Biotech in Geneva.

References

Advanced Market Analytics (2021), 'Global Neuromorphic Chip Market', available at: https://www.advancemarketanalytics.com/reports/3762-global-neuromorphic-chip-market (last accessed 8 April 2022).

International Human Genome Sequencing Consortium (2001), 'Initial Sequencing and Analysis of the Human Genome', *Nature*, 409(860–921), available at: https://www.nature.com/articles/35057062 (last accessed 10 March 2022).

Kant, Immanuel (2000), *Critique of the Power of Judgment*, ed. Paul Guyer, trans. Paul Guyer and Eric Mathews, Cambridge and New York: Cambridge University Press.

Kurzweil, Ray (2005), *The Singularity is Near: When Humans Transcend Biology*, New York: Penguin.

Le Monde (2001), 'Le génome humain cache de "vastes déserts"', *Le Monde*, 13 February, available at: https://scholar.lib.vt.edu/InterNews/LeMonde/issues/2001/monde.20010213.pdf (last accessed 10 March 2022).

Malabou, Catherine (2008), *What Should We Do With Our Brain?*, trans. Sebastian Rand, New York: Fordham University Press.

Malabou, Catherine (2019), *Morphing Intelligence: From IQ Measurements to Artificial Brains*, trans. Carolyn Shread, New York: Columbia University Press.

Modha, Dharmendra S. (2016), 'Introducing a Brain-inspired Computer', *Radio Locman*, 29 November, available at: https://www.radiolocman.com/review/article.html?di=162687 (last accessed 10 March 2022).

Murray, William (2013), 'IBM's Neuro-Synaptic Chips Mimics Human Brain', *EE Times*, 18 September, available at: https://www.eetimes.com/ibms-neuro-synaptic-chip-mimics-human-brain/ (last accessed 10 March 2022).

Schwarz, Jeffrey M. and Sharon Begley (2002), *The Mind and the Brain: Neuroplasticity and the Power of Mental Force*, New York: HarperCollins.

Waddington, Conrad Hal (1968), 'The Basic Ideas of Biology', in *Towards a Theoretical Biology: Prolegomena*, vol. 1, Edinburgh: Edinburgh University Press, pp. 1–32.

Index